Pedagogical Sciences

Pedagogical Sciences

The Teaching of Language and Literature, Education, Values, Patrimony and Applied IT

Editor

MSc Miguel Ángel Olivé Iglesias

Associate Professor. Holguin University, Cuba

QuodSermo Publishing

First Edition

Library and Archives Canada Cataloguing in Publication

Title: Pedagogical sciences : the teaching of language and literature, education, values, patrimony and applied IT / editor, MSc Miguel Ángel Olivé Iglesias, associate professor, Holguin University, Cuba.
Names: Olivé Iglesias, Miguel Ángel, 1965- editor.
Description: Includes bibliographical references.
Identifiers: Canadiana (print) 20210183446 |
        Canadiana (ebook) 20210183497 |
ISBN 9781989786338 (softcover) |
ISBN 9781989786345 (PDF)
Subjects: LCSH: Language and languages—Study and teaching. |
       LCSH: Literature—Study and teaching. |
       LCSH: Moral education. |
       LCSH: Educational technology.
Classification: LCC P51 .P43 2021 |
       DDC 418.007—dc23

QuodSermo Publishing
www.HiddenBrookPress.com
quodsermo@gmail.com

Pedagogical Sciences: The Teaching of Language and Literature, Education, Values, Patrimony and Applied IT

Editor – MSc Miguel Ángel Olivé Iglesias

Proofreading – Julio César Rodríguez Peña, María Elena Ayala Ruiz, Pedro Antonio Machín Armas, Jorge Alberto Pérez Hernández
Translations from Spanish – Miguel Ángel Olivé Iglesias, Jorge Alberto Pérez Hernández
Cover Design – Richard M. Grove
Cover Image – Richard M. Grove
Layout and Design – Richard M. Grove

Subjects:The teaching of language and literature, education, values, patrimony, applied IT

Editorial Staff:
MSc Miguel Ángel Olivé Iglesias. Associate Professor
PhD Julio César Rodríguez Peña. Associate Professor
PhD María Elena Ayala Ruiz. Full Professor
PhD Pedro Antonio Machín Armas. Full Professor
BEd Jorge Alberto Pérez Hernández. Instructor

Typeset in Calibri
Printed and bound in Canada

Table of Contents

The Teaching of Language and Literature

Education, Values and Patrimony

Applied Information and Communication Technologies

Acknowledgements

I am deeply indebted to many movers and shakers in the original conception and making of this book. I thank the publisher for his bigheartedness and foresight of the book´s scope. I thank every contributor whose work I received and honored these pages.

A special thank you to first publishers, who kindly allowed to republish papers previously issued. Finally, I thank my Editorial Staff for joint revision and collaborative translation, and the layout and design artist for a job finely done. Thank you all for your full support to the project.

Dedicated to:

Miguel Ángel Olivé Fonseca, my father,
for his lifelong dedication to work, study, reading, learning,
and for his unyielding ethics despite context or circumstances

Prof. Erie Thomas Ibarra (in memoriam),
PhD Alberto Medina Betancourt (in memoriam) and
PhD Manuel Velázquez León,
exemplary doyens of human values, exceptional
teaching and committed research in the educational field

All true men and women of science, research and
teaching worldwide regardless of time and place

The Editor
MSc Miguel Ángel Olivé Iglesias

Editor´s Foreword

The Holguin University in Cuba has over fifty years of undergraduate and graduate teaching experience and of conferring academic and scientific degrees recognized nationally and internationally to national and foreign students. Professionalism and seniority are key professorial signatures successfully leading the institution through accreditation processes. The Teacher Education English Department is a certified major with faculty doing research and publishing scientific material worldwide. Its accumulated results and scientific standing paved the way to embark on the demanding task of preparing a volume like the one I proudly present now.

Pedagogical Sciences is a book born out of friendship, awareness and objective insight into our "human project," understood as what we, a group of concerned and committed professionals, have been able to construe, conceive, build, preserve and treasure for the future. It condenses some of the achievements and huge potential forged throughout years of accumulation of scientific-technological-cultural wealth in the fields of the teaching of language and literature, education, values, patrimony and IT implementation in the educational area.

Friendship offered the bridge, the means and the supportive international cooperation. Awareness cleared out any questions about quality and friendship being incompatible in the paths of science. Objective insight cemented the confidence in the product presented here.
The book is divided into three sections, which, as will be seen, are closely interrelated:
The Teaching of Language and Literature
Education, Values and Patrimony
Applied IT

Theory, practice and culture go hand in hand in each and across the three sections. Therefore, particular and general criteria are argued in scholarly articles where the teaching of language and literature, education, values, patrimony and applied IT evidence a high professional outlook and careful analysis. Moreover, the sections are channeled towards an unveiling, clarification, concretion and contextualization of their significance in terms of scientific input to the mosaic of culture the human kind should bequeath to the next generations.

Reading these academic papers will disclose further thanks to the authors´ expertise in linguistics, didactics, pedagogy, values, patrimonial studies and applied IT, with a creatively approached, down-to-earth tone, respect and appreciation for human creation.

The book is a compilation conceived from a breakthrough perspective in line with the world´s most urging needs and humanistic tendencies. Its self-standing parts move smoothly from specific academic dissertations on the teaching of language and literature to broader educational, values and patrimonial concerns, along with applied IT papers, all of them meant to add a modest contribution to science. As a comprehensive whole, it focuses on bringing to the forefront and salvaging the most important resource: human beings and their creation. Without them – without us – there would be no language, no literature, no education, no values, no technology and no patrimony to safeguard.

There should be no higher pressing aspirations for humanity than to honorably and harmoniously live, coexist and be spiritually enlightened. Language is central to attaining such goals. Language unites. Education must indeed accompany any pursuits aimed at furnishing people with the necessary tools, values, to peacefully cohabit, exchange, learn and grow as individuals within a civilized context. Education and values edify. Patrimony, science, literature, technology and arts in general, created, inherited and preserved by society to be enjoyed today and tomorrow, embrace the former elements contained in the tangible and intangible heritage in and by which we live. Our patrimony is the offspring and solemn pledge of prosperity, peace and pleasure for humankind. They all are worth saving and sharing.

One outstanding strength of the book is the formidable bibliographical references each article registers at the end. Here too context, time and geography give us the possibility of further readings which will enrich our scientific culture and significantly fuel the potential academic exchanges I envision will be activated among authors. A second forte is the injection of youngness in the book. We have students from different majors coauthoring the papers, and graduates who are taking their first steps also as researchers. I look forward to seeing these new professors write articles and head the lists of upcoming editions. A third strong point is, undoubtedly, the presence of national and international authors with PhD, Spec. and MSc degrees, and senior teaching ranks (Full, Associate and Assistant Professors).

The book's first section presents some of the most systematic, active academics teaching, doing research and writing papers – publicized in national and international forums and publishing formats – that reveal their acute observations, analyses and experiences in the teaching of language and literature. The topics are as varied as the disciplines at play and the authors' stances and countries of origin; they cover the teaching of English as a foreign language as well as of Spanish and literature.

Didactics (viewed as the theory of teaching and learning) and culture (seen as the tangible-intangible patrimony historically conceived, created and accumulated by mankind) are at the center of these papers in well-conceived proposals that blend theory, practice and applied studies. Themes like skill development (listening, speaking, reading and writing), method-approach debates, lesson planning, the role of teachers and students in teaching and learning in a quality-education context, a welcome confluence of contributing sciences (Psychology, Sociology, Linguistics), discourse analysis and intercultural studies that favor the inclusion of fine Canadian literature (prose and poetry) in the university curriculum, etc., fill the pages dedicated to this topic.

The viewpoints herein expressed by the authors are valid and fully open to respectful academic exchange. This section especially reflects the maturity of science and researchers, their insight into matters and sources – in time and context – they approached and took valuable information from to produce their scientific corpus. Their statements and conclusions were drawn aided by both comprehensive and updated exploration, objective consideration and committed spirit of sharing and being receptive to suggestions. True science can only thrive in this atmosphere.

The second section lays intentional stress on present-day issues regarding education and values formation, nurtured by the endless fountain of elevation and ethics to be found, masterfully exposed by the authors, in three patrimonial assets: arts, literature and education, hence the sections' overlapping character. As commented above, mankind's survival largely depends on what we are able to do as an "intelligent race;" as a "project," to ensure there is a tomorrow. Interestingly enough, the previous section included the study and didactic channeling of a novel by a Canadian author where one of the chief concerns is the environment (indisputably at the top of any social agenda today), plus allusions to human conflicts and scourges, like moral corruption, drugs or murder, and a study of a well-known Canadian writer where vice and virtue, in the words of the essayist, are portrayed towards a constructive analysis.

As a valuable extra, this second section includes a related article on the promotion of reading as a tool to learn, grow and assume critical stances before the world and absorb the universal heritage at our disposal. In addition, the section features a paper on the teaching of English from a cultural perspective (the presence of Gallicisms in the English language), as a useful didactic approach to the link between language and culture, and how Gallicisms are to be interpreted, so learners acquire an all-around linguistic-cultural legacy, and a remarkable article on the development of professional skills in students to complement their academic formation with a professional-axiological formative conception. Finally, we close with an article that explores and proposes community work related to the learning of English from a cultural perspective that responds in its entirety to the essential aims of language teaching.

Therefore, the papers seek out to bring to center stage the role of moral and learning in terms of education socially speaking, and how effective they are as core tools to endure in a world we must save. Experiences gathered for this book by professors working in Cuban universities, and one working in a Chinese university, are modeled and presented enabling readers to reach conclusions and voice their own views.

The third section deals with outstanding contributions made by researchers and professors in the Information and Communication Technology (IT) area. Technology is widely used in applied studies to boost educational pursuits. The authors prove to the point of excellence how much can be done exploiting the endless purview of computer programming, teaching media and software development to favor teaching, learning and education in its broadest sense.

This section's extent brings to us applied IT proposals for the teaching of English as a foreign language (first section's domain) and the actual application of the advantages of IT to education. Articles of the utmost quality are collected here, which range from profound historic and epistemological studies on the topic to creative, relevant works on the conception and implementation of software, videos and learning objects to teach English as a foreign language, unveiling and putting to use interdisciplinary tenets. Additionally, the papers stand as a priceless contribution to explain IT related realities, model strategies and support technologically the efforts made in Cuba towards the improvement of learning in general.

The exploitation of IT is basic in the attempts to enhance education. It provides tools, channels knowledge, spurs motivation and sets a strong foundation and fulcrum for further elaboration and implementation according to the country's needs and aspirations. The papers included in this section feature necessary appendixes with a welcome illustration of theoretical elements discussed in them.

Fifty-one authors offer part of their prized written legacy in forty-three papers. Readers will be positively impressed by the essential commonality found in the articles as a whole. Their interconnectedness is evident, which is proof of an undeniable universal interlinkage exposed here thanks to science.

As editor, I find gratification in what we have been able to condense in this book. It discusses unavoidable, pertinent issues nowadays about which devoted Cuban and foreign professors and researchers express their informed views. It is a legacy that corroborates there is well-structured cohesion, sense, trajectory, purpose, objectivity and spirituality in our thoughts and actions.

Notes:
Aware of the obvious multiplicity of sources and notions in the scientific prose style, the Editorial Staff respected the original structure of the papers as they were submitted by the authors.

Authors are fully responsible for their language, views, opinions, statements, copyright violation and legal actions of any kind in their papers. Neither the publisher nor the editor have accountability for any transgressions detected in the future. There are no royalties implied in or ensuing from the publication of their papers in this book. They were properly notified since the issuing of the book's call.

Academic and scientific degrees are generally translated into English as BEd (or B.Ed.); Prof. (in Cuba it is a first-level college degree similar to a BEd or BA); BA (or B.A.); MSc (or M.Sc., M.S.); Spec. (in Cuba it is a second-level college degree similar to an MSc); and PhD (or Ph.D.).

To be in line with international titles, we include a practical reference guide for worldwide readers. The first three denominations (BEd; Prof.; BA) are similar to the terms we use here (As was noted, Prof. is not a teaching rank in Cuba). The fourth one (MSc) may be found as MSc, Master of Education (M.Ed.), MA (Master of Arts) or Master of Arts in Teaching (M.A.T.). The fifth one (Spec.), Educational Specialist (Ed.S.); and the sixth one (PhD), similar to the terms we use here, or Doctor of Education (Ed.D.), or Dr.

MSc Miguel Ángel Olivé Iglesias
Associate Professor. Holguin University, Cuba
Author, Editor, Reviewer

"Man's only worthy manuscript
is the one he bequeaths
in the books he writes"

José Martí

"Science is organized knowledge"

Herbert Spencer

"Books must follow sciences,
and not sciences books"

Francis Bacon

"Good teaching is…
about doing your best to keep on top of your field,
reading sources, inside and outside of your areas of
expertise, and being at the leading edge…
bridging the gap between theory and practice…"

Richard Leblanc

The Teaching of Language and Literature

The English Language Classroom Scenario: Context Bangladesh

PhD Shireen Huq. Full Professor
MA Sheikh Zobaer. Professor

In 1947, the subcontinent of India freed itself of colonial rule and was partitioned into two independent nations: India and Pakistan. Geographically it was a strange division, Pakistan having two parts, East and West, divided by the big land mass of India. Religion was an important bonding factor between the peoples of East and West Pakistan, Islam being practiced by a majority of the people but there were other minority religious and ethnic groups in both wings of the country; however, culturally and linguistically East and West Pakistan were poles apart. Immediately after independence in 1947, the Pakistani rulers tried to impose Urdu as the sole state language of Pakistan though numerically the Bengali population was more. The Bengali population of East Pakistan protested strongly. This movement known as the Language Movement of 1952 was spearheaded by the students of Dhaka University. On 21st Feb.1952, police opened fire on a procession of protesting students and many were injured and killed; many female students were harassed by police. This fight for their mother tongue strengthened the spirit of nationalism among the Bengalis, which ultimately played a crucial role in the liberation of Bangladesh. Multiple factors, particularly economic exploitation and linguistic oppression of East Pakistan by West Pakistan, led to increasing strife and bitterness between the peoples of the two parts of the country, leading finally to a nine-month long brutal war which saw the emergence of Bangladesh as an independent nation.

After independence in 1971, Bangladesh adopted the policy of 'one state one language', the country being predominantly monolingual in Bangla, though the presence of other small ethnic groups should not be overlooked. Bangla became the State language, to be used at all levels and English was relegated to the sidelines. The status of English was very dubious for a while. Understandable at this point, considering the earlier linguistic oppression at the hands of the Pakistani rulers. Full of the spirit of nationalism, the Bangladeshis set about rebuilding their country with their mother tongue Bangla at the core of their dreams and emotions. However, this had a backlash and led to a serious decline in English proficiency in the country. Moreover, the research and development of the Bangla language, along with necessary translations required for higher education and learning did not take place. Understandable again, for a newly – independent nation has multiple problems to grapple with, so that language research may not get the necessary priority it required at that time.

However, English language was still required for global communication, for trade and commerce, higher education, and international employment and the decline in English competence in the newly independent country led to some problems not anticipated before. Students were refused admission in good Western universities for being unable to achieve required TOEFL scores or being unable to handle the language content of the courses in their programs and while others, especially doctors and nurses, found themselves being refused employment abroad and particularly in the Middle East which had been an important source of remittance for the country. This led to rethinking of the status of English and English language teaching/learning in the country. At the primary and secondary levels, there were field surveys to determine the gap between the expected level and the existing gap in language competence, discussions and re-discussions on teaching methodology, teacher training, curriculum designing, textbook development, etc. Foreign experts were brought in to help.

The British Council played an important role here, followed by the USIS (United States Information Centre, now the American Cultural Centre). In this regard, the name that comes immediately to mind is that of Clive Taylor who came to Bangladesh in the mid-70s under the auspices of The British Council and spent a lot of time and energy with tertiary level teachers in the country to develop a set of textbooks, pre-eminent among them being Advancing Language Skills. Other language experts followed with their recommendations particularly for ESP (English for Specific Purposes). There was much thinking then, globally, on pedagogy and curriculum of Teaching/Learning of English as a Foreign (EFL)/Second (ESL)/ International Auxiliary Language (EIAL) to the so-called *Third World/Underdeveloped/developing*) countries where English was not the mother tongue. In the context of English language teaching, the tradition in Bangladesh had been to learn language through a study of literature.

The curriculum had been entirely literature-based, more specifically British literature-based. American literature, not to mention literature of other countries, was included in the syllabus much later with the return of teachers who had gone to do their PhDs from universities in countries other than in the United Kingdom. Consequently, teachers at all levels were not specifically trained to teach language as we understand pedagogy today. For the first time, people started becoming aware of these problems and the need to do something about the situation.

Sadly, the language policy with regard to the teaching/learning of English was inconsistent for a long time. The form of ELT in Bangladesh – English as a Second Language (ESL) or English as a Foreign Language (EFL) – is still a matter of debate among researchers. ESL refers to countries where English is widely used in public places and parliament, such as in India where it is used along with the state languages. In EFL, on the other hand, the language use is mainly confined to classrooms, and as a medium of instruction, not widely used in the community. Some scholars maintain that the use of English in Bangladesh is between a Second and Foreign language while others put it as a foreign language. A certain section of people use it for conversation and everyday use; to them it is a status symbol. Students who study in English medium schools also use English for everyday purpose. The people on the streets do not use it, neither do salespersons or street vendors or transport workers or servers in restaurants except in some exclusive establishments. In short, English is a language used for everyday purpose only by a small minority of people, particularly in the urban areas.

In the mid-1990s, there was a shift to CLT, Communicative Language Teaching, from the Grammar-Translation Method. Unfortunately, this was done without adequate preparation. Traditional classrooms in Bangladesh are teacher-centered with theatre style seating with students facing the teacher, the black/white board behind the teacher. Style of teaching is lecture style reminding one somewhat of the *guru-shishho* (disciple) relationship in the Middle Ages. The teacher wields unquestionable authority in terms of both discipline and knowledge. Students are not encouraged to ask questions but unquestionably accept the knowledge handed down by the teacher. This restricts the teacher-student interaction, puts a restraint on the natural inquisitiveness of students in the formative years of their lives. It inhibits them from speaking as we can see when they come to tertiary levels.

This situation is gradually changing today in more conducive environments in some private schools, but this is the scenario in the vast majority of schools in the country particularly in the rural areas. To say the least, this style of teaching and classroom is not at all suitable for CLT and till today, teachers face many difficulties to do the required CLT activities. Moreover, class sizes are usually very large and it is difficult for the teachers to give one-on –one attention to the students and make them practice the four skills. There may not even be space for the teacher/facilitator to move around the class during the lesson. In the rural areas, particularly, teachers of other subjects in adjoining classrooms, divided by temporary partitions, may complain of disturbance from the English language classroom during CLT activities and this again inhibits both teachers and students.

Teachers hardly spend time on developing speaking and listening skills of students (Shurovi 2014). In addition, during the rainy seasons, both teachers and students may have to wade through mud and water and might even be tired before the class begins; as such, they might find it easier to follow the traditional methods. These are important factors and should have been looked into before moving into CLT.

For CLT to be successful, it is very important to have well-trained, committed teachers and it is very important to create the right mindset in teachers , that is, to change them from the teacher –in-control mindset to the teacher –as-facilitator mindset. There are still doubts as to whether a large number of teachers have been able to acquire this mindset, and prepared to accept a situation where they are no longer in supreme control of the class. Regarding teacher training, there are both pre and in-service government run programs in the country but their outcomes are not satisfactory as discussed by Rahman (2018), Ali & Walker (2014). Moreover, the donor-sponsored projects have not had the desired outcomes and failed to attain the success claimed by them, as pointed out by Anwaruddin (2016). There has been criticism of the testing done in the Secondary and Higher Secondary level examinations, with no component of the listening and speaking skills as discussed by Nasrin Sultana (2018).

So this is the background English language teaching scenario at the primary and secondary levels in Bangladesh. Now what do we, classroom teachers, find when the students come to us in the entry level (tertiary) after twelve years of schooling? Most English classes are heterogeneous with students coming from the different schooling systems in Bangladesh: Bangla medium, English medium, and the Madrasahs. There are further subgroups, Bangla medium, Bangla medium English version, urban schools, and rural schools.

Close observation, after many years of experience of teaching English language at this level, has led the researchers to a few conclusions. First, let us take the writing skill. It is important to mention here that the students coming from the urban-based English medium schools have fewer grammatical errors than the others in the class though they are not error free and generally have more coherence and unity in their essays. With regard to grammar, they have five major mistakes, which are made frequently, the most frequently made one being the error in subject-verb agreement. Sentence structure errors come next followed by errors related to the misuse of tense. Another important type of error is the one to the misuse of preposition and the influence of mother tongue.

As English is limited mostly within the confines of academic educational system in Bangladesh, students who come from Bangla medium educational system do not get enough opportunity to practice English. As mentioned before, more grammatical mistakes can be found in the writings of Bangla medium students than that of students who come from English medium educational background. Since majority of the grammatical mistakes stems from errors related to subject-verb agreement, it points to the students apparent inability to distinguish between singular and plural subjects which makes them choose the wrong verb.

Consider this example: "He is one of my best friends." Most of the students would choose the word "friend" instead of "friends". Students particularly struggle with sentences that are lengthy, and where the subject and the verb are not close together. This is the reason why students struggle to construct long sentences, which in turn discourages them to try to overcome the problem. Here is an example taken from a student's written assignment: "Dhaka have many problems, and traffic jam is one of them." Here, it is clear that the student used the verb "have" thinking that it has a connection with the plural noun "problems." Here is another example: "Bangladesh is one of the most populous countries in the world and have many other problems apart from overpopulation."

Here again, the distance between the subject "Bangladesh" and the verb "have" (which should have been "has") has confused the student. Such problem works as a vicious circle that many students struggle to break free from until they are almost half way through their undergraduate studies. Sentences with correlative conjunction, prepositional phrases between the subject and the verb, indefinite pronouns, and interrogative sentences seem to be the most troublesome ones to the students.

Sentence structure is another problematic area for the students and English sentence structure particularly problematic when it comes to constructing long sentences. Short assertive sentences are found to be the least troublesome ones and students are frequently found to turn to short simple sentences and avoid complex and compound ones. Consider this example taken from a student's assignment: "Famous local railway market near of my town . which is i hate most . Because of public used to shopping too much and they are not safty."

There are several problems here. Firstly, the student fails to demonstrate proper understanding of the difference between a complete sentence and a sentence fragment. This is one of the most frequent problems found among students who perform at a below-average level. Secondly, the student fails to use correct forms of verbs and includes unnecessary words as well. Finally, the student also fails to maintain proper order of words. These are some of the most frequently-found problems among students who have not yet reached intermediate level language proficiency.

Consider another example containing similar language errors: "I hate the new market area of Dhaka. Most time busy the place. There is always a jam here and people are in a hurry. People cannot reach on time due to traffic jam. Lots of people going to new market for shopping and much gather people working are a problem." Similar syntactic and sematic mistakes can be found in this example.

A large number of students often struggle when it comes to constructing interrogative sentence and passive voice. Surprisingly, even in creative writing assignments, students hardly use optative and exclamatory sentences even though these types of sentences are frequently in use in Bangla – both in academic as well as in creative writing. As a result, it can be argued that students' lack of the use of imperative, optative, and exclamatory sentences stems from their apprehension of sentence construction, not from mother-tongue influence. Another frequently made error is getting the syntactical order of the words in a sentence wrong, particularly when a sentence is longer than they are used to writing.

This problem is due to the students' lack of exposure to English texts. As Bangla is the official language in Bangladesh, and English is very much neglected in Bangla medium curriculum, students often feel discouraged to read English books and newspapers – the two most available sources – which obstruct their progress in learning English. Due to this phenomenon, most of the students cannot get past the intermediate level, while a significant number of them get stuck at the beginner level.

Use of tense is a highly problematic area. Most of the Bangladesh students have a hard time maintaining the right sequence tense of their writings. The problem gets worse in longer sentences, as students often conflate between present and past tense in one sentence and end up using different forms of verbs incorrectly. Consider the following example: "I love playing cricket because I love outdoor sports and I also liked to play football in the afternoon." Here, the student wrongly used both present indefinite and past indefinite tenses in the same sentence. Students particularly struggle with perfect and perfect continuous tenses due to their lack of use in Bangla and also due to the fact that the sentence structure of perfect and perfect continuous tenses are very different from that of Bangla.

Consider the following example from a student's paper: "I did not want to go outside because it was raining for almost three hours that day." In Bangla, "it was raining" and "it had been raining" have the same syntactic construction. As a result, students often avoid using perfect continuous tense and use continues tense instead. Things get more problematic with regards to passive voice and interrogative sentence in perfect and perfect continuous tenses. As a result, most of the students avoid using perfect continuous tense and choose to use continuous tense instead. Similarly, they also tend to avoid using present perfect and past perfect tense, and use either present or past tense instead. Not only does such practice yield grammatical error, but also limit the students' ability to express themselves in a proper way, using proper expressions. As a result, their writings lack depth, nuance, and linguistic maturity – even if the students possess conceptual maturity. In most of the Bangla medium schools, students are made to memorize the rules of constructing different tenses. But memorizing the rules without using the language simply does not work, and results in an utter failure in understanding the inner mechanisms of a language. This hinders fluency.

Even though both English and Bangla belong to the same language family (Indo-European Language), there are some significant differences between them in terms of sentence structure. This mother-tongue influence is one of the major reasons behind a significant number of grammatical mistakes that Bangladeshi students make, and one particular instance where Bangladeshi students' mother-tongue influence in their English writing manifests itself the most is in the use of auxiliary verbs. In Bangla, auxiliary verbs are almost non-existent. They are never used in writing, let alone in speaking. But in English it is quite the opposite. As a result, Bangladeshi students struggle to a great extent when it comes to the proper use of the auxiliary verbs in English. Similar problem exists with the use of verb to have. Many students often use verb to have instead of using an auxiliary verb due to the influence of Bangla. Consider the following example: "There has a major problem in Dhaka." The student used the verb "has" instead of using the auxiliary verb "is" because firstly, auxiliary verbs are never used in Bangla, and secondly, the Bangla word for the word "has" means to possess, own, or hold something.

This is the reason why the student used the word "has" in this sentence, instead of using the auxiliary verb "is". Syntactical differences are also a major reason behind mother-tongue influence. The typical English sentence structure is subject + verb + object. However, in Bangla, a typical sentence structure is subject + object + verb. Due to such a major difference in sentence structure, many elementary-level Bangladeshi students of English struggle to escape from their mother-tongue influence and learn English incorrectly, which takes an enormous effort for them to unlearn when they progress through the stages of learning.

The final category among the five most frequently made grammatical mistakes is the misuse of prepositions. Prepositions are an integral part of English language, but in Bangla, prepositional words do not exist. Instead, the purposes of prepositions are served by a group of inflections. Because of this major linguistic difference, Bangladesh students have a hard time grasping the rules of using prepositions correctly. For example, in English, there are different prepositions for time and place. But in Bangla the same inflection is used in order to indicate both time and place. As a result, a Bangladeshi student is more likely to say, "Meet me in 11 AM in the shopping mall." Moreover, in English, the rules of using appropriate prepositions are as arbitrary as it gets, which makes it even harder for Bangladeshi students to master the use of prepositions. As a result, students tend to limit their use of prepositions to the most commonly used ones. Many students get frustrated to the point that they eventually give up trying to learn the proper use of prepositions.

Furthermore, students are not organized in their writing showing a lack of both unity and coherence. They tend to repeat and jump back and forth between points. Memorization of essays on specific topics from easily available essay books leads to this problem. In schools, students are not given enough practice in writing essays; large classes could be a reason for this with teachers being unable to keep up with the corrections. Instead, certain topics are given to the students and they memorize them for the examinations. So excepting in a few schools, the writing skill is not developed adequately in the students.

When it comes to the speaking skill, the students from the Bangla medium schools are inhibited to speak. In the traditional education system, students are not encouraged to question teachers in class. Some conservative teachers may interpret this as rudeness on the part of the students; unfortunately, such mindset has not fully changed even till today. Thus, at the tertiary levels, even when the teaching environment is more conducive, the inhibition works. They are afraid to talk. Also, in many cases they think others might laugh at them if they mispronounce a word. So, multiple factors work to prevent them from being interactive in class. The sad part of this is it impacts upon classmates' relationships negatively. A few tend to dominate the class, others feel threatened and sometimes leads to jealousy and animosity between friends. This is not a healthy atmosphere in a class.

Reading, a very important skill at the higher levels, is frequently neglected, eventually leading to a fear of reading in the students. This makes them slow readers and generally speaking, deters them from doing the volume of reading they are expected to do at this level. The 'cut' 'paste' from internet type of plagiarism could be an outcome of this. Most students struggle over their English courses throughout the undergraduate years and do marked improvement in their senior years. However, in their junior years, the English courses cause them a lot of stress, which impacts on their other courses and their overall CGPA.

The authors of this article have a few recommendations to help the students develop their language skills, and these recommendations are going to be particularly helpful for the students who come from Bangla-medium background. First of all, the language skill the students lack the most is speaking, but unfortunately the opportunity to practice speaking is extremely rare for most, in the context of Bangladesh. Watching English TV series, rather than movies, seems to be more helpful in terms of providing the students with enough instances of conversations that have a wide contextual variety. Apart from reading books to improve their vocabulary, word-choice, and expression, students can also listen to podcasts where academics and intellectuals are invited to talk. This will provide the students a wonderful opportunity to listen to some of the world's leading intellectuals, and can learn from the way they speak.

Finally, listening to radio shows can be surprisingly useful because unlike an academic lecture, radio shows tend to be light-hearted where speakers usually talk very fast, laugh, crack jokes, and even engage in heated arguments – all of which will give the learners a priceless access to a very different dimension of the language which they otherwise would not get if they only listen to academic talks and read books that deal with serious subject matters. Finally, reading as a habit seems to be on the decline globally and it has happened in Bangladesh also. Technology has too many attractions and it has lured them away from books. A conscious, concerted move has to be made by all stakeholders to rejuvenate this habit again; reading and writing skills will both improve. We believe that if Bangladesh students follow these steps throughout their undergraduate period, they will be able to overcome most of their limitations when it comes to learning English.

References
Ali, Md. Maksud & Walker, Ann L. (2014). *Bogged down ELT in Bangladesh: Problems and Policy. English Today*. June 2014.
Anwaruddin, S.M. (2016). *ICT and language teacher development in the global south: A new Materialist discourse analysis. Educational Studies.*
Rahman, M. M., Islam, M. S., Karim, A., Chowdhury, T. A., Rahman, M. M., Prodhan, M. I. S. S. & Singh, M. K. M. (2019). *English Language Teaching in Bangladesh today: Issues, outcomes and implications. Language testing in Asia.* 2019.
Shurovi, M. (2014). *CLT and ELT in Bangladesh: Practice and Prospects of Speaking and Listening. Journal of Language Teaching and Research*, 5(6), 1263-1268.
Sultana, N. (2018). *Test review of the English public examination at the secondary level in Bangladesh. Language Testing in Asia.* 30 Aug. 2018.

Academic Literariness in Mexican Humanities and Sciences

PhD Elia Acacia Paredes Chavarría
MSc Héctor Ernesto Jaimes Paredes
BA Carmina Paredes Neira

Today, it is common in university contexts to talk about literariness or academic literacy. The concept has been researched and implemented in recent years, chiefly in universities abroad. In Latin America, a salient researcher is Paula Carlino, from Argentina, one of the most active promoters in the area. She authored *Escribir, leer y aprender en la universidad. Una introducción a la alfabetización académica* y fundadora del GICEOLEM, (*Grupo para la Inclusión y Calidad Educativas a través de Ocuparnos de la Lectura y la Escritura en todas las Materias*).

At this point, it is relevant to define literariness (or academic literacy). It means that each discipline has a specific field-related stock of books that students have to read and write about in class, especially in college. This statement issues a first premise: there must be a clarification and classification of which texts are essential for each discipline and major; and a second premise, the relevance of professorial updating about comprehension, structure and writing in order to prepare students in class.

Carlino leads the group that propounds for regional subject-classification, mainly in college, on the basis that there must be a distinctive correlation of book distribution per educational levels and majors.

For example, note taking differs in senior high school and college. Professors must consider this element in their context. In senior high, usual procedures include reading a book and writing about it; however, in college, students have to consult a variety of sources. Oftentimes, their opinions are not sufficiently solid so readers have to discover their rationality and reach conclusions only by themselves.

In college, many professors take for granted students already know things, so they do not have to teach them. For example, faculty professors assign papers that demand quoting and referencing bibliography; nevertheless, they do not furnish students with tools to accomplish the task, like what theoretical corpus they must follow, which models can be of assistance in writing the papers. Such dilemma brings about disorientation and by extension, higher dropout rates.

On the other hand, reading and writing are considered separately – despite their interconnectedness. It is a general belief that a textual product is only an intellectual process, and professors fail to see that writing serves as a path towards learning.

A survey was applied in Argentina to find out if professors were interested in reading and writing for their students. The results rendered most of them were interested, only a few were not and a few implemented activities in class to achieve that end. In practice, what is really happening is professors do not focus on accompanying the student in the process. In Mexico, the necessary act of monitoring the student in reading and writing is key to attain solid knowledge. It cannot be either circumstantial or occasional: students understand complex concepts when they rewrite them in their own words. Consequently, they learn through reading.

Reading and writing contribute to learning in each discipline. Academic literacy demands that professors work with reading comprehension and writing about discipline-related texts. Teacher-student interaction is essential for understanding and reaffirmation by means of writing.

Carlino's group advocates redistribution of shared and cross responsibilities, supported by writing projects in the different subjects. The researcher explored teaching techniques in academic writing and institutional representatives. She accessed 103 Canadian and U.S. university sites and studied a set of on-line material featured by many academic entities.

Her findings rendered that many of these colleges offer composing courses and writing programs to encourage the learning of "writing through the curriculum," that is to say, via every curricular manifestation. To that end, universities put in practice three systems:
   Writing tutorials
   In-subject writing partners
   Intensive writing subjects

Organizationally speaking, there are differences between these systems. Yet all three are in charge of orienting and providing feedback for the written production of discipline contents the students have to learn.

Thus, writing is viewed as an epistemic tool, involved in learning, and each discipline contains a system of notions and methods, inherent discourse practices necessarily subject to teaching. All of these encompass inclusion situations in the teaching of writing within subjects whose objectives do not consider reading and writing. Bailey & Vardy (1999) and Zadnik & Radloff (1995), among others, analyze joint programs with curricular experts and composition specialists to integrate writing into the subjects' core syllabus.

All universities accessed by Carlino feature a "writing requirement," that is, the demand that graduates must have completed matters related to writing, or have certified their academic literacy by means of a formal assessment form (tests, essays, etc.). These universities contend students learn more when they write about the contents of a subject matter than when they do multiple-choice tests. Hence, if assessment situations the different majors propose include writing tasks, these must be added to the curriculum.

For students, the volume of writing they have to complete in a subject, plus the professor's support to carry it out, is the most prominent factor towards student involvement, measured in terms of time, intellectual stimulation and interest sparkled in the student.

Sometimes, group or small-group tutorials are activated, where production and guidelines are discussed for improvement. From there, each student revises and rewrites his/her text, and afterwards hands it over to the professor. Thus, pair-work allows a moment of rereading and revision of integrated writing in the subject. Duke University follows this tenet.

There was a Latin American Congress (XII) in Puebla, Mexico in early September 2013 for the Development of Reading and Writing, and an Iberian-American Forum (IV) of Literacy and Learning, where Carlino quoted the work submitted by a Physics and a Language professor about asking the students to write a paper for a school congress. The students fully took over in organizing the reception committee, designing the program, distributing promotion, etc. They invited foreign lecturers and acted as hosts and MCs. It is evident cross-disciplinary work may prove very useful.

Based on the U.S. and Canadian experiences, Carlino points out that teaching writing is a shared responsibility of all subjects that consider writing as a constituent of their own disciplines and attach the term "intensive writing" to them. These subjects with "intensive writing" – besides imparting discipline contents – should have characteristics, presented in the university statutes. This implies a significant curricular change. For example:
1. There must be a minimum of formal writing tasks. The work is to be developed and checked in drafting phases, teacher-oriented and guided (teachers will provide written comments and tutorials, organize in-class group analyses and pair-comments, etc.).
2. Time must be allotted in class to discuss writing procedures, assessment criteria, model texts and most frequent problems, as well as providing feedback in the students' composing.
3. Students must be allowed to participate in one or more individual tutorials with the teacher.

4. Reading material cannot go beyond a set number of pages per week, so that students can have time to read it.
5. Each teacher must have a limited number of tutees so their work can be properly assessed.
6. The program will include writing activities and assessment procedures.
7. Credits are granted upon completion of intensive writing courses, which will in turn enable the students to complete writing requirements established by the university.
8. Professors in charge of these subjects will take seminars on literariness, academic literacy, so they are qualified to lead the writing process in their students.

Carlino describes briefly the instituted systems in the Canadian and U.S. universities to teach students how to write academic texts. She contrasts this intensive writing against low written production in Latin American schools, even in Spain. Carlino notes that the implementation of these programs derives from a defined awareness of considering writing as a central tool and an indispensable one to learn any subject.

She emphasizes that writing is a key tool to learn, reconsider, develop and reorganize knowledge about a subject matter. Writing cannot be deemed only as a means to register knowledge; it must go beyond, identifying discourse practices inherent in each discipline, and its practice accompanied by the professor in his role as tutor and students as authors and peers. Writing is not just remedial work; it is above all curricular essence.

In *Escribir, leer y aprender en la universidad,* Paula Carlino (2010), describes four activities she developed in class linking writing products to reinforce content internalization in college students:
1. Synthesis-rote elaboration of the lesson.
2. Group writing tutorials.
3. Exam preparation.
4. Written response to bibliography-related questions.

In **synthesis-rote elaboration of the lesson**, the teacher explains a topic and a couple of students registers the development of the lesson to write the synthesis, which will be handed in, in slides, to the group at the beginning of the next lesson. The couple reads the synthesis and both group and teacher make comments to improve the text. The class revisits the previous lesson and gets feedback from the notes taken. As background, the teacher presented a task sample and delivered printed models to the students to show basic structures.

The student-writers follow up a writing plan related to the subject's contents. They have real readers and submit their product to group assessment, which implies the revision of one work per student. This is an elaboration task. Its public revision will develop critical thinking too if they are asked to give their opinions about the contents.

Group writing tutorials includes treatises or research papers. It is the development of a well-defined topic based on documentary information about a specific issue, social, literary, scientific, historic, etc. Carlino explains there is a general agreement for structuring the treatise: introduction, development, conclusions and bibliography. She insists it is vital students are told how to structure it and what to include in each section.

Exam preparation refers to preparing the students to face an exam. Carlino explains it is a good thing to deliver potential exam questions. These will demand a higher level of abstraction and generalization. Students must reveal text-author and bibliography-lesson topic relations. Drills are implemented to identify incomplete answers and work towards improvement.

Written response to bibliography-related questions. Three questions are asked about specific texts as bibliography to write a paper that remarks the most important elements. The teacher reads response samples and identifies-comments recurring difficulties. Names are not mentioned; only answers from a formal and content perspective.

These activities are proposed by Carlino for college students. However, they can be useful to work in senior high. The proposals made allow us to state a few points:

- ✓ In senior high, there are generalized discourse forms that must be addressed, tutorially or with accompaniment, to help students. PhD Rojas details the most common techniques used in senior high: questionnaires, summaries, glossaries, critique, synthesis, treatises, text commentaries, essays.
- ✓ Other forms that can be implemented are research reports, historiographical analyses, etc. These documents have a higher degree of specialization so they are left for university junior and senior students.
- ✓ There are subjects with no continual format of written texts, as the above-mentioned ones. Such is the case of Physics. In this subject, students must decode, interpret, comprehend and elaborate non-continual-format texts (terms used by PISA, Programme for International Student Assessment): texts in charts, boxes and graphs,

16

for example. Academic literacy will consider the contextual needs and the requirements of each subject.

✓ Texts types, even similar ones, are not treated equally. In senior high, there is still confusion between summary and synthesis, review and essay, as confusion is detected in approaching theoretical conceptions. The same applies regarding data registration, where traditional Latin abbreviations are used yet sometimes APA (American Psychological Association) is required. This latter form has gained preference internationally.

As a conclusion, academic literacy or literariness today demands we "write through the curriculum" focusing on specific discipline-related texts. For that reason, finding paths towards upgrading personnel in the identification, analysis, implementation and development of useful strategies to teach reading, thinking and learning in our schools is paramount in the improvement of our educational pursuits.

References

Carlino, Paula. (2005) *Escribir, leer y aprender en la universidad. Una introducción a la alfabetización académica.* Buenos Aires: Fondo de Cultura Económica.
Varios. (2013) *Memorias del XII Congreso Latinoamericano para el Desarrollo de la Lectura y la Escritura y IV Foro Iberoamericano de Literacidad y Aprendizaje.* México: BUAP.

Incorporating the External School Environment to Develop Language Skills with a Culturally Diverse Class

Graham Ducker. Teacher, Poet, Lecturer

In the late sixties, the Ontario Government consolidated the small school boards. Mr. J. M. Steele, the Director for the Fort Frances-Rainy River Board of Education, was determined to ensure equal access for all children in the district. One initiative was the introduction of all-day, everyday Kindergarten classes into the rural areas that had never had Kindergarten. The two-room Morson Public School was set aside for Kindergarten and Grade One. The students came from the surrounding villages of Bergland, Minahico, and Morson, and the two First Nations Communities of Big Grassy and Big Island. The 50-50 Indigenous-to-Non-Indigenous student ratio presented a unique challenge, especially given the Director's mandate:

- Design a comprehensive Language Development Program that reflects and responds to the cultural and social diversity within the Morson-Bergland community.
- Develop an all-inclusive flexible program that meets and adapts to the individual needs of every student.
- The progress of each student must be easily ascertained and readily available.
- The classroom atmosphere is to be relaxed, stress-free, and comfortable; the students must feel secure.
- The merging of the two cultures is to be gentle and unobtrusive.

To meet these goals, two primary pedagogical questions needed to be addressed: 1) How would one create a language program that combined the various aspects of cultural diversity? and 2) Was there a commonality that could be utilized? The approach that addressed both considerations eventually became clear: incorporating the external environment. What follows is a deep dive into the specific challenges and considerations that influenced the ultimate decision as well as a sample lesson on language development.

Factors to consider

My philosophy is that the first encounter with school should be — *must* be — a happy relaxing experience. This, then, begs the question, *how does one create a calm, stress-free environment? Further to that, what influences contribute to a relaxed classroom?*

To answer these questions, one must first consider common pupil factors, as follows:

- All pupils are influenced by the home environment.

- Although there are variations in learning abilities, there are universal similarities among children.
- All children pass through the same development stages, as scholars like Piaget have long asserted.
- Interest levels tend to be about the same, but may differ in mixed groupings.
- All children need love, security, and understanding.
- Most children worry about making mistakes.

Given the context of a classroom with an approximately 50-50 Indigenous-Non-Indigenous split, various cross-cultural factors also needed to be considered. This led to the creation of the following guiding principles:

- The children must be in an environment that allows them to communicate freely.
- The classroom environment must be relaxed and happy.
- There must be a non-competitive atmosphere, although friendly rivalries may develop naturally.
- Teacher sincerity and friendliness must be genuine; children quickly see through deception.
- A consistent high performance should be expected of each student, consistent with the pupil's learning ability.
- The teaching style must be warm and friendly.
- Without being discernible, cultural groupings must be avoided.
- There should be no rush for answers, written or oral.
- Employ short one-on-one sessions.
- Listen more, talk less.
- Be ready to accept silence.

With all of these factors under consideration, two main goals emerged:

- to provide the non-threatening relaxed atmosphere in which language development would flourish.
- to provide opportunities for discussion and sharing which would unobtrusively blend the cultures.

This exploration would be incomplete, however, without acknowledging the specific pitfalls of a Kindergarten class, namely that the classroom area can be constraining and that variety among activities can become too routine. Despite having stations such as a sandbox, bins of materials, a science station, a paint station, a kitchen area, a Lego station, and a library, as well as activities like discussion time, circle time, story creation, and music/action songs, the Kindergarten room still seemed to be incomplete. Was there, then, another area...

...that could be utilized?
...that would appeal to all children?
...that would stimulate language?
...that was familiar to both cultures?
...that presented relaxed conditions?

It was from these final guiding questions that the over-arching answer appeared: incorporating the external environment — the school yard, the large fields, the treed areas, the ponds, and especially the immense rock outcrop to the north.

"The Rock" and "Magicland"

Two hundred feet from the school began "The Rock," a huge outcrop of Precambrian Shield with its typical hollows of grasses, mosses, junipers, and Jack Pines. A variety of animals resided there such as American Red Squirrels, Snowshoe Hares, and Red Foxes. This became one of the main teaching areas. On many excursions, we ventured out here where the warm, relaxed conditions allowed for conversations around topics that were bothering the children.

On the north side was a fairly large region of poplar trees, shrubs, and ferns growing among scattered large boulders. This was Magicland and the children loved it. In the spring, it was very interesting as one could see through the area where the children were running and chasing each other along the many little paths around these boulders. As the spring progressed, the bushes gradually filled in all the spaces, except for these paths. Soon, under shady poplar trees, the brush formed low canopies over the well-travelled trails. It wasn't long before all you could see were little treed entrances, about four feet high, leading into Magicland. You could hear squealing children, but you couldn't see them. Once in a while, a little one would come out of one opening, and vanish into an adjacent one. It was their private little world. It was only when the bell rang did the tunnels disgorge their precious inhabitants.

To appreciate the intricacy and wonderment of Magicland, one had to bend over and follow a trail. I remember going in, sitting down somewhere out of the way, and watching "the ants" zipping along the tunnels. In there, time had a way of standing still. When school resumed in the fall, it wasn't long before Magicland was re-established. I often think of Magicland and "the ants."

The Straw Routine
A typical language development lesson

Part 1: Observations
- The class goes outside where, in the tall-grass area, each student selects a piece of grass (straw).
- Different aspects of the straw are discussed with no description ignored or scoffed at by anyone.
- Sometimes in the excitement, a child is asked to "hold that word" or it is jotted down to be used later.
- Leading questions are asked, and all answers are accepted. This is particularly important. A useful guiding question could be, what can we say about our straws?

"Long" could lead to "tall and high."
"Skinny" could lead to "thin, narrow, slender, slim."
"Dry" could lead to "crunchy, cracklie, feels flakie."
"Break" could lead to "snap, brittle, breaks easily."
"Smells like hay, like straw, like grass."
"It looks yellow, tan, brownish, yellowy."
"Tastes like..."

The goal is to extrapolate on the initial words, meaning teacher creativity is important. It is also essential to record the words so that once the conversation is pretty well exhausted, pupils return to the classroom and use the words in a chart story.

Part 2: The chart story

The words are written in a chart story. Descriptions of the straw are reviewed. These words become sight or reading words. Repetition of the descriptions reinforces the language. Such impromptu lessons become the best occasions that spur language development.

It should be noted that this lesson can be easily adapted by substituting a piece of grass for a rock, some moss, a twig, new grass, sand, a pine cone, pussy willow, a berry, a fly, a Wood Tick, different types of leaves, pieces of bark, etc. With this age group, "bugs" can be a real blast!

Both the considerations that influenced the decisions made and the sample lesson on language development I propose have served to fulfill the objectives set for this paper.

Circles in the Spiral: How life offers opportunities for reconnection, recovery, and redemption

PhD & MSc Ronald Mackay

Shane Joseph's choice of title for his most recent novel can be understood as a metaphor for a perspective on the nature of life and the fortuitous breaks that it affords us. Redemption lies within our grasp if only we recognise, seize, and act upon these moments.

Circles in the Spiral (Blue Denim Press Inc.) suggests that our lives are not constrained to follow the temporal links in a metaphorical chain in which earlier events restrict subsequent opportunities so that our future is inescapably predetermined. The word *Circles* in the title, conveys the idea that life is structured like a carrousel, returning to us opportunities that we earlier handled badly; that life is cyclical and so offers us a second, even a third, chance to get things right. The word *Spirals* complements *Circles* by adding the potential of upward stirring, of reaching, of the opportunity to strive for and embrace betterment, our own and that of others.

Thesis

In this essay, I argue that *Circles in the Spiral*, despite the failure and demoralization especially in the earlier chapters, offers the reader an ultimately reassuring view of life, one in which we as individuals are afforded the opportunity to review our past, acknowledge our present, amend our ways, forgive those who have trespassed against us, and make the world a better place.

The early chapters of the novel focus on the cyclical nature of lives grown out of deception, neglect, and desecration. In the later chapters, the potential for redemption is revealed. Nevertheless, throughout the entire novel, the author scatters crumbs of hope that suggest, rather than promise, a path to reparation. *Circles in the Spiral* tells a story of contemporary life in Canada and the modern world beyond any single country. It is a story of vice but also of virtue. It portrays in the most graphic and immediate of ways the dereliction of moral duty, of self-absorption that extinguishes empathy, of disregard, dishonesty, carelessness, apathy, treachery, malevolence, and despair. It shows a world in which our moral sentiments have been taken over by market value. Nevertheless, true to the title, it ascends – or rather, clambers clumsily – towards the promise, if not the realisation, of what Western classical and Christian culture has always encouraged: a firm disposition to aspire to that which is good through the practise of virtue, in particular the virtues of prudence, justice, temperance, and courage; of faith, hope, and charity.

I support these arguments by revealing some of the ways and means by which Shane Joseph's *Circles in the Spiral* successfully conveys this initially bleak but ultimately affirmative view of life and the redemptive implications it has for the characters and, by extension, for us readers.

Outline

First, I summarise the premise of the novel and the roles the protagonists play in the dramatic plot and some of their circular and spiral movements. Then I discuss the evolving moral perspective demonstrated by the action, and the recurring opportunities for personal and social betterment offered to the main characters. Finally, I draw a broad conclusion about the importance of this book as a work of contemporary Western, and particularly Canadian, fiction.

Synopsis adapted from the novel

Will Smallwood, a writer suffering from the dreaded writer's block as well as tormenting dreams, is plunged into a living nightmare when he is swept up into a misinformation campaign aimed at hijacking the Canadian Federal Election.

On the run, Will is forced to confront his personal demons: his suppressed childhood, his stalled career as a historical fiction writer, his lost love, Jacqueline, and the malaise of his aimlessness. He is offered a second chance to put things right when he is drawn to a yoga retreat and meets the promiscuous painter, Divine Secrets (Dee), along with a motley group of academics, alcoholics, and ascetics. The key to his deliverance lies in his uncovering the identity of the mystery person with the Twitter handle @abandonedchild97 stalking him on social media.

From an idyllic lake to a series of dashes between Ottawa and Toronto, pursued by mobsters and police, Will assembles the pieces of the puzzle while coming to the realization that his dysfunctional past and complicated present are connected, that people and events are re-entering his life for a reason, and that to open his mind and heart without cloaking them in fiction or fake news is his only road to redemption.

Techniques used by the Novelist

Will Smallwood is the sole narrator. Occasionally, he admits to being self-serving in his account of events, suggesting that he is not entirely reliable. The action takes place cyclically in three locations in chronological time: at Guru Swaminanda's lakeside retreat located in cottage country north of Ottawa; in the National Capital Region of Ottawa; in Canada's most populous region,

Greater Toronto; and then back in Ottawa until the dénouement at the guru's retreat once more.

The plot is complex and original. It makes use of recurring events, the apparently random but multiple appearance of the same characters and a sweeping circle through the same places from beginning to end.

The story is told within twelve lucid chapters. Overall, events are shown in chronological order. The principal exception is an account of a crucial period of Will's life when he was married to Jacqueline, like Will himself, a damaged being. Jacqueline committed suicide shortly after giving birth to Roy. The author offers this chapter as a deeply moving piece of reminiscence and introspection on Will's part. From time to time, the principal characters, Will, Dee, and Roy – and the secondary characters: Guru Swaminanda, Professor Darlington, Phil and Marge Davis, and Roy's social worker, Peggy Smithers – provide essential information about their backstories in conversation and flashbacks.

Discussion
Will Smallwood, a twice-divorced novelist whose earlier good fortune and creativity have dried up, spends his few remaining dollars to attend a rural spiritual retreat run by Guru Swaminanda. Swaminanda is "full of secrets and contradictions." He apparently indulges an unseemly appetite for the more attractive women attending his events. Once there, Will meets other souls like himself – lost and damaged individuals seeking serenity, respite, and whatever else they can grasp to make the expense worth their while.

Dee is a commercial artist fatigued by the corporate world, pursuing self-knowledge, sex, and liberation from the material. The widower, Professor Darlington, enjoys viewing naked bodies through his binoculars and casting aspersions on the sincerity of the Guru and everybody else. The Davis couple, Phil and Marge, appear to seek no more than a change of venue where they can vent the resentment they harbour for their ungrateful, dependent, adult children, as well as for each other.

In addition to successfully wooing Dee from the Guru's bed to his, Will experiences a mild epiphany. He recognises the futility of his life as a writer of formulaic historical fiction. He vows to abandon this genre and replace it with more current, penetrating writing about "real people and the things that matter in their lives."

One of the few insights that Guru Swaminanda offers his guests during the retreat is that life is cyclical, the same people and similar circumstances continuously re-present themselves. This, he suggests, foretells future encounters among the members of this small group and the recurring opportunities they offer each other to readjust their lives.

Will Smallwood's sexual affair with Dee continues when they return to Ottawa. However, neither Will nor Dee fulfil the resolutions they made to change their lives. Will had resolved to write novels based on immutable truths and real people; Dee, to abandon the commercial world of decorative art in which she had been successful but frustrated, in favour of more personal and fulfilling creativity.

As if to highlight the repudiation of his resolution, Will accepts an offer to write highly-paid, positive spin for social media on behalf of a department within the office of the Prime Minister of Canada. It turns out that Professor Darlington, he of the binoculars, runs this office for the purpose of preserving and polishing the reputation of the Prime Minister to ensure that he and his party will win the upcoming election and remain in power. Will also toys with writing a commercial blog funded by advertisements.

Equally neglectful of her resolution, Dee accepts a lucrative artistic assignment to decorate the headquarters building of a major corporation in Toronto. Before Dee leaves for Toronto, it becomes clear that their relationship is more carnal than intellectual, certainly on Will's side. "After all," Will reflects, "Dee and I were just meeting to have sex"; and again, "Sex was our substance." Dee, for her part, tries to get closer to Will by telling him about her own unhappy and abusive childhood. She tells him that she admires him, "for reaching upwards. That's attractive in a man." Dee herself is taking the first steps to rise, to confide in another person and to form a trustful relationship.

Will's hovers on the brink of revealing his past to Dee but is unable to revisit his childhood hell. He fails to reciprocate the confidences she shares with him and reflects to himself, "I knew I was running away from my past..."
Will is merely circling, repeating superficial relationships. Dee, too, is circling but striving, now, to rise into the spiral.

It is at this point that the author uses flashback. In an entire chapter, one of the most important in the novel, Will reflects on his early life as a way of explaining his inability to connect closely with Dee. As a child, he was shunted from one foster home to another. He suffered psychological and physical abuse. As a young adult, he fell in love with Jacqueline, a fractured woman who had herself never recovered from a background of parental rejection that led to social disfunction and mental instability. She becomes pregnant and uses her pregnancy to torture Will by suggesting that he may, or may not, be the father of the child she is carrying. Shortly after the child, Roy, is born, Dee commits suicide. Will, unable to cope, allows Roy to be adopted and washes his hands, though not his conscience, of the entire episode.

Back to the present. In his well-paid government work as a writer of promotional social media, Will is harassed online by a troll whose Twitter handle is @abandonedchild97. The troll's communications suggest that the Prime Minister of Canada has engaged in duplicitous behaviour, which, if revealed might cost him and his party the election.

Alerted by the evocative title, @abandonedchild97, Will suspects that the troll may be Roy, the child he discarded. With help from Guru Swaminanda who runs an ashram in Ottawa, Will tracks Roy down. They talk. Roy assures Will that his twitter tag was stolen, and that he knows nothing about it being used to harass Will or to threaten a disinformation campaign against the Prime Minister. The swift but frank reunion serves to form the beginnings of a bond between Will and Roy. Will admits that he abandoned Roy and that he may be the boy's father. Indeed, a DNA test later proves them to be father and son. The bond between them is strengthened by their relationship, the abusive childhoods they share, and by Will's desire to make amends.

This represents the crucial point at which Will begins, excruciatingly slowly and against his natural inclination, to spiral out of the cyclical trap within which he has been imprisoned for most of his life: "Deep down inside me," he reflects, "despite my protests, jubilation was gurgling. I had a son."

Meanwhile, Professor Darlington, now Will's boss, turns out to be unsound. He may have assisted in the death of his own wife to inherit her life insurance, his university post has been withdrawn, and he associates unaccountably with a repugnant Russian called Igor. By accident of circularity, Will encounters the two of them together in an Ottawa restaurant. Darlington lacks the capacity – or is it the will? – to manage the department established to ensure the success of the Prime Minister and his party in the upcoming election and shows himself unable – or unwilling? – to counter the false news about the PM's political integrity. Most alarmingly, Darlington encourages the finger of accusation for leaking information, that can only help the campaign of false news, to be pointed at Will. To Darlington's satisfaction, an agent of the Canadian Security Intelligence Service appropriates Will's laptop to search for evidence of collusion with those shadowy characters seeking to influence the election.

In panic, Will flees from Ottawa to Toronto where Dee is working temporarily. That Dee welcomes him and offers him sanctuary is another hint that she is in the upward spiral, willing to trust and help take Will with her.

However, when Will is alone, the mysterious Russian, Igor, breaks into Dee's suite with two henchmen. They transfer their captive to a motel. Will's captors are so inept that they fail to deprive him of his cell phone. Unwilling to contact the police for fear of being accused of treachery, Will calls the only person he believes may help – his son, Roy.

Will is starting to experiment with trust.

Here, the rising spiral effect becomes more prominent. Circumstances are transforming Roy from child abandoned into saviour of the very man who abandoned him – his own father. Roy is developing into a redeemer.
These are instances of the circular and spiral essence of the plot sufficient for the purpose of the essay to this point.

Discussion of some of the vices and virtues depicted
In what ways is *Circles in the Spiral* a contemporary story of vice and virtue?
I start with vice since the author gives a great deal more space to demonstrations of self-absorption that extinguishes empathy, neglect, dishonesty, carelessness, apathy, treachery, malevolence, and despair.

In the first chapter, at Guru Swaminanda's lakeside retreat, the author presents characters almost entirely devoid of virtue.

Will is bitter at having been jilted by his second wife, Susan, for a lover more capable of providing her with a stable, decent, and comfortable life, and fathering children she can take care of with his financial and emotional help. Will is bitter also about his "achieve nothing life" and about "losing his groove," resulting in his failure to develop as a successful author. Will's motivation for signing up for Guru Swaminanda's retreat is more escapism than a search for spiritual renewal. He is attracted to Dee for "her curvy bottom swaying under the flimsy pastel dress" and wonders if this preliminary encounter "would extend to sex."

After Will and Dee couple, then depart for Ottawa together, their relationship becomes largely devoid of the close, human "I to thou" exchange of equals seeking to know each other, to love, trust, and share. Will appears to be unable to relate to Dee as anything more than a sexual object; Dee appears more willing to view Will as a subject to whom she might connect with as a person. To that end, Dee recounts the neglect and abuse she suffered as a child and asks Will for a reciprocal account of his life. But Will is incapable of mirroring Dee's confidences. He himself admits, "I was also avoiding my own unravelling to Dee. … I knew I was running away from my past, not the one with Susan, but the one that had come before, the one that even Susan knew nothing about." Will has lived most of his life without a trusting relationship.

Will tries to work on the more meaningful novel he had resolved to write, but his efforts diminish as he realises that "after all, Dee and I were just meeting to have sex." Indeed, sexual encounters seem to count for more than communicating profoundly with words. Dee and Will barely know each other, principally because Will cannot find a way of trusting his confidences to another. Especially in the case of Will, this is a strategy employed by the author to have us appreciate how difficult, even unthinkable, it is for him to revisit the trauma of his youth as an abandoned orphan farmed out to foster homes who cared only about the profit for their efforts and not for the well-being of the subjects entrusted to their safekeeping. Several times, after Dee or Roy has unburdened themselves to Will and sought a like confidence, none is forthcoming. Will has suffered what might be Post-Traumatic Stress Syndrome and copes only by refusing to revisit his past.

The first real person-to-person communication occurs when Will has found Roy but their relationship as father and son has not yet been confirmed by the DNA test. For the very first time, Will is able to reveal the hardship of his own childhood to Roy. This is the low turning point of the story. This is essentially part of the recurring circle but most importantly it is the beginning of the spiral that will allow Will to begin an upward trajectory towards his essential humanity and allow himself to relate to others, Roy and Dee in particular, in meaningful human relationships created out of trust, perhaps even leading, ultimately, to a relationship with the eternal *Thou* of transcendental importance.

Will begins to trust more when he becomes a suspect in the disinformation campaign. His first trusting step is to put his life in Dee's hands by escaping to Toronto and going into hiding in her hotel suite while she is fulfilling her contract. Still too wary of the police, the very institution created to inspire confidence and uphold certainty, to ask for their help when he is kidnapped by the Russian goons, Will takes his second step towards trust when he calls Roy and asks for his help.

Will, like Dee and Roy but with far greater difficulty, is slowly emerging from a repetitious and deleterious circularity into the spiral that may lead to his redemption.

Guru Swaminanda, head of an ashram and host of retreats dedicated to divine aspiration, comes across as a flawed character. On the one hand, he is a shallow imposter as much intent on personal gain – whether it be free sex, money, or ownership if a lakeside resort in which to host his retreats – as on providing spiritual and moral guidance to his paying guests. On the other hand, his rejection of the material life, however pleasurable or painful it may be, in favour of "facilitating spiritual evolution," raises him to the status of guardian angel and liberator, if only in his own eyes.

Roy is one of the most intriguing characters in the novel. Despite all that he has suffered at the hands of his biological parents, his foster parents, and then from the clients who paid for his sexual services, he has retained a certain purity, an improbable integrity. These qualities are at one and the same time both the purity of the blameless child and the purifying wrath of the Angel of the Lord that "stretched out his hand upon Jerusalem to destroy it" in 2 Samuel 24.16. When Roy frees Will by killing the Russian goons, Will marvels: "Why are you doing this for me, Roy? When all I did was abandon you?"

At that point, Roy seems to grow to the dimensions of a biblical saviour. He is in the upward spiral.

In the end, the most corrupt character of all turns out to be Professor Darlington. Throughout, he is gradually revealed to be spiralling in a direction opposite to the others. The route he is taking is downwards and away from virtue into the depths of degradation and treachery.

With this contrasting portrayal of Darlington, the author is showing that circles in the spiral have the capacity to move in either direction.

By tracing some of the depictions of vice and virtue through this novel, I have tried to demonstrate how the author has used narrative structure to transform our perception of the characters and of the world they inhabit. We, the readers, change our perception because the characters have been induced to change theirs.

In this paper, I have shown some of the literary techniques and creative ways by which veteran novelist Shane Joseph draws our attention to the fundamental thesis of *Circles in the Spiral* -- that the interplay intrinsic to all human relationships are founded upon continuous exchange. If such exchanges are reduced to mere "goods" in "markets" – such as Will's initial preoccupation with the pursuit of sexual satisfaction from whoever could provide it at a cost he could afford; in the purely financial link between the Davis couple and their grown but still dependent children that causes resentment; in Roy viewing his body as a commodity to be offered to whomever for economic rent; in Dee's frustration that her artistic creativity has been hijacked by the highest corporate bidder – then humanity is adrift.

Exchange considered in this narrow way leads inexorably to moral degradation and societal breakdown. On the other hand, exchange can, Joseph shows, be considered more broadly and more in keeping with the expressed intention of Adam Smith, the great 18th century moral philosopher and economist. This broader interpretation incorporates, necessarily, the exchange of communication and mutual respect; communication by means of meaningful conversation and personal regard through the reciprocation of mindful esteem of the other, so establishing trust.

In the novel, Will, Dee, and Roy gradually acquire this appreciation of what true exchange must mean and how they must realise it in practice. On their part, resolution to act on that appreciation will bring them a long-awaited redemption. The author's cunningly slow reveal that this is the direction his protagonists choose, is why the reader can enjoy this novel as a tribute to hope rather than as a condemnation of despair.

Circles in the Spiral demonstrates that our future does not have to be dependent on our past if we choose to replace vicious circles with alternatives more virtuous. In this accomplished novel, Shane Joseph captures the essence of the principle that has shaped and continues to shape the personal, social, and political temper of Canada – the resolve to "get things right".

Bibliography
Wood, James. (2008) *How Fiction works*. Picador, New York.
Fritz, Stephen Martin. (2019) *Our Human Herds: The Theory of Dual Morality*. Dog Ear Publishing, Indianapolis.
Haidt, Jonathan. (2013) *The Righteous Mind: Why Good People are Divided by Politics and Religion*. Vintage Books, New York.
Scruton, Roger. (2017) *On Human Nature*. Princeton University Press. Princeton, New Jersey.

Controversy between FLT Approach and Method in the Cuban Context

PhD María Elena Ayala Ruiz. Full Professor
PhD Pedro Antonio Machín Armas. Full Professor

In the last decades, foreign language teaching has had a long history of discussion on teaching methods. Nowadays, when teachers are asked about the method they use, most of them say that they do not follow a method at all, but an approach. Some of them will state that their teaching obeys the principles that emerge from the communicative approach, but in many cases, the procedures and techniques they follow contradict their intention.

The above assertion raises a question in contemporary methodology about the implications that the misapprehension of the categories *method-approach* has for the management of the teaching-learning process. If it is true that there must be flexibility for contextualizing this process, it is too risky to let teachers make their own decisions when they are not sufficiently trained. Although many graduate courses and methodological sessions have been carried out on the theme, there are still difficulties, mainly in novice teachers, that interfere the logical coherence of lesson planning and teaching. Some of these deficiencies can be summed up in the following way:

- The devised activities frequently focus on grammar.
- Teachers follow the students' textbook session sequence, and this makes them dependent on this source and unaware of a methodological conception.
- Despite the fact that teachers write the *communicative approach* as a methodological conception of the lesson, not all of them master its precepts.
- There are still limitations in sequencing and ensuring a logical transition through stages during the implementation of exercises and tasks within a unit of language contents.

The previous deficiencies allowed the authors to determine the objective of this paper: to examine how the terms method and approach enter the post method era, for their appropriate implementation in the English foreign language teaching in the Cuban intermediate school.

Many researchers have developed important studies on this theme: Carro, F. Manuel. (1995); Douglas Brown, H. (2002); Brown, H. D. (2002); Kumaravadivelu, B. (2006); Bell, D.M. (2008); Can, N. (2009); Richards, J.C. (2013); Cadario, E. (2014); Soto, M. (2014); Didenko A. et al. (2015); Khafidhoh, A. (2017); Liping, W. et.al (2018), among others. They all refer to universal principles and theories concerning how languages are learned, or how language

itself is structured, applying principles and approaches for the design of language teaching programs, courses, and materials. They also highlight the controversy among the terms *approach* and *method* and their attempt to clarify their differences. One of the deepest studies was developed by an American, applied linguist Edward Anthony (1963), who identified two levels of conceptualization and organization, termed *approach* and *method,* as follows*:*
"...within the teaching method framework, the approach is constituted by those theoretical principles on which the curricular design is based..."[1] Richards (2002: 25). Thus, an approach is usually understood as the body of linguistic, psychological and pedagogical theories which inspire the teaching practice, while a method includes the approach, design and procedures. *Approach* is also assumed as a set of correlative assumptions dealing with the nature of language-teaching and learning. An *approach* describes the nature of the subject matter to be taught. "...*method* is an overall plan for the orderly presentation of language material, no part of which contradicts, and all of which is based upon the selected approach. An approach is axiomatic, a method is procedural. Within one approach, there can be many methods. .."[2] Richards (2002: 33).

It means that the term *approach* includes the whole orientation of teaching. It is wider than the term *method,* since it provides the philosophy to the whole process of education and sets expectations to the whole spectrum of the teaching-learning process. In addition, it places the general rule or principle to make this process possible; while *method* with the corresponding techniques and procedures are just its components. In this respect, it can be assumed that "... *approach* is the level at which assumptions and beliefs about language and language learning are specified; *method* is the level at which theory is put into practice and at which choices are made about the particular skills to be taught, the content to be taught, and the order in which the content will be presented..."[3] Anthony (1983: 63).

From their studies, it can be inferred that *approach* is the theoretical basis, which comprises the theory about the nature of language and that about language learning which explains the psycholinguistic and cognitive processes that take place in learning a foreign language, as well as the conditions that favor such processes; so that, it may be said that *approach* is more general than *method*, in the sense that the latter is determined by the principles and precepts offered by the *approach* that teachers assume. Its assumption is vital, since it contains crucial guidelines for making didactic decisions, which are not concentrated on specific operational determinations; hence, *method* is being

---

[1] Richards J.C. 2002 p.25
[2] Richards J.C. 2002 p.33
[3] E.M. Anthony. 1983 p.63

confined as organized, orderly, systematic, and well-planned techniques and *procedures* that are designed to fulfill a given objective, which represents an anticipated teaching and learning result.

In spite of what the studies clearly reveal, *method* is still somehow controversial. The study developed by Bell, D. M. (2003) deserves teachers' reflection, since he states that although the notion of *method* no longer plays a significant role in the thought of applied linguists, it still plays a fundamental role in the thinking of teachers. To support this assertion, it is convenient to resort to General Didactics and its classical conceptions about method as a didactic category. "…method is a way of mediating between the students and the contents, which is also determined by psychological factors that prevail in a group of students or even in each of the students…"[4] Each teaching method and each methodological procedure has a particular psychological structure, and it is effective when the teacher takes into account psychological aspects in a concrete teaching situation.

Method is not only oriented to the students' intellectual development, but also to their skills and values education. It has to be determined by an objective in the direction of the teaching-learning process and is implemented taking into account the students' level of development and the other non-personal components of the pedagogical process. On the other hand, it should not be confused with the subjective form that teachers assume when teaching, with their teaching personal style; it has to be seen as the most important didactic tool for guiding the teaching-learning process. All what teachers have to do is to "track" the inner logic of the learning process, so it can be managed in such a way that the students apprehend the content by means of their own activity. From this perspective, *method* is the way that the teacher follows for managing a well-planned and systematic teaching-learning process for the apprehension of the teaching content.

Taking the previous explanations into consideration, it is opportune to explore more recent approaches to language teaching. Other methods and pedagogical approaches to foreign language teaching continue to proliferate in this post-communicative era. In Cuba, the developmental approach plays a prioritized position together with the communicative and interdisciplinary approaches which are inscribed in the same position as the action-oriented approach, which seems to integrate the most recent theoretical precepts for teaching a foreign language.

Many scholars agree with Kumaravadivelu (1994) who identified what he called the *post method* condition: a result of the widespread dissatisfaction with the

---

[4] Klingberg Lothar et al. 1975 p.28

conventional concept of *method*. Although post method teachers adjust their approach to contextual factors, the concept of *method* has not been replaced. More recently, Richards J. (2013) refers to *post method* as the term used to refer to teaching which is not based on the prescriptions and procedures of a particular method, but which draws on the teachers' individual conceptualizations of language, language learning and teaching, the practical knowledge and skills teachers develop from training and experience, the learners' needs, interests and learning styles, as well as the teachers understanding of the teaching context.

In this respect, Kumaravadivelu (2001) advocates that any *post method* pedagogy ought to be particular, in the sense that language pedagogy must be according to a particular group of teachers, a particular group of learners following particular objectives, within a particular institutional context embedded in a specific sociocultural environment. This concept highlights the importance of providing teachers with a broad didactic framework based on updated theoretical conceptions that allow their autonomous behaviors when devising for themselves a systematic, consistent, and pertinent methodology, taking into consideration other important variables: learners' attitudes, motivations and other personality resources; such as, perseverance, flexibility, reflection, and open positions for learning.

From this perspective, Soto M.A. (2014) assumes that teachers tend to develop their own context-bound methodologies; however, it has been suggested that without proper teacher education programs, the *post method* condition might entail the risk of ELT practitioners, adopting some sort of "my-own-method" style, which might result in a "hybrid". Her position aims at teachers' integral preparation for conceiving and implementing their own methodologies in an era when the death of methods is being understood by some professionals in the field of foreign language teaching.

If it is true that *method* has been discredited in the thought of scholars, it certainly keeps a great deal of vitality and has to be part of the teachers' worries all the time. It cannot be taken as a single set of theoretical principles, but as a potential resource that has an important inner structure, whose vitality is given by teacher' choices as solutions to particular contextual needs and the resulting set of practices; thus, *post-method* does not imply the end of method, but a better understanding of its limitations.

Teachers should be exposed to all methods and they themselves would 'build' their own methods or decide what principles they would use in their teaching; thus, there is a challenge of training *post method* teachers (Cadario, 2014). This author states that the big challenge for teacher trainers at the university is to equip future teachers with the conceptual knowledge and competences that will allow them to make methodological decisions that suit the different contexts where they will soon be teaching. Theoretical foundation, at many different levels, is required for practitioners to be able to satisfy their students' learning needs and styles and also their own teaching identities.

As Cadario very well says, future teachers need to gain access to a big bulk of theoretical knowledge and develop their critical thinking skills to be capable of putting theories, principles, teaching techniques and strategies into the different teaching contexts they will face. *Post method* teachers must be reflective and critical if they are to become autonomous in the decision-making processes and be sensitive, not only towards their students and teaching contexts, but also towards their own identities.

Some of the aspects that teachers should bear in mind for deciding their own methods could be the following:

a. For accomplishing the communicative approach of the lesson, they must ensure that:

- The objective of the lesson is expressed in terms of communication, expressing a communicative function.
- The lesson topic orients the students towards a theme or topic for communication rather than on grammatical forms.
- The topic is of interest to the learners (motivation).
- The students know what they have to do in every activity or task. They know what they will be able to do at the end (orientation).
- The lesson focuses on communicative functions.
- There are communicative situations to introduce each task.
- Dialogues or passages are used to contextualize the language to be studied or practiced (contextualization).
- There are interaction techniques in the lesson (pair work, group work).
- The learners are motivated to take part in the activities and they get involved.
- There is often a purpose for listening, speaking, reading or writing (Communicative purpose).
- Drills are meaningful.
- There are activities that elicit opinions, feelings and beliefs from the learners.
- There is information gap; that is the students exchange information among them.
- The students have language choice to say what they want to express.
- There are tasks that integrate skills.
- The teacher is available and ready to offer help.

b. For integrating communication with the principles of the Developmental Approach, teachers' attention should be focused on:

- The cognitive independence of the students and their protagonist role; they should have autonomy and get involved.
- The development of creativity
- The unity between affective and cognitive aspects
- The promotion of self-reflection and self-evaluation
- Development of thinking skills
- The role of motivation
- The role of communication and activity in the students' integral formation

c. The communicative lesson is developmental when:
- The activities included are slightly beyond the current developmental level of the learners.
- Tasks are devised according to the students' level.
- The teacher creates possibilities of cooperation and interaction among the learners.
- The students are asked about what they do not know.
- The teacher promotes discovery learning through heuristic dialogs.
- The students are taught how to study the language more effectively.
- Thinking questions are used.
- The learners monitor and correct among them.
- Self-evaluation and co-evaluation are used before giving them their marks.
- The teacher carries out reflection sessions about how to learn.
- Values education is promoted through the lesson contents and activities.
- There is flexibility in class and respect for pupils' viewpoints.
- Diversity is taken into consideration.
- Teachers use opened-ended questions.
- They establish a good atmosphere of collaboration and trust.
- They include tasks that promote divergent thinking.
- They use correction techniques properly.

d. For fostering the Communicative Approach and the Developmental Approach from an interdisciplinary perspective, teachers should:
- Take into consideration the other subjects of the curriculum.
- Work with authentic texts that deal with cross-curriculum themes.
- Establish relationships to exchange ideas with other subject teachers to solve common problems in the content area.

There is a tendency of some foreign language teachers to follow the sequence of course books, rather than assuming a conscious decision-making process to determine the best methodology that may adjust to their students´ needs; hence, the importance of having an awareness of *approach* and *method*. These two concepts have been clearly defined and characterized in the current literature; the former, as the interdisciplinary philosophy that supports foreign language teaching and learning; the latter, as the system of techniques and procedures which find applications in practice as supported by the approach or approaches.

In the post method era, language educators prefer to use the term methodology which encompasses the system of techniques and procedures based on the teachers´ beliefs and assumptions about language teaching and learning. This body or system of techniques, procedures, actions and attitudes must be coherently integrated and organized in order to meet the learning needs of a particular course, group of students and their learning objectives and conditions. A methodology should be flexible enough to adjust the teachers´ teaching style and the students´ learning styles.

Bibliography

Abad, J.V. (2013). *Pedagogical factors that influence EFL teaching: Some considerations for teachers´ professional development*. Profile, 15(1), 97-108.

Atherton, J.S (2011). *Learning and teaching; Bloom's taxonomy*. Retrieved March 3, 2011 from http://webcache.googleusercontent.com/search?q=cache:jacyEcDDPKkJ:www.learninga.

English language teaching in the post-methods era: Selected papers from the 39th FAAPI Conference / Banegas, Darío Luis ... [et.al.]. (2014). 1a ed. - Santiago del Estero: Asociación   de Profesores de Inglés de Santiago del Estero. E-Book. ISBN 978-987-24550-1-9

Bell, D.M. 2003. '*Method and post method: Are they really so incompatible?*' TESOLQuarterly 37/2: 325–36. Ohio University. 143 p ELT Journal Volume 61/2 April 2007; doi:10.1093/elt/ccm006 2007. Published by Oxford University Press.

Bell David M. (2005). *Do teachers think that methods are dead?* Final revised version received August 2005.

Brisida SEFA. (2017). *The Importance of Communicative Method in English Language Teaching*. In Interdisciplinary Journal of Research and Development, Vol. 4, no. 4.

Brown, H. D. (2002). '*English language teaching in the "post-method" era: toward better diagnosis, treatment, and assessment*'. In J. C. Richards and W. A. Renandya (eds.). Methodology in Language. Teaching: An Anthology of Current Practice. Cambridge: Cambridge University Press.

Can, N. (2009). Post-method Pedagogy: Teacher growth behind walls. Proceedings of the 10th METU ELT Convention. Ankara. Turkey. Accessed from: http://dbe.metu.edu.tr/convention/proceedingsweb/proceedings.htm

Cadario, Elisa. 2014. *Eclecticism in the "new" foreign language classroom: re-thinking practices and developing an awareness of context in teacher training college*. Universidad Nacional de Río Cuarto.

Carro, F. Manuel. (1995). *Enfoque, método y técnica en la enseñanza de idiomas*. *Actualización de definiciones*.

Criado, R., & Sanchez, A. (2009). *English language teaching in Spain: Do textbooks comply with the official methodological regulations? A sample analysis*. International Journal of English Studies.

Douglas Brown, H. (2002). *English language teaching in the "post-method" era: Toward better diagnosis, treatment and assessment*. In Richards, J. C. and W. A. Renandya,

(Eds.), Methodology in language teaching (pp. 9-18). Cambridge: Cambridge University Press.

Didenko Anastasia V. and Pichugova. (2015). *Post CLT or Post-Method: major criticisms of the communicative approach and the definition of the current pedagogy*. Web of Conferences 01028   SHS 28 RPTSS 2015

Eisenchlas, S. (2010). *Conceptualizing "communication" in foreign language instruction*. Babel, 44, pp.13-21.

E.M. Anthony. (1983). *Approach, method and technique*. English Language Teaching. Vol 17. January. pp 63-67.

Harmer, J. 2007. *The Practice of English Language Teaching*. Fourth Edition. Harlow: Pearson

Hiep, P. H. (2007). *Communicative language teaching: Unity within diversity*. ELT Journal, 61(3), 193-201.

Khafidhoh Ahmad Dahlan. (2017). *A Critical Review on Post-Method Era in English Language Teaching for Indonesian Context.* In METATHESIS, Vol. 1, No. 1, April 2017. ISSN: 2580-2712, e-ISSN: 2580-2720.

Klinberg, Lothar. Et.al. (1970). *Didáctica General*. Pueblo y Educación. La Habana.

Kumaravadivelu, B. (2003b). *Critical language pedagogy. A post method perspective on English language teaching.* World Englishes, 22(4), 539-550.

Kumaravadivelu, B. (2006). *TESOL methods: Changing tracks, challenging trends*. TESOL Quarterly, 40. 5981.

Kumaravadivelu, B. (2006). *Understanding language teaching: From method to postmethod*. Mahwah, NJ: Lawrence Erlbaum.

Larsen-Freeman, D. (2001). *The joy of watching others learn. An interview with Diane Larsen-Freeman by William P. Ancker*. English Teaching Forum 39. P. 2–9.

Liping Wei. Et.al (2018). *Communicative Language Teaching (CLT) in EFL Context in Asia*. (2018). Asian Culture and History; Vol. 10, No. 2; 2018 ISSN 1916-9655 E-ISSN 1916-9663 Published by Canadian Center of Science and Education

Richards, J.C., Renandya, W.A. (2002). *Methodology in Language Teaching: An Anthology of Current Practice*. Cambridge: CUP.

Richards, J.C. (2013). *Curriculum approaches in language teaching: Forward, central, and backward design*. RELC Journal, 44. Pp. 5-33.

Rogers, T. (2001). *Language teaching methodology, online resource* (http://www.cal.org/resources/digest/rodgers.html), Sep. 2001.

Soto, María Alejandra. (2014). *Post-method pedagogy: Towards enhanced context-situated teaching methodologies*. Facultad de Humanidades, Artes y Ciencias Sociales – UADER

Strategic Reading: A Challenge for Lifelong Learning

PhD María Elena Ayala Ruiz. Full Professor
PhD Pedro Antonio Machín Armas. Full Professor

In Cuban universities, the study of English as a foreign language has become a compulsory requisite in curriculum design due to its implications in the future professional job. It has brought about greater attention to the scientific management of the foreign language teaching-learning process, which demands an increasing didactic training of teachers. Consequently, many studies have been carried out about this theme that focus the attention on current approaches, whose principles guide teachers in their decision-making, and impose higher reflection on their teaching practices to favor students' learning.

Nowadays, the higher education system implements a developmental didactics "...which takes into account the link between instruction and education; the importance of an integral diagnosis; the role of communication; the activity and the establishment of interaction and interrelation in which cognitive, affective and volitional aspects are implied..."[5] This conception of *developmental learning* is the support of Cuban Pedagogy, which is now enriched with an action-oriented approach, proclaimed by the Common European Framework (CEFRL).

Both approaches are considered vital tools for teachers, since they offer the theoretical foundation for planning appropriate activities, in which the student is the center of attention; there is greater consciousness on the learning process and on diversity among learners; differences are viewed as resources to be recognized and respected for learning; the social nature of learning is taken into account, rather than students as separate individuals and the uniqueness of each context is the most important concern, where the institution is connected with the world beyond the classroom.

The previous assertions aim at promoting holistic education with a conception of learning as a *lifelong* process, rather than learning to pass an exam. The students' integral development, the progressive transition from their dependence to their independence and the acquisition of learning tools are three basic criteria to guarantee lifelong learning.

The theme has called many scholars' attention; so, many sources deal with it: Cros, F. (1999), European Commission (2001), Castellanos, D. (2005), Meyer, Ch. (2018), among others. *They reveal the importance of facilitating lifelong learning as a paradigm of teaching for personal development, which can be*

---

[5]Castellanos et al. 2005 p.33

obtained whenever the students are provided with learning strategies that allow them to develop skills for discovering and learning on their own.

With the previous intention, there have been very serious articles that describe the writers' thoughts about this topic in different countries. They emphasize *the importance of reading in the foreign language as a priority with great implications on everlasting learning.* They all assume that the students should be offered the opportunity to widen proficiency in reading comprehension for fostering critical reasoning, study skills, and reading skills, indispensable for success in academic and career development.

In spite of the efforts made at the university to teach reading well, there are still limitations in reading practices:
- There is not always a good motivation for reading.
- The same types of activities are repetitively used.
- Although the reading stages are usually covered, they are not explicitly taught.
- The students are seldom conscious of their own reading strategies.
- The students commonly read for answering questions; sometimes these questions do not meet their expectations.

These limitations allowed the authors to determine as the *objective* of this paper to propose a set of methodological tips for calling teachers' attention to the instruction of reading strategies as a premise to favor lifelong learning.

Development

Many researchers underscore that a skillful population is the solution for a country's sustainable development and stability. They all agree with the fact that motivation to read, the consciousness about one's own skills and the existence of reading strategies are a precondition for successful and lifetime learning. That is why reading effectively in a foreign language takes priority in university students, since it helps them be successful in their learning process at the institution and in their lives, in general.

Due to the great importance attached to reading, it has become a challenge to teach reading well, which requires particular knowledge and skills. "…adequate preparation needs to be given to teachers through both their pre-service teacher education and ongoing professional development that includes teachers' understandings of reading instruction as well as their capacity to assess reading strategies and regulate the reading process…"[6] This is a consensual viewpoint that the Cuban university assumes and implements by means of curricular strategies.

---

[6] Honan. 2015 p.92

The studies in this field reveal that reading constitutes an important pedagogical device to teach and learn English as a foreign language through which the students are prepared for reading critically, for assessing what they read, and for expressing themselves clearly both verbally and in writing, and understand different types of materials, as a way they have for their own lifelong learning. This assertion can be supported by conceptions and beliefs assumed by different authors:

"... reading is the most important skill for foreign language learners in the academic contexts. In academic settings, reading is the central means for acquiring new knowledge and gaining new access to alternative explanations and interpretations. If a student cannot read and comprehend a written language, she/he cannot be expected to be good in other content areas which will crucially require some reading skills..."[7] This assertion places reading as one of the most multifaceted tasks. Learning to read in a foreign language presupposes awareness that allows the students to deal with reading as a thinking process, in which reading skills and strategies should be taught explicitly in an authentic reading process through authentic reading materials and tasks.

"...the use of reading is a different methodological experience that challenges both instructors and students to explore their own capacities of understanding texts that are related to their field of study or proficiency. Reading increases students' skill to understand more technical and general vocabulary, improving the other language skills, vocabulary, and expanding knowledge in their majors."[8] It is particularly relevant in higher education due to the diversity of studies; when teaching, reading should be aimed at teaching the students to be critical, confident and independent; to make learning a process of self-improvement that explicitly recognizes the learner's social context where the exchanges that take place are the foundation for developing critical professional readers.

In Cuba, the didactics for teaching reading assumes Vygotsky's sociocultural theory, which highlights the essential role of social interaction in the development of cognition. Such developmental advancements in the field of reading depend on the cultural and reading tools provided by the teacher through the right use of the zone of proximal development, contextualized to this topic as the distance between the actual development of reading skills and the students' reading potentials under the teacher's guidance or in cooperation with more experienced peers.

---

[7]Decker. 2007 p.17
[8]Pluck. 2013 p.38

41

There are many authors who focus on the significance of acquiring reading strategies that help students become strategic readers: Pardo 2004; Alyousef (2005); Cassany, D. (2006); Erler, L. & Finkbeiner, C. (2007); Cubukcu, F. (2008); Grabe, W. (2009); Harvey, S. & Goudvis, A. (2013); Mason, L. (2013); Garcia, J. & Cain, K. 2(014); William et. al. (2015); Iwai, Y. (2016); Boyraz, S. & Altinsoy, E. (2017), among many others. They put emphasis on the teacher's responsibility of providing the students with comprehension strategies, when to use them, and giving the students with opportunities to practice and apply them.

They all agree that in the way learners become strategic readers, they will be more efficient, creative, and flexible to acquire the foreign language more easily. They also refer to metacognitive reading strategies, in such a way that the students can regulate and control the reading progress. This sort of strategies enables the students to acquire metacognitive skills, which give them the consciousness of how, when, and where to use strategies to support their comprehension and self-correct misunderstanding through feedback. They involve motivation to read and judgment of their own reading processes as significant requirements, apart from demonstrations by teachers of what to do, how and when.

Due to the indiscriminate use of the terms *reading skill* and *reading strategy*, it is convenient to define *strategy* as a general plan selected deliberately by the reader to accomplish a particular goal or to complete a given task (Paris, Wasik, & Turner, 1991). When students are able to select and use a strategy automatically, they have achieved independence in using the strategy. Along with the strategies that expert readers use, they also use a number of comprehension and study skills. It is clear from research that readers develop the use of strategies and skills by reading and writing and being given the support they need to grow in these processes (Wells, 1990).

Many scholars in this area have offered various definitions of reading strategies. They have been valued as actions, techniques, thoughts, and behaviors that are required to improve reading comprehension. No matter the definition assumed, these strategies have become an important component in the reading teaching-learning process, since successful students should count on a repertoire of reading strategies to select, and use correctly in varied reading contexts. It can be said that both terms *strategy* and *skill* are always associated, rather than separated actions from the act of reading itself; they should be embedded in the context, practiced together so the learner can apply them in contexts outside the classroom. According to Williams & Moran (1989), skills are focused on the text itself, strategies are focused on the reader.

In the associative process of reading and lifelong learning, the studies reveal that students read best when they are placed in an environment that is sensitive to their pre-existing structures, and that is flexible enough to adapt reading strategies to their individual needs. This promotes *lifelong learning*, which is defined as all learning activity done throughout life, with the purpose of cultivating knowledge, skills and competence, within a personal, community, social and/or job-related perspective.

From this viewpoint, lifelong learning is seen as a permanent process, which takes place from elementary to higher education; where it is expected that the students are better equipped for learning, since they have apprehended learning tools and skills for innovation and adaptation of learning to future work environments; learning to live together and with others; learning to know, to do and to be, which is self-directed and personal.

The studies developed by a large group of researchers make known a wide variety of reading strategies that should be taught to the students in order to favor conscious reading tools for lifelong learning, so they are pre-requisites for proposing the following *methodological hints* for professors of English as a foreign language in higher education:

- Diagnose the students' reading potentials when they enter the university. It allows professors to design a good strategic and individualized plan according to the students' level of development.
- Incorporate strategy instruction as a part of the reading lesson. Model the use of strategies in reading properly and provide the students with enough practice and feedback.
- Explain why and when the students should use a comprehension strategy, and provide them with opportunities to practice and apply them.
- Define the objective for reading each text.
- Include authentic purposes and materials according to the students' needs and interests and text readability, as the purpose is specified for knowing why a text is being read.
- Revise question typology after analyzing the type of text and deciding the purpose for reading the text as well as its structure and meaning, adapting your questions to the corresponding level of comprehension.
- Establish cooperative or reciprocal learning in reading lessons to allow the students to learn reading strategies reciprocally, with their teacher and other students. In that way, good strategies can be maximized, while inappropriate strategies are minimized.
- Ensure the students' awareness of the strategies they use when performing a reading task. Evaluate them to decide which strategies

worked best when they had difficulties to comprehend the text, and what suitable strategies can be chosen.

- Have the students understand by thinking, reflecting, revising and integrating their reading strategies. Take into account that reading is a subjective process, so an idea can have multiple interpretations.
- Promote mental independence to openly share how other minds work: to recognize and direct inner processes for understanding issues, to express ideas and beliefs, to make decisions and solve problems.
- Practice heuristic dialogues for self-discovery, so the students can learn from their own experience. Ask questions that stimulate thinking.
- Challenge the students by cultivating the habit of mental receptivity in the first stage of active reading and being critical and creative in the other stages.
- Develop inferential and creative thinking: to draw inferences from careful observation; to draw conclusion from evidence or premises, so train the students to observe, analyze, reason, contextualize, conceptualize, synthesize, evaluate, communicate, research and solve problems.
- Provide the students with techniques to infer word definitions, so they can fully understand the necessary words for understanding similes, slang or other such abstract language, then teach directly the meaning, prior to introducing the content.
- Observe the way the students read critically and evaluate reasoning and understanding. Take into account clarity, accuracy, relevance, reliability, completeness and fairness.
- Monitor and assess students' level of reading skills regularly for grading the system of reading comprehension activities properly, according to pre-determined objectives.
- Develop sessions aimed at systematic reflections by student-teachers to identify common problems, and their possible causes and solutions, to redesign action plans for continuous improvement.
- Respect and recognize the students' viewpoints and how they shape the content of the message. Include questions like Who said that? Where is this coming from? What do they want of me?
- Conceive self-reflection and self-evaluation activities.
- Monitor the students´ own understanding of the text to be aware of when they do not comprehend something, and teach the students how to monitor their own understanding of the text to become conscious of when they do not understand something, identifying where the problem occurs in the text.

Train the students to:

- Preview by using visual clues in the text such as pictures, tables of contents, appendix, preface, chapter and paragraph headings, charts or graphs, and to look at headings or subheadings used throughout the passage. Explain them the value of previewing as a strategy that facilitates predictions about what they will read, in which brainstorming plays a vital role. Think about text structure.
- Use graphic and semantic organizers; such as, graphs, story maps as a way to visualize, construct and represent ideas from the text or establish relations.
- Have a purpose in mind when reading: of predicting, anticipating through text mapping, and summarizing, in order to activate their previous content schemata as they have to use their prior knowledge of the text topic.
- Take an overall view of the text to see what it is about before reading it.
- Recognize key information by using typographical features like bold face and italics. Underline or circle important information in the text and use graphic and semantic organizers; such as, graphs or story maps, to assist with comprehension.
- Observe the structure of paragraphs to determine the essential: the topic sentence, the body and the closing sentence.
- Generate questions about the text and monitor self-understanding by questioning, thinking about, and reflecting on the ideas and the information provided in the text.
- Extract salient points to summarize. Summarizing helps students identify and relate main themes, eliminate unnecessary information and retain what they read. Explain how to do it: determine the main ideas; organize them hierarchically and paraphrase.
- Generalize from facts and inferences; how to separate the relevant details from the irrelevant.
- Discover facts and their correspondence with reality to describe them accurately.
- Discern fact from fiction.
- Make assumptions; that is, to assume, take, adopt or accept.
- Assess the text: something that they like or they do not: use the words judge, appraise, estimate, value and evaluate; to examine and judge, appraise, estimate the value of something according to a standard that involves comparison.
- Determine the key word definitions that they need for getting the gist of the text.
- Use the dictionary effectively if they cannot get the meaning from context.
- Find out the word connotations according to the context to guarantee clear thinking.

- Infer the meanings of unfamiliar words in the text; guess the meanings of the unknown words by looking at the title, the adjacent words and by considering the context of the text to draw conclusions, make predictions, and reflect on reading.
- Observe the familiar and the unfamiliar forms carefully to see details that they might have missed. Careful observation can help discover new knowledge and learn new things. It requires them to be conscious, take their time and attention for self-understanding and creativity.
- Discover analogies, as comparisons of something familiar to something unfamiliar in order to find or explain a common principle.
- Construct hypothesis as an explanation or tentative conclusion derived through reasoning.
- Argue only after defining key ideas; formulating and understanding definitions comprise a large part of learning.
- Define words and concepts. They provide adequate vocabulary to express and learn new ideas.
- Identify genre as a way for knowing the nature of the text in order to predict form and content.
- Recognize and use pronouns, referents, and other lexical equivalents as clues to cohesion.
- Be aware of the structure and organization of the text: cause and effect, comparison and contrasts, description, narration, argumentation, classification and categorization, as a means to understand content and organize the structure of the information of the text: logical or chronological.
- Draw conclusions by putting together information from parts of the text and inducing new or additional ideas.
- Take notes while reading, using symbols and abbreviations to highlight the gist of the text.
- Judge the accuracy of a passage distinguishing facts from opinions and express reading opinions based on reasons or feelings.
- Construct arguments and value assumptions to defend ideas and persuade others to believe in them.
- Spot incongruities as things they observe that do not meet their expectations or assumptions.
- Think about information in both English and their mother tongue when they read.
- Ask questions to clarify, wonder and determine author's style when the reading gets confusing in order to synthesize new information, and to determine the importance to be actively involved in the reading process; also, to read with a purpose, and to go further into comprehension. Students ask themselves questions about the text whose answers can be found within it. By generating questions,

students become aware of whether they can answer them and if they understand what they are reading.

· Stop from time to time and think about what they are reading and go back and forth across the text to find relations between its parts.

By following the above tips, teachers can improve their reading teaching practices, ensuring a better training of the students as independent readers.

The Cuban university follows a developmental approach that demands the urgent need of providing the students with reading strategies that will allow them to learn independently throughout their lives, under precepts that aim at promoting a holistic progress with a view of learning as a lifelong process.

Reading effectively in a foreign language is one of the most demanding activities for university students. It helps them be successful in their learning process at the institution, and in their lives in general. It requires highly trained teachers with an understanding of evidence-based reading instruction and the didactic competence to implement it in the classroom.

There is a considerable quantity of research that has been conducted into efficient reading instruction, whose main concern is the insertion of reading-strategy training, so the students can develop reading skills for dealing with any type of text, as a means for becoming independent readers.

The methodological suggestions offered may help university professors reflect on their daily reading teaching practices, so they contribute to a lifelong learning from their action and developmental perspective.

Bibliography

Alyousef, H. S. (2005). *Teaching reading comprehension to ESL/EFL learners*. The Reading Matrix, 5(2), 143-154.

Boyraz, S. & Altinsoy, E. (2017). *Metacognitive awareness of reading strategies in EFL context*. International Journal of Language Academy, 159-167.

Cassany, Daniel. (2006). *Tras las líneas*. Barcelona, ES: Editorial Anagrama.

Castellanos, Doris. Et al. (2005). *Aprender y enseñar en la escuela: Una concepción desarrolladora*. Ciudad de la Habana: Ed. Pueblo y Educación.

Effective Reading Instruction in the Early Years of School (2017). Centre for Education Statistics and Evaluation GPO Box 33 Sydney NSW 2001. Australia April.

Common European Framework of Reference for Languages: Learning, Teaching and Assessment. Council of Europe. Cambridge University Press. ISBN: HB 0521803136 - PB 0521005310 www.uk.cambridge.org/elt

Decker, S.M. (2007). *Academic Literacy Instruction*. Portsmouth, NH: RMC Research Corporation, center on Instruction.

Teaching reading, report and recommendations (2005). Department of Education, Science and Training report prepared by K Rowe and National Inquiry into the Teaching of Literacy.

Ebrahimi, S.S. (2012). *Reading Strategies of Iranian Postgraduate English Students.*

Erler, L. &Finkbeiner, C. (2007). *A review of reading strategies: Focus on the impact of first language.* Oxford, UK: Oxford University Press.

Garcia, J & Cain, K 2014, '*Decoding and reading comprehension: A meta-analysis to identify which reader and assessment characteristics influence the strength of the relationship in English*', Review of Educational Research, vol. 84, no. 1, pp. 74-111.

Grabe, W. (2009). Reading in a Second Language: Moving from Theory to Practice. New York: Cambridge University Press.

Honan, E (2015). *This is how Australian teachers are taught how to teach children to read.* Edu. Honan, E 2015, EduResearch Matters, Australian Association for Research in Education, viewed 22 March 2017, < http://www.aare.edu.au/blog/?p=922 >.

Hudson, T. (2011). *Teaching Second Language Reading.* Oxford: Oxford University Press.

Hong-nam, K. & Page, L. (2014). *Investigating metacognition awareness and reading strategy use of EFL Korean University students.* Reading Psychology, 195-220.

Janzen, J. (2002). *Teaching strategic reading.* In J.C. Richards, & W. Renandya (eds.), Methodology in Language Teaching (pp.287-294). New York: Cambridge University Press.

Kutluturk, S. (2016). *An Investigation on the Effects of Using Cognitive and Metacognitive Strategies.*

Mason, L 2013, '*Teaching students who struggle with learning to think before, while, and after reading: Effects of self-regulated strategy development instruction*', Reading & Writing Quarterly: Overcoming Learning Difficulties, vol. 29, no. 2, pp. 124-144.

Vander C. (2017). *10 Reasons Why Lifelong Learning is the Only Option.* January 20, 2017

Pardo, L (2004). *What every teacher needs to know about comprehension.* The Reading Teacher, vol. 58, no. 3, pp. 272-280.

Pluck, G., (2013). *Teaching Psychology through English. Incidental improvement in academic reading comprehension.* Journal of Educational Services in Psychology. Vol.LXV, Nº 1/2013, 38-42

Cubukcu, F. (2008). *How to enhance reading comprehension through metacognitive strategies.* The Journal of International Social Research. 83-93.

Ellis, R. (2015). *Understanding Second Language Acquisition.* Oxford. Oxford University Press.

Geva, E. & Ramirez, G. (2015). *Focus on Reading.* Oxford. Oxford University Press.

Harvey, S., &Goudvis, A. (2013). *Comprehension at the core.* Reading Teacher, 432 439. doi:10.1002/TRTR.1145.

Iwai, Y. (2016). *Promoting strategic readers: Insights of preservice teachers' understanding of metacognitive reading strategies.* Scholarship of Teaching and Learning, 1-10.

Elken M. (2008). *Lifelong Learning- a Core Activity for Universities.* Institute for Educational Research, Faculty of Education. University of Oslo.

Tavakoli, H. (2014). *The effectiveness of metacognitive strategy awareness in reading comprehension: the case of Iranian University EFL students.* The Reading Matrix, 314-336.

Williams, M., Mercer, S., & Ryan, S. (2015). *Oxford handbooks for language teachers: Exploring psychology in language learning and teaching.* UK. Oxford University Press.

Vygotsky, L. S. (1978). *Mind in society: the development of higher psychological processes.* Cambridge, MA: Harvard University Press.

Inter-Linguistic Dimension of Communicative Competence in Teacher Training

PhD Pedro Antonio Machín Armas. Full Professor
PhD María Elena Ayala Ruiz. Full Professor

Foreign language learning has become common practice worldwide and bilingualism a universal phenomenon rather than an exception. People need to learn second or foreign languages for multiple purposes or reasons. The literature on the field of language teaching and learning is rich and diverse and has a long history of research. The studies in this field started with the influence of Linguistics and Psychology and have extended to such disciplines as Sociology, Education and Neurosciences.

A historical *promenade* along the theoretical foundation shows that the studies now comprise not only the descriptions of the complexities of language – as in earlier times – but they focus on the learner and the processes involved in learning. Contrastive analysis theory and error analysis are now insufficient to language teaching practitioners; thus in the last decade one can observe a tendency towards research on learners' interlanguage (interlanguage analysis theory). This type of analysis brings to light a clearer and wider view of the process in which the learner has an active participation and responsibility.

The hypothesis that learners construct a system of their own is a true general fact about foreign language learning subjects, but in the case of foreign language teacher training, it is of paramount interest and concern, for the process of teacher preparation is more sophisticated than the regular language learner's preparation. Language teachers need metalinguistic awareness and metacognitive comprehension on how the process occurs. They assume more responsibility for their own learning and for using those experiences and strategies to teach others. Hence, in teacher training at the universities, two basic directions must be consciously observed: 1) the procedures and strategies for shaping their linguistic and communicative competence, and 2) the training in the mastery of the English language focusing on complexities, which require special didactic treatment in the teaching-learning process.

By reading these notes you (as language learners and teacher trainees) will get important information about what characterizes your language learning process, what kind of relation should be established between you (subject) and the language (object of learning); thus, you will have a clearer view of the process that you should manage in your own leaning and in teaching others. First, let's have a brief view of two important theoretical aspects you should be aware of: contrastive analysis and error analysis.

The roles of contrastive analysis (CA) and error analysis (EA)
The role of the native language has since long ago been considered significant by language teaching practitioners. Lado, R. 1957, stated "...individuals tend to transfer the forms and meanings, and the distribution of forms and meanings of their native language and culture to the foreign language and culture". The predictions of learner's errors were based on differences between the two systems (Mother tongue and foreign language). However, partial dissatisfaction with this theory gave rise to error analysis. It is concerned not only with inter-lingual errors (those occurring due to transfer from the native language), but also those caused by interferences within the system of the foreign language (intra-lingual errors, such as overgeneralization of rules). These conceptions have been systematically treated by Selinker since the 1970s, and Gass and Selinker (2008). These authors offer a historical overview of this process.

As a language learner, you have probably noticed that there are aspects of language that are more difficult than others to be learned. In other words, contrastive analysis helps the teacher to predict areas that will be difficult or easy for learners. However, according to studies discussed by these previously mentioned authors, not only did errors occurred that had not been predicted by theory, but there was also evidence that some predicted errors did not occur. Error analysis provides a broader range of possible explanations than contrastive analysis for teachers to account for errors, and there are two main error types within that framework: interlingual and intralingual.

Selinker and Gass state that one of the major criticisms of error analysis was directed at its total reliance on errors and the exclusion of other information. [...] one needs to consider non-errors as well as errors to get the entire picture of a learner's linguistic behavior. A second difficulty with error analysis is the determination of what an error is. In sum, error analysis *per se* cannot provide us with full information, because an assumption of error analysis is that correct usage is equivalent to correct rule formation. However, it only sees a partial picture of what a learner produces of the foreign language; i.e., a learner may use a rule correctly in one context and incorrectly in another.

An interlinguistic dimension of communicative competence in a foreign language
Since your language production may be influenced simultaneously and *in extenso* by multiple sources, it is convenient to integrate the different theoretical views about your developing foreign language system. It is clear that there are other factors that affect foreign language learning; these factors, according to specialists, may be attitude towards learning, motivation and aptitude. Considering the previously mentioned limitations of CA and EA, the latest tendency has been research based on the study of the learners' interlanguage. As stated by Selinker and Gass, "learners do not have a uniform

starting point, their utterances vary in degree of syntactic sophistication and their interlanguages are unique creations".

The theory of interlanguage has been systematically studied by different authors in the last two decades: Selinker (1990s); Selinker, L. and S. Gass (2008); López V. (2000); Fernández, J. (2006); Cenoz, J., Hufeisen, B. and Ulrike, J. (2003), among others. Interlanguage development may be referred to as the different stages learners go through in the process of approaching the foreign language system. Interlanguage has an individual nature, so every individual student gradually constructs his/her interlanguage. It has a non-lineal, variable and a temporary character as the student goes through different stages of development. It shares characteristics from both the mother tongue and the target language and in particular cases, a third language.

There are two types of research studies on interlanguage development that teachers can do. One is based on longitudinal studies and the other on cross-sectional studies. Samples of these studies are offered by many practitioners, like White, L. (2000); Ayoun, D. (2000); Lindström, E. (2003); Tello, L. (2006); and Westing, W. (2009). Despite the complexity of this process of data collection, identification of errors, classification, determination of sources and remediation strategies, the study of interlanguage development reveals crucial information for language teachers as well as for learners. It must be a systematic practice of foreign language teachers. It requires a more personalized attention to learners; more opportunities for extended input, feedback and remediation. Eventually, we see an improvement of the interlinguistic system.

A review of research experiments described in the revised literature, led to the synthesis of the following observations, which you (as an experienced language learner) may have probably undergone:

- Learner interlanguage production may be influenced simultaneously by two different sources (the mother tongue and the target language). That is, apart from the negative transfer from the mother tongue there are interferences within the system of the foreign language.
- There are interlanguage phenomena that do not have their origin in either the native language or the target language (confusions, avoidance of English-like forms, communication strategies, and simplification of target language structures). Learners tend to avoid complex and specific forms of the target language, such as phrasal verbs, collocations, idioms, and others.
- Learners impose structure on the available linguistic data and formulate their own internalized system (known as interlanguage). That is, they build up utterances with the available linguistic resources they have in their repertoire. In other words, they produce communication using the

language forms they know, which may or may not be the appropriate ones.

- Learners reach generalizations that justify their deviant language forms and rules (known as interlanguage hypotheses). Then they produce utterances and expect to get evidence of whether their production is right or wrong; that is, they expect to be monitored and corrected. This allows restructuring the created system, or in other words, improving interlanguage production.

All these data leads us to understand the communicative competence of a foreign language learner as a *sui generis* configuration, when compared to that of the native speaker. It reflects a dynamic and continuous developing process, in which the learner approaches successively the target language system, but they will never reach the proficiency of the native speaker in all its dimensions. Cook, V. (2002) refers to the characteristics of the foreign language speaker as a language user who should be able to communicate internationally in expressing their ideas and culture. So, your expectations should be to get as close as possible to the native speaker proficiency, but keeping in mind that you will have a unique configuration determined by your individual cognitive structure and social-affective characteristics.

From the very moment you start learning English as a foreign language you become a member of the bilingual community. You are building up a communicative competence in that language which is characterized by an interlinguistic-nature component. This had not been considered in previous conceptions of the concept. Therefore, **inter-linguistic competence** is proposed as a new dimension to integrate the four traditional areas because of the great significance it has from the linguistic and didactic points of view for the language teacher. It is considered as a subsystem of the communicative competence and a necessary quality, which a foreign language teacher must develop. It is the essential aspect that distinguishes the communicative competence of the bilingual speaker from the monolingual one.

One obvious fact is that an adult learner already possesses an intellectual development and a native linguistic code to communicate their reality, thus the complexity is in learning a new language code to express their thought. Studies in Neurosciences show that in the case of adults learning a new language, new brain areas assume these functions; while in the case of bilingual children, the two languages are represented in the same brain area. This indicates that the younger the subject, the more efficient their learning will be. The process for establishing an appropriate association between the acoustic or graphic symbol and its meaning demands a systematic and meaningful practice through communicative learning tasks, which should be linked to the professional pedagogical performance.

The formation and development of communicative competence in a foreign language has similar characteristics among learners, but at the same time it is a unique process in each individual. Every individual produces their own interlinguistic system, which they gradually shape to reach higher stages in the approximation to the target language system through the solution of contradictions and confusions. An important requirement for this to happen is that you need mediation; that is, the help of other more advanced learners or the teacher. So, asking questions, and using different sources (books, recordings, dictionaries, etc.) will always help you and give you cognitive orientation to enjoy your learning process.

You will not always learn one linguistic form by a single encounter with that form; you need systematic encounters and then consciously try to use it in practice. You will notice that little by little you will be able to structure your speech and that the system you are building is taking shape.

You may have probably noticed that there may be as many similarities as differences between the structural patterns of English and Spanish. It must be clarified that similarities are not absolute; there are always some distinguishing features. There is a great variety of interlinguistic phenomena which, as a good language learner you should try to discover. Teachers can help and give priority to teaching many of them, but it will be quite hard to cover all of them during class time. This makes evident the fact that 'once a language learner, you become a long-life learner' if you do not want your interlanguage system to fossilize.

Among the forms you need to pay special attention to and gradually learn are the specific forms (idioms, collocations, specific syntactic constructions, phrasal verbs, proverbs), among others. In order to be able to do that, you should dynamically interact with the foreign language through listening and reading and observe carefully, compare forms and patterns, try to infer meanings of words and phrases from context, make deductions and reach generalizations; though, it is advisable to be careful with the overgeneralization of specific forms and patterns. You can verify this by checking your hypothesis with more advanced learners or the teacher. These are cognitive strategies that improve appropriation of knowledge, habits and skills that benefit your communicative and interlinguistic competence.

Inter-linguistic competence is interpreted as a configuration of linguistic and sociolinguistic knowledge, habits and skills, which allow the activation of psycholinguistic mechanisms to minimize the influence of negative transfer; and avoid other deviations (errors), confusions, simplification of complex patterns in the communicative act, and thus be able to convey the message. In accounting for general deviations, one can mention as the principal causes the system of the native language in the mind of the learner, the target language system and the inter-linguistic system the learner is creating.

As you may have realized so far, the role of the student has a great significance in learning a foreign language. They must develop and use their own learning strategies. In so doing, they have to establish the appropriate connections with the existing network in their cognitive structures by applying thinking processes, and asking questions, and establishing associations. When connections cannot be established within the system of the foreign language, then representations from the mother tongue are activated.

Learning a foreign language is a complex process for any individual. It has a multidimensional character, that is, many factors influence the amount and quality of what we learn. Learning tasks should demand the involvement of learners in an active, conscious process where they assume responsibility to learn; where they develop cognitive and metacognitive strategies combining learning styles, analyzing linguistic phenomena in meaningful context, and integrating skills to perform communicative acts.

Learners avoid complex structures in the foreign language and choose simple or more transparent forms. This phenomenon is known as avoidance. This determines what structures a learner produces and which are not produced. The differences between the native language and the target language may be a source for avoidance; nonetheless, the complexities of the foreign language have been found to be a great source for this interlinguistic phenomenon. For instance, Spanish speakers learning English tend to avoid phrasal verbs and resort to those forms that are semantically more transparent (like the use lexical items from Latin).

Not all linguistic phenomena require the same focus of attention. Specific language forms and patterns of the target language should be purposefully treated. Here we are referring to English-like constructions and forms, which are not parallel with Spanish forms and constructions. The learner needs to interact with other subjects and with written and oral texts and receive new and repeated input, as well as appropriate feedback in order to be able to reconstruct the linguistic system they are building up. This interlanguage system gradually approaches the target language system, giving rise to a communicative interlinguistic competence.

There are certain affective and intellectual qualities that a foreign language teacher-trainee should develop. These qualities are related to some linguistic abilities, both being promoted through specific learning-task items.

Some qualities of a language learner and teacher trainee:

- Linguistic sensibility, curiosity for linguistic phenomena through discovery learning of these forms and meanings, leading to a linguistic intelligence
- Linguistic and didactic knowledge and abilities, as determined by the variety of exercises, which are samples to the development of creativity
- Metalinguistic capacities in both languages acquired through observation, analysis, comparison and deduction
- Respect to linguistic diversity and love for the mother tongue and the foreign language culture
- Admiration of the aesthetic and stylistic values in the use of certain linguistic forms in the communicative act
- Associating inter-linguistic abilities with creativity and the modeling of learning tasks
- Motivation for the pedagogical profession and the teaching of a foreign language in particular

Some abilities that a teacher trainee should develop:

Learning tasks should integrate linguistic and communicative aspects, which derive from some of the following interlinguistic abilities:

- Identify distinctive graphic and phonic features in equivalent, transparent lexical items and use them adequately (Example: English: *strategies* – Spanish: *estrategias*)

- Comprehend / differentiate the use of similar lexical items in both languages but with different semantic uses. Example: *to process* (v), when stressed on the second syllable means to parade in procession

- Comprehend / use lexical forms from other languages orally and in writing, examples:

- Some that are already part and parcel of English vocabulary (From French: *promenade, coup d' état*). This implies familiarizing with the pronunciation, which may be the original one, or the accommodated pronunciation to the English language.
- Words and expressions which are used internationally, like some Latin words and expressions, examples from Latin (*per se, status quo*), or from French (*déjà vu, laissez-passer*)

- Identify / employ appropriately English words whose similarity with Spanish may activate false equivalent representations, for example: *actually* – which does not mean *actualmente*

- Discriminate distinctive orthographical features between English terms and their adaptations to the Spanish language, examples are *baseball–béisbol, football–fútbol.*
- Recognize and articulate appropriately Spanish lexical items which have been assimilated by English but which have suffered orthographic and phonological adaptations, example: *corridor, machismo.*
- Comprehend/use adequate syntactic structure parameters of the English language, which are different from the mother tongue, examples:
  - Colocations: Spanish: *tomar una decisión*— English: *make a decision*
  - Phrasal verbs: *turn up*
  - Idioms: *I couldn't help but feel a deep sense of loss* …
  - Question patterns
- Comprehend/employ English proverbs appropriately which may not be transparent with their Spanish equivalents, example: *"better the devil you know tan the devil you don´t"*
- Identify/employ neutral linguistic forms, which are common between languages. The perception of the learners about the distance between L1 and L2, or their considerations about similarity or difference makes them hesitant in decision-making related to the real positive transfer potential of some linguistic elements, for instance the Spanish term *universidad acreditada.* By previous experiences in perceiving distance between Spanish and English, the learner may doubt whether it could be *accredited university*.

Methodological procedures for interlinguistic development in teacher training
The main reason for IL analysis and remediation is to facilitate development and avoid fossilization in language learning or in particular aspects of language. Hence, it is convenient to turn to the aspect of teaching and remediation. The concern here is with teachers of English to be, who (unlike second language acquisition learners) are learning the language in a country where English is a foreign language. That is, they rarely have contact with native speakers if they ever do. It means they are more systematically exposed to foreign language users (Spanish speakers who are teachers of English as a FL) or to other interlanguages (in the interaction with peers), despite the use of native speaker audio-texts.

The following proposal of methodological procedures is intended to achieve a more efficient interlinguistic development of students in the pre-service English language teacher-training course. They are the result of the systematization of the interlanguage theory and the consideration of the role of the learners in creating an individual system. They are specially devised for foreign language teacher trainees. So, as language learners you should:

- Expose yourself and your learners to sufficient native speaker input (either oral or written input). Sometimes the cause of deviations may be lack of sufficient input.
- Use input intentionally to focus on selected language-specific information (these are language items a learner views as unique or particular to the language, and so it requires more analysis and practice than language-neutral forms or language universals).
  • Use techniques to reflect or make the learners react to such language-specific items; for example, if it is a syntactic form, verify if it is semantically transparent, reflect on its structure, analyze it, compare it to the native language equivalent form and even to the interlanguage (IL) form that you or they would produce in that situation, and discuss the probabilistic difficulties your prospective learners will have in trying to use this form.
- Devote enough time to elicit particular language-specific items by using the appropriate elicitation technique (question and answer, interview, conversation, etc.)
- Request and give appropriate feedback through positive or negative evidence. That is, the former by the teacher's approval or model utterances as additional input; the latter through direct or indirect correction of the deviant utterances
- Carry out reflection sessions on non-English like and English like constructions. Analyze the causes of deviations with the classmates and your learners
- Make sure that you learn the necessary metalinguistic information that can be used as a self-learning and teaching tool.
- Reflect on the objective of each procedure to add to your professional-pedagogical competence.

Learning tasks for teacher trainees
The following tasks are only a sample of the great diversity that may be employed. They are based on literary text extracts, as reading comprehension tasks which comprise several exercises and procedures. They can also be derived from listening interactional texts, as well. The ones presented here are only a sample that is suitable for the post intermediate and advanced levels, that is fourth and fifth year students. They integrate the different skills.

TASK 1:
Read the extract of the text and do the following exercises:
'Did you mount her?' The agent asked, looking over.
Langdon glanced up, certain he had misunderstood.
'I beg your pardon?'

'She is lovely, no? The agent motioned through the windshield toward the Eiffel Tower. 'Have you mounted her?'

'Langdon rolled his eyes. 'No, I haven't climbed the tower'

'She is the symbol of France. I think she is perfect'

Langdon nodded absently. Symbologists often remarked that France -a country renowned for machismo, womanizing and diminutive insecure leaders like Napoleon- could not have chosen a more apt national emblem than a thousand-foot phallus. (Taken from The DaVinci Code, p. 33)

a) The verbs (*look over* and *climb*) are used in this extract, the author uses synonyms for each as well. Can you identify these synonyms?

b) Identify a fixed formula used to ask the speaker to repeat what he said. Reflect on the difference with the Spanish equivalent

c) Pick out a word with a prefix. What type of word class is it? How does the prefix affect the meaning of the word root?

d) Pick out a compound word whose graphic representation is motivated by the elements that are combined to form it. How does this compare to its Spanish equivalent?

e) Identify a word from Spanish, accepted in the English vocabulary. Find out how it differs in pronunciation from its Spanish equivalent.

f) Pick out a two-word adjective. How does it differ from its Spanish equivalent in terms of syntax and morphology?

g) What word does the author use to refer to the Eiffel Tower in a figurative sense? Look up the word in the dictionary, what meaning applies to the word in this context, its denotative or connotative meaning? Explain.

h) Say true or false according to the meaning expressed in the conversation extract, give the necessary comments and explanations:

- The police agent seems proud of their symbol of France_____
- Langdon understood the agent from the very start_____
- Langdon showed a great interest on the topic_____
- Symbologists consider the Eiffel Tower is a suitable symbol for France_____
- There are opinions that men and women are equally treated in France_____

TASK 2:

Read the extract to do the following exercises:

Langdon stared at the picture, his horror now laced with fear. The image was gruesome and profoundly strange, bringing with it an unsettling sense of déjà vu. A little over a year ago, Langdon had received a photograph of a corpse and a similar request for help. (Taken from The DaVinci Code, p. 26)

- a) This extract describes: 1) a pleasant situation 2) an unpleasant moment 3) An interesting experience
- b) Underline all abstract nouns in the text
- c) Pick out all the adjectives
- d) Pick out two regular verbs in past that may be converted into nouns

e) Pick out two prepositional phrases
f) Which line contains an adverb qualifying an adjective?
g) Which line contains a French expression meaning ´the illusion of having previously experienced something´.
h) What is the intension of the author in using this foreign expression?
A. To give local color (the French context where this takes place)
B. To make the idea stand conspicuously
C. To exalt the expression of the idea and to elevate the language

TASK 3:

Read the extract and do the following:

Langdon could not help but feel a deep sense of loss at the curator´s death. Tonight´s meeting had been one Langdon was very much looking forward to, and he was disappointed that the curator had not turned up.

a) Identify all the noun forms by underlining them. Which are unknown to you? What can you do to infer their meaning?
b) How do the syntagmatic relations help identify them as nouns?
c) What word combination (lexical set) is an idiom?
d) Which is a suitable translation for the idiom? a)…no pudo ayudar pero si sentir una sensación … b) no pudo evitar sentir una sensación
e) Pick out a phrasal verb formed by V ing+adv + prep. Identify the direct object (D.O) of this verb. Translate this sentence and reflect on the similarities and differences with the Spanish structure
f) Which of the several meanings in the dictionary of the phrasal verb *turned up* (V +adv.) best suits this context? What synonym can replace it?
g) Prepare an oral report about this topic: Something I can´t help but feel a strong desire to do is....
h) Describe something you are very much looking forward to

TASK 4:

Read the following extracted sentences from the main text (The Da Vinci Code). As you read analytically, try to spot one specific English language form per sentence to express certain meanings. Reflect on the grammatical structure used if possible and determine a suitable translation for each. Later use these forms in sentences of your own.

a) *As they ascended, Langdon tried to focus on anything other than the four walls around him.*
b) *We planned to meet after my lecture, but he never showed up.*
c) *The man was taking dead aim at Sauniere´s head.*
d) *Last month, much to Langdon´s embarrassment, Boston Magazine had listed him as one of that city´s top ten most intriguing people.*

e) *Langdon had once walked the Louvre´s perimeter; it was an astonishing three-mile journey.*

f) *Sauniere looked remarkably fit for a man of his years.*

g) *Without taking his eyes off Sophie, Fache produced his own cell phone and held it out.*

h) *The boy grew into a powerful young man*

i) *Fache waved Sophie off.*

TASK 5:

Read the extract and do the following:

Musee du Louvre.

Langdon felt a familiar tinge of wonder as his eyes made a futile attempt to absorb the entire mass of the edifice. Across a staggeringly expansive plaza, the imposing facade of the Louvre rose like a citadel against the Paris sky. Shaped like an enourmous horseshoe, the Louvre was the longest building in Europe, stretching farther than three Eiffel Towers laid end to end.

a) Why does the author use French words in this description? 1) because he speaks French 2) as a stylistic resource to give local color 3) because his readers are French people

b) The following words are accepted in English vocabulary and they appear in English dictionaries (edifice, façade, and plaza). The author uses them because A) They have no English synonyms B) He wants to elevate and make exact use of the language in the belle letters.

c) The word façade has kept its French pronunciation in English. Look it up in the dictionary

d) Pick out a prepositional phrase formed by prep. + art + adv + adj + noun. Translate it.

e) Translate the following phrase at the end of the extract: ...laid end to end.

f) In this extract the author is trying to remark:
   - The beauty of the Louvre Museum
   - The enormous size of the building

g) What phrases or sentences helped determine your choice in the previous item?

h) Write a description of a huge monument/building you have seen, and then prepare a spontaneous monologue to be used with your students as a listening comprehension task.

Learning a foreign language is a complex multi-faceted process having an interdisciplinary character. In this process, the individual learner has a crucial role in constructing a new system with the help of mediators, and this system is called interlanguage (IL).

Teachers in preparation need and interlinguistic competence, which will help them be more efficient and permanent language learners and teachers for this competence, has an impact on the metalinguistic and didactic capacities.

The integration of the theories of contrastive analysis and error analysis to interlanguage analysis becomes a valuable tool in the teacher's hands for understanding the process learners undergo, and make important decisions in the management of the process. It offers a different view on the errors the learner produces which obey to his/her unique self-created system. Interlanguage development undergoes different stages in the process of approaching the foreign language system.

The process of foreign language teacher training requires special attention and systematic interlanguage analysis. It should cover metalinguistic and interlinguistic analyses, reflection on differences and similarities, reflection on language-specific information and the teaching implications.

Interlanguage analysis suits the teachers in preparation with pedagogical tools to direct their teaching focus on the aspects that require learning, either for themselves as language learners or for their future professional practice.

There are items of language that require less attention than others. This can be revealed with more precision by interlanguage analysis with the passing of years, and once an in-service teacher, it will add a lot of experience to teachers' linguistic and methodological background. The methodological procedures and tasks proposed here are intended to contribute to this goal; especially through the discipline Integrated English Practice.

Bibliography

Ayoun, Dalila. *Web-based elicitation tasks in SLA research*, University of Arizona, [available online at Language Learning & Technology, Vol. 3, No. 2, January 2000, pp. 77-98] [Visited 27/3/2012, 12.22 p.m.]

Cenoz, Jassone, Brita Hufeisen and Ulrike Jessner. *The multilingual Lexicon, Why investigate the multilingual lexicon?* University of the Basque Country, Spain, 2003. 133 p. [available online at: http://books.google.com.cu/books] [visitado 30/3/2013, 8.27 a.m.]

Fernandez, L. Justo. *Interlingua*, 2006, [available online in: http://culturitalia.uibk.ac.at/hispanoteca/lexikon%20der%20linguistik/i/INTERLINGUA%20Interlengua.htm] [Visitado 30/3/13, 8.30 a.m]

Kleinmann, H. *Avoidance behavior in adult Second Language acquisition*. Languague Learning, 27, 93—107 [https://www.google.com.cu/search?q=avoidance+behavior+Kleinmann&ie=utf-8&oe=utf-8&rls=org].

Lado, Robert. *Linguistics across cultures*: Ann Arbor: University of Michigan Press, 1957.

Lindström. Eva. *Language complexity and interlinguistic difficulty*, Department of Linguistics, Stockholm University, 2003. [Available online www2.ling.su.se/staff/evali/complexity-abs.html]

Selinker, Larry and Susan Gass. Second Language Acquisition: an introductory course. Routledge, New York and London, 2008.493 p.

Tello Rueda Leyla Yined. Análisis contrastivo e interlingüístico de peticiones en inglés y español, en: Íkala, revista de lenguaje y cultura, Universidad de Antioquia, Colombia, 2006. Vol. 11, N.º 17 (ene.-dic., 2006) pp. 91-116 [Disponible Online http://www.redalyc.org],. [Visitado 30/8/12, 12.25 p.m.]

Westing Wang. *Interlanguage Theory and Emergentism: reconciliation in Second Language development*, National University of Defense Technology, China, [Available in www.ccsenet.org/journal.htm, vol. 2, No. 1, March 2009. [Visitado 5/2/13, 1.02 p.m.]

White, Lydia. *Universal grammar in Language acquisition*, McGill University, 2000. [available online] [Visitado 6/02/11, 10.26 p.m.]

21st Century Canadian Literature: An Analysis of the Novel Mistaken Identity, by Norah McClintock, from a Cognition-Discourse-Society Didactic Approach

PhD José Reinaldo Marrero Zaldívar. Full Professor
MSc Dalquis María Rodríguez Díaz. Associate Professor
MSc Miguel Velázquez Hidalgo. Associate Professor

The study of Canadian literature is central for the development of an integral culture in the students of the Cuban university. That is why this paper approaches Nora McClintock so her name is included in the university curriculum. The quality of her work allows us to enter contemporary topics: ecology, false identity, teenage concerns, money laundering and parenthood issues, among others.

McClintock is a Canadian author who has written detective stories mainly for youngsters. She was born in Montreal on March 11, 1952. She lived in Toronto where some of her novels are set. She graduated from McGill and has been awarded the Arthur Miller Award five times. One of her most well-known novels is *Mistaken Identity*.

She was honored with a membership of the Canadian Society of Authors, Illustrators and Artists for Children and the Crime Writers of Canada. She also wrote articles for charity newspapers. Her death on February 6, 2017, left a legacy and a faithful readership.

The present paper analyzes her work as a representative example of Canadian literature, revealing its potential to use it for the development of text comprehension skills and literary competence.

The plot

The novel is about a sixteen year old girl names Zanny, who lived with her father, Mitch Dugan. For reasons initially undisclosed to the reader, they are constantly moving and traveling across various provinces. An unexpected event, a pro-environment strike, turns her into a public figure and she is recognized by people who were not aware of her whereabouts but were hopeful they would find her someday.

In a distant city, Chuck Benson, a journalist, recognizes Zanny as the possible daughter of Mike Alexander. He gets in touch with Special Agent Wiley who, upon reading the missing persons file, notices her remarkable similitude with Melissa Alexander. Zanny´s life changes overnight when one day she arrives home to find police cars and ambulances. Her father is dead. She becomes a foster kid tormented by solitude and the thought that her father, Mitch Dugan, was not who she had imagined; rather a possible thief and killer called Michael Alexander. From that moment on, a series of events and developments mark the novel and Zanny's life: drugs, ill-gotten money, murder, etc. The outcome is favorable for the girl, who finds a happy way out and restarts her life.

From narrative frame to literary analysis

Mistaken Identity creates a dynamic of harmonic combination where narration, description and dialogue, as well as recurring motives and intrigue as leitmotif, put forth an attractive atmosphere involving reader, text and author. The first two chapters present a chronological map of the characters; yet the following chapters are an intentional rupture based, linguistically speaking, on a repetition of time adverbs, place descriptions, surprising dialogues, anticipatory expressions and causal connections. These elements give way to an investigative ambience as a reflection of a culture characterized by national identity traits that range from culinary aspects to psychological ones.

Symbolism plays a key role in the novel: tomato sauce red to suggest blood in a murder, a broken egg to hint upset states of mind. Instead of just words, actions aim at making the reader explore between the lines. The author skillfully handles the dramatic method to introduce apparently meaningless affairs, which synthetically leave clues to move from the plot to the denouement. Supporting characters reach a notable significance to prop the necessary precedents of the main action in the story.

The rally to save the planet, the novel's introduction, in which Zanny's face is displayed, is a substantial resource to open the plot and unchain what follows. Like this, many other means are used to intrigue the reader. Colloquial language is also added as a feature. The unexpected outcome stands as a fulfilled conclusion and explanation of the novel's title.

Didactic approach to the novel

Cognition, society and culture need language, discourse and communication (Van Dijk, 2000(a): 52). Based on this integrative conception, description, analysis and explanation must cover all angles of the triangle and unveil their nexuses.

Likewise, the proposal is based on Bakhtin's precepts about ideological-dialogic character: it stems from considering culture as a system or systems of signs within which language has a leading role (Lotman, 1979:22). This perspective allows viewing cultural processes as communication processes, transcending space and context of human-social communication (Eco, 1988:24). It also gives the reader a discourse optic of reality. In addition, these notions are closely linked to a cross-disciplinary focus of linguistic studies, originated in the very cross-disciplinary nature of human knowledge. It assumes the tenets of discourse linguistics and discourse analysis, which allow to see the discourse-cognition-society relationship (Van Dijk, 2000).

To understand the novel as a higher level of narrative, it is necessary, from a didactic standpoint, to use procedures and techniques that set the reader in a world-view mode. This would activate background reading experiences and feelings. Therefore, the professor´s wise orientation is fundamental to achieve further purposes in comprehension. These include translation, interpretation and information transfer.

Text comprehension enriches intellectual, affective and communicative growth. It broadens *lebensraum*, gives access to other places and historic periods, and offers ground for visualizing other cultures, spotting differences and learning to respect diversity and unity. It also contributes to discover and dialogue with universal values such as truth, solidarity, intrigue, eco-friendliness, beauty, honesty, justice and freedom.

School contexts lead to a reflexive and contextualized appropriation of cultural heritage, assumed in the perception we have of the world through a code system: language and culture are two inseparable units. This cultural unity and the dynamics of learning are mediated by the text as a communicative element. In the text is delimited, expressed and structured a system of meanings revolving around a theme. The intention is to let these meanings be perceived and socialized in a given historic-social and cultural context. Thus the text is a communicative unit.

The cognitive frame technique

This technique is recommended to work towards an understanding of the text as a cognitive, cross-disciplinary unit, as it sees the text as a unit made of general components that can be present in any text typology. The most usual text elements are:

Subjects: those about who something is said.
> Actions (or Processes): the act of doing, creating, producing, contributing, transforming, forming, inventing, conceiving or discovering.
> Problems: contradictory situation, unknown or confusing state that needs to be solved through actions.

Aims: ends, purposes that prompt actions.

Object: character, place, inanimate or animate things, abstract or concrete, fictional or real.

Circumstances: time, modes and space coordinates necessary to comprehend facts, situations, characters, etc.

Outcome: positive or negative consequences, solutions or failures determined by certain actions exerted upon an object or subject.

Tasks to elaborate the cognitive frame

The following are identification questions based on *Mistaken Identity*, by Norah McClintock:

1. What is the text about?
2. Which character stands out since the beginning?
3. List the characters as they appear in the plot.
4. List the action/s of each character.
5. Write if you notice in the characters´ behavior: concern, doubt, intrigue, agitation, anger, melancholy, sadness, understanding, solidarity, protection, hatred, revenge, ambition.
6. Define the problem that impelled the characters to act. These notes may help you: solve a family conflict, balanced relation in the couple, sharing space, saving the planet, overcoming obstacles to reach a goal, evade persecution and death, fight a virus or an epidemic, fight for social justice, etc.
7. Draw a chart where you transfer, in your view, relations established (Character / Action / Character benefited or affected).
8. According to the way the plot unfolds, analyze which the objective of the characters´ essential actions is.
9. After defining the actions´ aim, mention the character´s achievement. Follow these patterns: irreparable psychological damage, death of an innocent person, a character´s recovery, environmental destruction, separation of a couple, cheating in a couple, doubt, disagreement, intrigue, etc.
10. Comment on the following assertion: "Lies can run a hundred years; the truth will catch up in just one day." (African proverb)

These procedures favor the development of the students´ first level of performance. Capacities are activated towards the fulfillment of cognitive activities in a stable way, and they are given the possibility to repeat and reproduce. Questions may be elaborated to:
✓ Identify explicit relations in the text.
✓ Select main ideas.
✓ Recognize distinctive traits of a concept.
✓ Classify characters, objects, places, processes, procedures, etc.
✓ Describe or enumerate elements, features, properties.
✓ Recombine ideas, facts, etc.

✓ Identify in-text explicit elements (names of places, characters, dates, historic allusions, properties of objects, phenomena, facts, situations).
✓ Recognize text typology and elocution forms.
✓ Identify key words.

Free, open questions can be asked, also closed, multiple choice ones. If the aim is at checking explicit comprehension of larger information volumes, true-or-false questions can be included.

Contemporary Canadian narrative has great potential for multicultural studies. McClintock´s oeuvre is a clear example of the power of writing for the expression of an underlying culture inside text structure, as a way to present universal values and conflicts.

The implementation of methods used by analogical hermeneutics and literary analysis allowed bringing off the objective of the cognitive-frame technique for a dynamic understanding of texts through tasks. This permitted the authors to help in the solution of the problem of intercultural text studies via the linking of the semantic, syntactic and pragmatic dimensions.

Introducing this in the subjects "Didactics of Language and Literature" and "Comprehension and Construction of Meaning" is a valid input to the teaching-learning process and the enrichment of literary competence in university students.

Bibliography
Adam, J. M. (1985) *"Réflexion lingüistique sur les types de textes et de compétences en lecture."* In *L'orientation scolaire et professionalle*, 14, 4, 293-304.
Alonso Tapia, Jesús (1995). *La evaluación de la comprensión lectora*. Pp. 63-78. In *Textos de Didáctica de la Lengua y La literatura*. No 5. Julio. Madrid.
Álvarez Álvarez, Luis (1996) *La lectura ¿pasividad o dinamismo?* pp. 11-14. In *Educación*. No. 89. La Habana, septiembre-diciembre.
Cairney, Trevor H. (1996). *Enseñanza de la comprensión lectora*. Ministerio de Educación y Ciencia. Ediciones Morata, SL. Madrid.
Cassany, Daniel (1999). *Enseñar Lengua*. / Daniel Cassany, Marta Luna, Gloria Sanz Barcelona: Editorial Graó.
Dijk Teun Van (1989). *La ciencia del texto*. Barcelona: Editorial Paidós.
Fabelo Corzo, José Ramón (1989). *Práctica, conocimiento y valoración: La naturaleza del reflejo valorativo de la realidad*. La Habana: Editorial de Ciencias Sociales.
Heras León, Eduardo (2007) *Los desafíos de la ficción: técnicas narrativas*. Ciudad Habana. Editorial José Martí.
Hernández Sanchez, José Emilio (2010).*La comprensión de textos: Un desafío teórico y didáctico actual*. In *Renovando la enseñanza-aprendizaje de la lengua española y la literatura*. (p.117). Ciudad de La Habana. Editorial Pueblo y Educación.
Lotman, Y. (1979). *Semiótica de la cultura*. Madrid: Ediciones Cátedra.

McClintock, Norah (2005) *Falsa identidad*. Bogotá. Grupo Editorial Norma. (*Mistaken Identity*)

Montaño Calcines, Juan Ramón (2010) *Renovando la enseñanza-aprendizaje de la lengua española y la literatura*. Ciudad de La Habana. Editorial Pueblo y Educación.

Palincsar, A.S. Y A.L. Brown (1984) *Reciprocal teaching of comprehension-fostering and comprehension-monitoring activities*. In *Cognition and Instruction*, 1, 117-175.

Pearson, D.P. Y M.C. Gallagher (1983) *The Instruction of Reading Comprehension*. In *Contemporary Educational Psychology*, 8, 317-344.

Ricoeur, Paul (1995). *Teoría de la interpretación: Discurso y excedente de sentido*. España: Siglo Veintiuno Editores.

Roméu Escobar, Angelina (1999). *Aplicación del enfoque comunicativo en la Escuela Media*. pp.10-50 In *Taller de la Palabra*. Ciudad de la Habana: Editorial Pueblo y Educación.

Solé I. (1992) *Estrategias de lectura*. Barcelona, Graó/ICE.

Van Dijk, Teun *et al* (2000(a). *El discurso como estructura y proceso. Estudios sobre el discurso*. Barcelona: Gedisa.

Developing Foreign Language Professional-Pedagogical-Oral Communicative Competence in English Major Students at Holguin University

PhD Julio César Rodríguez Peña. Associate Professor
MSc Miguel Ángel Olivé Iglesias. Associate Professor
Spec. Marlene Mora Delgado. Associate Professor

The new models for the formation of English teachers – freshman, sophomore and junior years are pre-service academic training then in-service practice teaching during the senior year for the completion of the major´s requirements – demand that they reach levels of formation and development of communicative competence in the foreign language that will allow them to use it as the basic instrument for teaching.

Assessment processes in forming and evaluating graduates-to-be have been approached by previous research (Medina, A. 2004; Pérez, J. 2006; Rodríguez, R. 2006; Cruz, H. 2008 y Velázquez, M. 2010). It has been proved that the levels of communicative competence reached do not meet the goals expected for the students to continue their formation, mainly during practice teaching. Linguistic limitations they have affect their performance in in teaching. Consequently, it was necessary to address the problem to guarantee adequate efficiency and proficiency levels in the learners.

Doctoral and Master studies made by the authors allow to state that oral expression has been widely treated (Rodriguez, J. C. 2008, Fuentes, C. 2008, Medina, O. 2008); however, it has not been sufficient. Nevertheless, the last decades have seen an increase of analyses to solve issues emerging in the teaching-learning of foreign languages.

Among the most significant contributions by the afore-mentioned investigators can be mentioned techniques and procedures for the learning of pronunciation, specific characteristics of oral language, how to treat pronunciation errors, the role of accuracy and fluency, requirements and typology of exercises for oral expression from communicative perspectives with emphasis on interactive and cooperative aspects, and the definition that the purpose of this skill is the development of fluency, given its import in the communicative approach.

The teaching of English based on the communicative approach, should favor the formation of four main communicative skills in language learning: listening comprehension, oral expression, reading comprehension and written expression. Within the key objectives of the teaching the foreign language, oral expression is given priority. These abilities should be formed to foster an appropriate communicative competence.

Valid criteria on the relevance of communicative abilities have been declared by different authors. Among them, internationally, are Brumfit, Ch. (1985); Coll (1985); Richard-Amato, P. (1988); Abbott, G. *et al* (1989); Brown, G. (1989); Byrne, D. (1989); Finnochiaro, M. (1989); Terroux, G. (1991); Nunan, D. (1991); Brown, D. (1994); Richards, J. (1995); Ur, P. (1997); Ellis, R. (1998); Léia, I. (2000) y Jenkins, J. (2001). In Cuba, the most outstanding are Antich, R. (1975 y 1986), Acosta, R. (1996), Faedo, A. (1988, 1994, 1997, 2003), Santiesteban, E. (2004), Medina, A. (1999, 2004, 2006) y Pérez, A. (2008).

An aspect frequently forgotten is the line to be followed in the Integrated English Practice lessons during freshman studies: the professional-pedagogical approach. If this approach is correctly applied, learners will gradually adapt and improve speaking so they can communicate with their own students. This approach includes speaking in a clearer and slower way, using simplified pronunciation and discourse, reformulating the same message several times.

In the didactics of foreign languages, the new interpretation of this phenomenon has led to introducing a new term, *teacher talk.* In relation to the object of this investigation, it refers to the satisfactory use of English as a foreign language. This implies the application of communicative strategies and linguistic registers that are in correspondence to the increasing needs and possibilities of the teacher and the students. The teachers of English have to be correct models: they are the "mirror" for the linguistic formation of the students in the language they study.

The professional-pedagogical approach in the teaching–learning of English. Theoretical support

The use of the language by teachers in class accompanied by objects, pictures, model scales and other teaching media permits to establish a link between words and concrete objects or phenomena being studied, it strengthens the representations, stimulates operations of analysis and synthesis at the perceptual as well as at the rational level, and facilitates comprehension and communication in the teaching-learning process.

The English language is assumed as a basic instrument of communication. Consequently, the communicative approach, departing from the **Special didactics for the teaching-learning of foreign languages**, is assumed as one of the essential supports, epistemologically speaking, for the present investigation. This assumption is focused on the tenets embraced in the international arena and in Cuba: the communicative-systemic approach .

Such assumption implies that communication is the principal function of language. Thus it should be learned bringing the students as close as possible to real communicative acts, in such a way that they learn to communicate in an authentic manner. This must be taken into account for content selection, what should be done from a functional, graded and concentric perspective, considering all areas of the communicative competence, so that it is significant and in harmony with the students´ needs and how they will use the language. It is also vital for organizing learning activities with an interactive character, in which information gaps and the use of authentic texts should predominate.

According to Medina, A. (2006), *communicative competence* is a configuration of capacities, knowledge and linguistic and extra-linguistic abilities and habits manifested during the communicative act in the foreign language to satisfy individual and collective communicative needs, in correspondence to the required linguistic, sociolinguistic, discourse and strategic norms.

Due to the singularity of the object of the present investigation, it is necessary to explicitly add the professional-pedagogical component to the above definition. That is, to say that learners in their formative process – a major in English – are competent from the communicative point of view in this foreign language, they should be able to use the language as the essential vehicle to direct the teaching-learning process. In this investigation the authors considered it essential to deal with theoretical elements of the category **professional-pedagogical approach.**

The professional-pedagogical approach is multidimensional and includes factors such as:
- Methodological instruction
- Development of capacities such as self-preparation from a didactic point of view
- Pedagogical and curricular mastering of contents
- Alternative thinking

Taking into consideration the contributions made by several researchers, the authors of this paper consider it pertinent to highlight the following features of this concept:
- It is a general organization and management that supports the system of educational influences of the teachers who interact with students at any level, focusing on integrating pedagogical training since students´ first year in the teacher education majors
- It takes into account the true formation of the communicative-methodological foundation for students to face their pre- and in-service activity. Special didactics of foreign languages, in recent years, has been profusely using a term for the type of communication to be used by the teacher of foreign languages in class. This is *'Teacher Talk'*, which should not be overlooked for its

impact on the teaching-learning process of English. It is not considered a competence in itself; it is rather in all the actions of a foreign language teacher. It consists of four language areas: phonological, lexical, syntactic and discourse.

This paper aims at complementing the notions exposed here about communicative competence with a new perspective, the **professional-pedagogical-oral communicative competence.** It is approached as an integration of skills, knowledge, and linguistic and extra-linguistic patterns that occur during the act of communication in the foreign language.

Objective of developing the professional-pedagogical-oral communicative competence is to direct the teaching-learning process of oral communication in foreign languages at any educational level, demonstrated in the integration of the academic, professional-investigative and on-campus-and-community activities that define students´ future role as teachers and communicators.

Content of the professional-pedagogical-oral communicative competence in English:
  - Linguistic dimension: pronunciation, grammar and vocabulary.
  - Paralinguistic dimension: facial expressions, kinesics, and kinesiology.
  - Sociolinguistic dimension: knowledge of cultural norms, linguistic styles, linguistic registers, adapting the text to the message, and evidence of cooperation in the interaction.
  - Strategic dimension: beginning of the communicative act, identifying strategies to compensate for limitations in other areas, and closing the communicative act.
  - Ethical and professional dimension: treatment of language mistakes, respectful manner comply with the standards of professional ethics.
  - Psychological dimension: particular attention to students´ individual characteristics, distribution of tasks and responsibilities according to needs and possibilities of students nowadays.

Means for the development of the professional-pedagogical-oral communicative competence

Within the main means teachers access we can mention educational software, such as Rainbow and Sunrise, for Junior and Senior High respectively; textbooks of Integrated English Practice; Spectrum series (both textbooks and workbooks); NewClass Laboratory; texts of methodology of the teaching of foreign languages; texts on research methodology; material devised by teachers; thematic internet; DVDs; listening texts; songs in English; on-line classrooms and computers.

Evaluation of the development of the professional-pedagogical-oral communicative competence

The main skills to be evaluated are the professional ones, which in their development must move to higher levels as students advance to the next academic year. For this process of evaluation, the dimensions of the professional-pedagogical-oral communicative competence in English should be taken into account, with indicators, instruments and scales of measurement.

Proposal of tasks for the development of the professional-pedagogical-oral communicative competence in English as a foreign language

1. An English teacher can make use of a variety of teaching aids, including technological ones. However, the blackboard continues to be a basic means for the transmission of knowledge. Every teacher should know how to exploit it efficiently.
   a) Consult the books Metodología de la enseñanza de lenguas extranjeras by Antich, page 159, also Olivé, Rodríguez and Mora (*"Improving the Teaching of Foreign Languages. Thoughts and Pointers"* in *Pedagogical Sciences*),
   b) to investigate about the necessary requirements for the use of the blackboard,
   c) be ready to comment on them briefly,
   d) demonstrate with some examples how to use the blackboard.

2. Language games can be used to improve the learner's command of a particular item of language.
   a) Consult the book *Teaching Oral English*, by Donn Byrne, pp.100-103 to investigate about this topic.
   b) Prepare a brief report about it and be ready to say it orally.
   c) Imagine you are a teacher. Choose a game and implement it in class with your classmates.
   d) How did you feel playing the role of a teacher? Share your experience with your classmates.

3. Sometimes the students feel tired in class.
   a) Find out causes and consequences of this problem with your Pedagogy teacher.
   b) Prepare a brief report about it and share it with your classmates.
   c) Consult the book *Five-Minute Activities* by Penny Ur, pp. 2-5 and choose one activity that will help you to change the students' mood.
   d) Be ready to implement it with your classmates.
   e) How did your classmates react? How did you feel about that?

4. Learning the pronunciation of English sounds we don´t have in our mother tongue is a difficult task for some students. However, practicing them in an amusing way, by means of tongue twisters, for instance, can bring about excellent results.

    a) Consult the booklet *Creating a Language Learning Classroom* by Jane Kinegal and choose a tongue twister to practice the sound / ʃ /.

    b) Imagine you are already a teacher, and practice it with your classmates.

    c) What was your classmates´ reaction?

5. In the process of formation as English teachers some students feel they take too many major-unrelated subjects.

    a) What is your opinion about that?

    b) Should English teachers know only English?

    c) Investigate with each of your teachers the main objective of the subjects you take.

    d) Lead a debate in class about the importance of those subjects in your process of formation as English teachers.

6. In your *Integrated English Practice* lessons you usually carry out activities to develop oral expression. These activities are characterized by the presence of communicative situations in which there are information gaps to fill.

    a) Work in small groups to plan a role play that reviews the language contents of one or two of the units already studied.

    b) Be ready to play the role of a teacher to guide the activity. Your classmates will perform the role of your students.

7. Your teacher assigned situations to be acted out in class. You and another student will play the role of the teacher.

    a) Write down the aspects you will take into account to evaluate your classmates.

    b) Evaluate them.

    c) Share opinions on the grades given.

    d) How did you feel evaluating?

    e) What was difficult?

8. You are a teacher. You enter your classroom and see a student crying. You approach him and he describes how another teacher slapped him for bringing a frog to class and creating disorder.

    a) What do you think about the way in which the teacher handled the situation?

    b) Consult sources about educational methods.

    c) Share your findings with your classmates.

9. Imagine you are teaching nine-grade students. They are deciding on how to continue their studies. The principal asks you to lead an activity which will promote their interest towards pedagogical studies.

    a) How do you feel about such responsibility?

    b) Read *Propuesta de actividades para estimular la motivación hacia la profesión pedagógica en los estudiantes de la Facultad de Secundaria Básica* by Delvia Castellanos.

    c) Choose one of the activities she proposes and implement it in class with your classmates.

    d) Have them tell their opinion about the activity you chose.

    e) Comment on the importance of promoting your students' interests towards teaching as a profession.

10. Text *"Can Teachers Take Accessibility Too Far?"*

In her classroom, Courtney Cook establishes no hours to finish her work. Instead, she takes her students out for ice-cream and gives them her home phone number in case they need her. She also makes frequent visits to parents who are often absent from school and from their homes.

"I make myself very accessible to kids", says Cook, 28, who teaches Mathematics to fourth and fifth graders at the Buena Vista School in San Francisco. "I say if you are ever in trouble, I want you to feel you can come to me".

"Kids are very perceptive people, they know who cares, they know who doesn't", she says.

But to some teachers there should be clear limits between teachers and students.

"I do feel there's a line with teacher's involvement ", says Anna Knapp, a Biology teacher. "It should be at school and certainly not outside it, certainly not to the point where students are going to teachers' homes". Knapp thinks personal problems should be handled by social workers, not by teachers.

Post Reading Activities

a) Work in teams to comment on the following phrases.

    • Kids are very perceptive people.

    • There's a line with teachers' involvement.

b) Would you act like Courtney Cook or like Anna Knapp? Why?

c) Read Pedagogía de la Ternura by Turner and Pita (CDIP). Prepare an oral presentation on the general ideas of the book.

The development of the competence we have studied in this paper is a necessity for solving the inconsistencies and limitations detected both theoretically and empirically. The integration of crucial processes of pedagogical higher education (academic, professional-investigative and extra-curricular) has a direct impact on the development of the professional-pedagogical-oral communicative competence in English for the Teacher Education English Major students. Besides, it contributes to the formation of a professional with a broader profile in the educational area beyond the classroom.

Bibliography

Abbagnano N. (1963): Diccionario de Filosofía. Edición Revolucionaria. Instituto Cubano del Libro. Vedado, Ciudad Habana, Cuba.

Abbott, Gerry *et al* (1989): *The teaching of English as an International Language*. La Habana. Cuba.

Acosta Padrón, R. et al. (1996): *Communicative Language Teaching*. Belo Horizonte. Brasil.

Addine, F., González, A. y Recarey, S. (2002): Principios para la dirección del proceso pedagógico. En Compendio de Pedagogía. La Habana: Pueblo y Educación.

Álvarez de Zayas, C. (1999): La escuela en la vida. Soporte electrónico.

Alexander, L.G. (1974) *Practice and Progress*. Ed. Pueblo y Educación. La Habana. Cuba.

Antich de León, R. (1975): *The Teaching of English in the Elementary and Intermediate Levels*. Ed. Pueblo y Educación. La Habana. Cuba.

Antich de León, R. (1986): Metodología de la Enseñanza de Lenguas Extranjeras. Ed. Pueblo y Educación. La Habana. Cuba.

Añorga Morales, J. et al. (1994). Glosario de Términos de la Educación Avanzada. CENESEDA. Material impreso. La Habana, Cuba.

----- (1995): Proyecto de Mejoramiento Profesional y Humano. Conferencia dictada en el 1er Taller de Educación Avanzada, Ciencia y Técnica. Material impreso. La Habana, Cuba

Byrne, D. (1989): Teaching Oral English. Ed. Revolucionaria. La Habana.

Carter, R. and Mc Carthy (1997): *Exploring Spoken English*. Cambridge University Press.

Cassary, Daniel. et al. (1998): Enseñar Lengua. Editorial Grio. Barcelona. España.

Colectivo de Autores. (1989): Temas sobre la actividad y la comunicación. Editorial de Ciencias Sociales. La Habana. Cuba.

Cook, V. (1996): *Second Language Learning and Language Teaching*. Second Edition. Printed by JW Arrowsmith LTD, Bristol. Great Britain.

Cruz López, H. (2008): Una Concepción Teórica para evaluar la Calidad de la Formación Inicial del Profesional en la Carrera Licenciatura en Educación Especialidad Inglés. Tesis en opción al Grado Científico de Doctor en Ciencias Pedagógicas. Centro de Estudio de Educación Superior "José de la Luz y Caballero" Holguín.

Forteza, R. (2000). Indicadores para el diagnóstico del desarrollo de la habilidad de escritura en estudiantes de la EMS. Tesis en opción al título de máster en teoría y práctica del inglés contemporáneo. ISP. José Martí. Camagüey, Sede Holguín.

Fred N. Kerlinger *et al* (s. f.): Evaluación Educativa. Universidad Pedagógica Nacional.

Fuentes González, H. (2000). El proceso de investigación científica. U. Oriente: CEES. Soporte electrónico.

-------------------; Alvarez Valiente, I; Matos Hdez, E. La Teoría Holístico Configuracional en los Procesos Sociales. Rev. Pedagogía Universitaria. Vol. 9, No. 1, 2004. Soporte electrónico.

Giovannini, A. et al. (1996): Profesor en Acción. Edelsa. Grupo didascalia. S.A. Madrid.

González Maura, V. (1995): Psicología para Educadores. Ed. Pueblo y Educación. La Habana. Cuba.

González Rey, F. (1995): Comunicación, personalidad y desarrollo. Ed. Pueblo y Educación. La Habana. Cuba.

Hughes, A. (1996): *Testing for Language Teachers*. Cambridge University Press. Printed in Great Britain.

Hutchinson, T. y Alan Waters (1996): *English for Specific Purposes*. Cambridge Language Teaching Library. Cambridge University Press. Printed in Great Britain.

Leontiev, A. N. (1975) Actividad. Comunicación. Personalidad. Editorial Pueblo y Educación. La Habana. Cuba.

Madden, C.G. y Theresa N. Rollick (1997): *Discussion and Interaction in the Academic Community*. En http://www.tccolumbiaedu/academic/tsol/webjournal/sl.html. To alberto@cristal.hlg.sld.cu: Consultado 28 Feb 2007.

Medina Betancourt, Alberto R. (1998): La Competencia Metodológica del Profesor de Lenguas Extranjeras. Revista de los centros de Profesores de La Palma. Canarias. España. No. 24.

_____ (2006): Didáctica de los Idiomas con Enfoque de Competencias. Ediciones Cepedid. Colombia.

_____ (2012): *Glossary: Improve your methodological technical register with more than 800 terms*. Universidad de Ciencias Pedagógicas José de la Luz y Caballero, Holguín. Cuba.

Paez C, V. (2007): Modelo Pedagógico de Autodesarrollo por Competencias para Profesores de Lenguas Extranjeras en Ejercicio. Tesis en opción al Grado Científico de Doctor en Ciencias Pedagógicas. Centro de Estudio de Educación Superior "José de la Luz y Caballero" Holguín.

Pérez Sarduy, Y. (2005): El desarrollo del modo de actuación interdisciplinario en la formación inicial de profesores de Lenguas Extranjeras. Tesis en opción al Grado Científico de Doctor en Ciencias Pedagógicas. Centro de Estudio de Educación Superior "José de la Luz y Caballero" Holguín.

Richard Amato, Patricia A. (1996): *Making it Happen*. Longman. Cambridge University. New York.

Richards, Jack C y Rogers Theodores (1995): *Approaches and Methods in Language Teaching: A Description and Analysis*. Cambridge University Press. Printed in Great Britain.

Rodríguez Deveza, Rafael A. (2005): Concepción Teórico – Metodológica para el Diagnóstico – Formación de las Generalizaciones Gramaticales en la Carrera Licenciatura en Educación, Especialidad de Lengua Inglesa. Tesis en opción al Grado Científico de Doctor en Ciencias Pedagógicas. Centro de Estudio de Educación Superior "José de la Luz y Caballero" Holguín.

Terroux, Georges and H.Woods (1991): *Teaching English in a World at Peace*. McGill University. Quebec.

Vygotsky, Lev. S. (1995): Obras Escogidas. Tomo Cinco. Ed. Pueblo y Educación. La Habana. Cuba.

The Role of Learning Strategies in Foreign Language Teaching

Spec. Hilda María Reyes González. Associate Professor
Spec. Marilús González Borjas. Associate Professor
Spec. Marlene Mora Delgado. Associate Professor

A strategy is defined as the set of procedures used for achieving a plan, goal or objective. In learning, a strategy is the sequence of procedures used to facilitate learning. We use strategies every time there is an attempt to learn something new. Strategies are also used to control the direction and amount of attention a given task requires, as well as to motivate ourselves. Most research efforts have concentrated on the identification of effective strategies used by language learners in different contexts and their performances during work with different kinds of tasks.

Learning strategies are also special thoughts or behaviors that individuals use to understand, learn or retain new information. The use of appropriate strategies ensures greater success in language learning. How well students learn a language ultimately depends more on their own efforts than on the teacher's. Thus, any attempt to understand effective language teaching must consider the issue of effective language learning.

Learning strategies promote and facilitate language learning. Language learners are the actual agents in the use and choice of strategies as they are directly affected by them. As learning in general, language learning has to be internalized and the results obtained are related to the efforts developed by the agents involved in the process. Learning strategies are flexible and can be taught, so learners can be trained in their management. That is why it is possible to speak of strategy training or learner training as techniques teachers use to make learners become aware of their own strategies, and train them in their practice.

The language teacher is not simply a transmitter of knowledge; like a coach, the language teacher needs to assist students in understanding the task before them, staying motivated, building discipline, and learning how to pursue the task on their own. These thoughts are starting points to support the relevance of developing learning strategies in the foreign language class.

Language learning should be student-centered firstly because students are individuals who differ in significant ways. They differ essentially in language knowledge and skill development. Secondly, students have different learning styles and strengths. Finally, students differ greatly in their levels of motivation, their attitudes toward study in general, and their feelings toward language study in particular. Consequently, the reasons for a student's success or failure differ from person to person. Inevitably, no teacher-designed, one-size-fits-all lesson or program will meet the needs or suit the styles of all of the students in class. Instead, as much as possible, students need to take responsibility for their own learning, choosing goals that fit their needs and strategies that work for them.

It has been proved that students learn more effectively if they are active participants in the learning process. Much language study and practice takes place when the teacher is not around to give instructions or to check up on students. Students who actively take advantage of out-of-class study and practice opportunities will make much more long-term progress than students who consider them a chore to deal with as quickly as possible. Students who take responsibility for their own learning will improve not only their language skills more effectively throughout the course, but also will have the skills they need to continue studying after the course ends.

Another reason to support the role of the students in language learning is that few English as a foreign language programs are long enough to guarantee that students will master the language studied before they leave the program. In many countries, English is taught in middle school and even primary school – often as a required subject – but students study English only a few hours a week and have little opportunities to practice what they learn. Even the students who complete a university major in English still usually have gaps in their English skills when they graduate, and students who are not in an English major, or who study in a night school, have even less English training and practice. Therefore, if a high level of proficiency is the goal, students will probably have to continue studying English long after they leave the educational context, and the students who most likely keep making progress toward mastery of English are those who are already accustomed to designing and carrying out their own language study plans.

Of the many points one could make about language learning, we focus on four that deserve special attention, because they are central in language teaching and because they are points that foreign language learners can easily lose sight of in the learning continuum:
- language is a tool for communication,
- learning a language involves mastery of both skill and knowledge,
- learners need to give serious consideration to the impact of feelings on language study,
- learners vary considerably in their preferred approaches.

The last aspect is central. As learners vary considerably, there is no reason to believe that they should all go about language learning in the same. It means their learning styles must be considered. A wide range of variables has been identified to contribute and determine the success of learning. Some of these have to do with cognitive, affective and socio-cultural factors (Brown, 1987). Among them, the learning style is a collection of cognitive parameters, which refers to a person's consistent tendencies or preferences in learning, and sensory preference is one of the significant characteristics.

A contrasting set of learning styles that has been given attention, has to do with learners' sensory preferences. Learners are categorized in four groups: visual learners (those who learn best by seeing), auditory learners (those who learn best by hearing), kinesthetic learners (those who learn best by moving and doing things), and tactile learners (those who learn best through feeling and touching). Classroom language teaching usually involves visual and auditory stimulus. Auditory students are comfortable with lectures and oral activities.

In contrast, visual students benefit tremendously from instruction with visual backup. Studies have shown that the provision of appropriate contextual visual aids significantly facilitated both listening and reading comprehension in students of lower proficiency levels (Omaggio, 1979; Mueller, 1980; Liu, 2004; Abraham, 2007).

Another set of learning style categories has to do with learners' personality types. Some learning style contrasts suggested include the following distinctions: extroverted versus introverted learners; thinking versus feeling learners (this is a distinction between learners who are more cognitively oriented and those who are more affectively oriented); closure-oriented and judging learners versus open and perceiving learners (the former would strive for clarity, results, and closure; the latter are more comfortable with ambiguity for longer periods and feel less internal pressure to resolve questions any time soon).

Success in learning a foreign language, unlike success in first language acquisition, is very variable. Learner strategies, as conscious actions in learning and using the language, are one of the variable factors that have profound effects on how individual learners approach language learning and how successful they are. The more we learn about learner strategies, the more we gain a sense of the complex system of language learning and teaching.

Foreign language learning strategies have been a subject of interest in scientific research. When facing a foreign language, learners use a number of different strategies acting as tools, which make language learning more successful, self-directed and enjoyable. They assist learners in mastering the language forms and functions necessary for understanding and using the language in real life situations. The element of choice seems to be one of the key features of language learning strategies. Learners use strategies intentionally with the aim of making learning more successful. They consciously employ strategies that suit them most.

Learning does not happen when students simply sit in a classroom and listen. As has been pointed out, it is essential to make them active participants in the learning process instead of passive recipients waiting for information to be given. Language teachers should act as facilitators or guides, who demonstrate and provide students with explicit guidelines.

Along with the advances of technology and the prevalence of smart classrooms, the integration of multimedia makes classroom presentation appealing and informative. Inquiry teaching accompanied by visuals or multimedia provides prompt or extra support to the content being discussed, makes learning more comprehensible and invigorates the interactive spirit.

The Common European Framework of Reference for Foreign Languages (2018) links strategies with effective communication. Strategies are considered as a means that the language user exploits to mobilize and balance own resources, to activate skills and procedures, in order to fulfill the demands of communication in context and successfully complete the task in question in the most comprehensive or most economical way feasible depending on his other precise purpose.

Many researchers on the field of learning strategies have analyzed their characteristics. One of the most accepted criteria is Rebecca Oxford's (2011), who lists the following basic features of learning strategies:
- They contribute to the main goal: communicative competence.
- Strategies allow learners to become more self-directed and to develop autonomous learning; they affect the process of learning: the learner's success or failure in learning.
- They expand the role of language teachers in a way that the traditional role of the teacher in the educational process changes and the role of facilitator is assumed by helping, advising, diagnosing, coordinating learning and participating in communication.
- They are problem-oriented, i.e. oriented towards a specific language task.
- They are specific actions taken by the learner.
- Strategies involve many other learner aspects, not just cognitive.
- They support learning both directly and indirectly.
- They are not always observable, they can be concealed.
- They are often conscious.

- Strategies can be changed, i.e. the existing ones can be adapted, new ones learnt and acquired and unsuccessful ones abandoned.
- They are flexible.

Many researchers have emphasized that the development of learning strategies depends on a number of factors: level of language competence influences their choice, learner's age, gender, nationality and ethnic background, learning environment, learning context and the way of teaching. It is also worth noting that language aptitude has considerable impact on the choice of learning strategies. General (cognitive) learning style may also influence the choice of learning strategies, as well as previous language learning experience, level of education and level of motivation. It is important to stress that affective factors, like language anxiety, significantly influence choice and application of learning strategies. The selection and use of learning strategies is also affected by personality traits, such as intelligence and personal beliefs.

Oxford (1990, 2011) divided learning strategies into two main groups: direct and indirect, which are subdivided into six main groups. In Oxford's opinion, direct strategies involve new language directly and these are classified in memory, cognitive and compensation strategies. All direct strategies require mental processing of the language. Indirect strategies do not directly affect the target language, but have a significant role in language learning. This author included memory, cognitive and compensation strategies into the category of direct strategies, while the indirect strategies include metacognitive, affective and social strategies.

Memory strategies involve the mental processes for storing new information in the memory and for retrieving them when needed. These strategies entail four sets: creating mental linkages, applying images and sounds, reviewing well and employing action.

Cognitive strategies require conscious ways of handling the object language and fall into four groups: practicing, receiving and sending messages strategies, analyzing and reasoning, creating structure for input and output. These strategies are the mental strategies used to make sense of the learning.

Compensation strategies fill knowledge gaps a learner may have, either in speaking or in writing, to help overcome language difficulties. As Oxford says, compensation strategies are employed by learners when facing a temporary breakdown in speaking or writing. These strategies are divided into two groups, guessing intelligently and overcoming limitations in speaking and writing.

Metacognitive strategies enable learners to control their own cognition by using different strategies such as focusing, arranging, evaluating, seeking opportunities, and lowering anxiety. These strategies involve overviewing and linking with material already known, paying attention, delaying speech productions, organizing, setting goals and objectives, planning for a language task, seeking for practice opportunities, arranging, planning and evaluating your learning.

Affective strategies are concerned with the learner's emotional requirements assisting them to cope with their emotions, motivation, and attitudes related to learning. These strategies entail lowering one's anxiety, encouraging oneself and taking one's emotional temperature.

Social strategies lead to increased interaction with the target language. These promote language learning through interactions with others. Every language conveys a form of social behavior. So learning a foreign language requires a correct interaction. As Oxford states, it is extremely important that learners employ appropriate social strategies in this process. Social strategies comprise asking questions and cooperation with others.

Although the classification proposed by Rebecca Oxford is the most widely accepted, there are others like the one offered by O'Malley and Chamot. It is similar to the classification proposed by Oxford. The aforementioned classification comprises three major groups: cognitive, metacognitive and affective strategies. According to these authors, cognitive strategies refer to the mental processes learners use when learning a language and are limited to specific learning tasks (e.g. repetition, translation, grouping, writing notes, deduction, induction, determining key words, contextualization, concluding).

Cognitive strategies help learners understand their course material, including interaction with course contents as well as usage of the certain techniques in solving language tasks. They refer to direct and indirect tasks in the learning process, and include direct manipulation or transformation of learning material. Unlike cognitive strategies, the authors claim that metacognitive strategies include executive functions like focusing attention on relevant contents, selective attention; functional planning of the learning process, supervision and evaluation of what has been learnt. As opposed to cognitive and metacognitive strategies, they highlight that social-affective strategies enable interaction with other learners. Among these strategies, they include cooperation with other participants to complete language tasks, group work interaction and debate.

As individuals who differ in their learning styles, students should be exposed to a wide range of learning strategies and assume their own language learning.

However, teachers have to find ways to make room for student initiative in the classroom. Language is a tool for communication, that is why teachers should help students use the language for genuine communication as often as possible. It is a fact that mastery of a foreign language involves developing language skills through practice, but to reach this goal students should be highly motivated and be given opportunities to practice in class through engaging tasks designed in accordance to their strengths and limitations in the language.

There are many ways to encourage students to take initiative, for instance:
- Have students keep their own vocabulary list,
- let them choose their own books for reading practice,
- have them choose topics for writing or discussions,
- ask them to tape their own listening material
- have them design and carry out their own study plan as a component of the course.

Teachers should try to build their students' intrinsic motivation by encouraging them to consider rewards that come from within themselves, such as a sense of accomplishment, the love of learning new things, the love of creating, or the desire to pursue their curiosity and interests. In fact, many researchers suggest that intrinsic motivation is a more powerful driving force than extrinsic motivation (Brown & Lee, 2015).

Examples of material used for developing learning strategies in beginners from the Bachelor in Education English Major at the University of Holguin
The texts presented below have been used in the subject Integrated English Practice I during reading comprehension lessons. This selection responds to the need of developing reading comprehension skills and presenting the students strategies they can exploit to become independent and more effective language learners.

Text # 1: Strategies for Learning English
Have you ever felt discouraged because it's hard to speak and understand English? Don't give up! Here are three strategies to help you learn faster and remember more.

Strategy 1. Set goals
Have you ever set goals for learning English? When you set goals, you decide what you want to learn. Then you set a plan to help you reach your goals. Maybe your goal is to learn more vocabulary. There are many ways to do this. For example, you can read in English for 15 minutes every day.

Strategy 2. Look for opportunities to practice English

Talk to everyone. Speak with people in the store, at work, in the park. Don't worry about making mistakes. And don't forget to ask questions. For example, if your teacher uses a word you don't understand, ask a question like "What does that word mean?"

Strategy 3. Guess

Don't try to translate every word. When you read, concentrate on clues such as pictures or other words in the sentence to help you understand. You can also make guesses when you are talking to people. For example, look at their faces and hand gestures – the way they move their hands—to help you guess the meaning.

Set goals, look for opportunities to practice and guess. Do these things every day, and you will learn more English.

Taken from Ventures in English

Text # 2: Strategies for Learning New Words

Have you ever felt discouraged because there are so many new words to learn in English? Have you ever set goals for learning new words? Here are some ideas to help you practice and remember vocabulary.

Strategy 1. Keep a vocabulary notebook

Buy a small notebook. Take it with you everywhere. When you see new words around you in the street, on an advertisement, or in a newspaper, writ the new words in your notebook. Use clues to guess the meanings. At the end of the day, use your dictionary to check the meanings. Write an example sentence or draw a picture to help you remember the new words.

Strategy 2. Make vocabulary cards

Have you ever felt bored waiting in a line or taking the bus? Use the time to practice vocabulary. Choose five words from your English class or from a newspaper magazine. Write each word on a small card. Write the new word on one side of the card. Then write the definition or translation on the other side of the card. Test yourself on the definitions.

Strategy #3 Use new words in conversation everyday.

Choose one new word from your notebook or vocabulary cards every day. Try to use it in a conversation some time during the day with your friends, classmates, family, or with your teacher. Using the words you learn will help you remember them.

Taken from Ventures in English

An essential way to help students become better language learners is to help them explore different methods and strategies for language learning. In part, this involves sharing what language teachers know about language learning from personal experiences, both positive and negative. However, it is equally important to encourage students to explore new methods on their own and share with each other what works and what does not. Often, the analysis of these experiences in the classroom expands students' horizons and stimulate learning.

Learning strategies allow students to become more independent and autonomous, encouraging them to play an active role within the new language acquisition process; they give ownership to students which produce quite a positive stimulus in learning. The teacher is no longer seen as the authority, but as a facilitator and a guide for the students. Strategies, like the complex skills of language learning, can be learned through formal instruction and sustained practice. In language classrooms, it is possible for teachers to help their students learn strategies that will make learning more effective and often more fun.

Bibliography

Addine, Fátima and others. Didáctica, teoría y práctica. Editorial Pueblo y Educación. Ciudad de la Habana, 2004.

Abhakorn, Jirapa. *The Implications of Learner Strategies for Second or Foreign Language Teaching*. In: https://research.ncl.ac.uk/media/sites/.../arecls/abhakorn_vol5.pdf

Antich de León, Rosa. Metodología de la enseñanza de lenguas extranjeras. Editorial Pueblo y Educación. 1986.

Castellanos, Doris y otros. Aprender y enseñar en la escuela. Editorial: Pueblo y Educación. Ciudad de la Habana, 2002.

Common European Framework of Reference for Languages: learning, teaching, assessment. Companion Volume with New Descriptors. Council of Europe, February, 2018. www.coe.int/lang-cefr

Dilkova, T.S. *Learning Strategies in Foreign Language Teaching: Using Translation in English Language Teaching*. 14-Journal of the University of Chemical Technology and Metallurgy, 45, 4, 2010, 449-452. In: dl.uctm.edu/journal/node/j2010-4/14_Dilkova_453-456.pdf

Kramer, Aleidine. *Principles of Language Learning and the Role of the Teacher*. In: *https://hrcak.srce.hr/file/266316*

Lee, Horng-Yi. *Inquiry-based Teaching in Second and Foreign Language Pedagogy*. In: Journal of Language Teaching and Research, Vol. 5, No. 6, pp. 1236-1244, November 2014 © 2014 ACADEMY PUBLISHER Manufactured in Finland. doi:10.4304/jltr.5.6.1236-1244 *.www.academypublication.com/issues/past/jltr/vol05/06/03.pdf*

Oxford, Rebecca. *Language Learning Styles and Strategies: an Overview*. Ventures in English. Cambridge University Press, 2008.

Developing Communicative Competence in Foreign Language Teaching through the Task-Based Approach

Spec. Hilda María Reyes González. Associate Professor
Spec. Marilús González Borjas. Associate Professor
Sophomore Student Daniela Aitana Domínguez Reyes.

Task-based learning, also known as task-based approach, is a model that can transform the teaching-learning process, traditionally based on the teacher, in a process centered on the learner. From this perspective, learners have a leading role in their learning process, with greater involvement in setting goals and taking the necessary actions to achieve them. The solution of problems and the accomplishment of tasks close to their personal and professional experiences stimulates his motivation and promotes meaningful learning.

The task-based approach proposes the organization of the course in terms of a final task or set of tasks, which enables the treatment of different contents. In its implementation, learners develop the skills and competences required for their linguistic training. From this conception, the active role and autonomy of the student ponders, as well as cooperation and exchange to foster innovation and creativity to achieve the goals planned.

Task-based language teaching proposes the use of tasks as a central component in the language classroom because they provide better contexts for activating learner acquisition processes and promoting foreign language learning. Richards and Rodgers (2001) state that this is because tasks are believed to foster processes of negotiation, modification, rephrasing, and experimentation that are at the heart of second language learning.

This approach considers language learners as social agents, that is, as members of a society, who have tasks to perform in given circumstances, in a specific environment and within a specific field of action. It is based on the execution of tasks, carried out by one or more individuals, through the use of their skills, to achieve a specific result. The action-based approach, therefore, also takes into account cognitive, emotional and volitional resources, as well as specific capacities that an individual applies as a social agent.

The use of language – which includes learning – comprises the actions carried out by people who, as individuals and as social agents, develop competences, both general and communicative- linguistic, in particular. To achieve these purposes, they use skills that are at their disposal in different contexts and under certain conditions and restrictions. Hence, in order to carry out activities that involve the use of the language to produce and receive texts related to topics in specific areas, it is advisable to use strategies that seem more appropriate for carrying out the tasks to be performed. The control of these actions by the participants produces the reinforcement or modification of their competences.

From the conceptions of the communicative approach, the development of communicative competence is the final goal in the teaching-learning process of languages. This is achieved through the development of necessary procedures for the learner to enhance the four linguistic skills, based on the interdependence between languages and communication (Richards and Rodgers, 1998). In the eighties, researchers began to present a wide variety of studies related to the task-based approach, which has been considered as the natural evolution of the communicative method. This approach is based on the existence of a task and an objective to be achieved after solving tasks that will guide the language learner towards the fulfilment of a given goal while developing linguistic and pedagogical tools necessary for its resolution.

Richards (2001) considers the task-based approach supports on communicative and interactive tasks as central units for the planning and development of instruction. According to this researcher, tasks should provide the foundation for learning from one language to the demand of meaningful communication, negotiation and sharing of meanings and enable students learning grammar as a result of their involvement in the use of language authentically. This approach is an extension from the principles of the communicative approach.

The task-based approach, as a didactic orientation, takes the language learning needs as a starting point to determine what students may be able to do with the language, which tasks are essential in situations relevant to them, and what level of performance is required for its successful realization. In this sense, tasks are primary units of description for the selection of targets, rather than certain components of the language system such as learning the grammar rules or the vocabulary.

Communication and learning involve the performance of tasks that are not solely language tasks, even though they involve language activities and make demands upon the individual's communicative competence. To the extent that these tasks are neither routine nor automatic, learners require the use of strategies in communicating and learning, as well as processing (through reception, production, interaction or mediation) of oral or written texts.

Addressing this approach requires the analysis of the term task, assumed by many researchers to designate the interaction between student and language content in the teaching-learning process. The proposals of Nunan (1989), Willis (2001), Richards and Rogers (2001), Breen (2006), Oxford (2006), Medina and

Fernández (2012), Ramírez and Faedo (2017), provide elements of interest for the purposes of the present work.

For Nunan (1989), the task is a part of class work that involves students in understanding, manipulating, producing or interacting with the target language, while attention is focused primarily on meaning rather than on form.

Richards (2002) assumes the task as an activity that is designed to achieve a certain learning objective and its dimensions influence its use in the teaching of a language. These dimensions include objectives, procedures students use to complete a task, expected results, learning strategies that its execution demands, the way in which the result will be evaluated, and participation, related to its development individually, in pairs or in groups.

Ellis considers the task as a work plan that requires students to process language in a pragmatic way to achieve a result that can be evaluated. This involves attention to meaning and use of the linguistic resources available to the student, although the design of the task can require the use of particular forms. The CEFR defines the task as any intentional action that an individual considers necessary to achieve a specific result in terms of solving a problem. Task accomplishment by an individual involves the strategic activation of specific competences in order to carry out a set of purposeful actions in a particular domain with a clearly defined goal and a specific outcome.

Tasks actively involve learners in meaningful communication, are relevant and challenging but feasible, and have identifiable outcomes, which are real and practical. Students can track their progress in developing language skills by their ability to carry out realistic tasks that help them interact communicatively and purposefully. The difficulty of a task depends on a range of factors including the previous experience of the learner, the complexity of the tasks, and the degree of support available.

As Willis states, tasks can have a variety of starting points: they may be based on a written text, or a recording of spoken data, or visual data, and/or they may draw on learners' own input, on their personal experience or their knowledge of the world. They could be games, demonstrations, interviews or a combination of several of these.

Tasks can be varied in nature, and may involve language activities to a greater or lesser extent. On the other hand, they may be quite simple or extremely complex and may involve a number of steps or embedded subtasks. Consequently, the boundaries of a task may be difficult to define. A task intends to provoke the use of the language very similar to the way in which it is used in the real world and can involve productive and receptive skills, orally or in the written form, and different cognitive processes.

Communication is an essential part of the tasks in which the participants carry out activities of interaction, expression, understanding or mediation, or a combination of two or more of them. Communicative tasks require students to understand, negotiate, and express meanings in order to achieve a communicative objective. Its realization is related to both the meaning and the way it is understood, expressed and negotiated. Therefore, there should be balance in the attention given to meaning and form, to fluency and correction, when selecting and sequencing tasks.

Communicative tasks of a pedagogical character (as opposed to the exercises that specifically focus on decontextualized practice of formal aspects) involve learners in meaningful communication, pose a difficulty, but are, in turn, feasible and have identifiable results. These tasks may include meta-communicative tasks or subtasks, that is, a communication about the implementation of the task and about the language used to carry it out, which also includes the implication of the student in the selection, control and evaluation of the task, in a language learning context.

In the consulted literature there is consensus in recognizing the potentialities of the task-based approach in the field of education and school. Its many attributes and features will give a capacity analysis viable, useful and meaningful, as they are small units that cater to very important aspects within the curriculum (Long, 1985). The conceptions offered by Long, assumed in this work, emphasize the potential of the task for:
- diagnosis and monitoring of the student's needs.
- critical analysis of curricular contents and the planning of actions that promote personal and professional growth of the student.
- the acquisition of the foreign language, in an environment of negotiation and exchange, which allows the determination of goals attainable by the student in a certain period of time.

Tasks are also an educational activity, so they should be attractive and motivating for foreign language learners. They are supposed to involve the learner in such a way that, while acquiring a command of the language, he develops the required competencies and gets in touch with the cultural elements of that language. This is another demonstrative element of the relevance of addressing questions regarding the way of designing, sequencing and organizing tasks presented to the learner.

As an educationally appropriate activity, tasks should have a close link between what is discussed in the classroom and what exists in the real world. Tasks designed by language teachers must be related to those situations and credible contexts that surround the student. For this reason, they have to involve the student in active and spontaneous use of the language as a user, and not as a learner (Van der Branden, 2006). In Cuban Higher Education, a context in which the authors develop their professional activity, the task must, in addition to promoting the development of communicative competence in English, prepare the students to meet the standards required in the certification process, which establishes CEFR level A2 as a goal.

The traditional presentation-practice-production (PPP) teaching/learning cycle was at one time virtually the only acceptable for task sequence. In the PPP cycle, grammar presentation came first, followed by controlled and less controlled practice and then by actual production. However, Willis' (1998) task-based model offers a task cycle that opposes the PPP sequence. In this model, which effectively combines meaning and form, the communicative task comes before the focus on form (language analysis and practice). Another significant feature is that the learner not only performs the task but also reports it.

Task-based learning has a holistic approach. The students carry out a communicative task making use of the linguistic resources available to them. Research on the subject suggests that it is only after the cycle of tasks has been completed that students' attention is directed to specific forms of language. Willis' framework consists of the following:
  - Pre-task - introduction to the topic and task.
  - Task cycle: task planning, doing the task, preparing to report on the task and presenting the task report.
  - Language focus - analysis and practice (focus on form).

Johnson (1996), Skehan (1998), and Willis (1996) discussed sequencing of tasks according to methodological task features, such as extent of communication (negotiation of meaning), task difficulty, and amount of planning allowed. Others

have discussed how to sequence tasks to reflect the developmental sequence of language acquisition. Skehan (1999) suggested targeting a range of structures rather than a single one and using the criterion of usefulness rather than necessity as a sequencing criterion.

Another aspect to be considered when analyzing the foundations of the task base-approach is learners' individual differences such as learning styles, learning strategies, age, gender, and culture, which are factors that influence the development of language learning. Among those variables, learning styles and learning strategies are variables relating to learners' performance in completing their language tasks. Moreover, learners' learning styles influences their choices of learning strategies (Ehrman & Oxford, 1990).

What are, then, the basic assumptions of task-based language teaching? Feez (1998) summarizes these as follows:
- The focus of instruction is on process rather than product.
- Basic elements are purposeful activities and tasks that emphasize communication and meaning.
- Learners learn language by interacting communicatively and purposefully while engaged in meaningful tasks.
- Activities and tasks can be either those that learners might need to achieve in real life or those that have a pedagogical purpose specific to the classroom.
- Activities and tasks of a task-based syllabus can be sequenced according to difficulty.
- The difficulty of a task depends on a range of factors including the previous experience of the learner, the complexity of the tasks, and the degree of support available (quoted in Richards and Rodgers, 2001).

The study developed on the topic is essential for implementing CEFR premises, with the necessary adjustments to any particular context. The examples of tasks provided in the paper respond to the conceptions assumed by the authors. The tasks meet the requirements of the A1 (Starter) level of the CEFR and have been designed and implemented with first year students of the Journalism Major in the University of Holguin. The tasks are aimed at treating the content of this level and correspond to the requirements stated in the descriptors. Although the tasks presented are aimed at promoting the development of oral expression, they also enhance its integration with the other aspects of the verbal activity.

The tasks proposed are organized in three phases. The authors assume the cycle proposed by Moore and Lorenzo (2015), which includes a preparatory phase (preparation task) that provides orientation and activates previous knowledge, the development phase (task) and the final phase (post task). During the different moments that the task goes through, the instructions are simple, clear and sufficient and tasks are carried out in pairs and/or groups. This facilitates communication and mutual collaboration between students. The tasks also contribute to the treatment of the topics, the structures of language and the typology used in the certification exams that are applied, which favors the students training for their successful completion.

Task 1: Meeting new people
Preparation task

1 Say your names. I'm Ali. I'm Thomas.

2 Stand up in alphabetical order and say your names.

I'm Ali. I'm Birgit. I'm Thomas. I'm Zak.

Tasks
1. Group work: Ask the students, first in groups and then as a whole, to come up with ten questions, answers to which they would like to have in order to get to know someone in the classroom. Once the class has agreed on a list of questions, send the students back into their groups to put these questions into a logical order. Come back together again and agree upon an order. At this point, each student should pair up with another student, preferably one from a different group. They should ask each other the questions, making note of the answers -so they can introduce their partner to the class as a whole.

Post task:
A. Which of the following greetings are typical in your country? Tick the ones you think and compare with your partner.
   a) a hug
   b) a handshake
   c) a pat on the back
   d) a kiss on the cheek
   e) a bow

B. Work in pairs. Write the name of a country where these greetings are used.

C. Get ready to dramatize a dialogue about personal information. Use the greetings above.

D. Class activity: Take notes on the information provided by your classmates and get ready to report orally.
"Their names are... They live in ... "

Task 2: Talking about families

<u>Preparation task</u>: Make word webs about **family** and **jobs**. Write a sentence about each word. Then compare with your partner, use the example below as a model.

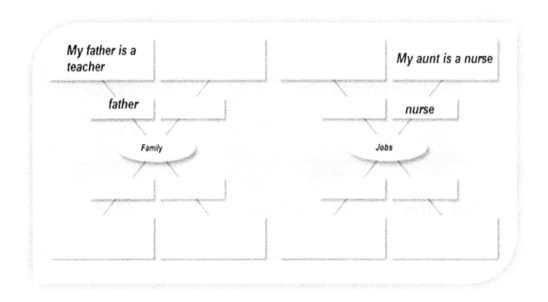

Tasks

1. Class activity: Go around the class and find this information. Write a classmate´s name only once. Ask follow up questions on your own.

Find someone...
- who is an only child (Do you have any brothers or sisters?)
- who has a brother and a sister
- who lives with his/her grandparents
- whose mother/father works long hours
- who has a family member with an usual job

Class activity: Compare your information.

2. Group work. The students bring pictures of their families. One student shows the pictures and his/her group mates ask questions. Then they take turns showing their pictures and exchanging information about them.

<u>Post task</u>: Tell the class about your family.

"I have one brother and two sisters. My brother's name is Paul, he is a lawyer, he loves his job. My sister ..."

Task 3: Describing routines

Tasks:
Group work. Number the free time activities below from 1 (you like the most) to 6 (you like the least).
_____ watch TV
_____ listen to music
_____ go to the gym
_____ go out with friends
_____ help with the housework
_____ play video games

    A. Add two more activities to your list.
    B. Get ready to read your list to the class. Support your selection.
    C. Listen to the lists proposed by your classmates and get ready to ask follow up questions (What are your favorite TV programs? When do you go to the gym? How often do you clean the house? What kind of music do you prefer?)

Post task:
Group work: Take a poll of your routines. Take turns asking each person these questions.
    a) What time do you get up on weekdays?
    b) How do you travel from home to school?
    c) Do you ever exercise? How often do you do it?
    d) What do you do after school?
    e) What do you do on weekends?
- Class activity: Compare your routine with your classmates' routines. Whose schedule is the most like yours? Tell the class.
- Suppose you have a pen friend who lives in England. Write a letter telling him/her about your routine. You may use the previous questions as a guide for writing.

The management of the teaching-learning process from the postulates of CEFR gives special attention to the task-based approach. Under these conceptions, the foreign language learner uses a wide and varied range of resources and procedures to achieve a specific objective, while developing the skills and competencies necessary to cope with the demands made under the teacher's guidance.

The task-based approach fosters high levels of communication between students and between them and the teacher, who as a guide, mediator, facilitator of learning, leads a process focused on the students, their strengths and needs in foreign language learning. The task-based approach also potentiates constant assessment of the results achieved and the search for alternatives that may require a student to overcome their limitations from the linguistic point and set new goals, promoting the development of strategies to learn independently.

The tasks planned under the conceptions assumed in this approach encourage language learning and skill training. The fulfilment of tasks demands the use of the learners´ own communicative abilities to shift from their mother tongue to the target language. Besides, tasks provide opportunities for learning in a cooperative way and prepare the students to use the target language with specific professional purposes. The tasks presented contribute to the development of the students' communicative competence at an early stage of the language learning process, providing them a natural context for language use and increasing their motivation towards the language lesson.

Bibliography
Barturén, N. (2019): *El aprendizaje basado en tareas como método para desarrollar la expresión oral en estudiantes de inglés de un instituto superior tecnológico de Lima*. Tesis para optar el grado de maestro en educación con mención en docencia e investigación en educación superior. Lima: Perú.
Common European Framework of Reference for Languages: learning, teaching, assessment (2018): *Companion Volume with New Descriptors*. Council of Europe. www.coe.int/lang-cefr.
De Gustín, N. (2019): *El enfoque de enseñanza de idiomas basado en tareas (TBLT)*. Trabajo de fin de grado en Educación Primaria. Mención lengua extranjera: inglés, Facultad de Educación y Trabajo Social. Universidad de Valladolid.
Edwards, C. and J. Willis (2005): *Teachers Exploring Tasks in English Language Teaching*. Published by Palgrave Macmillan.
Ellis, R. (2003): *Task-based language learning and teaching*. Oxford: Oxford University Press.
Forero, L. y K. Hernández (2012): *El aprendizaje basado en tareas como enfoque metodológico para mejorar la inteligibilidad en la pronunciación de sonidos vocálicos del inglés como lengua extranjera*. Proyecto investigativo para optar al título de Licenciado en Educación Básica con Énfasis en Humanidades e Idiomas. Universidad libre de Colombia. Bogotá D.C. Lavery, Clare. British Council Language Assistant. ISBN 086355 4873.
MacCarthy, M., J. MacCarten and H. Sandiford: *Touchtone 1*. Cambridge: Cambridge University Press.
Medina, A. (2012): *Formación de hábitos lingüísticos y desarrollo de habilidades comunicativas en el aprendizaje de lenguas extranjeras*. En Revista Electrónica Luz. Edición 50; Año X I. No. 4. Oct-dic. II Época. RNPS 2054. ISSN 1814-151. Holguin. Cuba.
_____ (2012): *Glossary: Improve your methodological technical register with more than 800 terms*. Universidad de Ciencias Pedagógicas José de la Luz y Caballero, Holguín. Cuba.
Nunan, D. (2004): *Task-based language teaching*. Cambridge University Press.
Oxford, R.: Task-Based Language Teaching and Learning: An Overview. Asian EFL Journal Press, Volume 8, Number 3. Descargado de

https://www. asian-efl-journal.com.

Parnrod, U. & others: *Styles, Strategies & Tasks: Are They Related?* Volume 47 January-June 2014. Descargado de

https://www. researchgate.net/publication.

Ramírez, I., Faedo, A. and others (2017): *Tareas para la comunicación oral en inglés para estudiantes universitarios. Una tipología.* Editorial Mar Abierto. Ecuador.

Recino, U. y Laufer, M. (2010): *Task Based Learning in Communicative Foreign Language Teaching*. En Revista Electrónica Edumecentro. Volumen 2. No. 3. Sep.-dic. RNPS 2234 RNSW: A0319. ISSN 2077-2874.

Richards, J.: Interchange Intro, Fourth Edition. Cambridge: Cambridge University Press.

Richards, J. & Rodgers, T. (2001): *Approaches and methods in language teaching*. Cambridge: Cambridge University Press.

Terroux, Georges and Woods, H. (1991): *Teaching English in a World at Peace*. McGill University. Quebec.

Using the CEFR. Principles of Good Practices. University of Cambridge. ESOL Examinations. October 2011.

Van den Branden, K. (2006): *Task-Based Language Education: from Theory to Practice*. Cambridge University Press.

Willis, D. and Willis, J. (2007): *Doing Task-based Teaching*. Oxford: Oxford University Press.

Willis, J. (1996): *A framework for task-based learning.* Harlow: Longman.

Leading the Blind to Listen in an FL Lesson. Theory and Methodology

MSc Miguel Ángel Olivé Iglesias. Associate Professor
Senior Student Arianna Rosa Leyva
MSc Idania Leida Leyva Pérez. Associate Professor

Language is a characteristic capacity of human beings to express thoughts and feelings by means of the word. In today´s world, English is a language spoken in many countries, even in those in which it is not a first or official language. It is considered as the international language of diplomacy, business, science, technology, medicine and tourism. Today it is essential to learn English: it is used more and more in almost all areas of knowledge and human development. Practically, it can be argued that it is the language of the world.

The Cuban System of Education considers English as a subject to be taught in all educational levels. Nowadays, the English subject in our system of Education is in correspondence to the political, social-cultural and economic importance of foreign languages. Cuba develops relations of cooperation and interchange with many countries concerning technical, political, scientific, educational and cultural fields.

The teaching of English must contribute not only to linguistic efficiency but also to the ability of constructing and reconstructing knowledge. It implies to develop knowledge, habits and skills in the learners so as to allow them to communicate appropriately in a foreign language; that is, to understand oral and written information, express themselves orally on familiar themes and write simple and brief messages.

The success of the study of English as a foreign language requires a high motivation in learners and teachers. A motivated learner will develop a positive attitude, the same way as motivated teachers will bring motivation to their students.

It is imperative to make teaching and learning culturally relevant and to enable access to prior knowledge upon which new skills and concepts can be built. It is critical for educators to understand the ways in which learners´ cultural and linguistic backgrounds profoundly influence their experiences in the classroom. This is especially true when it comes to teaching blind learners in the Cuban system of Education.

Internationally, a number of researchers on teaching the blind may be mentioned: Carney, S., Engbretson, C., Scammell, K. and Sheppard, V. (2003); Waterfield, J. and West, B. (2008); Hojan et al (2012); Coşkun, A (2013);

Niwagaba, G (2014); Kane, S. and Bigham J. (2014); Kocyigit, N and Sabuncu Artar, P (2015); Konga K, Kaha Kore and Aheinga K (2015).

Nationally, authors who have studied and researched on education for the blind are N. Barraga (1983), Delgado (1994), M. García (1998), M. Bueno (2004), Santos (2004). As well, we have consulted the works of C. González (1994), A. Santaballa (1997), I. Fernández (2001), X. García (2002), C. Hernández (2003), D. Martín (2004), G. García (2005) y L. Menéndez Navarro (2008), S. Alonso (2008), E. Vives (2007). In Holguin, L. Almaguer (2009), S. Alonso (2009), A. I. Cordero (2010), Y. B. Calero (2010), Y. Leyva (2010), C. M. Aguilera (2011), C. Vicente (2011), T. Arcos (2012) and D. Alas (2018).

The authors of this paper thought of a way to help blind learners learn the language and develop a skill in class that is hardly used in actual practice, listening. Listening in itself is advantageous. Blind people sharpen their other senses to fill the gap that is left by not being able to see; hearing is one of them. The problem of listening comprehension has been addressed by prestigious national and foreign investigators in the fields of pedagogy, general didactics, and foreign language teaching, it has also been dealt with in Term and Diploma Papers at Holguin University: Talizina (1983), Wipf (1984), James (1984), Antich (1986), Abbott et al (1989), Dunkel (1991), Feyten (1991), Morley (1991), Ur (1998), Rost (2002), Anderson and Lynch (2002), Medina (2003, 2006, 2012), Córdova (2005), Causarás and Olivé (2016, 2017), among others.

Special Education is devoted to people with special needs due to their high intellectual talents or because of psychological disabilities, physical, sensory-receptors-related or more complex. It implies specific educational policies, and calls for a didactics for people with special needs in any context. Special education in Cuba basically aims at incorporating children, teens and young people with any disability to social and work activities.

Special Education Management for the blind and the visually limited people is in charge of education in children, teens and young people with visual deficiencies. Departing from a special psychology, a special pedagogy for the blind is elaborated, plus techniques for rehabilitation so those people can be integrated in society.

The structure of the education of blind and low-vision students in Cuba encompasses:
1. Pre-school grade, two-year course for blind children, a year for children with low vision. Its fundamental objective is their preparation for school.
2. Primary education, from 1st to 6th grade. Two cycles, the first one from 1st to 4th, mainly preparatory; the second one from 5th to 6th, when

students deepen on the knowledge acquired in the different subjects. They receive vocational guidance in this cycle.

3. The third stage ranges from 7th to 9th grade. A general education is guaranteed to assure a proficient incorporation of the graduate to advanced studies.

Besides these levels, there are classrooms to work through a preparatory stage with those students whose loss of vision happens during school age (late blindness). They arrive in school without specific necessary preparation to face the process of learning without knowing the Braille system. This stage allows students to enter the grade and level that best fits them.

The teaching of the visually-affected is carried out in several types of classrooms: for the blind, for students with low vision, strabismus and amblyopia. There are also mixed classrooms.

Special schools have the same general objectives that govern general school, since their operation is ruled by laws similar to the learning process of students who can see, with specific demands such as guided objectives in sight correction and compensation.

The study program for the education of blind students and those with low vision includes the subjects of study of General Polytechnic and Industrial Arts Education, with special subjects of study, like Braille Stenography, Boldface Typewriting and Context Awareness. The development plan for this specialty for the blind (MINED, 2004) includes visual stimulation, orientation and mobility, the possibility to continue studies, and information technologies. This guides the teaching-learning process toward assisting the blind in accessing general education.

Some psychological and pedagogical characteristics of the blind

Visual deficiency in children is defined as: "Vision disorders provoking limitations in the process of perception of the world around." The degree of affection is varied: from practically no influence on the child's development, to deep limitations creating educational needs in special schools. Visual deficiencies result from ocular anomalies, eye-refraction diseases and other illnesses.

The loss of eyesight can be provoked by diseases or traumatic injuries to the human organism. Some diseases are:

1. Diseases of the organ of sight (anomalies of refraction, which may imply a marked visual lesion, glaucoma, blurred cornea, vascular and retina diseases, atrophy of the optic nerve, etc.).

2. Diseases of the central nervous system (meningitis, encephalitis, meningoencephalitis, brain tumors, etc.).

3. The organism's general diseases (measles, scarlet fever, diphtheria, the flu, scrofula, tuberculosis).

4. Traumatic injuries in peripheral sight, nervous passages and cerebral cores.

The loss of eyesight implies a much more intense activity by the other senses to compensate the decrease of received sensations. They also add serious alterations in social life, in relating with other people, etc. Because of the lack of a rich sensorial experience, there is a reduced amount of representation of objects and surrounding phenomena. Besides, these can be poor and inaccurate. Absence or limitation in adequate space orientation is typical, resulting in movement to be highly dependent on kinesthetic sensibility and touch; walking is unstable and posture is not totally erect. In general, slowness in movement is observed.

Students with visual deficiencies, either the blind or those visually limited, have all of the possibilities of development if education takes their specific characteristics into account:

- Thinking with great verbal development and much less practical experience.
- Limited capability of mobility.
- Further development of their still operational senses (touch, taste, smell).
- Better use of their still operational senses to carry out theoretical and practical activities.
- Sharpened tactile ability.
- Affectivity characterized by depressive cyclic crises during development.
- Preference for oral activities where they have better performance possibilities.
- Increase of audition and tactile memory.

Conditions must be created at school and in family for the joyful compensatory adaptation of the blind. It is important to remark that blind students may attain a psychological development functionally equivalent to that of students who can see via alternative ways of learning and developing. This means that teaching and learning in students who can see and those who are blind are not identical processes but they can reach related results through different options.

The listening skill
Ability comes from the term *"habilítas."* It makes reference to the capability and disposition for something. It is the set of complex actions that favor the development of capabilities. It is a complex system of psychic and practical

activities necessary for the regulation of activity, knowledge and habits that the individual possesses and should develop.

While "to listen" is seen in terms of attention and silence, "to hear" has more to do with the perception of sound and the faculties of the ear (see Lipari, 2010) and the response (Bodie & Crick, 2014). This distinction often helps separate the focus of work by audiologists who study the physiological components of hearing from those, like communication scholars, who study the individual and relational components of listening. Language learning depends on listening. Listening provides the aural input that serves as the basis for language acquisition and enables learners to interact in spoken communication.

Authors who analyze listening recognized it as a multidimensional construct that consists of complex (a) affective processes, such as being motivated to attend to others; (b) behavioral processes, such as responding with verbal and nonverbal feedback; and (c) cognitive processes, such as attending to, understanding, receiving, and interpreting content and relational messages (Halone, Cunconan, Coakley, & Wolvin, 1998).

According to Debra L. Worthington & Graham D. Bodie (?) the listening skill has been defined by different authors. They propose the following systematization:
- Tucker, 1925: An analysis of the impressions resulting from concentration where an effort of will is required.
- Rankin, 1926: The ability to understand spoken language.
- Nichols, 1948: The comprehension of expository materials presented orally in a classroom situation
- Barbe & Meyers, 1954: The process of reacting to, interpreting, and relating the spoken language in terms of past experiences and further course of action.
- Brown & Carlson, 1955: The aural assimilation of spoken symbols in a face-to-face speaker audience situation, with both oral and visual cues present.
- Barbara, 1957: A definite, usually voluntary, effort to apprehend acoustically.
- Spearritt, 1962: The active process involved in attaching meaning to sounds.
- Barker, 1971: The selective process of attending to, hearing, understanding, and remembering aural symbols.
- Weaver, 1972: A process that takes place when a human organism receives data orally. The selection and retention of aurally received data.

- Kelly, 1975: A rather definite and deliberative ability to hear information, to analyze it, to recall it at a later time, and to draw conclusions from it.
- Steil et al, 1983: Consists of four connected activities – sensing, interpreting, evaluating, and responding.
- Wolff et al, 1983: A unitary-receptive communication process of hearing and selecting, assimilating and organizing, and retaining and covertly responding to aural and nonverbal stimuli.
- Wovin & Coakley, 1988: The process of receiving, attending to, and assigning.
- Brownell, 1994: An overt behavior that conceptualizes the teaching and training process.
- ILA, 1996: The process of receiving, constructing meaning from and responding to spoken and/or nonverbal messages.
- Cooper, 1997: Listening competence means behavior that is appropriate and effective. Appropriateness means that the content is understood and effectiveness deals with the achievement of interactive goals.
- De Ruyter & Wetzels, 2000: [as perceived by customers] A set of interrelated activities, including apparent attentiveness, nonverbal behaviors, verbal behavior, perceived attitudes, memory and behavioral responses.
- Brown, 2001: An important skill through which language learners internalize linguistic information without which they cannot produce language.
- Bostrom, 2011: Acquisition, process, and retention of information in interpersonal contexts.

Medina, 2006, states: "It is a process through which the listener (student) actively interacts with the audio-text, he perceives and recognizes the linguistic units in order to construct meanings out of them through top-down and bottom-up processes. During the processing of information through his/her mental activity, the listener constructs the meanings or messages by a critical evaluation of the information according to his/her cultural background."

Listening skills vary as the context of communication differs. Wolvin and Coakley (1988) propose five different types of listening:
- Discriminative listening helps listeners draw a distinction between facts and opinions.
- Comprehensive listening facilitates the understanding of oral input.
- Critical listening allows listeners to analyze the incoming message before accepting or rejecting it.
- Therapeutic listening serves as a sounding board and lacks any aspect of critiques.

- Appreciative listening contributes listeners to enjoy input and receive emotional impressions.

Listening is a vital component of the oral communication, or the interactive process in which the individual takes the roles of speaker and listener through a verbal and non-verbal component. As an utterance unfolds, listeners take advantage of both linguistic and extra-linguistic information to arrive at interpretations more quickly than they could, using the spoken language alone. For instance, listeners have been shown to use visual (exophoric) information about the scene (Tanenhaus et al, 1995), the goals and perspectives of their partners (Hanna et al, 2003), and spatial constraints about how objects in the world can be manipulated (Chambers et al, 2002) during language understanding, all of which serves to restrict the set of potential interpretations that need to be considered.

The listening process refers to how listeners interpret input in terms of what they know or identify what they do not know, as well as the way in which learners use different kinds of signals to interpret what is said (Flavell et al, 1981; Brown et al, 1985; Rubin, 2011). Like the reading process, listening includes three types of processing: *top-down processing*; *bottom-up processing*; and *interactive interpretive processing* (parallel processing).

Top-down processing is the listening processing during which the learner draws upon his background knowledge and expectations of what will follow next in the discourse, and then infers what the intentions of the speaker may have then (Rost, 2005). Through top-down processing readers and listeners utilize real-world knowledge and refer to various types of schemata [plural of schema: a mental structure of preconceived ideas] that help them predict what will follow in the discourse.

Bottom-up processing is the listening processing during which the learner analyzes the various morpho-syntactic elements of the discourse from the phonemes of the language to the syllables, words, phrases and sentences that make up the discourse. These activities require processing of all of the linguistic structures of the target language (Field, 1999). Rahimi, 2012, argues that "as more sounds occur, the listener can eliminate more and more possibilities until he arrives at the single, more accurate match to the input sounds, and this matching may occur before all of the sounds have been heard because of the elimination process."

Interactive interpretive processing is also known as 'parallel processing'. Scholars argue that 'top-down' and 'bottom-up' – as two types of comprehension processing – operate in an interactive, reciprocal way and complement each other at all levels of analyses simultaneously (Brindley, 1998; Dunkel, 1991; Grabe, 1991; Lynch, 1998; Mendelsohn, 1998; Morley, 1995; Perfetti, 1988).

Park's Interactive Process model shows how it takes both top-down processing coupled with bottom-up processing for comprehension to take place. Park argues that 'bottom-up' requires linguistic knowledge and 'top-down' occurs when background knowledge is activated (Park, 2004).

Language Learning Strategies

Listening strategies are techniques or activities that contribute directly to the comprehension and recall of listening input besides can be classified by how the listener processes the input. In the communicative approach to language teaching, this means modeling listening strategies and providing listening practice in authentic situations: those that learners are likely to encounter when they use the language outside the classroom.

Goals and Techniques for Teaching Listening

Instructors want to produce students who even if they do not have complete control of the grammar or an extensive lexicon, can fend for themselves in communication situations. In the case of listening, this means producing students who can use listening strategies to maximize their comprehension of aural input, identify relevant and non-relevant information, and tolerate less than word by-word comprehension.

Integrating Metacognitive Strategies

Before listening: Plan for the listening task
- Set a purpose or decide in advance what to listen for
- Decide if more linguistic or background knowledge is needed
- Determine whether to enter the text from the top down (attend to the overall meaning) or from the bottom up (focus on the words and phrases)

During and after listening: Monitor comprehension
- Verify predictions and check for inaccurate guesses
- Decide what is and is not important to understand
- Listen/view again to check comprehension
- Ask for help

After listening: Evaluate comprehension and strategy use
- Evaluate comprehension in a particular task or area
- Evaluate overall progress in listening and in particular types of listening tasks
- Decide if the strategies used were appropriate for the purpose and for the task
- Modify strategies if necessary.

Using Authentic Materials and Situations: Authentic materials and situations prepare students for the types of listening they will need to do when using the language outside the classroom.

According to Terroux, G. and Howard Woods (1996) the following five-step approach should be considered when planning a listening comprehension exercise:

1. Preparation: the teacher prepares the students for the listening exercises to arouse their interest and makes any clarification.
2. Demonstration: the teacher demonstrates how the activity works to make sure the students know what they have to do. This step may be optional if the teacher considers it is not necessary to demonstrate
3. Listening: the students listen to the text to complete the task that has been set
4. Correction: the teacher helps the students see if they have completed the task successfully. This helps the teacher determine difficulties and prepare remedial work.
5. Integration: the teacher organizes some kind of follow up task related to the listening text. This could involve a listening activity, a speaking activity or the integration of several skills together.

Before listening students will be asked to:
- Distinguish individual sounds, word boundaries, and stressed syllables
- Identify thought groups
- Listen for intonation patterns in utterances
- Identify grammatical forms and functions

Before listening students will be asked to focus on:
- Listening for gist, main ideas, topic, and setting of the text
- Listening for specific information
- Sequencing the information

Didactic considerations

Many authors have emphasized on the different phases involved in the development of the listening skill process. Causarás and Olivé, 2017, analyzed:

Pre-Listening: A well-designed listening activity should be broken down into carefully sequenced "phases" that build on each other. The initial pre-listening phase should prepare students by helping them activate their background knowledge and clarify their expectations and assumptions about the text. An ideal pre-listening task is one in which the teacher, through carefully constructed questions, helps students to activate background information and language components needed to comprehend the text without "giving" this information to the students.

While Listening: "Global comprehension" refers to understanding the very general idea(s) or gist of the listening text after the first or second listen. While the students might pick up some details after the first listen, our aim should be to help them focus on the general meaning first, so that they can establish a preliminary framework that will enable them to get more details in the subsequent listens.

Post-Listening: A post-listening activity represents a follow up to the listening activity and aims to utilize the knowledge gained from listening for the development of other skills such as speaking or writing. If we have listened to a TV program presenting a certain point of view regarding health care, for example, we can ask the students to do some research and identify some opposing views to present them in class. Alternatively, we may want to engage the students in a discussion of the merits of the views that were expressed in the listening segment.

Like post-reading activities, post-listening activities allow for recycling and further activation of vocabulary and structures as long as they are interesting and engaging and are carefully thought out.

For our students to become proficient listeners they need to be exposed to tremendous listening input and they need training (especially at the lower levels of proficiency) on how to develop effective listening strategies. Be sure to:
- Allocate ample time for listening activities the same way you do for speaking or grammar practice.
- Engage the students in discussions of the strategies they use and allow them to learn from each other.
- Make listening a "regular" part of homework.

Focusing on listening is one of the best investments you can make as language teacher, as it will help your students develop more confidence in their language ability. Listening is a challenging skill, yet, with constant practice, support, and encouragement, your students will develop both strategies and confidence.

The authors assume the following orientations and recommendations given by Chok Sengs (?) about the teaching learning process of blind students:

First and foremost, teachers have to understand the visual condition of their blind student. Teachers do not need to understand the medical implication of the student's blindness, just how much residual vision he or she has.

The next thing to do is to learn the background of the student. How and when he or she became blind. If the blind student became blind when he or she was, for example, at the age of eight or nine, he or she has certain visual memory. He or she will conceive ideas and images differently from someone who was blind at birth.

When confronted with a totally blind student do not despair. Read teaching material to the blind student and get him or her to Braille the material before lessons. The problem of a shortage of material in Braille has always plagued teachers for the blind.

In the classroom, the blind student cannot see the board so the teacher has to be more vocal and say out every word he or she puts on the board including direction of where the words are. For example, teaching the format of a letter say out, 'On the left hand corner of your page you write the address. The address of this college is number twenty-nine, Green Lane'. Remember the blind student cannot see the board but he or she can hear well. When plans or diagrams are used, you can emboss them for your students by sticking string to cardboard. Here teachers may have to use their ingenuity.

Teaching tips
- Use talking books and taped dialogues for reading comprehension lessons.
- Use real objects in the lessons.
- Check in on them regularly to see if they need help, but only provide help they request.
- Assign a mobility helper if needed.
- Speak directly to the blind student.
- Minimize background noise.
- Eliminate physical objects in aisles and doorways and reduce overall clutter.
- Highlight all main points of a lesson orally.
- Identify name of student who is speaking.

Blind students may be visually impaired but their other senses are intact – they even over-activate and sharpen – so teachers of the blind should utilize the other senses. Learning a language is very much tied up with culture, exposure and experiences. Blind students may not be able to acquire exposure and experiences the same way as sighted students. So teachers of the blind may have to do a little more than other teachers. Bring experiences and exposure to the blind students.

There are many tools and aids that can be beneficial for blind students. These students may have some of their own mobility aids. Here are some tools and devices that teachers may want to consider having available for blind students language learners:
- Braille devices
- MP3 players
- large print books
- magnified screens

- real objects
- large wall charts
- podcasts
- audiobooks

It is recommendable to begin the English classes with an activity related to games that help to center the learners' attention and serve like a preamble to the theme to be developed.

As to the utilization of audiovisual material, like movie films, television or videos in Internet, make sure that students with visual disability are located in a place where they may listen clearly. Describe only the imagery that you consider more relevant.

Descriptions must be brief and simple, utilizing "obvious" English, according to their level of understanding. If you are going to utilize series of slides or some other half a graphic to complement the exposition, describe the images that illustrate the presentation.

When you utilize visual help like drawings or graphics, try always to do the description of images or graphics, mentioning the most essential characteristics and omitting those details that do not contribute important information. Avoid utilizing demonstratives or adverbs: "Here, there, this or that" when you refer to objects or places. Utilize the real names of the objects and adverbial phrases that provide to the blind learner one referent space like: "On the right, upper left, behind me, etc." If it is possible, work with real objects. For example, if the theme of the classroom is names of fruits, find those you are going to teach and permit students to explore and recognize fruits tactilely, while you pronounce the correspondent name. This strategy is functional, not only for the blind student and or with low vision, but for the students in general.

Finally, students with visual impairments achieve much of their learning through listening. Develop listening skills in the following areas:
- Auditory perception;
- Sound discrimination;
- Sound location;
- Association of sounds and objects or situations;
- Interpreting auditory information;
- Listening for sequence;
- Listening for detail;
- Listening for main ideas;
- New vocabulary;
- Listening to follow instructions;
- Learning to listen to audiocassettes;

- Using earphones to minimize distractions;
- Reading the questions to be answered before listening to the information;
- Playing short portions of a tape and stopping to make notes; and adjusting the speed of the tape player.

The authors have tried to compile valuable information for the FL teacher who works with visually limited or impaired children. Both the theory that supports practice and the methodology that channels it are pillars that lead the way towards understanding and implementing procedures and techniques, which will allow this type of learner to succeed.

Listening plays a significant role in achieving this goal. The skill is the threshold to language imitation, correction and proficient use. Given the fact that the blind do enhance their other senses, listening then becomes a useful tool to teach the listening skill in the foreign language.

Bibliography
1. Anderson. A & T. Lynch. *Listening.* Oxford: Oxford University Press. 1988.
2. Antich, R. Metodología de la Enseñanza de Lenguas Extranjeras, Editorial Pueblo y Educación, La Habana. 1986.
3. Barraga, Natalie. Disminuidos visuales y aprendizaje.- España: Editorial ONCE, 1985.
4. Causarás, Daymara and Miguel Olivé. Audiotexts and Exercises for Listening Comprehension in English in 8th-grade Students at René Ibarra Font Junior High School in Holguin. 2017.
5. Chamot, A.U. The Cognitive Academic Language Learning Approach (CALLA): An update. In P.A. Richard-Amato & M.A. Snow (Eds.), *Academic success for English language learners: Strategies for K-12 mainstream teachers* (pp. 87-101). White Plains, NY: Longman. 2005.
6. Chamot, A. U. *Electronic Journal of Foreign Language Teaching,* Vol. 1, No. 1. pp.14- 26. 2004
7. Chamot, A.U., & El-Dinary, P.B. Children's learning strategies in immersion classrooms. *The Modern Language Journal, 83*(3), 319-341. 1999.
8. Chamot, A. U. Learning strategies and listening comprehension. In. D. Mendelsohn and J. Rubin (eds.).*A Guide for the Teaching of Second Language Listening.* CA: Dominie Press. 1995.
9. Chamot, A.U., Barnhardt, S., El-Dinary, P.B., & Robbins, J. *The learning strategies handbook.* White Plains, NY: Addison Wesley Longman. 1999.
10. Cohen, A.D. *Strategies in learning and using a second language.* London: Longman. 1998.
11. Enríquez O´Farril, Isora y A. Pulido Díaz: Un acercamiento a la enseñanza del inglés en la Educación Primaria, Ed. Pueblo y Educación, La Habana, 2006.
12. Graham, S., & Harris, K.R. Students with learning disabilities and the process of writing: A meta-analysis of SRSD studies, In L. Swanson, K.R. Harris, & S. Graham (Eds.), *Handbook of research on learning disabilities* (pp. 323-344). New York: Guildford. 2003.

13. Grenfell, M., Harris, V. *Modern languages and learning strategies: In theory and practice.* London: Routledge. 1999.

14. Harris, V. Adapting classroom-based strategy instruction to a distance learning context. *TESL-EJ, 7*(2). Retrieved from http://www-writing.berkeley.edu/TESL-EJ/ej26'al.html. 2003.

15. Lynch, T. Theoretical perspective on listening. Annual review of applied linguistics, 18, 3-19. 1998.

16. Mendelsohn, D. Teaching listening. *Annual Review of Applied Linguistics, 18,* 81-101. 1998.

17. O'malley, J. M., & Chamot, A. U. Learning strategies in second language acquisition. Cambridge, UK: Cambridge University Press. 1990.

18. O'malley, J. M., Chamot, A. U., & Kupper, L. Listening comprehension strategies in second language acquisition. *Applied Linguistics, 10*(4), 418-437. 1989.

19. Oxford, R. L., & Burry-Stock, J. A. Assessing the use of language learning strategies worldwide with the ESL/EFL version of the Strategy Inventory for Language Learning System, *23*(2), 153-175. 1999.

20. Oxford, R. L., & Burry-Stock, J. A. Assessing the use of language learning strategies worldwide with the ESL/EFL version of the Strategy Inventory for Language Learning System, *23*(2), 153-175. 1995.

21. Oxford, R. L. Language learning strategies: What every teacher should know. Boston MA: Heinle & Heinle. 1990.

22. Park, G. P. Comparison of L2 listening and reading comprehension by university students learning English in Korea, *Foreign Language Annals,* vol. 37, no. 3. 2004.

23. Pérez, G. & Nocedo I. Metodología de la Investigación Educacional. Editorial Pueblo Educación. La Habana. 2001.

24. Rahimi, A. H. On the role of strategy use and strategy instruction in listening comprehension. *Journal of Language Teaching and Research*, Vol. 3, No. 3, p. 550-559, May 2012.

25. Rost, M. L2 listening. In E. Hinkel, *Handbook of research on second language learning and teaching.* (pp. 503-527). Mahwah, NJ: Erlbaum. 2005.

26. Rost, M. *Introducing Listening.* London: Penguin books. 1994.

27. Rubin, J. A review of second language listening comprehension research. *Modern Latzgziage Journal,* 781 2: 199-221. 1994.

28. Rubin, J. Study of cognitive processes in second language learning. *Applied Linguistics, 11,* 117-131. 1981.

29. Rubin, J. What the "good language learner" can teach us. *TESOL Quarterly, 9,* 41-51. 1975.

30. Stern, H.H. What can we learn from the good language learner? *Canadian Modern Language Review, 31, 304-318.* 1975.

31. Terroux, G. and Howard Woods. Teaching English in a World at Peace. Professional Handbook. Montreal: McGill University. 1996.

32. Vandergrift, L. Facilitating second language listening comprehension: acquiring successful strategies. *ELT Jorrnal* 5313: 168176. 1999.

Skill Development in Foreign Language Teaching. Theory and Proposal

MSc Miguel Ángel Olivé Iglesias. Associate Professor
PhD Julio César Rodríguez Peña. Associate Professor
MSc Katiusca Ceballos Bauta. Associate Professor

Skill formation and development in FLT, the theory underlying both processes and their didactic crystallization, has always been a must on the map of foreign language teaching. Central to a discussion on the matter is the notion that skills are defined as the *know-how*, or are called the *learn-to-do*, according to UNESCO standards. This is translated as putting to use the knowledge acquired.

In an educational context, skill development means that the student acquires knowledge and applies it in a specific field. Álvarez de Zayas (1996) states that skills, as a part of the contents, allow to characterize didactically speaking the operations performed by the students, as they interact with their object of study, transforming it, passing on to it their human influence.

The mastering of a foreign language involves, for example, knowing the rules for verb conjugation. But, the learner must also practice it to internalize habit and skill so that language command reaches the levels desired or expected. Therefore, foreign language teaching gives special prominence to skill development through the integrated practice of the language in communicative situations. The previous statement is fundamental for an understanding on how the process operates. As a constituent of contents, skills stand as man's practical performance within a certain field of knowledge amassed in the vast cultural mosaic of humankind. A preliminary approach from a psychological standpoint reveals that skills are the actions and operations mastered by an individual – the learner – with a definite objective in mind.

It must be pointed out that skill formation and development is by no means the exclusive possession or prerogative of foreign language teaching. Any learning activity presupposes the acquisition of knowledge and the development of general and particular skills, depending on the reality and perspective of the process.

Recent studies on skill formation and development carried out in the specific field of the Teacher Education English Major, rendered elements that explain why this work came to life. While it is a fact that the official documents perused show clearly the multifarious aspects related to teaching and learning, and the teaching staff is one of seniority and dedication, there is still much to be explored in the areas of theory and contextualized practice to enhance the process. This paper is an endeavor towards that end.

Stepping into the concept of skill implies first and foremost an analysis from a compilation of definitions. Obviously, this work cannot list all of them. It will propose a selection and disclose coincidental points.

Petrovsky (1978) states that skills are the mastery of a system of psychical and practical activities, which are necessary for the conscious regulation of activity, knowledge and habits. Danilov & Skatkin (1978) clarify that skills are an extremely encompassing and complex pedagogical concept, and view them as the capacity acquired by man to creatively use his knowledge and habits in theoretical and practical activity. They were able to summarize the definition in saying that skills are *knowledge in action*.

González (1995) defines these as the mastery of psychical and practical operations that allow rational control of activity. She adds that they are the result of systematization of actions under such conditions that their constant development is guaranteed. They are actions which are embedded in learning and assure efficient human performance.

Álvarez de Zayas (1996) says that skills are the mastery of the content that reveals human behavior in a specific context. For him, they are actions and operations mastered by the individual, with a goal in sight. Oramas (?) posits that skills are developed within the activity, and therein are included cognitive activity, practical activity and valuation activity. Ortiz & Mariño (2009) present them as a dimension of contents showing man's behavior in a specific field of knowledge.

A critical reading of these definitions leads to mark words that are essential to the analysis: action, practice, activity, use of knowledge and habits, behavior, acquired capacity. In other words, the study of the very concept brings to light that the process occurs as follows: from practice to the psychical plane and back again. Furthermore, skill development is a full combinatory exchange between the outside and the inside, a dialectical harmony between psyche and reality. It should be noted that Danilov and Skatkin refer to "capacity". Delving into this is not the scope of the paper, but it must be clarified that today specialists place capacities beyond the restricted meaning of skill, and logically envelop it.

A constant in the definitions is the fact that many authors include skills within the contents, discerning what is to be taught and what is to be learned. For González, Recarey & Addine (2004) contents are the product of mankind's contribution during its historic development.

They include:

> ➢ Systems of knowledge.
> ➢ Systems of skills and habits.
> ➢ Systems of relations with the world (values, feelings, attitudes).
> ➢ Systems of experiences (affective and motivational) in activity.

There are no skills and no habits without previous knowledge: the latter is the foundation upon which the former form and develop. Knowledge comes first then you teach how to operate with it in a given reality and a given practice. Knowledge and skills are coherently connected. These are modeled and developed. Rephrasing it, knowledge is a key premise for the development of the skills.

Skills are a form of assimilation of activity. Alongside with habits, they enable people to carry out a given task. So, when they carry out an activity they acquire a system of procedures and methods that are useful for the performance of a variety of tasks. They also begin to master actions piecemeal, as they exact their performances. Only with a feedback on what has already been learned – knowledge and habits – will they be able to perform better.

Skill manifests itself in the most perfect and elemental way of acting. At a higher level it is considered as the mastering of the whole process, and presupposes the acquisition of knowledge and the formation of habits as essential components. An effective skill formation includes systematization through repetition of actions and steady reinforcement, together with continual improvement.

Skills are therefore a systematization of actions and these are subordinate processes of a conscious objective, as was previously stated. It can be said that in the case of the skills, automatization is not reached: this is a characteristic of habits. The fulfillment of skill-related actions demands conscious regulation by the individual. Skill development implies the possibility to choose and put in practice the different methods and the knowledge acquired in correspondence to the final goal and the conditions of the task.

A further analysis of skills in the teaching and learning of a foreign language should refer to Leontiev *(Taken from Antich et al)*. He states that the learning process is a complex activity with two aspects, a methodological and a theoretical one:

1. The acquisition of knowledge (the premise of the existence of previous knowledge to move to the next level).
2. The formation of habits and skills (formed and developed on the basis of the previous knowledge).

To understand how teaching and learning work and which their cycles are for presentation and exploitation in a lesson, we must firstly depart from the theory of verbal activity. It is based on the general theory of activity defined by Vygotsky and his followers (Leontiev, Luria, Galperin). Verbal activity has four aspects: listening, speaking, reading and writing. From these elements the system of teaching is organized, that is, we speak about a reading comprehension, a speaking, a writing and a listening comprehension lesson, depending on the leading skill involved.

It should be pointed out that even when there is a leading skill in a lesson, they act in combination through the process: it is impossible to develop a pure skill when in real life they overlap in communication. It is clear that there is no such thing as a pure one-skill lesson. The students will do tasks of all types and will navigate back and forth the skills of the language during the hours allotted. However, there is always a beacon skill that predominates because that is what you seek as a teacher and that is what the syllabus suggests as contents to be taught. That skill is the header in each lesson.

This idea cannot be forgotten in the teacher's formulation of the objective of the lesson. Teachers must have in mind what they will achieve in the students at the end of the lesson, the system of lessons, the unit, and the course. The four skills will be maximized and minimized at intervals, but one will be the ruler.

In the last decades listening comprehension has been focused as complex operations that integrate different components of perception and linguistic knowledge in a process science has not deepened into yet. Medina (2004) states that the close relationship between listening comprehension and oral expression has put authors and researchers to work together. He also says that the insufficient approach to the former has affected the development of the latter.

Authors who have studied the skill are: Antich (1975); Winitz (1978, 1986); Ahser (1984); Krashen et_al (1984); Wipf (1984); Faedo (1988); Abbott (1989), Brown (1989); Byrne (1989), Finnocchiaro (1989); Terroux (1991); Nunan (1991); Brown (1994); Acosta (1996); Ur (1997); Ellis (1998); Medina (2004, 2006, 2012, 2014).

Oral expression has been widely studied in the last decades. The development of the skill has gained solid ground within foreign language teaching. Its formation and development implies two aspects: a receptive one (listening) and a productive one (oral expression). Therefore, it is a two-way process that includes the speaker (who codifies the message) and the listener (who decodes the message).

Authors doing research on the skill are: Antich (1975, 1986), Richards (1983), Coll (1985), Richard-Amato (1988), Abbott *et al* (1989), Brown (1989), Byrne (1989), Finnocchiaro (1989), Terroux (1991), Nunan (1991), Brown (1994), Acosta (1996), Ur (1997), Ellis (1998), Jenkins (2001), Ramírez (2009), Gerard (2010), Ronda (2013), Medina ((2004, 2006, 2012, 2014).

Linguistic as well as pedagogical materials have given room to the development of reading comprehension in the mother tongue and foreign language teaching. Medina (2004) quotes several authors that have worked with reading comprehension. Among these: Álvarez (1996); Almaguer (1998); Medina (1998); Fernández (2001); Rivera (2001); Ayala (2000, 2005); Montejo (2003, 2004, 2005); Medina (2004, 2006, 2012, 2014); Sales (2007); Hernández (2008); González, 2009) and Acosta (2011).

Written expression, or writing, has had a lower treatment as compared to the rest of the skills. Olivé (2011) comments that of these four, writing has, for the longest time, remained in the shadows. He adds that writing has seen the other skills bask in the sun of wider acceptance and more hours of practice. Rivers (1970); Antich (1986); Abbott *et al* (1989); Acosta (1998); Medina (1998, 2004, 2006); etc., are relevant names in this skill.

All this theoretical rationale finds practical ground in the teaching and learning of foreign languages, especially English, which is taught in the Teacher Education English Major of Holguin University. The view held by the professors of the Discipline Integrated English Practice is that of forming and developing skills in communicative situations. These situations respond to communicative functions – a reflection of the multiplicity of contexts occurring in real life – carrying in themselves the discrete elements of the language (pronunciation, vocabulary, grammar), and are by extension vessels of the target culture.

It is the duty of foreign language teachers to put their students in an environment that facilitates the acquisition and development of the systems of knowledge, skills and values afore-mentioned. A language classroom is a context for exchange that will move across these systems, and will provide for progress in every sense, including that of the communicative skills that will ensure adequate communicative competence. The activities and tasks conceived by the teacher and done by the students ought to be conducive to high competence in the language and to personal growth.

As conclusions it can be said that each skill has been approached in the teaching and learning of a foreign language. It is obvious that oral expression and reading comprehension outstand, receiving special attention and emphasis within the four skills. The suggestions have a practical value for the teachers in their attempt to form and develop the communicative skills in English. How skills are organized will depend on the contention that their development operates with internal-external dynamics, that is to say, a psychical-practical sequence. The harmony reached will guarantee the level of development of the skill. The language teacher will have to consider both the formation of the habit and the development of the skill itself while introducing, for example, linguistic rules and leading the students into an intensive practice. Working with the different skills means developing each and integrating them.

Skill development in the teaching-learning of English is not an end in itself. It must be at the service of a pedagogical, professional, formative, and interdisciplinary approach to the lesson. Furthermore, the skill is not developed *per se*, but as a means to improve communicative competence, which will allow the students themselves to teach English in the different levels of the system of education.

Following are presented the tasks that were modeled for the discipline, mainly for fourth year, even though they can be adapted to specific needs and objectives in the different years. These tasks observe the precepts mentioned in the previous paragraph, without disregarding the development of the skills. The students will have to use all four skills to accomplish them.

I. Prepare a lesson where you present a text for ninth-grade students so that:
   a) From a lexical analysis you make them understand the words *successful, discomfort, personality, talented*. Show how you convey their meanings.
   b) From a social perspective they are motivated to be good professionals.
   c) From a psychological viewpoint you elucidate for them the bases of talent as a human capacity.
   d) From an axiological stand you are able to touch their hearts.
   e) From a methodological viewpoint they understand the whole text, and you interiorize the principles of the teaching of reading.
   Be ready to present your lesson in class.

II. Simulated Situation: You are a teacher already. Suppose you have a pupil who is very shy in class and sits apart from the rest of the class. They are neither for nor against him. How would you help the boy and the rest of the class come together? How would you treat the boy? Make a list of actions you would follow. Give advice. Consult your Pedagogy and Psychology professors. What pedagogical, psychological and axiological elements helped you in the educative strategy you followed to help your pupil?

III. Consult with *the Grupo de Salud Escolar* (School Health Team) professors about brochures and articles you can read so you write a letter to prospective students you will have next academic year, who you know are beginning to have sexual relations. You will talk to them about the responsibility that comes with age and sexual relations, and the imperative need to use condoms and IUDs. You will explain to them in detail why it must be so, by reading for them and distributing material about using contraceptive devices and the condom.

IV. Simulated Situation: You have eleventh-grade students with many different opinions about having sexual relations. One boy says that to have sex with many girls is good because he learns more. A girl says to use condoms will hurt her and she won't feel the same. What can you do to help them both and the group in general? Prepare a list of solid reasons to prove the boy he is wrong and the dangers he exposes himself to, and to show the girl the advantages of the condom. Would you discuss your students' doubts with their families? When? Explain. Remember you are a teacher and an educator. Use scientific information.

V. Carry out a survey in your community clinics. First consult the book at CDIP *Metodología de la Investigación Educativa* (Methodology for Research on Education) to find out about requirements to survey someone. Then find out the work done in terms of sexual education. Compare it to what is done in your university. Prepare a report to be handed in on your findings where you present how teachers in the schools can help in the sexual education of the young generations.

Skill-integrating tasks derived from the situations above:
1 - Read the situations analytically and detect all the conflicts, dilemmas and problems encountered by the characters. List them.

2 - Prepare a five-item "strategy" that leads to the accomplishment of the following:
➢ Showing a degree of solidarity and support with the affected character.
➢ Approaching critically the behavior of all the characters.
➢ Proposing concrete ways (steps) to influence on the characters' verbalizations, attitudes and behaviors.
➢ Finding possible solutions to all the problems posed in each situation.
➢ Designing a plan to help and guide the affected students and support the families.

3 - Write out a report on the work done to be presented orally in plenary session.

4 - Write notes, letters or customized points to be told personally to the families that include:
- ✓ How he or she feels about the problem as a teacher, a member of an educational institution, and as a human being.
- ✓ How the family should face the problem and help the young boys and girls.
- ✓ An outline of the difficulties ahead and how they can be overcome.
- ✓ An offering of unconditional counseling and help.

5 - Prepare expositions with the elements below:
- ❖ Contrasting the bad models given in the situations with good ones, bringing the latter ones to the foreground, taking them from personal experiences, anecdotes.
- ❖ Emphasizing the good points of the characters and how these can be channeled positively for common welfare.
- ❖ Presenting other situations beyond the contents of the ones they have faced in the simulations, which are new points of departure for analysis and solution.

Research done on the matter of skill formation and development rendered insufficiencies that affected the fulfillment of specific objectives in the Teacher Education English Major of Holguin University within the Discipline Integrated English Practice. The present paper aimed at contributing a properly contextualized proposal.

An approximation to the problem started with the contextualization of the analyses made. Empirical and epistemic inquiry into the category led to systematization, assumption and modeling of a theoretical and methodological proposal to channel the results didactically and offer a set of integrated tasks according to the needs and realities of the Teacher Education English Major of Holguin University.

Bibliography
Addine Fernández, Fátima; Ana María González Soca; Silvia C. Recarey Fernández (2202) *Principios para la dirección del proceso pedagógico*. In Compendio de Pedagogía. Editorial Pueblo y Educación.
Álvarez De Zayas, Carlos (1996) *La escuela en la vida*. Editorial Pueblo y Educación.
Antich De León, Rosa; Dariela Gandarias Cruz; Emma López Segrera (1986) *Metodología de la enseñanza de lenguas extranjeras*. Editorial Pueblo y Educación.
González Soca, Ana María; Silvia Recarey Fernández; Fátima Addine Fernández (2004) *La dinámica del proceso de enseñanza aprendizaje mediante sus componentes*. In Didáctica. Teoría y práctica. Editorial Pueblo y Educación.
Ceballos Bauta, Katiusca; Miguel Ángel Olivé Iglesias (2013) *Aproximación al desarrollo de las habilidades comunicativas en inglés en los estudiantes de la carrera de lenguas extranjeras inglés*. Monografía.

Medina Betancourt, Alberto (2004) *Modelo de competencia metodológica del profesor de inglés para el perfeccionamiento de la dirección del proceso de enseñanza-aprendizaje del nivel medio.* Tesis de Doctorado. UCPH.

Olivé Iglesias, Miguel Ángel (2011) *Writing: The Cinderella? Experiences with Fourth-year Students of the Teacher Education English Major of Holguin University.* Scientific Paper. Holguin.

Olivé Iglesias, Miguel Ángel (2013) *Programa Analítico de la Asignatura Práctica Integral de la Lengua Inglesa para 4to año, CRD.* Syllabus. Teacher Education English Major of Holguin University. Scientific Paper. Holguin.

A Neglected Skill in FLT: Writing

MSc Miguel Ángel Olivé Iglesias. Associate Professor
MSc Katiusca Ceballos Bauta. Associate Professor
MSc Guillermo Ronda Velázquez. Associate Professor

The organization of a foreign language lesson is generally based on the formation and development of four language skills: listening, speaking, reading and writing. Such distribution responds to psychological, didactic and linguistic premises that have guaranteed teaching. All four skills are tributary to an ultimate goal, which is to provide teachers-to-be with the tools for an adequate crystallization of the teaching-learning process of the foreign language.

Of these four, writing has, for the longest time, remained in the shadows. It has seen the others bask in the sun of wider acceptance and more hours of practice. Much has been written about listening, speaking and reading; less about writing. The skill has been neglected not only by teachers. Students are, in vast majorities, allergic to it. Experience – unhappy one – has it. Abbott *et al* (1989) say that writing should be fully integrated, and never neglected.

This paper intends to reveal some experiential views about writing in class. After an exploration on the issue, it lists suggestions that proved effective with senior students, and offers examples of what was done to amend the conspicuously poor status of the skill.

Historically, emphasis has been put on the first three skills. Writing has been the Cinderella in the family. There is a variety of reasons:
The teaching cycle moves from listening to speaking to reading to writing. If any setbacks come along and cuts must be made in the process, writing is the one "sent to the kitchen to do the dishes" because it *takes time, so let's leave it for homework, let's leave it for tomorrow, let's make it simpler, let's skip it, let's forget about it.* The saddest part is that the students do notice that the teachers underrate it. Abbott *et al* (1989) warn that often written exercises are left just for the end of the lesson, done in a hurry and hardly ever finished in class.

The opposite also occurs. Writing is crippled when time is short. Nevertheless, when a sizable quantity of minutes is left to finish the lesson (which many times amount to half an hour!), the teacher improvises by driving the students into a writing session that will make do for the lapse –to the teacher's self-indulgence and the boys and girls' fracture of whatever affection they had for the Cinderella. Again, Abbott *et al* (1989) are explicit in saying that written work is squeezed into the lesson.

Students generally engage in listening, speaking and reading activities with a degree of motivation that plummets drastically when the teacher announces, *"Now we are going to write."* The act of exerting physical effort on creating sentences, paragraphs and compositions in a foreign language is contrary to the students' natural bias: they evade having to write; even in their mother tongue. The writing tasks in class fall short of variety, concrete aims and realization of the importance of the skill to support and cement the others, and to help marshal mentally ideas that will come out "in a better shape" orally.

Writing is compressed sometimes in the routine teacher assigns topics or titles-students protest-teacher imposes-students take refuge in the solitary crusade versus a blank paper sheet. The obvious fact? They will toy with the pencil – and the teacher – until the period is over, like Penelope doing and undoing her weaving.

The truth is that few students enjoy writing and find it complementing and profitable. When left for homework, the written pieces rendered are mostly mere copy-and-paste replicas (from an original produced by the good student) with desperate variations. Again, the sad part, teachers grading in a rush too, fail to notice the *"plagiarisms."*

The advanced level students are not alien to this odyssey. Doomed to confront the Cinderella with crescendo complexity in terms of word count and themes, they sweat through the minutes, and in the end hand in bleeding samples of their literary output with unsatisfied – yet relieved, because they´re leaving! – looks.

What to do to overturn this reality? How to insert the Cinderella in the family, so that students welcome and embrace her as a part of their linguistic enrichment? Why this phobia that infests both teachers and students? Why must Cinderella stay and scrub the floor when she has beauty to display before her sister skills?

Evidently, writing in a teacher-training context cannot be deemed as an elite preparation towards professional writing. It is a substantial constituent of a larger mosaic where the other abilities and educational targets are clearly inlaid. Therefore, writing for a teacher-to-be is a complementary weapon for the mastery of a foreign language. It is a path leading to the exacting of the oral skills, a door to unleash one´s imagination and creativity, and to expand horizons.

Attempts have been and are being made, serious ones. Devising cross-curricular proposals, enhancing existing syllabi with fresh exercises, giving up the closed pattern of testing direct compulsory writing topics and letting the students – for the sake of result and simplicity (and yielding to the students´ complains that the topics are too difficult) – choose themselves almost always what they want to write about.

Now, what tips can be offered? Let´s reflect on the following:
- ✓ Writing **is not** the Cinderella; or at least if it is, we must release her from her stepmothers´ oppression and fast-forward the movie to her marrying the prince. Changing the mental frame is the move.
- ✓ Make sure beforehand that your lesson plan includes a properly balanced weight of oral and writing tasks. Do observe the precept of the primacy of the oral over the written. Kinegal (2006:13) introduces a key principle: *"Achievement in one skill area enriches and reinforces progress in all others..."*
- ✓ Give writing a well-grounded purpose, a solid foundation.
- ✓ Guarantee that the skill is not conveniently filling a gap in the system, or avoid that it was planned but then discarded because time was over. Both are destructive maneuvers.
- ✓ Both free and directly assigned topics and titles ought to be present in the session diet, planting gradually the spark of challenge before circuitous topics.
- ✓ Vary the proposals. Do not dwell on one type of task.
- ✓ Writing is not only for producing monologues. If a student writes a dialogue, with characters interacting, that is also practice. Teachers forget that.
- ✓ Provide your students with catchy springboards to write from. For example, story texts they can modify not just the end of, but also the beginning. This variant is not sufficiently exploited.
- ✓ Plant in your students a sense of success and improvement, as little as it may be.
- ✓ Show your own motivation: write out your own versions and share them. Let the students know that you practice writing too. It encourages them.
- ✓ Writing does not mean being alone, at least not all the time. It can be approached in two's or more, even in teams, or in a constant exchange with the teacher. Looking at a white leaf with a forced upon title on it is devastating if the student is told to write, write, write and that´s it. Abbott *et al* (1989) warn that the teacher cannot just write.
- ✓ Select impact texts every time you can. Those which will touch the students´ feelings and emotions. A quality motivational start for writing could trigger the minds of the slowest, the shiest, the laziest and the most recalcitrant ones. Kinegal (2006) states the need for emotionally engaged students. Motivation is a fire starter. Do not underestimate it.

- ✓ Disclose for your students the potential of using dictionaries such as Webster´s and Roget´s. Marshall (2006) mentions the must of including in class resources such as dictionaries. Language power comes from reading, consulting, absorbing the cultural wealth that underlies in those sources and writing therefrom.
- ✓ Balance the assignment of long and short writing in class. Gauge your students´ motivation, language proficiency, atmosphere, to decide whether you should put them to write long materials or not. Many teachers leave long ones for homework, short ones being dealt with in class; but they can start with the introduction of a story and carry on at home. Do bear in mind, though, that, as Abbott *et al* suggest, time spent on written work in class is not wasted. Just diagnose, and balance, wisely.

Examples of tasks that can be proposed to the students are summarized here. These proved effective with senior students currently involved in the process. Much is still to be done and attempted, as language errors are plenty and motivation can be improved.

TASKS:

FROM A LISTENING PASSAGE: THE STORY OF TELLY
Prepare in writing the following notes:
1. For Telly. Give her comfort, consolation in her problem and a way out to solve it.
2. For Telly's parents. Criticize them constructively and give them hints on how to help Telly to overcome her fears.
3. For the storyteller. For her exquisite performance.
4. For someone you know who has phobias. Give advice and support.
5. For yourself. In a moment you know you had of fear.
6. Prepare a dialogue between you and Telly where you talk with her about her fears.
7. Prepare a dialogue between you and Telly's parents where you explore her state of mind and you offer solutions.
8. Write a report that begins with: "*I have a student who…*" where you present difficulties you had with a pupil and how you helped him or her overcome fears.
9. Write a beginning for the story. Insert new characters and variations.
10. Write a new ending for Telly's story starting when the door opens and the voice steps in. Be ready to story-tell it.

FROM A READING PASSAGE: DEAR ABBY
1. Prepare a written comment of the social, educational, ideological and axiological perspectives of the passage.

2. Write a hundred-word paragraph on the impact the story had on you.
3. Prepare a dialogue where you interview Abby on the courageous task she has and your viewpoints on the different issues she explores and mentions.
4. Write a letter to Abby acting as if you were a reader in trouble. Present your problem. Ask for advice.
5. You are a journalist. Prepare a written report where you present your criteria and support to Abby´s column in the paper.
6. The stories depicted in Dear Abby are diverse and many times very strong and shocking. Some are: stepfather in love with stepdaughter, terminal illnesses, unfaithfulness, and homosexuality. Choose one of these and write a short heartfelt article on the matter. Be respectful, tactful, ethical and constructive.

FROM A LISTENING PASSAGE: HARVARD UNIVERSITY
1. Elaborate in trios a dialogue among Cuban students who are willing to know about Harvard. One of them is familiar with the University.
2. Write a letter to the imaginary Dean of the Faculty of Languages at Harvard University. Introduce yourself and your University. Talk about it. Show pride.
3. Enquire about the history and organization of our University. Prepare a written report.
4. Interview Professor Rafael Rodríguez. Find out about his experiences in other universities abroad (Venezuela, England). Outline an interview guide.

FROM A READING PASSAGE: CHARLES DARWIN
1. Prepare a dialogue with a classmate. You are a scientist advocating Darwin's premises. Your classmate is a student of yours willing to know more about Darwin and evolution (seven lines each character).
2. Simulated Situation: You are a teacher. One of your students in class gets angry and offended at Darwin's theories because he is a devoted Christian. Prepare a short dialogue where you recreate such situation. Be highly respectful.
3. From the previous situation. Write a note to the student's parents (they are Christians too) on the issue and provide ideas on how to cope with the issue and come up with educational solutions. Propose to meet them.
4. Imagine you can time travel back to Darwin's times. Create a conversation between you two on his findings, your position and the impact they had on you. Be respectful in case you do not agree with him.
5. Prepare a written report on the essences of life, education and need for understanding and tolerance and caring among people, no matter what their vision of the world is, or their sex, preferences, skin color, origin, etc.

FROM A LISTENING PASSAGE: THE LAW OF LIFE

1. Simulated Situation: A pupil of yours is having trouble concentrating and she is getting C's in her exams. You have tried to contact her parents but they never show up. It seems there is neglect on their part. She is an adolescent. Write a carefully composed letter to her parents summarizing the girl's situation and the need to have a family-school meeting to help the girl.

2. From the previous situation. Prepare a private dialogue with the girl. Introduce your worries and suggestions you have to help her out. Offer unconditional support.

3. Does the Cuban society disregard its citizens? Do a little research, and present your informed arguments in an essay.

FROM A READING PASSAGE: THOU SHALT HONOR THY FATHER

Write notes to:

1. The writer of the story. Compliment him on the positive change and make personal comments and suggestions.

2. The father in the story. Compliment him on the boy he has and the importance of a healthy relationship parent-child.

3. A student of yours who has publicly been haughty and recalcitrant with his mother (he is 16, she is 40).

4. Write in two's a conversation between the father and the son after they made up and are at home together celebrating recovery, life and their love.

5. Prepare an essay to be told orally on: The role of parents in upbringing their children. Write about challenges, rewards, joys, pains.

FROM A READING PASSAGE: ARROWSMITH

Simulated Situation: You have a friend who does not like studying. In tests he is always asking you to provide all the answers. You owe him favors, but cheating is wrong. You want him to stop and study.

1. Prepare a dialogue in couples where the previous problem is illustrated.

2. Prior to approaching your friend, you seek counseling in a teacher friend. Elaborate a conversation between you and the teacher where she advises you on how to deal with the situation.

Write a letter to:

3. Fatty. Admonish him. Advise him.

4. An American student. Reveal for him the asset that is the Cuban system of education.

5. Prepare a dialogue with personal and educational glimpses between you and the American student in task 4 who comes to visit you.

FROM A LISTENING PASSAGE: JOURNALISM
1. Create a dialogue (interview-like) with both sides (journalist-interviewer) out of the information you have gathered so far.
2. Write four paragraphs (Introduction, Development, Conclusions) where you lay down your opinions about teaching. Bring to the surface its good side and the many challenges.
3. Prepare cards to offer homage to professors you admire. Be sure to condense what you feel about them. The cards will be read in public.
4. Prepare cards for your parents as well with similar characteristics.

Observant of the very tips offered, the author moved along these tasks in the lessons. The students showed degrees of interest and applied to the different proposals with an acceptable intention. Their skills with dictionary consultation were poor as well.

The experiential notes poured on this paper are a clue to the urgent necessity of exploring ways to motivate students – who seem to have lost the road to it – back to the essences of language learning and practicing. Given the circumstances, it is not an easy undertaking.

Writing particularly deserves more credit. It is the teacher´s role to give a happy ending to the Cinderella story, unveiling new strategies to "lure" the students into the act of writing.

The activities devised and implemented did make a difference in the senior students class. Motivation and involvement were the push. However, the path to improvement in terms of language and higher levels of motivation itself is bumpy. Cinderella will have to get up, get rid of the apron and get a pair of new shoes to meet her prince.

Bibliography
Abbott, Gerry et al (1989) *The Teaching of English as an International Language*. A Practical guide. Edición Revolucionaria. La Habana.
Brown, H. Douglas (2001) *Teaching by Principles*. University of San Francisco. U.S.A.
Finocchiaro, Mary and Christopher Brumfit (1989) *The Functional-Notional Approach. From Theory to Practice*. Edición Revolucionaria.
Kinegal, Jane (2006) *Creating a Language Learning Classroom: From Theory to Practice*. British Columbia Teachers´ Federation. Canada.
Marshall, Sondra (2006) *Communicative Approaches to Evaluation in Foreign Languages*. Teaching.British Columbia Teachers´ Federation. Canada.
Terroux, Georges. *Teaching English in a World at Peace* (1989) McGill University. Canada.

Improving the Teaching of Foreign Languages.
Thoughts and Pointers

MSc Miguel Ángel Olivé Iglesias. Associate Professor
PhD Julio César Rodríguez Peña. Associate Professor
Spec. Marlene Mora Delgado. Associate Professor

Today's conceptions on the teaching of English at any educational level nationwide are a repository of historic approaches, methods, tendencies, which have prevailed, overlapped or smelted in an unending effort to extract the best from each and mould them into a solid produce.

University curricula apply a didactics for higher studies that harmonizes traditional and contemporary views on teaching, whose corpus is an optimized version of both to improve learning. The teaching of English as a major enters too the realm of integration of methods, styles, notions. Specialists in the field, like Abbott *et al* (1989), warn that there are no royal roads to language, and Eble (1988) states that he cannot conceive of any one way of teaching that excels all others. Only an efficient, adequately sifted combination of these would bring about quality lessons and quality learning.

It goes without saying that the role – and responsibility – of teachers is fundamental, no matter what their actual prominence in a classroom may be. Whichever stance is followed, they are there, and they chart the course even when the activity is predominantly student-centered. According to Eble (1988), the teacher's performance remains essential to most teaching and learning. He emphasizes that the most important things in a classroom are the teacher and the students.

The remembrances of many students of English cherish the image of grand professors with grand styles. Back then the premises of teaching accentuated the teacher's role, and language teaching was mechanical and repetitive. But they remember, though, active professors proposing mechanical drills for the discrete elements of the language, dialogues learned by heart, lab headphones that chimed prompting them to respond, etc.

Those professors prepared lessons marked by the paradigms of the moment. The "public" secret of accomplishment was in their attitudes and styles, so when they entered the classroom they regaled their students with their gifted teaching. Those teachers' lesson plans are in many aspects different from today's lessons, but students did learn their bit of English in that context, and were proud of the way they did it and of the teachers they had.

That is the core of this paper: like teacher, like lesson. A good teacher will teach a good lesson; a good lesson will bring about good learning. The aim is then to ponder on the fact that appropriate learning comes from an appropriately-planned lesson, and such lesson comes from a devoted, flexible, fun, informed professor. That notion is discussed here and enriched by tips to be followed in planning and teaching a foreign language lesson.

Times gone by have bequeathed to the new generations a hall of fame of outstanding teachers, each with his or her style. Take one lesson plan, hand it over to three teachers and visit, unseen, their class. None will teach the same, none will get equal responses, none will focus on it similarly. It means that they stamp a unique imprint on the act of concretizing what is written on paper in a live instant of interaction with the recipients of the thought-out model in hand. They have their *style*, which according to Eble (1988) is the characteristic way a teacher goes about his or her work.

In the closing sentence of the introduction were outlined four qualities that define a good teacher. They are not the only ones, yet a review of these would be healthy:

1. Devoted. Teachers must commit brawns and brains to the task of planning a lesson. The deterrents to a complete dedication to that moment are multifarious. Eble (1988) alerts that teaching at the top of one's abilities is exhausting. However, only devotion will bear fruit. He who applies himself to a task will concentrate, will shut out interferences and will make time and room to write; let alone that he will find it rewarding from a personal and professional perspective. Devotion is, in the words of Leblanc, about caring for your craft.

2. Flexible. Teachers must be open to change and options. Their flexibility will enable them to accept differences, to choose wisely from alternatives, to restudy critically sources of knowledge, to discern the possibilities and limits of the existing reality. Flexibility is by no means unleashing. It is being aware of the tension of the leash, knowing when to tighten it, knowing when to loosen it up. Or, as Leblanc puts it, it is *not* having a fixed agenda and being rigid but being flexible to react and adjust.

3. Fun. For Leblanc good teaching is about humor. A lesson running on entirely strict terms, with students regarded as robots, not just embraces authoritarian precepts of teaching, it also knocks out the motivation they ought to encounter in relaxing, smiling and enjoying inside a classroom. That they laugh in class from time to time is not a breach of discipline: administer fun in productive doses.

4. Informed. The introduction made a pass at traditional and contemporary teaching. The boundary between them seems diffuse and hazardous if improperly assessed. The bulk of data at a person's disposal is immense and timeless. So, a carefully selected theoretical, academic,

methodological posture out of conscientious, analytical reading will turn that person into an informed one, equipped to make decisions in the direction of teaching.

Now, how do teachers lay down in black, white – and hues of grey – that avalanche of rationale? What general tips could guide them into do's and don't's while planning and teaching a lesson? Mind these:

I. PLAN EVERYTHING YOU WRITE DOWN

Whatever you finally write on your lesson sheet must have been thoroughly planned. Once the ink dries you might have to live up to and account for it. Planning is what separates humans from animals:

    a) Teachers mentally conceive and organize strategies and tasks before they articulate them or zap them into a screen in this computer era.

    b) Teachers mentally ready themselves up to champion what they write. What is on paper should have a reason, a platform, and a foundation.

So, plan what you write is translated as: "Be sure you know well what's underneath the skeleton of your lesson". You already burned your ships: there is no coming back.

II. WRITE DOWN EVERYTHING YOU PLAN

No wordplay. Brainstorms in you will need to be materialized, literally. If language is the material realization of thought, your planning must be a reflection of that. The more your planning is blueprinted and enriched, the less you leave to incidentals.

Truly enough, a bustling class will always be far more teeming with an infinite range of probabilities and multiplicities of situations than a lesson constricted by space and frozen in a few hundred terms; nonetheless, the more your preparation allows you to write, the more you tread into that range and reduce it by mastering it.

III. GUARANTEE YOUR STUDENTS ARE WARMED UP

Motivation has to touch every minute of the lesson and every heart of every student. It cannot be an ingredient separately inserted into the *hors d'oeuvre*, or the main dish, or dessert. It must be added to all the courses and during table talk too. Abbott *et al* (1989) mention that a teacher must create motivation by providing interest, fun and a sense of achievement.

Attention here must be directed to the need of influencing the individual – the student – so that he or she willingly performs a task, and behind his or her acting there are factors such as interest towards the activity, fun, sense of success.

IV. DO NOT LINGER SOLELY ON TOP STUDENTS

It is well known that teachers want their lesson plan to be on the hit play lists. So, they constantly return to the active students and relegate the shy, silent, C ones. They are ignoring that their first flaw in teaching is precisely that.

Keep your "invisible" students in permanent check, move around, ask directly, encourage when students make mistakes, praise when they do fine. Do keep in mind that timid and C students need special attention, although they must increasingly be treated to the feast that is a language lesson.

If the professor always recurs to the salient students, the others will slowly recede into oblivion, false sense of safety (or the contrary: they might feel neglected), and into lack of language practice.

V. ORGANIZE AND EXPLOIT THE BLACKBOARD

These are apparently simple actions that escape main concerns in class. They imply three things:
1. The blackboard is a frequent source of reference to the students. Keep it organized, exploit it to emphasize the landmarks of your lesson, erase what was already discussed and when you are moving on; except for reinforcement points you would be willing to leave on it at all times.
2. Use it for the professional "hatching" of your students. Send them to the blackboard (on a useful assignment), let them feel they are teachers too, tell them to write on it and socialize as teachers-to-be.
3. A note of advice: After you or they write something on the blackboard, walk to the end of the classroom, reread it to spot possible mistakes. This procedure has proven to be effective to many teachers for years.

VI. MAKE THE HEADING OF THE TASKS CRYSTAL CLEAR SO THEY STRIKE HOME

A heading is a guide. Experience has shown that even after presenting the heading in detail, students ask, minutes into the task, about what they have to do and what the heading means. For this and many other reasons, make sure that:
1. The verb opens the statement (you can <u>underline</u> the verb, CAPITALIZE it, put it in *italics*, etc.).
2. The statement is brief and precise. Briefness also implies simplicity: use one verb per heading, one command.
3. Preferably, the heading stays on the blackboard for students to turn their eyes to every time they need feedback.

VII. WEAN YOUR STUDENTS PROGRESSIVELY

Get your pupils off your hair gradually. They will never be a nuisance to you, but they need and deserve to grow as independent and future teachers themselves: the lesson is the best context for them to rehearse.

You should keep your lesson on the student-centered mode. Student-centered lessons involve them more, they glue and engage them personally to the tasks. Also, student-centered lessons provide much practice on their side, much dynamics from the true protagonists of the activities: they will always be the ultimate *raison d'être* of the process.

Sit among your students, become one of them. Mingle so they feel confident; do not sit at your "throne" during a foreign language lesson. Even when you notice that your age is proportional to gravity and your teacher seat calls you, do stay on the move passing on to your students tasks, assignments, things you usually do and they can do instead.

What can students do in class?
- Write date, topics and tasks on board.
- Read out headings, items, examples, texts, etc.
- Give out cards, arguments.
- Circulate around tables helping out others.
- Prompt classmates.
- Explain doubts.
- Make corrections.
- Act as teachers during segments of the lesson.
- Present situations.
- Captain teams.
- Monitor the process.
- Volunteer information from extra sources (books, dictionaries).

VIII. APPLY ZEALOUSLY AND TIMELY APT CORRECTIVE TECHNIQUES

A self-respected teacher has to study for ever. Knowing the grammar, vocabulary, phonetics, and culture of your lesson – and a bit beyond these – is unavoidable – and unforgivable if you don't do it. Wisdom is an ever-moving target you are aiming your sights at and certainly not always hitting.

Translation: Never say never, consult books and sources, admit what you don't know and admit it when you are wrong.

Corrections of phonetic and grammar mistakes can be made public on the board – with extreme tact and treatment – and generalized from a professional angle. When you correct and how you correct will largely depend on the students' characteristics. Diplomacy and opportunity ought to be weighed by you; and your zeal to do it justly must accompany the act.

The English language is very rich and supple, open to variations, variants, and turns. Teachers have to continually cross that threshold by studying. Of course, teachers are not walking encyclopaedias, they do not know it all, but the bull's eye of knowledge and mastery must be pierced time and again with attempts at scoring points in this peculiar archery quest. Do teachers always shoot?

IX. IDENTIFY, POSITIVELY, THE OBJECTIVE OF YOUR LESSON
Are you sufficiently clear on what your students are really going to do in class? Is your lesson a reading, listening, writing or speaking one? Which ability prevails over the others?

First and foremost, it is clear that there is no such thing as a pure one-skill lesson. The students will take on tasks of all types and will navigate back and forth the skills of the language during the hours allotted. A lesson's objectives have to be clear and attractive, says Eble (1988).

However, there is always a beacon skill that predominates because that is what you seek as a teacher and that is what the syllabus dictates as contents to be taught. That skill is the header in each lesson. This notion must be kept in mind in your resolution on what to formulate as the objective of your lesson. Be careful; think hard about what you will achieve in your students at the end of the lesson, the system of lessons, the unit, and the course. The four skills will be maximized and minimized at intervals, but one will be the ruler.

The teacher's qualities and the tips proposed are not a straightjacket for the reader: they are a must for the ones in charge of implementing didactic and methodological goals in the lesson. What remains a truth is that the theoretical and experiential notes poured on this paper are a clue for teachers to see the necessity of reflecting on and exploring ways to plan and teach better lessons and motivate students.

These tips are a guide for those willing to embark on the adventure that is teaching a foreign language lesson, especially to young people. They are experienced-based suggestions that can be followed. The far-sighted teacher will tailor them according to his/her reality.

Bibliography
Abbott, Gerry et al (1989) The Teaching of English as an International Language. A Practical Guide. La Habana. Edición Revolucionaria.
Brown, H. Douglas (2001) Teaching by Principles. U.S.A. University of San Francisco.
Eble, Kenneth E. (1988) The Craft of Teaching. U.S.A. Jossey-Bass Inc. Publishers. San Francisco, California.
Finocchiaro, Mary And Christopher Brumfit (1989) The Functional-Notional Approach. From Theory to Practice. La Habana. Edición Revolucionaria.

Kinegal, Jane (2006) *Creating a Language Learning Classroom: From Theory to Practice*. Canada. British Columbia Teachers´ Federation.

Leblanc, Richard (?) *Good Teaching: The Top 10 Requirements*. (single page) Canada. York University. Ontario. (?).

Marshall, Sondra (2006) *Communicative Approaches to Evaluation in Foreign Languages Teaching*. Canada. British Columbia Teachers´ Federation.

Olivé Iglesias, Miguel Ángel (2011) *Writing: The Cinderella? Experiences with Senior Students of the Teacher Education English Major at Holguin University, Cuba* Cuba. Article. University of Pedagogical Sciences. Holguin.

Teacher and Learner: Roles Revisited

MSc Miguel Ángel Olivé Iglesias, Associate Professor
PhD Julio César Rodríguez Peña, Associate Professor
MSc Marisela Rodríguez Calzadilla, Associate Professor

Time-honored approaches of teaching have long considered strict notions on what teachers should expect – and demand – from their pupils. Hardly ever do we see it the other way around: pupils expecting – or demanding! – this or that from teachers. A review of manuals, materials, regulations, books, lesson plans, will invariably render the implicit conception that the objectives are formulated for the learner. Eyebrows will rise at any attempt to overturn that deeply-seated view.

Obviously, the customary way to formulate lesson objectives prevails here, heavily. However, let us argue against that placid accommodation: if the heart of the lesson is the student, not the teacher – why not display then demands from the latter, given that the former are central to the process? This work intends to maximize an angle of the teaching-learning process where the primary focus is on the discussion this time of what teachers must achieve to face class as professionals, and which "objectives should be set" for them to win the affection and respect of their pupils and leave a mark that is worth commending and long-lasting.

An analysis of the issue must start at what specialists say. Eble (1988:78), for example, states that: "The teacher's performance remains essential to most teaching and learning", and "...the most important things in a classroom are teachers and students". It goes without saying that the role –we add the responsibility – of teachers is vital, no matter what their actual prominence in a classroom may be. Whichever stance is followed, professors are there, they are the guidance.

If a teacher's performance is so relevant, then what he or she does leaves a mark, an imprint, so his or her conduct and preparation will be something to consider. Now, which elements ought to be a part of a teacher's repertoire during his or her preparation and at the time of imparting knowledge and crystallizing educational pursuits? Our notion of a "complete" teacher may begin with the following proposal:

A teacher must be *devoted*. Teachers must commit brawns and brains to the task of planning a lesson. The deterrents to a complete dedication to that moment are multifarious. Eble (1988:81) alerts: "Teaching at the top of one's abilities is exhausting." However, only devotion will bear fruit. Those who apply themselves to a task will concentrate, will shut out interferences and will make time and room to write; let alone that they will find it rewarding from a personal and professional perspective.

Devotion is a*bout caring for your craft*, says *Leblanc*. Caring is to be concerned, to have thought or regard for something or someone, to have an inclination or liking for that or those you are related or have a commitment to. Therefore, when teachers care, both their brains and hearts are engaged, harmoniously, in the endeavor of education. Devotion will also spark creativeness and passion for what they do, and there will be no room for weakness or frustration.

Devoted teachers will plant on their students a sense of success and improvement, as little as it may be, and most of all will show motivation in the learning of the language by, for example, writing out their own versions of the tasks proposed and sharing them with their students. They will let their students know that they practice the language too. It encourages them a lot, and hardly ever do we see teachers do that.

A teacher must be *flexible*. Teachers must be open to change and options. Their flexibility will enable them to accept differences, to choose wisely from alternatives, to re-study critically sources of knowledge and doctrines, to discern the possibilities and limits of the existing reality. Flexibility is by no means unleashing. It is being aware of the tension of the leash, knowing when to tighten it, knowing when to loosen it up. Or as Leblanc puts it, *not always having a fixed agenda and being rigid but being flexible to react and adjust*.

Flexible teachers will be aware of a reality always richer than planned notes: a bustling class will be by far more teeming with an infinite range of probabilities and multiplicities of situations than a lesson constricted by space and frozen in a few hundred terms. So, they must adapt, re-consider, teach and educate "on the go," but with their feet on the ground, as is discussed later in this paper.

A teacher must be *fun*. Notice that we write *fun*, not *funny*. Teachers are not there to make students laugh all the time so discipline is undermined, compromising learning and respect. Leblanc says that *good teaching is about humor*. A classroom is a meeting place with many different vibrant souls together, and it must be a place of solace where people meet for learning in a relaxed manner.

A lesson running on entirely strict terms, with students regarded as robots or prisoners, or empty boxes, not just embraces authoritarian precepts of teaching, it also knocks out the motivation they ought to encounter in relaxing, smiling and enjoying inside a classroom. Kinegal (2006) states the need for *emotionally engaged* students. That they laugh in class from time to time is not a breach of discipline: administer fun in productive doses. Eble (1988) says that the teacher's task must be to determine the most profitable blend of freedom and discipline in a group. It will work wonders. Teachers will have to gauge them wisely.

A teacher must be *informed*. The introduction referred to traditional and contemporary teaching. The boundary between them seems diffuse and hazardous if improperly assessed. The bulk of data at a person's disposal today is immense. Therefore, a carefully selected theoretical, academic, didactic posture out of conscientious, analytical reading will turn that person into an informed one, equipped to make decisions for the benefit of the teaching-learning process and the agents involved.

Timing, type of lesson, type of student, are all switches of the lesson mode. Well-informed teachers are those who grasp all – and lose little – getting the most out of it. They profit from the whole and decide on it sagely. No one can take apart a teacher's well-knitted mind and lesson if it meets the musts of the process and renders palpable results. Yet, who best sums up the relevance of information is Leblanc: *"Good teaching is ...about doing your best to keep on top of your field, reading sources, inside and outside of your areas of expertise, and being at the leading edge...bridging the gap between theory and practice..."*

Self-respected teachers study forever. Knowing the grammar, vocabulary, phonetics, and culture of the lesson – and beyond these – is unavoidable, and unforgivable if teachers do not observe this. Wisdom is an ever-moving target we are relentlessly aiming our sights at and certainly not always hitting. Translation: Never say never, revisit books and sources you think you know so well, admit what you do not know, and admit it when you are wrong.

Corrections of mistakes can be made public on the board and generalized from a professional angle. When teachers correct and how they do it will largely depend on the students' characteristics. Tact and opportunity ought to be weighed by teachers; and their zeal to do so must accompany the act.

The English language is very rich and supple, open to variations, variants, and turns that we must learn by studying. Of course, we teachers are not walking encyclopaedias, we do not know all, but the bull's eye must be pierced time and again with our attempts at scoring points in our archery quest.

A teacher must be a *'teacher-talker'*. Adequacy in the use of English as a foreign language by the teachers is essential, and teacher-talk has much to do with it. Using it as a basic instrument in teaching and contributing to reach higher levels in the use of communicative skills, implies the application of communicative strategies and linguistic registers that are in correspondence to the increasing needs and possibilities of the teacher and the students. The teacher of English must be a correct and precise model. He is the basis for the linguistic formation of the students in the language they study.

In this respect, teachers must keep in mind the so-called *professional-pedagogical approach.* This is a multidimensional concept and includes factors such as:

Methodological instruction.

Development of capacities, such as self-preparation, from a didactic point of view.

Pedagogical and curricular mastering of the systems of knowledge.

Development of alternative thinking.

Taking into consideration the contributions of several researchers in the field, the authors of this paper consider it pertinent to highlight the following features of the concept:

It is a general organization and management that supports the system of educational influences of the teachers who interact with students at any level of education, focusing on integrating pedagogical training.

It takes into account the correct development of the communicative and methodological formation for students to face their pre-service and in-service professional performance, with a comprehensive and contextualized character.

Didactics of Foreign Languages, in recent years, has been using profusely a term for the type of communication to be used by the teacher of foreign languages: *teacher-talk.* It should not be overlooked for its impact on teaching. While it is not a competence in itself, it is present in a foreign language teacher´s performance. It is considered the socio-linguistic variable used by the teacher to be understood in the classroom. It consists of four language areas: phonological, lexical, syntactic and discursive. A deeper analysis into this concept revealed an essential gap: the non-inclusion of *traditional body language* as an important element that adds intention and meaning to the word. Body language is an inherent cultural component of the Cuban context because of the emotional nature of this type of communication and its ethical implications, as well as other elements within the language that would meet the specific needs of prospective teachers of English.

A teacher must be *competent*. While this notion is implicit in the previous ones, further explanation is deserved here. Teachers must be an example in the integration of skills, knowledge, linguistic and extra-linguistic patterns at play during the act of communication in the foreign language, through their appropriate use as a key for teaching.

The focus must be on integrating pedagogical training, on having –as the students´ priority– to identify and solve difficult situations, on taking into account communicative training to face their actions with a comprehensive and contextualized character, that is, to direct the teaching-learning process of oral communication in foreign languages at any educational level. This is to be evidenced in the integration of the academic, professional, research and on-campus-and-community-activity components, all of which stimulate the students´ future role as teachers and communicators.

It is important for teachers to be aware, while planning lessons, that the process of communication has to be coherently conceived, not only in its affective and regulatory functions, but also in its informative (instructive) function. The way in which the selection of the non-verbal means of communication (pictures, objects, model scales, gestures, etc.) is done, allows defining verbal communication.

The use of language by teachers in class – supported by objects, pictures, model scales and other teaching media – permits to link words and concrete objects or phenomena. It strengthens representations, it stimulates the operations of analysis and synthesis at the perceptual as well as at the rational levels, and it facilitates comprehension and communication in the teaching-learning process.

As a summary, this paper intended to open a window towards the teaching-learning process where the primary focus is on the discussion of what teachers must achieve to face a class as professionals, and which "objectives should be set" for them to win the affection and respect of their pupils and leave a mark that is worth commending.

The authors hope they were able to reach that point, and certainly expect many teachers and teachers-to-be (those in the teacher education majors) to ponder these views with an open mind. Teachers must have goals for themselves much responsive to the needs and interests of those who are under their supervision, so the imprint they leave serves and honors their students and the ultimate goals of learning and education.

Bibliography

Abbott, Gerry *et al* (1989) *The Teaching of English as an International Language. A Practical Guide*. Edición Revolucionaria. La Habana.

Brown, H. Douglas (2001) *Teaching by Principles*. University of San Francisco. U.S.A.

Eble, Kenneth E. (1988) *The Craft of Teaching*. Jossey-Bass Inc. Publishers. S. Francisco, California. U.S.A.

Finocchiaro, Mary and Christopher Brumfit (1989) *The Functional-Notional Approach. From Theory to Practice*. Edición Revolucionaria. La Habana, Cuba.

Kinegal, Jane. (2006) *Creating a Language Learning Classroom: From Theory to Practice*. British Columbia Teachers´ Federation. Canada.

Leblanc, Richard (?) *Good Teaching: The Top 10 Requirements* (single page). York University. Ontario.

Marshall, Sondra (2006) *Communicative Approaches to Evaluation in Foreign Languages Teaching*. British Columbia Teachers´ Federation. Canada.

Olivé Iglesias, Miguel Ángel (2011) *Writing: The Cinderella? Experiences with Fourth-year Students from the Teacher Education English Major*. University of Pedagogical Sciences.

Olivé Iglesias, Miguel Ángel (2012) *Experience-Based Tips for Planning and Teaching a Foreign Language Lesson in the English Major of the UPS of Holguin*. University of Pedagogical Sciences. Holguin.

Rodríguez Peña, Julio César (2014) *La competencia comunicativa oral profesional pedagógica en inglés de los estudiantes de la carrera Licenciatura en Educación Especialidad Lenguas Extranjeras Inglés*. Tesis en opción al título científico de Doctor en Ciencias Pedagógicas. Holguín.

Terroux, Georges and Howard Woods (1989) *Teaching English in a World at Peace*. McGill University. Canada.

Key Leverage: Motivation in FLT

MSc Miguel Ángel Olivé Iglesias. Associate Professor
PhD Jorge Ronda Pupo. Full Professor
Prof. Eladoy Oliveros Díaz. Assistant Professor

The early reminiscences of motivation go a long way back to the very existence of humankind and the attempts to adapt to the surrounding conditions, to change the environment and to develop. Deeply rooted in the platform of human need, interest and stimulation to do things, human beings have evolved from a multiplicity of occurrences, all of which were marked by their interference with the course of nature to modify it, thus modifying themselves.

Why does history record such progress in both social and personal maps? Why were humans compelled to transform reality, and by extension renovate themselves constantly? What invisible strings pulled their brains and hands to sow, build, create, write, love and reach beyond the stars? What *furnaces of Heaven* forged them and pushed them to the adventure of Life? The answer might very well have an explication in their motivations to do so, their drives, and their unending proclivity to explore and grow anthropologically speaking.

Whereas motivation has profoundly laid down philosophical and psychological foundations – not really the scope of this paper – the impact and study of this category expands to other branches, other disciplines. That is the case of motivation within teaching and learning, and within the teaching and learning of foreign languages, what leads us to methods and methodologies on how to teach and motivate students. How a student strives with a language challenges imagination. The paper aims at brushing upon one element that may be considered central to-day in the light of classic and recent studies and reflections, and in the experience of the author. Motivation is a power source to achieve goals and move along in the current of events, either in life or in a classroom.

General Remarks

Webster's Dictionary (1992) explains that the word derives from *motive,* a category registered in both general and specialized bibliography. Webster's enters it as *"needs, emotions or desires that cause a person to act."* From the start, it is evident that a variety of factors affect motivation:

> ➢ Needs: There are material requirements that are to be met by an individual, which lead him or her to secure them.
> ➢ Emotions: The inner mechanisms of people act as catalysts in their behaviour, urging them to react and behave.
> ➢ Desires: The strong wishes that accompany individuals in their quest also push them to take action.

These explanations are further clarified by Smirnov *et al* (1961:36) when they say that motives are: *"Aquello que (...) excita a actuar y dirige esta actuación a satisfacer una necesidad determinada"*[9]. Gonzalez *et al* (2001:25), on the other hand, state that motives are: *"Objeto que responde a una u otra necesidad y que, reflejado bajo una forma u otra por el sujeto, conduce su actividad"*.

Thus, motives do pull the strings of mankind and lead it to make decisions and to perform. But motives pass through the brain's sieve before they set humans in motion for the activity by means of which necessities are satisfied. Motivation then may be defined for the purposes of this article as: *"That which arouses an interest to act, and prompts an individual to accomplish an activity or a task in hand"*.

Four comments arise from this working definition. One is the recurrence of the term *interest*, seen as the significance that an object has for a person, the degree of influence that it may have on that person. Two, such interest will make the individual act towards the execution of the activity. Three, in a more general sense, motivation may encompass a group of individuals, not just one, from a social perspective. Four, the task in hand ought to be viewed to occur in a reality the individual is in connection with, and will proceed to modify.

These theoretical notes are applicable to specific fields in which motivation is at play. Such is the case of teaching and learning, especially foreign languages. What happens in a classroom filled with young people facing a considerable bulk of information they must digest and pass tests about? How to activate the keys that may ensure motivational attitudes to learn English in students with very low levels of interest?

A direct correlation can be established between motivation and learning, between academic results and the desire, either intrinsic or extrinsic, to perform adequately. Now, what elements can be discussed here to help teachers understand the phenomenon and reassess their lessons from a more motivational view? How to help, from the lesson and the attitude in class, the real and ultimate targets of the pedagogical process?

---

[9] Quotations in Spanish cited verbatim from Spanish translations of Russian authors or from the Cuban authors. Smirnov's: "What (...) prompts to act and directs actions towards the satisfaction of a specific need." González's: "What responds to some need which, reflected by the subject, directs his/her activity."

Looking Purposely at the Lesson of English

Setting and atmosphere of the lesson

The first step in motivating an English lesson is to dispose of all that is negative, and unproductive. Many are the deterrents of the process; we don't have to add more. You cannot force students – who are coming into the classroom from a Physical Education class – to concentrate in seconds flat on a listening text. Give them time to adapt (remember that is one feature of man's evolution), to reorient themselves in the new class compass. Giving time is not giving it *away*; it is flowing logically from one tempo to another, from one world order to another. According to Eble (1988:36) *"Establishing a good atmosphere for a class is an important aspect of teaching well."*

So, build a proper atmosphere that may begin with asking questions about what happened in the previous period, and what their expectations are on what they will do now (the very handling of questions might be crucial in creating that positive atmosphere), or simply by letting them know that you know they are human and need time and space to refocus.

Know your students' fortes and feeble points

Knowing your students well could be crucial in imparting knowledge to them. You are fully aware of their weaknesses and potentials, so you can use that for the best. You know who is shy and will respond to an entirely different type of correction or reference, and how that particular student will react. But you also know your active assets in the classroom. You will certainly be sure of how to elicit the highest from them. Pride of achievement and shyness are on radical ends but they both can burn your lesson status to the ground if improperly handled.

Allow calculated doses of fun to color your lesson

A lesson running on entirely strict terms, with students regarded as robots, not just embraces authoritarian precepts of teaching, it also damages the motivation they ought to encounter in relaxing, smiling and enjoying inside a classroom. Kinegal (2006) warns us of the need for *emotionally engaged students*. That emotional engagement is only attained in a relaxed environment – in a controlled manner! That they laugh in class from time to time is not a breach of discipline: administer fun in productive doses. Eble (1988:76) phrases it as follows: *"The teacher's task...is to determine the most profitable blend of freedom and discipline for each student in a group."*

That is probably the best recipe for a lesson to run smoothly: the magical combination of liberties and limits. We don't have to be afraid. Fun will work wonders, just balance it.

Make sure your students are warmed up for the lesson
The teacher must be *an anticipator of pleasurable experiences* in a classroom, as Eble, 1988, says. Motivation therefore has to touch every minute of the lesson and every student's heart. It cannot be an ingredient separately inserted into the *hors d'oeuvre*, or the main dish, or dessert. It must be added to all the meal courses and during table talk too. Suggestions here are plenty: anecdotes, personal glimpses, situations, recordings, dramatizations, allusions, etc.

Abbott *et al* (1989:59) mention that a teacher must *"Create motivation by providing **interest, fun** and a sense of achievement."* I direct the attention to the need of influencing the individual – the student – so that he or she willingly performs a task, and behind his or her acting there are factors such as interest towards the activity, fun, sense of success.

Two elements that may add to develop motivation, according to the previous authors (1989:61) are that there must be *"...some plausible reason (...) why the communication is being made..."* and that *"...we should constantly keep to the forefront the purpose of communication, the needs of the addressee, and the requirements of the...medium."* They emphasize the fact that a rationale must accompany the act of learning, as well as the concrete context and conditions in which it occurs.

Give your students their righteous place in the classroom – and in your heart
Don't forget you are training teachers-to-be. They must develop many professional skills to enter their own pupils' classrooms and worlds. Pass on to them as many tasks and assignments as possible. A list of what students can do in class:
- Write date, topics and tasks on board.
- Read out headings, items, examples, texts, etc.
- Give out cards, arguments.
- Circulate around tables helping out others.
- Prompt classmates.
- Explain doubts.
- Make corrections.
- Act as teachers during segments of the lesson.
- Present situations.
- Captain teams.
- Monitor the process.
- Volunteer information from extra sources (books, dictionaries).

But also open your heart to them. Each and every one of your students is a *terra incognita* that yearns – believe it or not – to be discovered and accepted and recognized and nurtured in his or her own degree and ego. The notion that closeness damages discipline and melts borders in the classroom is a myth, ill-treated and misinterpreted. Obviously, the teacher sets the "ground rules" according to the students' age, maturity and attitudes. Give them confidence to practice, to talk, to take flight and grow, and let them know you know who they are by their names and by their qualities.

Consult experts on the matter of motivation and apply your findings to class
Six interesting pointers towards motivation, according to De Camp (2010)[10], can be adapted as follows:
*"**Success** - Nothing succeeds like success. If students regularly experience success and have a healthy self-concept they need to have successful experiences approximately 75% of the time. In most cases teachers should sequence the learning from the easiest to most difficult – especially for students who are easily frustrated.*

__Concern__ - If zero concern exists there will probably be zero learning. On the other hand, too much concern and some students become frustrated; too little and some students become bored.

__Meaningful__ – The more the learning relates to the student's past, present or future knowledge and experience, the greater the chances the student will be involved in the learning. Also, sharing the purpose of the lesson with the student increases the chances the student will be motivated to participate. Other ways are through drama, role-plays, field trips, discussion, films and videos, etc.

__Positive Feeling Tone__ – If we make what is being learned a pleasant experience we increase the chances students will want to continue to learn.

__Interest__ – People are motivated to do those things that they find interesting. We attend to things we find novel, varied and vivid. Humour and enthusiasm are two teacher behaviours that create interest. Curiosity about something also peaks our interest. By showing interest in students we impact the feeling tone in the classroom.

__Knowledge of Results__ – When we know that what we are doing is being done well, or needs to be improved and we know what to do to improve and feel and believe we can do it, we are motivated to continue. How teachers respond to students´ responses provides guidance for the students to either stop or continue with a line of thinking."

Guarantee that your lesson plan includes a properly balanced weight of oral and writing tasks

---

[10] Taken by De Camp from Barrie Bennett.

Do observe the precept of the primacy of the oral over the written. Do not burden your students with tasks solely in one-skill mode. Vary the proposals both in terms of skill and richness. Research has proven, for example, that the students of the current generations are biased against writing, so the teacher's task is to find *the* equilibrium that is needed, moving in crescendo from speaking activities to writing ones.

Give what you do in class a well-grounded purpose, a solid foundation

Guarantee that the skill you are navigating is not conveniently filling a gap in the system, or avoid that it was planned but then discarded because time was over. Both are destructive maneuvers. Each step you take with your students in class must have a basis to stand on, or it will crumble.

Provide your students with attractive sources or assignments to work from

For example, story texts they can modify not just the end of, but also the beginning. This variant is not sufficiently exploited. The sources must activate the students' curiosity, their interest to know what's next and to discover what is new for them. Ways to draw out the motivation for a subject are described by Eble (1988:76): *"Curiosity, the way to unfold a subject's mysteries, arousing and satisfying curiosity, moving the student from understanding to doing, exemplifying and embodying..."*

Plant in your students a sense of success and improvement, as little as it may be

Kinegal (2006:12) introduces a key principle: *"Achievement in one skill area enriches and reinforces progress in all others."* And by achieving progress in the skills, the students will feel motivated. The act of motivating is a closed circle in which achievement and motivation affect each other proportionally. If students see their performance in the language is poor, their motivation will fade and they will shut out the lesson. On the contrary, a bit of praising for whatever it is that the student does right in class, or for the personality qualities he or she has that will help him or her overcome difficulties, could change the universe for them and set them on the track of motivation to go on and try to succeed.

Show your own motivation

Eble (1988:83) says that *"If teachers find teaching pleasurable, they probably communicate that sense in one way or another to students."* He goes further in stating that *"Humans are strongly motivated by other humans. Seeing someone doing something well is often the first step to wanting to do that thing well oneself."* And he clarifies: *"For professors to be motivated they have to believe in what they are doing."*

It is then vital that you shine in the classroom, that you reveal your motivations. Write out your own answer versions of the assignments and share them. Let the students know that you practice writing too, or that you look up the meaning of words in the dictionaries, that you have doubts too, that you tape yourself to correct your own mistakes, that you watch films and listen to songs and are fascinated by discoveries you make in them, phrases that you did not know. It encourages them a lot. It tells them that the person in front of them is human and finds joy too in language learning.

Select texts that involve the students

Find texts that touch the students´ feelings and emotions. A motivational start for practicing the language could trigger the minds of the slow, the shy, the lazy and the unruly ones. As stated elsewhere, Kinegal (2006) claims the need for emotionally engaged students. Motivation is a fire starter. Do not underestimate it.

Uncover for your students the magic of working with dictionaries

Marshall (2006) mentions it is vital to include in class resources such as dictionaries, thesaurus, etc. Language power comes from reading, consulting, absorbing the cultural wealth that underlies in those sources. Cuyas, Webster's, Roget's, Kenyon and Knotts, Collins, Oxford are powerful dictionaries that can be used in class or outside. Of course, freshmen will have to move cautiously along the stock of books, according to their needs and possibilities. But there are really no boundaries to opening a dictionary save those that come from the restrictions that a student might impose on him or herself. Those limits are expanded today by technologies.

Conclusions

The presentation of ideas on the issue of motivation and how to kindle it in class is not exhausted here. Motivation covers every corner of man's activity in formal and informal contexts, in every imaginable occasion and minute. It lies within him or her, and is fueled too from the outside.

The hints exposed here come from different sources. The reader is free to take or discard, enrich, modify, integrate. I certainly expect to have planted the seed of motivation in him or her.

Bibliography

Abbott, Gerry *et al* (1989) *The Teaching of English as an International Language: A Practical Guide*. Edición Revolucionaria. La Habana. Cuba.
De Camp, Maureen (2010) *Creating a Language Learning Classroom: From Theory To Practice*. British Columbia Teacher´s Federation.
Finocchiaro, M. (1989) *The Functional and Notional Approach: From Theory to Practice*. Edición Revolucionaria.

González Maura, Viviana y otros autores (2001) *Psicología para Educadores*. Editorial Pueblo y Educación. Ciudad Habana.
Kinegal, Jane (2006) *Creating a Language Learning Classroom: From Theory Practice*. British Columbia Teachers´ Federation. Canada.
Marshall, Sondra (2006) *Communicative Approaches to Evaluation in Foreign Languages Teaching*. British Columbia Teachers´ Federation. Canada.
Mc Donough, Jon et al. (1993) *Materials and Methods in ELT. A Teacher's Guide*. U.S.A. Blackwell Publishers Ltd.
Olivé Iglesias Miguel A. (2011) *Writing: The Cinderella? Experiences with Senior Students of the Teacher Education English Major at Holguin University, Cuba*. Article. UPS. Holguin.
Olive Iglesias, Miguel (2012) *Experience-Based Tips for Planning and Teaching an Integrated English Practice Lesson in the Specialty at the UPS in Holguin*. Article. Holguin, Cuba.
Smirnov A., Leontiev A., y otros (1961) *Psicología*. Imprenta Nacional de Cuba.
Penny Ur (1996) *A Course in Language Teaching. Practice and Theory*. Cambridge. University Press.

Skill-Integration in Foreign Language Teaching: Developing Oral Expression

MSc Miguel Ángel Olivé Iglesias. Associate Professor
BEd Yudisleidy Ruby Pupo Almarales
BA Milena Labrada Freeman

Language is a means of communication that allows social interaction. It shows people's ways of thinking and acting. Language is the way of expressing the system of symbols and codes that represent a cultural background. The great scientific and economic changes of the century, as well as the advances in the technological field, demand from any educational system new dynamics in which the teaching of foreign languages plays an important role as an instrument to approach knowledge, exchange ideas and communicate. English, particularly, has become an international language used by over 300 million people around the world. It is the official language of many nations and of most of the spoken and written business and scientific production globally.

The teaching of English as a foreign language not only contributes to linguistic accuracy but also to the construction and reconstruction of knowledge. In other words, it is the improvement of basic habits and skills that allow people to communicate in English.

Teaching and learning English is a priority in the Cuban System of Education. It responds to economic, social, cultural, political and diplomatic realities. The main goal of the English subject in terms of language is *to develop communication* and an acceptable level of communicative competence in the language, which takes place in the interaction between two or more persons. The subject contributes to the students' formation of their world-view. It will buttress the Junior High School curriculum by favoring the education of responsible and committed students.

A search for information related to the development of oral expression of English as a foreign language made it possible for the authors to determine that this topic has been delved with by linguists, professors and researchers at international, national, and local levels. Thus, such relevance has been analyzed in a variety of investigations addressed at determining the most effective strategies for developing oral expression within the English lesson.

The development of oral expression aims at achieving a better communicative competence. Authors such as, Antich, R. (1975, 1986); Richard-Amato, R. (1988); Faedo, A. (1988 y 1994); Abbott, G. (1989); Byrne, D. (1989); Finocciaro, M. (1989); Terroux, G. (1991); Ur, P. (1997); Medina, A. (1998 and 2006), among others, have offered valuable contributions.

Oral expression is used for many functions. Through oral expression, people can establish relationships, find out information and compare viewpoints. Oral expression is the key for communication. By considering what oral expression tasks can be used in class, and what specific needs learners report, teachers can help learners improve their oral expression and overall oral competence.

Skill integration is decisive in the learning of English and the development of an appropriate oral expression, as is revealed in the quotation below:

"… A simple but effective way of ensuring that skills are integrated is to get the learners to collaborate, in pairs or in groups, on fluency-focused tasks. Integrated skills activities are important because: they provide opportunities for using language naturally, not just practicing it, many pair- and group work activities call for a variety of skills, sometimes simultaneously, in order to involve all the learners, students seem to learn better when they are engaged on activities which involve more than one skill."[11]

Theoretical elements concerning oral expression and skill integration in foreign language teaching

Oral Expression

From an interpretation of what really happens in the communicative act, language teachers, among others, use the following terms, which describe the four skills of the language: listening, speaking, reading and writing. This is a generalized use. Some specialists still maintain it: Antich, R. (1975); Plattor, E. (1981); Jevel, R. (1966); Acosta, R. (1996); Cook, V. (1996); Hutchinson, T. (1996); Ur, P. (1997) and Jiménez, M. (2001).

In the 80s, other authors approached these skills as listening comprehension and reading comprehension. Brumfit, Ch. (1985); Antich, R. (1986); Abbott, G. (1989); Byrne, D. (1989); Terroux, G. (1991); Brown, H. (1994). Likewise, during this period oral expression and written expression began to be used too (Antich, R. (1986); Byrne, D. (1989); Brown, H. (1994)). This expresses in a better way the exactness of the content of the verbal skills. So, they are assumed by the authors in this paper.

Oral expression particularly is an interactive process of constructing meaning that involves producing and receiving and processing information (Brown, 1994; Burns and Joyce, 1997). Its form and meaning depends on the

---

[11]Taken from *Teaching Oral English* by Donn Byrne

context in which it occurs, including participants themselves, their collective experiences, physical environment, and purposes for oral expression. In order to know how to produce specific points of language such as grammar, pronunciation or vocabulary (linguistic competence), required by oral expression, learners should also understand when, what and in what ways to produce language (sociolinguistic competence).

Oral expression is a productive skill involved in a two-way process of oral communication (Byrne, 1989). The speaker has to encode the message he wishes to convey in appropriate language. A good speaker synthesizes this array of skills and knowledge to succeed in a given speech act.

Oral expression, its formation and development, implies two abilities: a receptive one (listening) and a productive one (oral expression), so it is a dual process which includes the sender or speaker (who encodes the message) and the receiver or hearer (who decodes the message). It is an interactive process in which in a dynamic way the roles are interchanged.

Byrne (1989) states that: "The main goal in teaching the productive skill of speaking will be oral fluency. This can be defined as the ability to express oneself intelligibly, reasonably, accurately and without too much hesitation (otherwise communication may break down because the listener loses interest or gets impatient)."

In reference to this topic, the authors supports that to attain this goal, you will have to bring the students from the stage where they are mainly imitating a model of some kind, or responding to clues, to the point where they can use the language freely to express their own ideas. The development of the oral ability is a good source of motivation for most learners.

Ur, P. (1997) stated that speaking is not just any skill, the author highlights that it is arguably the most important, and therefore should take priority in any language. Within this analysis it is stated that: "The role play is virtually the only way we can give our learners the opportunity to practice improvising a range of real-life spoken language in the classroom, and is an extremely effective technique if the students are confident and cooperative; but more inhibited or anxious people find role play difficult and sometimes even embarrassing."

Oral expression has gained space in the last decades within foreign language teaching. Its formation and development include both receptive and productive sub-skills. It is generally defined as *"An interactive process in which roles between people are dynamically changed."* (Medina, A. 2004).

Another definition given by Medina (2006) is: "Oral expression is the process through which the student-speaker in interaction with one or more persons and in an active position, carries out the double role of receiving and coding the message, with the aim of satisfying his communicative needs in the foreign language. The development of this skill covers a wide spectrum, from the approach based on language and which emphasizes accuracy, up to the one based on the message and which emphasizes meaning and fluency; and its highest aim is that the student should be able to develop communicative acts with the necessary competence. This is mainly the ruling skill in the teaching-learning process of foreign languages and its effectiveness depends on the integration with the rest of the verbal skills on the strong entailment between affective-motivational and cognitive elements."

These previous authors have offered important criteria for the development of English communication. The analysis of this information allowed the researcher to determine that there is an ample variety of proposals, approaches, techniques, procedures, principles, and exercises provided with the intention of improving the effectiveness of the teaching–learning process of English as a foreign language.

To be effective when teaching oral expression, some methodological aspects should be kept in mind because "The development of oral expression skills is a good source of motivation for most learners." (Byrne, 1989)
Points to pay attention to:
1) Demonstrate the learners that they are making progress in the language all the time.
2) Correction should not discourage the learners.
3) Encourage the learners about how to complement the knowledge they have got in the English language.
4) Teach patterns of real interaction.
5) Give guided preparation.
6) Teach interactional language.

Skill Integration
Medina (2006) proposes for the formation and development of oral communication in English a system of methodological principles for the direction of the teaching-learning process of English.

One of these principles is the **"Principle of the integral character of the communicative abilities for their formation and development."** It states that the four communicative abilities (Listening comprehension, Oral expression, Reading comprehension and Writing) cannot be separated and they have common aspects that make them a unit and they are naturally integrated in the act of communication.

In more specific terms, there are suitable proposals for the teaching–learning of this language with specific purposes. The context is favourable, given the right conditions and proposal of tasks, to integrate skills in class so that students find other ways to use the language and practice different skills at the same time.

Communication implies the acquisition of knowledge about the language system and the development of habits and skills within each of the language skills. Teaching should attempt to develop all the language skills in the sequence: listening, speaking, reading and writing since the beginning of the course, as they complement each other within the teaching-learning process.

While one of the skills is the objective of teaching, the others may act as a means for its development and develop themselves at the same time. Listening and speaking are treated first due to the primary character of oral communication, where listening is the basis for speaking. Reading precedes writing as the basis of it, and the latter is considered an instrumental skill. This means writing is not an objective in itself (except in specialized courses), but a means for the development of listening, speaking and reading. If we are looking for sources to talk, whether guided or free, it is apparent that many of these will come from reading and writing activities.

Students will, of course, need dialogues as conversational models but these are not necessarily the best stimulus for talk. A reading text on an interesting or relevant topic may be much more productive, often because the ideas are presented more directly. Through reading the learners can also greatly expand their receptive knowledge of the language, especially in the often neglected area of vocabulary. Similarly, a writing activity, done collaboratively in pairs or small groups, will be accompanied by a good deal of talk – talk that is needed to get something done.

Skill integration aims at achieving a better communicative competence. This theme has received attention both at national and international levels. Authors such as Antich, R. (1975, 1986); Byrne, D. (1989); Douglas Brown. H. (1994); Acosta, R. (1996); Ur, P. (1997); Medina, A. (2006); Machín, P. (2011); Olivé. M. (2013), among others, have offered valuable contributions.

Following is offered a working definition of *skill integration* for the purposes of this paper, given by Olivé. M. (2013): "The combination of two or more skills of the language in the teaching-learning process of English to attain a further goal, which can be the improvement of one particular skill; or their integration in follow-up stages to complete a sequence of learning or comprehension in the same process."

Speaking is one of the language skills to be developed in most of the school courses in English at all levels. The skill is either developed independently as a primary goal to be attained at the very end of learning and/or as a means for other skills such as reading. Consequently, as a general rule, speaking is a teaching point and this is reflected in the objectives of such courses.

Speaking relates intimately to the other language skills, but it is closely connected with listening. This connection between listening and speaking reveals itself in their character as parts of oral communication in which both of them – the receptive skill of listening and the productive skill of speaking – take part. In this process, both listener and speaker play different roles and, thus, while one is working on the encoding of the message, the other is decoding the meanings embodied in the language forms produced by the speaker and aided by non-verbal means such as facial expressions and gestures. In some situations, one person may do all the speaking and so keep up the flow of speech (transactional function of language) as, for example, in a lecture; and in other situations, such as in conversations, speakers constantly change roles (interactional function of language).

The above, however, does not mean, under any circumstances, that speaking does not relate to reading and writing within the natural process of communication. This is clearly seen, for instance, when you meet a foreigner from an English speaking country who is visiting Cuba. He gives you a book and after he has gone back to his country, you write to him. Here the exchange covers listening-speaking first, reading then, and finally writing. So the interrelation among the skills in the process of communication is evident.

Developing speaking requires knowledge of the language system skills in the mastery of language (linguistic skills) and skills in its functioning as speech (communicative skills). Thus, in learning a language as communication, the learner must assimilate its components – pronunciation, vocabulary and grammar – and use them in speech.

Learning to speak, then, requires much practice in the functions and forms of the language. The aim of the teacher is to develop linguistic and communicative skills in integration and progressively, until free and spontaneous speech is attained.

Listening comprehension is an exceedingly important skill; it makes up almost one third of people's language activities. Besides, listening is a very difficult skill to acquire when learning a language, because the listener has no control over what he hears (language content, complexity or speech). He cannot choose his pace; he cannot avoid structures he does not know; he cannot skirt around ideas he cannot express. Besides, spoken words do not stay to be scrutinized and puzzled over, as do written words. Speakers vary in the amount of consideration they show to foreigners in the clarity and care with which they express themselves. The main difficulty people face when visiting a foreign country is that they cannot understand what is being said to them.

The ability of listening comprehension is not acquired naturally; then, it must be taught. Listening practice is especially important in classrooms where English is taught as a foreign language; that is, in situations (like in Cuba and in Brazil) where English is not the language of the country, and where opportunities for hearing English outside the classroom are few. Students in such environment often learn to read and write English, and even to speak it, but they frequently have great difficulty comprehending English spoken to them.

Reading is one of the main skills that the learner should acquire in the process of mastering a language. Through reading the learner enriches his knowledge of the world around him. He increases his knowledge and understanding of the culture of the speakers of the language, their ways of thinking, and their contributions to many fields of artistic and intellectual endeavor. Reading develops learners' psychological processes such as analysis, synthesis, comparison, generalization, memory and imagination. Reading is a mighty weapon to develop in the learners´ qualities as patriotism, internationalism, responsibility, honesty, loyalty and love.

Findings of applied linguistics have stated that language is primarily oral, and writing is derived from it. Scientific procedures in language learning involve listening first, followed by speaking. Then comes reading, and finally writing. The assumption is that written language is a graphic representation of vocal signals, and therefore reading must come after one has acquired the habits to respond to vocal signals.

Reading is also a way to improve listening, speaking and writing. The introduction of reading permits to bring in carefully controlled writing exercises. These two reinforce each other and consolidate the aural-oral learning. The oral language is the constant factor in the reading process, and it is the teacher's primary task to ensure mastery of related audio-lingual exercises as a prerequisite to the introduction of reading. This aural-oral mastery will aid students in learning to recognize the written forms. Through the perception of the visual forms via the eye, the student must establish a relationship of meaning based on auditory signals.

Writing has for many years, even centuries, occupied a large place in teaching and learning procedures in school. To be literate has implied to read and write. Besides, writing exercises keep students busy and out of mischief. The exercises are easy to handle and poorly qualified teachers may take them directly from the textbook.

Writing is, in its simplest form, a graphic representation of speech; that is, letters or combinations of letters which represent the sounds one makes in speech. It involves the correct association of conventional graphic symbols with sounds which have no meaning and no significant interrelationship for the writer. In a more complicated process the graphic symbols (letters, numbers and diacritic signs) have to be arranged into words, according to certain rules. Words have to be arranged to form sentences and these are linked together in a certain way to form a text around a topic. In this sense, writing involves the encoding of a message for someone who is generally not physically present. Thus the writer has to ensure that what he writes can be understood successfully.

Generally speaking, writing as a simple process, is taught in the elementary level, while as a complex process is taught in the intermediate and advanced levels.

In non-specialized courses writing is not an objective in itself because not many students will need to write in English. In fact, in these courses writing is an instrumental skill at the service of reading, speaking and listening abilities, so it should not be taken as a major skill to be developed. Writing facilitates practice in the use of learned vocabulary and structures. It helps the students retain in the memory patterns of all kinds: graphemes, words, phrases, sentences, and texts.

The Importance of Integrating Skills

There is a tendency in language classrooms (although perhaps a diminishing one) to focus attention on one skill at a time: thus, in one lesson, or part of a lesson, special attention is paid to oral work; in another to reading and so on.

This sometimes reflects the apparent needs of the learners. Often, however, it is a pedagogical convenience rather than a necessity and probably reflects the way skills have been sequenced in the unit of work in the course book: speaking/listening+ reading+ writing. This kind of sequencing recycles and reinforces language items, but does not integrate skills in any real sense.

Notice that in 'real life' we do not use language skills in any set order or in any necessary conjunction with each other. For example, if we see an interesting advertisement in the paper for a holiday, we may discuss it with somebody and then perhaps ring up or write for more information. This nexus of activities, which so far has involved reading-+ speaking/listening either speaking/listening or writing, may continue or stop at that point. It can provide a model for integrating skills in a realistic way and is especially useful at a post-elementary level. Another simple but effective way of ensuring that skills are integrated is to get the learners to collaborate, in pairs or in groups, on many of the fluency-focused tasks. Finally, both simulation and project work provide a natural framework for integrating skills.

First, however, we need to see why integrated skills activities are important:
  (a) They provide opportunities for *using* language naturally, not just practising it.
  (b) Many pair- and group work activities call for a variety of skills, sometimes simultaneously, in order to involve all the learners.
  (c) Students seem to learn better when they are engaged on activities which involve more than one skill.[12]

It must also be clear that single-skill activities are not effective: there will in fact be many occasions when we ask the students just to talk or read or write, because this is appropriate. Equally, however, we should be looking for opportunities to knit skills together, because this is what happens in real lire.
Integrating the four main language skills (listening, reading, speaking, and writing) has showed to be very beneficial in the foreign language classroom. Considering that communication requires the integration of the four skills, it makes sense that language is taught in a communication-promoting way.

There are several advantages for using an integrated skill approach. It exposes English language learners to authentic language and challenges them to interact naturally in the language. Learners rapidly gain a true picture of the richness and complexity of the English language as employed for communication. However, with a segregated approach, it is difficult to use language in a meaningful way. For example, when students are focused on only one skill at a time, such as writing, it is not very meaningful or very likely that they will ever be focused on just writing while they are communicating.

Another advantage to using an integrated skill approach is that it stresses that English is not just an object of academic interest or merely a key to passing an

---

[12] Taken from *Teaching Oral English* by Donn Byrne

examination; instead, English becomes a real means of interaction and sharing among people. This also relates to motivation, and it is more likely for students to be motivated to learn a language if they are able to use it to interact, rather than to just have knowledge about the language. A third advantage of an integrated approach deals with the teacher's side of the process. Teachers are able to track students' progress in multiple skills at the same time. Also, skill integration allows for growth in all main skill areas at the same time, this allows students to be able to use their strengths in order to help them grow in their weaknesses. In other words, if a student is particularly strong in reading, they may be able to use this skill to help them with listening. This advantage also relates to motivation, because if the learner is a weak reader, but a very strong speaker, they may be prevented from becoming discouraged and unmotivated to continue learning the language. Integrating the language skills also promotes the learning of real content, not just the dissection of language forms. Finally, skill integration, whether found in content-based or task-based language instruction or some hybrid form, can be highly motivating to students of all ages and backgrounds.

An integrated-skill approach is obviously a more realistic approach to authentic language learning, whereas a segregated approach does not offer a meaningful understanding of language. Nor does it seem to be a motivating style to learning a foreign language.

Integrating the Language Skills

In order to integrate the language skills teachers should consider taking these steps:
* Learn more about the various ways to integrate language skills in the classroom.
* Reflect on their current approach and evaluate the extent to which the skills are integrated.
* Choose instructional materials, textbooks, and technologies that promote the integration of listening, reading, speaking, and writing, as well as the associated skills of syntax, vocabulary, and so on.
* Even if a given course is labeled according to just one skill, remember that it is possible to integrate the other language skills through appropriate tasks.

"With careful reflection and planning, any teacher can integrate the language skills and strengthen the tapestry of language teaching and learning. When the tapestry is woven well, learners can use English effectively for communication" (Orellana, ?)

Didactic considerations for the teaching-learning process of English oral communication

The authors assume that oral abilities should not be developed in isolation in the classroom. Classroom techniques that develop the students' ability to express themselves through speech would therefore seem an important component of all up-to-date language courses.

Characteristics of a successful oral exercise

1. Students talk a lot: As much as possible of the period of time allotted to the activity is in fact occupied by students' talk.
2. Participation is even: Classroom discussion is not dominated by a minority of talkative participants: all get a chance to speak, and contributions are evenly distributed.
3. Motivation is high: Students are eager to speak because they are interested in the topic and have something new to say about it, or because they want to contribute to achieving a task objective.
4. Language is of an acceptable level: Students express themselves in utterances that are relevant, easily comprehensible to each other, and of an acceptable level of language accuracy.

What the teacher can do to help solve problems regarding the development of oral expression:

1. Use group work.
2. Base the activity on easy language.
3. Make a careful choice of topic and task to stimulate interest.
4. Give clear instructions.
5. Keep students speaking the target language.

It must be added that the activities that are proposed in class should reflect reality, and whenever possible they should be presented in integration with other skills besides listening.

Pair work organization

Pair work activities provide the students with opportunities to talk to one another without constant supervision or correction from the teacher. It will provide the learners with the maximum amount of meaningful practice. At the same time, it will get the students to work on their own. There are two ways of getting the learners to work in pairs: fixed pairs and flexible pairs. To achieve successful pair work teachers should follow certain procedures:

- Make sure the students know exactly what they have to do.
- Divide the students into pairs (taking advantage as much as possible of the way they are seated).
- Carry out selective checking by walking round the class and listening in.
- Control noise level by stopping an activity and asking the students to start again more quietly.
- Gauge the amount of time an activity should go on for.
- Provide any necessary feedback.

Pair work is on the whole more suitable than group work, partly because the students do as much talking as possible and partly because it is usually easier to divide a class up into pairs. Pair work helps the students to increase their confidence in being able to say something in English. Also, the students learn from each other. This kind of activity provides more possibilities for correcting real communication. For developing pair work the students should be allowed to move around the classroom and to interact freely with other students in the classroom, but most of these activities work quite well if the students remain seated and interact only with those who are near them because it helps to control discipline.

Skill-integrated Activities to Develop Oral Expression
To conclude the paper, the authors present activities that can be introduced in class based on skill integration:

Activity I
Write on a sticky label your first name, your family name, your favorite color and your favorite hobby. Then, stick it on to your clothes and wander about the classroom until you find someone with whom you share something according to the label.

> a. Establish a conversation with the partner you selected and try to find as many things in common between you and your partner as possible: likes, dislikes, preferences, etc.
> b. Get ready to make a class report about any surprising discoveries and coincidences.

Skills involved: writing, oral expression and listening.
Activity II
Write on a piece of paper what you like to do the most. All the pieces of paper are going to be collected and put in a box.
a. Pick up one sheet of paper and try to guess who wrote it and why you think so.
b. The owner of the sheet of paper is going to confirm or deny your answer.
Skills involved: writing, oral expression and listening.

Activity III
Imagine the classroom is empty: no furniture, no people, nothing. Create your ideal classroom arrangement taking into account your preferences.
a. Share your project with your partners.
Skills involved: writing, oral expression and listening.

Activity IV
Select one of the following actions and draw a stick figure related to it:

- Painting.	– Cooking.	– Sweeping.
- Dancing.	– Watching TV.	– Swimming.
- Traveling.	– Cleaning.	– Running.

    a. Then, prepare a conversation by asking and answering questions on what the person in the figure likes to do.

    b. Act out the conversation.

Skills involved: writing, oral expression and listening.

Activity V
Work with the beginning of a story on a topic you enjoy.
a. Give it to your close partner, who is going to write an end to it..
b. Get ready to dramatize it in front of the class.

Skills involved: writing, oral expression and listening.

Oral communication is essential for the development of an appropriate culture and for exchange among human beings. Developing oral expression in a foreign language lesson from a skill-integration perspective will allow teachers and students to engage in activities that will favor the skill and open paths of communication towards an improvement of communicative competence.

The theoretical elements analyzed in this paper are based on valuable material consulted, and support the practical part, in which five activities were proposed to illustrate how skill integration can be fostered in a foreign language lesson and how it can serve the purpose of skill enhancement, oral expression in this specific case.

Bibliography
1. Abbott, Gerry *et al* (1989). The teaching of English as an International Language: A Practical Guide. Edición Revolucionaria. La Habana. Cuba.
2. Acosta Padrón, Rodolfo *et al* (1996). Communicative Language Teaching. Belo Horizonte. Brazil.
3. Antich de León, Rosa. (1975). The Teaching of English in the Elementary and Intermediate Levels. Editorial Pueblo y Educación. La Habana. Cuba.
4. Antich de León, Rosa. (1986). Metodología de la Enseñanza de Lenguas Extranjeras. Ed. Pueblo y Educación. La Habana.Cuba.
5. Brown, D.H. (1994). Teaching by Principles. An Interactive Approach to Language Pedagogy. Prentice Hall Regents. U.S.A.
6. Brown, O. and O, Yule. (1983). Teaching the Spoken Language. Cambridge University Press.
7. Burton Dwilight L. et al. (1975). Teaching English Today. Houghton Mifflin Company. U.S.A.
8. Byrne, Donn. (1989). Teaching Oral English. Edicion Revolucionaria. La Habana. Cuba.
9. Cassary, Daniel. *et al*. (1998). Enseñar Lengua. Editorial Grío. Barcelona. España.

10. Colectivo de Autores. (2003). Programa de Inglés para la Educación Secundaria Básica Ed. Pueblo y Educación. La Habana. Cuba.
11. Cook, V. (1996). Second Language Learning and Language Teaching. Arnold Group. London.
12. Douglas Brown, H. (1987). Principles of Language Learning and Teaching. U.S.A, Prentice-Hall Inc.
13. Ellis, Rod. (1998). Second Language Acquisition. Oxford University Press. New York.
14. Faedo, A. (2001). Comunicación Oral en Lenguas Añadidas: Un reto pedagógico actual. Curso 36, Evento Internacional "Pedagogía 2001". La Habana, febrero del 2001. Cuba.
15. González Castro, Vicente. (1989). Profesión: Comunicador. Ed. Pablo de la Torriente Brau. La Habana. Cuba.
16. González Maura, Viviana et al. (2001) Psicología para Educadores. Editorial Pueblo y Educación. Ciudad Habana. Cuba.
17. Hartwell, Patrick and Robert Bentley. (1982). Open to Language. Oxford University Press. New York. U.S.A.
18. Little Word, William. (1981). Communicative Language Teaching. Cambridge.
19. Mc Donough, Jon et al. (1993). Materials and Methods in ELT. A Teacher's Guide. U.S.A. Blackwell Publishers Ltd.
20. Medina Betancourt, Alberto R. (1998) Modelación de Factores Posibilitadores de la Competencia Metodológica del Profesor de Inglés para Dirigir la Formación y Desarrollo de la Habilidad de Comprensión Lectora en el Nivel Medio. Opción al Título Académico de Master en Educación Superior. Centro de Estudios "Manuel F. Gran" Universidad de Oriente. Santiago de Cuba. Cuba.
21. Medina Betancourt, Alberto R. (2004) Modelo de competencia metodológica del profesor de inglés para el perfeccionamiento de la dirección del proceso de enseñanza-aprendizaje del nivel medio. Tesis presentada en Opción al Grado Científico de Doctor en Ciencias Pedagógicas. Universidad de Ciencias Pedagógicas José de la Luz y Caballero, Holguín. Cuba.
22. Medina Betancourt, Alberto R. (2006). Didáctica de la lengua extranjera con enfoque de competencia. UCP Holguín. Cuba.
23. Nation, Paul. (2000). Designing and Improving a Language Practice. In Forum Magazine. Volum 38 Number 4.
24. Padron Pérez, Liudmila, et al. (2003). Frontal and Group Work Techniques for the Teaching of English Oral Communication in Secondary School. Diploma Paper. CDIP. UCPH.Holguín. Cuba.
25. Plattor, Emma et al. (1981). "English Skills Program" Gage Publishing Limited. Canada.
26. Richard-Amato, Patricia A. (1996). Making it Happen: Interactions in Second Language Classroom. From Theory to Practice, Second Edition.
27. Richards, Jack C. and Charles Lockhart (1995). "Reflective Teaching in Second Language Classroom". Cambridge University Press.
28. Rivers, Wilga M. (1977). A Practical Guide to the Teaching of English: Communicating" Cambridge, Mass. Urbane III. USA.
29. Roche Garcia, Dianelis, et al. (2001). A Proposal of Texts and Exercises for the Enrichment of Oral Expression in Eighth Graders, based on Reading Comprehension. Diploma Paper. CDIP. ISPH. Holguín. Cuba.

30. Seedhouse, Paul. (1999). Task-based interaction. In ELT Journal Vol. 53/3 July 1999. UK. Oxford University Press.
31. Terroux, Georges and Woods, Howard. (1991). Teaching English in a World at Peace. McGill University. Quebec.
32. Ur, Penny. (1996). A Course in Language Teaching. Cambridge University Press.
33. Ur, Penny. (1992). Five-Minute Activities: A Resource Book of Short Activities. Cambridge University Press.
34. Webster's Dictionary Including *Thesaurus*. (1992). Prentice Publishing Press. Canada.
35. Wyndhamn, Jan. (1993). Problem-solving revisited. Sweden, Linkköping University.
36. www. an integrated skills approach to language teaching and learning. monografías.com
37. www. the importance of integrating skills in the teaching of english as a foreign language. monografías.com

Canadian Presence in the Teaching of Oral Expression in the Preparatory Year at the University of Havana

MSc Guillermo Ronda Velázquez. Associate Professor
MSc Miguel Ángel Olivé Iglesias. Associate Professor
PhD Jorge Carlos Ronda Pupo. Full Professor

The Teaching of Oral Expression at the School of Foreign Languages in the University of Havana

Studying a foreign language in an unfavorable environment is not an easy task. "Language educators and program administrators agree that studying abroad is beneficial, and perhaps even essential, for students who want to improve their oral proficiency in a foreign language". U. Lindseth, M. (2010). For Cuban learners it is practically impossible to do so due to the blockade imposed by the USA for more than sixty years.

"The efforts made by professors and students in our country to improve the teaching-learning process of English can be said to be unique" (Prieto, 2017). The hardest of challenges is to prepare advanced users of the language at university level.

When students begin their preparatory-year at the School of Foreign Languages (S.F.L.), at the University of Havana (U.H.) they face some language shortcomings, mainly during the first semester. Oral Expression (O.E.) is the ability that hinders their linguistic evolution since they come from schools where the teaching of English is basically written. They begin the preparatory year at different language levels. Making matters worse, some students are not in the habit of studying, or sometimes the habit is very poor. Developing group activities is difficult. To start socializing in class is not easy at first, since students are going through the adolescence period. Adapting to the university requisites is an enormous challenge in their lives and not everyone does it successfully.

Students continue to use study guides as they did in high school, and try to learn everything by heart. This may be helpful to study reading comprehension, grammar or written expression but it does not meet their learning needs regarding oral expression. Besides, as stated before, they appear not to like group study activities because of shyness and fear of talking in front of other people. Sometimes, professors cannot develop group activities because cooperation among students is too limited. Along with these factors, it is important to mention the lack of books and updated study materials to aid in the oral expression ability at present.

Nevertheless, preparatory-year students achieve many of their goals during their ten-month course. For instance, they start the year as beginners; however, once students have finished the year, they get a B2 level, according to the European framework. Generally speaking, oral expression skills strengthen as time goes by and most students enhance their knowledge of the language. Sadly, not everyone feels the same sense of satisfaction.

Motivation represents another achievement in this course because students' motivation increases as the academic year moves forward. Due to motivation, students do different activities oriented by professors and they overcome shyness and stage fright as they move on in the second semester. Preparatory-year students learn to adapt to the S.F.L. environment quickly and they respect and maintain strong discipline patterns once they feel adapted to it.

Preparatory-year students become very cooperative during the year. They bring a variety of books, dictionaries, and different materials to class in order to contribute to their own teaching-learning process in oral expression. Finally, during the second semester they are able to correct their classmates. It is one of the goals of the semester. It definitely highlights the oral language level acquisition preparatory-year students achieve when they have finished the academic year.

As stated before, the process is not successful for everyone. If students want to become freshmen, they have to earn a passing grade. It can be four (4) or five (5). If they happen to get three (3), they should study some other major once the preparatory year is over. The National System of Education gives them the chance to select a new specialization. However, it should not be related to language learning at all.

Oral expression is taught with the aid of two main course books. In the first semester, students use Spectrum 1. Spectrum is a communicative course which contains fourteen units. It is based on the idea that "communication is not merely an end-product of language study, but rather the very process through which a new language is acquired" (Spectrum 1, iii).

Spectrum 1 has many advantages. The authors state the book involves students in the process of communication by providing them with useful, natural English along with opportunities to discuss topics of personal interest and to communicate their own thoughts, feelings, and ideas. Spectrum 1 is a very useful tool in class. The book constitutes a lesson plan itself. It provides structures for professors and students to follow. This can give students a sense of security and achievement as the class advances through the book.

Additionally, it offers a variety of contents developed through communicative situations.

However, Spectrum 1 has disadvantages as well. It is thought that it does not always meet every student's needs. Of course, it is impossible to write a book for every student. "Moreover, students dislike the same type of tasks that are used throughout the course book" (Castillo, 2017). Grammar sometimes is misleading because grammatical items are somehow unclear. Topics and language use are not always relevant and often need to be supplemented. Also, some of the illustrated vocabulary is not accurate and appealing to students because of unclear illustrations.

Evaluation in this term goes as follows: students face a mid-term test and a final test in the first semester. There are two exercises to be tested: dialogues and narrations. During the former, students have to imitate people involved in a communicative situation that may be similar to another one previously presented in the book. They have been trained to transpose the communicative situations in the book to a new one. In the test, each situation is briefly explained on a card, which offers detailed information for both students separately. Students, in couples, choose the card out of many displayed on the table. Then, students split the card into two separate smaller parts and each one gets an individual piece of information. They do not practice the dialogue. They only briefly study what they are supposed to ask or answer. Then, they meet in front of the examiners to develop the dialogue and be evaluated.

The latter exercise is similar, but it is an activity to be developed individually. Students choose a card from the table. The card will contain a dialogue. They may silently read it and be ready to report it. First, students have to tell the examiners what the conversation is about. Then, they are expected to transform every sentence the characters say to the third person singular. Both exercises are presented before two different boards of examiners.

During the second semester, students continue to practice the oral skill of the language. The book they use now is called Passages 1. This is an American course book as is Spectrum 1. The main difference is that it focuses on the individual performance of students. The book is divided into twelve units. Each one portrays controversial issues and provokes students' reactions to them. By the time students start the second semester, they have developed oral strategies to face the new activities and exercises in this book.

Students face a mid-term test and a final test in the second semester as well. One activity will be a presentation combined with an interview. Students pick up a card from the table and develop a three-step presentation about the topic selected. They have five minutes to get ready and three to present. After that, professors ask questions about the topic. The final test is similar. The presentation takes six steps this time and the interviewers ask questions that demand students to use the passive voice, the conditional sentences and the compound tenses in their answers. In addition to this exercise, there is a book report of a novel they would have selected at the beginning of the first semester. They have to follow ten steps to complete this activity. The rest of the students are active participants and may ask questions about the report if the examiners allow them to.

The rest of the abilities: listening comprehension, reading comprehension and written expression are evaluated by other examiners. Students have to achieve four (4) or five (5) in every test of every ability to become freshmen. Achieving two (2) or three (3) in one test, which are failing grades, means they will not be able to start majoring in English.

Characterization of the Pedagogical Situation in Prep Year prior to the Canadian Teachers' Contribution

The English Language is taught in the preparatory year as one subject. However, it is divided as follows: oral expression as the main ability, written expression, reading comprehension, listening comprehension, grammar and pronunciation. These last two aspects of the language are not considered abilities as the previous four are, but habits or subskills. All of them are taught by different professors. Oral expression is affected since students fear making mistakes in front of others.

The uniqueness of the English Language lays in its skills and subskills. Timing for evaluating is divided according to the complexity of the principal objectives of each one. It shows that, despite its decomposition, it is in many ways, an integration of the central basis of the language. Morley (1991) suggested that "students can be expected to do well in the pronunciation of English if the pronunciation class is taken out of isolation and becomes an integral part of the oral communication". Nevertheless, it is not until the second semester, when the school year is getting over that students come close to this point.

As stated before, the English language in the preparatory year is divided into several abilities and professors who teach the different skills. Even when professors specialize in specific areas of knowledge, they try to prevent students from studying each component of the English language in isolation. All lessons are taught in English apart from the ability being dealt with. So, they use strategies to integrate all subjects in class. In addition, these techniques let students develop spoken English easily. They can be used to meet the learner's individual future goals. Performing in class, however, is a major challenge for students in this level.

Let us take a closer look into the preparatory-year and its main difficulties in the teaching of oral expression. Firstly, reading comprehension and written expression are the abilities in which junior and senior high school students are better trained in our country. The other two abilities at those schools are rarely developed because they are not the target at those levels. Then, when students choose to study English at the S.F.L., they bring a passive repertoire of words they cannot pronounce, and other words that they mispronounce in most cases. Professors in charge of teaching oral expression have a challenge ahead of them. The first lesson includes teaching the alphabet, the verb **to be** and the personal pronouns. These are very basic contents students are supposed to have already grasped from previous levels, but it is not so. Students seem not to have dealt with sounds like: /ʤ/, /v/, /z/, /æ/, /ʌ/,/ə/, /đ/, /ɵ/ , /ʃ/ and others.

Using the different teaching media and materials available at the S.F.L. is not enough. The oral expression professors have to use the phonetic description method to explain to students how to use their speech organs to pronounce properly, but it has proven to be of little help. If students do not learn the right sound at this moment, they will continue to speak English using the Spanish alphabet and will not pass the preparatory year.

Regarding grammar, teaching how to pronounce the "s" or "es" in the third person singular in simple present, in the indicative mood is another difficult task. Even when it is one of the main goals in the first semester, students learn the theory by heart, so when the time comes to use what they have learned, they fail.

The "ed" participle in the regular verbs in simple past is something difficult for students to learn as well. The /t/, /d/ or /ld/ is very confusing to them. It is one of the main goals in the second semester. The past and past participles of the irregular verbs also hinder students' participation in class. As they have pronunciation problems, it is hard to understand audio texts and videos in class. Concerning vocabulary, they limit their language use to the words they find in the book, but finding new words in the dictionary, getting meanings across, using synonyms and antonyms is more than a challenge to them. This was one of the things Mr. Theriault considered when developing his strategy.

Canadian Volunteers' Cooperation in the Teaching of Oral Skills to Students Majoring in English

The wholehearted and friendly help offered by the Canadian volunteers to many people overseas became a reality at the S.F.L. in the U.H. A group of retired teachers from different high schools and colleges in Canada gathered to come to Havana and assist in the teaching of English as a foreign language. The vast experience of the group brought about positive changes in the way the language has been taught over the years in this school.

The group was composed by highly spirited people willing to help from their own viewpoints and experience on one of the purest tasks humans can devote their time to, teaching younger generations. As they were coming from different teaching levels, subjects and expertise fields, they gathered in smaller groups to help in different years of the major. The ones with more experience teaching English as a foreign language in Canada and overseas gave their contribution to preparatory year. Those who had taught different subject matters collaborated in the first and second years.

Therefore, the ones whose experience was closer to literature, history, and subjects related to more specific fields such as translation, interpretation or didactics gave their contribution in those areas of knowledge. Unfortunately, those were a minority, and not every time the visiting team brought teachers who could help students in these subjects.

Volunteers collaborated in the recording of a course book called **At Your Pace**, issued by Cuban professors of English in our university. The book was a valuable tool for teaching non-philologist students at the U.H. The voices of the Canadian teachers have been listened to and repeated by a huge number of students up to the present day. Thanks to them, students have been able to establish the phoneme-grapheme relationship of words, phrases and functions in the book. This task is highly remunerated in other countries; however, they did it for free in Cuba.

Volunteers also brought books, magazines and a variety of teaching media and material for the different levels they worked with. Some even worked jointly in the coaching of students for their performance in the **Willow Street Festival**, a cultural activity held by the preparatory-year students every year. They sing songs in English, recite poems, tell jokes, and perform roles in plays, among other activities.

This paper focuses on the group that collaborated in the preparatory year. Mr. Philip Theriault, the founder, heart and soul of this project, always gave his help in this level. He coordinated the group and encouraged other people in Canada to come along. Together with him, volunteer teachers Judith Haley and Sandra Bergeron were a permanent and unlimited help. They also encouraged other people to come to Cuban schools to help. In addition, we counted on the unconditional help of Sandra Watson and Valerie Vachynsky. All of them were able to captivate our students' hearts. Cuban professors had never experienced something like that before. When developing such tight bonds between those who teach and learn, professors can do marvelous things in class. Once students trust their professors fully, they walk along the valley of knowledge under their guidance and control completely at ease.

It is important to say that the Canadian volunteers did not fill in for Cuban professors. They established strong bonds with students both inside and outside the classroom. Lessons were taught on a fifty-fifty basis by Cuban and Canadian professors. The lesson plan Cuban professors had prepared before hand was sometimes transformed due to suggestions and advice given by their Canadian counterparts. As they brought with them new teaching material and new ideas to approach contents, the lesson plan was analyzed and modified in cases as was necessary. However, the objectives of the lessons were always kept the same.

In most cases, Cuban professors presented the new contents, guided the students in the drilling process and cooperated with individual cases and slow-learning students. Canadian volunteers contributed with the correction of mistakes and suggested new and attractive ways of saying words, phrases or sentences. To have native speakers of the language teaching in class is the closest way of learning the language spontaneously in a more realistic environment.

Most Cuban professors have learned English in Cuba, helped by other Cuban professionals who also learned English the same way. Even when there is a variety of new possibilities for students and professors to learn the language in a non-natural environment, the presence of a native teacher is irreplaceable. It is undeniable that students, and even professors, tend to use their native language to communicate outside class after the school day is over, and even during breaks. The presence of native English professors, even when sometimes they could speak Spanish, set the rules when it was time to speak.

The oral activity practice went even further. A month before the Canadian teachers were scheduled to come to Cuba, the team of preparatory-year professors had already arranged an outdoor schedule to promote the interaction of students with the native teachers outside class.

The schedule was presented to the Canadian teachers to see if it met their interests. Some of them did participate in the activities suggested. This enhanced the possibilities of a more guided oral practice. Students did not feel enclosed and under the strict control of professors. They rather viewed the activities as a practical way to really use and learn the language spontaneously. Language corrections were made differently. Most students did not even notice they were being corrected as the volunteer teachers demonstrated the proper use of the words or phrases students had mistakenly used before. Activities like that may come to substitute somehow the possibilities of learning abroad and staying with families for a term. As it may seem: "students' perspectives on the home stay experience have been extensively reported, with a trend toward positive affective outcomes" (Di Silvio, 2014). In the Cuban environment, students welcomed the Canadian volunteers at 8:00 a.m. in class and spent the whole day by their side, sometimes until late in the evening for fifteen days. They took them on tours to important places in Old Havana in the afternoon and in the evening. Students were asked to take a notebook and a pen to jot down new words and phrases they might learn during these social activities.

The Strategy Used by the Volunteers

Canadian volunteers always asked Cuban professors to let them know other ways in which they could help in the teaching-learning process more effectively. Mr. Philip Theriault took the initiative to contribute a language strategy to help the teaching of oral expression in the preparatory year. Based on his previous trips to Cuba, the lessons previously taught at the S.F.L. and the interaction with students in different levels, he proposed a strategy to strengthen the teaching of this ability. He saw that the acquisition of vocabulary items was a challenging issue for students in this important year. So, he oriented his efforts to contribute with this topic within the teaching-learning process in the preparatory year. After analyzing his proposal along with the oral expression professors of the year, minor changes were made and the resulting strategy was set as follows:

Vocabulary Acquisition Strategy

New Vocabulary Items
Mr. Theriault made a complete analysis of the fourteen units in Spectrum 1, the book used in the first semester of the preparatory year. The book as such, lacks vocabulary, but brings a fully elaborated artwork from which vocabulary items may be extracted if a careful description of it is made. He proposed a group of words per unit that could enhance students' active vocabulary in unexpected ways.

Synonyms and Antonyms

For every word he spotted, he offered either an antonym or a synonym or both, every time it was possible. However, that was not a teacher-centered activity since he fully interacted with students to promote their active participation in the development of the exercise as he explored their background knowledge in the field. The use of dictionaries was not allowed as the activity emphasis was entirely on the oral ability. Students were also not to read at the time.

Illustrative Sentences

It seems obvious that language does not function by offering words in isolated ways. Words are part of bigger language utterances. To pave the way for a better understanding and fixation of new items, he went ahead by placing them in sentences. As it may seem, students were also asked to collaborate in the elaboration of sentences that contained such words. Sometimes, students spoke sentences incorrectly, but the whole process was quite productive.

Idiomatic Phrases in Mini Dialogues

As idioms are part of the culture passed on to students through the teaching of a foreign language, Mr. Theriault prepared mini-dialogues containing the new vocabulary items used in sentences and phrases so that students could practice new conversations and solidify the learning of these items. As the conversations were short, students were told to enhance them under the professor's control. In so doing, they gave their personal contribution to the development of the activity and felt they were the real protagonists of the exercise. Mr. Theriault contributed with a list of more than five hundred idiomatic phrases to be used in other communicative contexts along the school year. He patiently gathered phrase after phrase by listening to the conversations of his family members, friends, coworkers, people on the street, radio, TV programs, and the like.

Role Plays and Monologues Suggested

Finally, Mr. Theriault prepared sets of dialogues and some monologues so students could interact and use the words, phrases and sentences practiced before in new communicative situations. The strategy was proposed to be enhanced and made better for its future application in the second semester. Other Canadian and Cuban professors embraced the strategy and have reported positive results on its further implementation and the development of their students' oral expression ability. "Since communication strategies can reduce gaps in L2 communication, it has been suggested that they can also lead to better oral proficiency in L2 learning". Fang-Yen Hsieh (2014)

Canadian Presence and its Role in the Teaching of English to Future Graduates

The preparatory-year students make progress in English due to the long hours of language practice spent in class. This is a paramount year in which students start to learn oral English practically from scratch and end with an ability that, according to European standards, resembles an A2 level.

The presence of Canadian volunteer teachers coaching the teaching-learning process and working with students in and outside class for fifteen days in a row really makes a difference. As one of those students said: "…and after practicing with the Canadians, my tongue rolls as if attached to a ball-bearing mechanism…" gives the idea that their presence and cooperation was not in vain.

This interaction with native professionals was an immersion into English that marked students positively. This was the result not only because of the wonderful English taught but because of the volunteers, the new refreshing ideas they put into practice and after-class interactions. It was because of the personal example of altruism the volunteers gave to all of us students and professors at the S.F.L.

The whole process did not finish after they left. Cuban students and Canadian volunteers exchanged emails and addresses and kept in touch during the years while learning at the S.F.L. and in many cases, after graduation. However, that was not oral communication. For that reason, not all students became engaged in this kind of interaction. Those who did not enjoy reinforcing the written ability dropped out. According to Blake, "a distant learning format is not the appropriate learning environment for everyone; the format self-selects for those who have both the ability and preference to work more independently" (Blake 2008)

The contribution made by the Canadian professionals has served to form more professionally prepared men and women who are now devoting their personal efforts to make great improvements in our society. Some became translators, interpreters or professors at the same school where years ago, they met this inspiring generation of Canadian volunteers.

The paper has tried to disclose how to sort out difficulties in the teaching of oral expression at the School of Foreign Languages in the University of Havana. A characterization of the pedagogical situation prior to the contribution of Canadian retired teachers and volunteers was offered, as well as the challenges experienced by the Cuban students and professors on their way to success. The strategy put into practice by the volunteers during their annual visit to the university proved to be valuable in many senses. Finally, the Canadian presence and contribution to the teaching-learning process of English in the preparatory year is considered a turning point in the preparation of English professors, translators and interpreters-to-be.

Bibliography

Blake, Robert, et al. (2008) Measuring Oral Proficiency in Distance, Face-to-Face, and Blended Classrooms. *Language Learning & Technology* http://llt.msu.edu/vol12num3/blakeetal/ October 2008, Volume 12, Number 3 pp. 114-127 Copyright © 2008, ISSN 1094-3501 114

Castillo Franco, C. (2017) New Artwork and Pictorial Procedures to Increase Students' Participation in Oral Expression Lessons in the Preparatory Year. School of Foreign Languages of the University of Havana. Diploma Paper. Havana, Cuba

Di Silvio Francesca et al. (2014) Foreign Language Annals, Vol. 47, Iss. 1, pp. 168–188. © by American Council on the Teaching of Foreign Languages. DOI: 10.1111/flan.12064

Fang-Yen Hsieh, Amy (2014) The effect of cultural background and language proficiency on the use of oral communication strategies by second language learners of Chinese journal homepage: www.elsevier.com/locate/systemSystem 45 (2014) 1e16

Web sites

1.-http://www.monografias.com/trabajos4/aprender/aprender.shtml. Celtic, Regional and Minority Languages Abroad Project

2.-http://www.cramlap.org/Documentation/Theory and Practice in Language Teaching and LearningA Task-Based Approach to Language Learning (TBLL) by Steve Walsh

3.-Aspects of Task-Based Syllabus Designed by David Nunan. Karen's Linguistics Issues, December 2001

Grammar Hurdles in Foreign Language Learning: English Double Negatives. Theoretical and Pedagogical Underpinnings

MSc Miguel Ángel Olivé Iglesias. Associate Professor
Prof. Eladoy Oliveros Díaz. Assistant Professor
PhD Julio César Rodríguez Peña. Associate Professor

Introduction

Learning an FL is a pleasant and challenging experience. English takes full credit for both characteristics. Some 800 million people use it as an FL for its academic and professional value and it is regarded as *lingua franca*. English is a formidable, "hospitable" language that has amply assimilated and molded features and vocabulary in its evolution coming from every point of the globe. Nearly half a century ago, Eckersley & Eckersley (1966) noted that "...English (is) a rich language with a vocabulary of already about half a million words, and growing daily."

Open to "immigrant" words from virtually every language, recent opinions set its vocabulary bulk on the staggering figure of 2 million words today. A contemporary dictionary, Webster's (1992), unabridged version, registers around 160 thousand entries.

The alluring yet daunting phonetic nature of English baffles, for example, Spanish speakers. While in Spanish we enjoy a comfortable one-to-one phoneme-grapheme correspondence, English takes our breath away displaying a two-way sound-written equivalent diversity that poses a conundrum even to the keenest learner.

Finally, grammar too looms menacingly over the student: "English syntax... is particularly difficult to grasp." *(Taken from 100 Common English Usage Problems. Knowledge Growth Support kgsupport.com)* We will not address fully here sociocultural implications beyond the discrete planes of language yet will brush upon some unavoidable associations therein.

Let's examine what Soloway (2001), editor of *Grammar Smart*, asserts: "... people can't stand grammar. We understand. It's boring... But grammar itself is not the problem—usually it's the way grammar is taught."

For the sake of illustration, we can mention four particularly salient grammar constituents of the English language that have proven hard to grasp: split infinitives, prepositions (use and position in phrasal verbs), idioms and phrasal verbs. An efficient command of these requires study, effort and meaningful training as much as, sometimes more than, other objects of learning.

This paper focuses briefly on an aspect of foreign language (FL) teaching and learning, which is an invariant in our classrooms, English grammar. Affected by dissimilar reasons, using negatives is but another of the many pitfalls of language learners slip into.

The authors disclose the problem, put it in context addressing it from different angles and offer valid sociolinguistic arguments for readers to analyze and inquire further. Besides, they singularize the topic by sharing experiences gathered from the Teacher Education English major in the Holguin University, Cuba.

Grammar hurdles: Double negatives in English
Venolia (1979) was quite aware of the grammar potholes both English native and non-native speakers bump into: "Certain types of grammatical errors occur repeatedly," while Professor Steve Ford, a well-known online teacher, warns us that there are many "traps to fall into" in learning grammar. *(privateenglishportal.com Test preparation 11, Singular vs. Plural)*

Harmer (1999) contends, "Grammar teaching has always been one of the most controversial and least understood aspects of grammar teaching." Consequently, the complexity of learning English grammar is universal. In their paper "The English Language Classroom Scenario: Context Bangladesh," professors Huq and Zobaer (2021) mention some of their students´ problems: "Sentence structure is another problematic area for the students and English sentence structure particularly problematic when it comes to constructing long sentences... Use of tense is a highly problematic area... The final category among the five most frequently-made grammatical mistakes is the misuse of prepositions."

Another author, Lovinger (2000), puts forward the following worth-considering facts: "The doctrine that whatever emerges from people's lips is the language and that many verbal wrongs make a right is not advocated here..." (he refers to his book) "... Nor is the cliché of English as "a living language" dragged in to justify bad English... On the contrary, I do not hesitate to distinguish between right and wrong usage when the difference is clear."

In the Cuban case, one of the most recurring difficulties students of English grapple with in an FL class, corroborated in practice (Teacher Education English major, Holguin University), is the use of negatives. In Spanish we say, "No le digas nada a nadie", a triple negative commonly accepted in that language. However, English is not that flexible (except in informal talk) so it is a "mistake" to say, "Don´t tell nothing to no one," a frequently heard utterance.

Lovinger is aware of this: "In some languages double negatives are considered proper. For instance, "I have no money" in Spanish is "Yo no tengo ningún dinero". The literal translation is "I don't have no money," which in English is considered ungrammatical; to make it grammatical, either scrap the "don't" or change "no" to any." *(ibidem, Lovinger)*

The origin of this problem lies precisely in the Spanish form. A phenomenon known as *interference*, more specifically "negative transfer," plays the role of the villain: students tend to pass, consciously or not, the linguistic patterns of their mother tongue (MT) (source language) into the target language.

This is how Cazabón (1974) sees the phenomenon: "Interference from the mother tongue... is possibly the greatest single handicap in the acquisition of a second language... negative transfer accounts for a good many of the mistakes made by students of a second language."

Nonetheless, double negatives make native and non-native teachers and students equally "pull their hairs out," as Steve Ford would say. Historically, there have been opposite stances. Grammarians have said much on this issue. C. E. Eckersley (1966) is final, "The double negative, e.g. *I did not meet nobody*, must never be used–though it may be heard in the speech of uneducated people."

Lovinger is less strict: "The English-speaking tradition is that a double negative is vulgar and improper, unless the speaker wants one negative to cancel the other and thereby produce a positive." (See below our comments on President Obama´s speech), and H. L. Mencken (cited by Lovinger) wrote: "Like most other examples of 'bad grammar' encountered in American, the compound negative is of great antiquity and was once quite respectable." (Mencken provides examples from Shakespeare).

As is argued in a VOA radio program, Everyday Grammar, "English teachers do not like double negatives because they can be confusing and illogical. Starting in elementary school, teachers tell students to avoid them. But many native English speakers still use double negatives..." *(Adam Brock as writer and producer for VOA Learning English, and Ashley Thompson as editor)*

In the broadcast, the presenters explain what double negatives consist in: "There are two types of double negatives. The first kind of double negative is when two negative words form a positive statement. When President Obama said, "Time is not unlimited," the negative "not" and the negative prefix "un" cancel each other out. What Mr. Obama meant is that time is limited for Iran.

Politicians, lawyers, and diplomats sometimes use this type of double negative in sensitive situations." *(Reference made to a speech by Obama)*
We feel a comment should be made in regards to Obama´s sentence. Stylistically speaking, what the President used is called *litotes* or *meiosis,* known as a rhetorical device. It is defined as an "understatement in which an affirmative is expressed by the negative of the contrary (as in "not a bad singer" or "not unhappy")" *(Taken from Merriam-Webster Collegiate® Dictionary).* It is termed "weak affirmative" by Webster's Dictionary of English Usage (1989).

Galperin (1981) states it is "a stylistic device consisting of a peculiar use of negative constructions... Charles Bally, a... Swiss linguist, states that negative sentences are used with the purpose of ´refusing´ to affirm." Examples the author provides are "not unlike," "not unpromising," "not displeased." *(ibidem)*

Brock and Thompson continue saying that "The second type of double negative is when two negatives form a stronger negative. For example, "I don't know nothing." When you place a verb between two negative words, the result is usually a stronger negative. But, if you told an English teacher, "I don't know nothing," the teacher would probably correct you with, "I don't know anything." This kind of double negative is taboo in professional and academic situations. Some people see it as a sign of being poorly educated." *(ibidem)*

Objectively presenting the pros and cons and what really happens in actual communicative environments, the radio speakers proceed to comment: "But the double negative is alive and well, especially in informal speech..." *(ibidem)* This is especially true, as people do watch popular TV series and listen to catchy lyrics transferring, while performing in class or socially, the language they are exposed to.

Even though there are numerous more (sometimes inappropriate) in all walks of life, here are some interesting examples (usage in these particular cases is not necessarily "inadequate"):

o Sheldon Cooper (actor Jim Parsons), in the American TV series The Big Bang Theory (Season 3, Episode 2), sarcastically uses a double negative: "I don't suck nothing."

o Taylor Swift, iconic American singer and songwriter, says "I don't trust nobody" in her song "Look What You Make Me Do" (album Reputation).

o Ed Sheeran/Eminem/50 Cents sing "Ain't noboby cold as me" in the song "Remember the Name."

o In the song "Love the Way You Lie," Eminem/Rihanna say "Never do nothing to hurt."

o Hollyn says "Don´t need no keys" in "Alone" and

o Bebe Rexha says "I don´t trust no one around us" in her song "I´m a Mess."

The list is endless. The point is double negatives exist in the language and seem to reach vast audiences and publics eager to mimic their idols. Lovinger explores that notion too: "Perhaps in a long-range, philosophical sense there is no verbal right and wrong. But that view does not help you and me in choosing our words and putting together our sentences clearly and properly according to the educated norms of society. Those holding the permissive views follow most of the norms themselves. They do not say or write, "Them guys hasn't came," or "I ain't did nothin nohow," although some people are apt to do so." He adds that "The double negative is sometimes a result of carelessness or hastiness, hence understandably more common in speaking than in writing."

An authoritative source mentioned earlier abounds on the double negatives. We extensively quote its criteria – based on historical studies, richness in examples and objective position – for their usefulness to understand this phenomenon (Webster's Dictionary of English Usage. 1989):

"Otto Jespersen, in *Negation in English and Other Languages* (1917), has an interesting observation. He notes that negation in a sentence is very important logically but that it is often formally unimportant in the structure of the sentence—in many instances in English it is marked by no more than an unstressed particle like old ne or modern -n't. Hence, there has long been a tendency to strengthen the negative idea by adding more negative elements to the sentence. This tendency is perhaps properly called *multiple negation*, but it is usually referred to in modern handbooks and commentaries as the *double negative*."

"The more effusive multiple negatives seem to have gone out of literary favor some time after Shakespeare, but the double negative kept in use: "... lost no time, nor abated no Diligence —Daniel Defoe, Robinson Crusoe, 1719 (in McKnight 1928)"

"It was during the 18th century that the double negative began to attract the unfavorable notice of grammarians. Leonard 1929 cites such early 18th-century grammarians as James Greenwood (*An Essay Towards a Practical English Grammar*, 1711), but it seems to have been Lowth (1762) who gave the classic form to the statement: ´Two negatives in English destroy one another, or are equivalent to an affirmative....´"

"The old multiple negative and the common or garden double negative were passing out of literature in Lowth's time. What was happening was that their sphere of use was contracting; they were still available but were restricted to familiar use—conversation and letters. And, since old forms persist the longest among the least educated, the double negative became generally associated with the speech of the unlettered. In modern use, the double negative is widely perceived as a rustic or uneducated form, and is indeed common in the speech of less educated people..."

"It still occurs in the casual speech and writing of more sophisticated and better educated people: There's one more volume which I hope will be the last but I haven't no assurance that it will be —William Faulkner, 5 June 1957, in Faulkner in the University, 1959" or "You can't do nothing with nobody that doesn't want to win —Robert Frost, letter, 20 Sept. 1962."

"The range of use of the double negative has shrunk considerably in the past 400 years—partly through the hostility of the 18th-century grammarians and their followers—but it has not disappeared. If it's part of your normal speech, you certainly don't need to eradicate it when talking to your family and friends. But it is not a prestige form; you are not likely to impress the boss, the teacher, or the job interviewer by using double negatives. But, as the examples above show, it does have its uses. You just have to pick your occasions."

The English major classroom realities. Theoretical and pedagogical underpinnings

Students from the aforementioned major struggle with the negatives too. It is customary to hear/read them say/write, "I won´t say it to you until you don´t come," an obvious "borrowing" from the Spanish equivalent, "No te lo diré hasta que no vengas".

Another hurdle is "I don't want nothing," a transfer from "No quiero nada". Here teachers have to work also on the omission in English of the pronoun, "I," as it is not necessary in Spanish. Students say "Don´t want nothing." We are confronted with two grammar traps in one sentence.

Oftentimes a simple explanation suffices to lead the students back to the "right" construction, but what really makes a difference will always be shifting from a formal theoretical, comparative analysis to practice. Exercises and plenty of practice will re-accommodate the Spanish model into the English one.

This will have positive effects: conscious practice, based on logical explanation, will assist firstly in the internalization of knowledge, then in the students´ appropriation of the necessary tools to "act in the language" and develop their linguistic competence, a stepping stone towards communicative competence: "The only way to develop a good command of the English language is to master its rules and apply them accordingly in your everyday speech and writing." *(ibidem, 100 Common English Usage Problems)*

Olivé, Rodríguez and Ceballos (2021) view it as follows: "The mastering of a foreign language involves, for example, knowing the rules for verb conjugation. But, the learner must also practice it to internalize habit and skill so that language command reaches the levels desired or expected. Therefore, foreign language teaching gives special prominence to skill development through the integrated practice of the language in communicative situations."

This pedagogical rationale becomes useful for teachers in class, in not only teaching grammar but also regarding cultural, technical and dynamic components of the process. Olivé, Rodríguez and Mora (2021:a) distinguish one critical side of teaching, which will safely and effectively shuttle teachers along teaching paths: "A self-respected teacher has to study for ever. Knowing the grammar, vocabulary, phonetics, and culture of your lesson – and a bit beyond these – is unavoidable – and unforgivable if you don't do it."

Expanding from a psycho-pedagogical and didactic outlook, the authors previously quoted reflect, in a new article (work-in-progress) (2021:b), on two critical components when teaching an FL lesson: "How a student strives to learn a language challenges imagination... two elements central today... Motivation and creativity are powerful sources to achieve learning goals and push the dial of knowledge forward, either in life or in an FL classroom."

The Common European Framework of References for Language (CEFR) posits these premises to progress in language, transitioning from being a basic user through independent to proficient:
"In order to engage in language activity, the communicative language competence includes;
> *Knowledge of the words*
> *Knowledge of the sounds*
> *Knowledge of the syntactic rules*

The ability to use
such knowledge
To understand and
produce language"
> *(Taken from CEFR and new National. English Language Teaching Syllabus)*

CEFR tenets give us room to introduce key pieces of advice before we finish. Language learning is usually associated with and chiefly responds to motivations, context and purpose. Furthermore, contents learned and skills developed in classroom conditions will have to be adapted to real, distinctive sociolinguistic environments.

Ronda (2016) finds theoretical and methodological support in Halliday: "Halliday (2004) is assumed, language is considered a layer system illustrated as a system of inclusive, successive planes: phonology/graphology, lexicon-grammar, semantics, situational context, cultural context and finally, as a higher layer, ideology..." *(Translated by the editor)*

What do I want to learn? What for? Where will I use my English? Therefore, what may be correct *here* may be incorrect *there*. Broadly, what will open doors and fast track a person´s life and career *here* will shut doors and be a deterrent for him/her *there*. Salvador et al (2018) cite Savignon (1987) in saying that "Communicative competence has to do with a real speaker/listener who interprets, expresses, and negotiates meaning in many, many different settings."

To overcome successfully language hurdles, alongside linguistic (or *grammatical* as Canale and Swain (1980) put it) competence, learners will have to acquire and develop other essential competences: strategic, discourse, sociolinguistic, etc. Ronda affirms: "To know how to produce specific aspects of language, such as grammar, pronunciation, vocabulary or text (linguistic competence) required for oral expression, students must understand when, what and how to produce the utterances (sociolinguistic and discourse competence)." *(ibidem, Ronda) (Translated by the editor)*

Ponder Lovinger´s analysis, "At times the difference between correct and incorrect usage is hazy. English has an abundance of words, more than any other language, and multiple ways to express almost any idea. Our language is so complex that nobody ever learns it all and that even its leading authorities occasionally stumble. They disagree and one finds fault with another. Their differences concern both specific points and standards of strictness or looseness in the use of words and grammar." Lovinger strongly advocates for "... precision over fashion, logic over illogic, and grammatical correctness over "political correctness." *(ibidem, Lovinger)*

Here are examples of double negatives in some texts in the syllabus for the subject *Integrated English Practice* for second year students:

Unit 6 *"Shopping for vegetables"*
   Audio text: "Going shopping with my wife"

..."It is not that I don`t like helping her buy new clothes." Her husband said

..."I shouldn`t wonder if it didn`t rain." The lady replied

   Text: "Happy birthday dear Martha"

..."Nobody didn`t go." She entitled the book

..."It is not impossible." The teacher said

..."It does not matter if it isn`t perfect." The teacher said

Unit 8 *"What kind of person are you looking for?"*
   Text: "Charles"

   ..."Did you learn anything today?" His father asked

   ..."I don`t learn nothing." The boy replied.

As has been surely noticed, the examples presented mostly reflect the spoken part of language. This is a distinction that should be made while addressing "grammar mistakes." The idea of what is wrong or right must go through the prism of context, communicative situation, etc. As Salvador et al state, "Since the advent of the communicative approach... there has been a shift of emphasis from correctness to appropriateness, from form to meaning..." *(ibidem)*

Given the fact that the authors´ analyses depart basically from a Cuban scenario where English-as-an-FL teachers-to-be are formed – language models who will cascade their learning in their professional practice – it stands to reason that they must be taught grammar (plus pronunciation and vocabulary), culture and behavior that adhere to a standard (quite a comprehensive area), generally accepted level of English. It means that both correctness and appropriateness ought to be harmonized. Propriety in speaking/writing – and in deportment – is always welcome, respected and embraced.

Conclusions

While grammar is considered by many students, authors, researchers and professors as a troublesome aspect of language in theory and FL teaching, it is central in learning the language. Hence, it ought to be focused on with a considerable amount of attention, willpower and contextualization.

How we acquire the grammar of our mother tongue as we grow differs from learning it in school, or as an FL subject. Gold (2002) avers, "Children do not learn grammar by repeating rules taught out of context. They learn it from speech patterns in their mother tongue." MT acquisition mechanisms are helpful in furnishing us little by little with the building blocks of the language, either acquired or learned. This is a valid didactical and inter-linguistic premise.

One of grammar's tricky contents is the so-called double negatives. They have been approached in this paper from a plurality of perspectives – geographical and temporal – including the authors' educational context. As well, suitable pedagogical pointers have been outlined, which emphasize the relevance of knowing the rules (grammatical, social) but above all of moving from rule to practice with a personal interpretation of social acceptability.

It is highly recommendable to reassess the ways in which grammar (be it in the MT or in an FL) is presented and practiced in school, or how parents contribute to a better "grammatical accuracy" in their children. The gist of the right-wrong dilemma is, as Ward warns, in picking "your occasions," and as we have tried to pinpoint from a didactical and pedagogical foundation, in being aware of context, purpose, register and propriety. The conversational or colloquial style (introduced by Dubsky, cited by Baez, 2006, and revisited by Salvador et al, 2018) is as valid as the scientific prose style or any other. Context will be *the* problem solver.

There are many factors involved in teaching and learning an FL: social, pedagogical, didactical, psychological, linguistic, cultural, etc. All of these must be channeled so they exert positive influence on learning grammar and language as a whole, imprinting, by extension, a significant and integral lifelong education where language and conduct are a person's appreciated hallmarks.

References
Cazabón, María J. et al. (1974). *A Comparative Analysis of English and Spanish*. MINED. Pueblo y Educación. La Habana.
Eckersley, C. E. & Eckersley, J. M. (1972). *A Comprehensive English Grammar for Foreign Students.* Pueblo y Educación. La Habana.
Eckersley, C. E. (1966). *A Concise English Grammar for Foreign Students*. Revised Edition. Longmans.
Enríquez O´Farrill, Isora et al. (2010). *Integrated English Practice 1*. Pueblo y Educación. La Habana.
Fitikides, T. J. (2002). *Common Mistakes in English with Exercises*. Pearson Education Limited. Longman. England.
Ford, Steve. privateenglishportal.com. Test preparation 11, Singular vs. Plural (on-line video).
Fowler, H. W. (1965). *Modern English Usage*. Revised Edition. Oxford University Press.
Galperin, I.R. (1981). *Stylistics.* Moscow Vyssaja Skola.
Gold, Joseph. (2002). *The Story Species.* Fitzhenry and Whiteside. Canada.
Harmer, Jeremy. (1999). *How to Teach Grammar*. Pearson Education Limited.
Huq, Shireen and Sheikh Zobaer. (2021). "The English Language Classroom Scenario: Context Bangladesh." In *Pedagogical Sciences. The Teaching of Language and Literature, Education, Values, Patrimony and Applied IT.* QuodSermo Publishing, 2021.
Knowledge Growth Support. *100 Common English Usage Problems*. kgsupport.com.
Longman Dictionary. 5th Edition. (2010). Pearson Education Limited.

Lovinger, Paul W. (2000). *The Penguin Dictionary of American English Usage and Style*. Penguin Books Ltd. U.S.A.

Merriam-Webster Collegiate® Dictionary. Digital Version.

Murphy, Raymond et al. (1989). *Grammar in use*. Cambridge University Press.

Olivé Iglesias, Miguel Ángel, Julio César Rodríguez Peña and Katiusca Ceballos Bauta. (2021). "Skill Development in Foreign Language Teaching. Theory and Proposal." In *Pedagogical Sciences. The Teaching of Language and Literature, Education, Values, Patrimony and Applied IT*. QuodSermo Publishing, 2021.

Olivé Iglesias, Miguel Ángel, Julio César Rodríguez Peña and Marlene Mora Delgado (2021:a). "Improving the Teaching of Foreign Languages. Thoughts and Pointers." In *Pedagogical Sciences. The Teaching of Language and Literature, Education, Values, Patrimony and Applied IT*. QuodSermo Publishing, 2021.

Olivé Iglesias, Miguel Ángel, Julio César Rodríguez Peña and Marlene Mora Delgado (2021:b). "Challenges in FL Classrooms: Outlining Motivation and Creativity." Article (work-in-progress).

Ronda Pupo, Jorge Carlos. (2016). Concepción teórico-metodológica para el proceso de evaluación de la expresión oral en la Práctica Integral de la Lengua Inglesa V. Tesis en Opción al Grado Científico de Doctor en Ciencias Pedagógicas. La Habana, Cuba. (Doctoral Thesis)

Salvador Jímenez, Bertha Gregoria et al (2018) *Discourse Analysis for Foreign Language Teacher Education*. Editorial Universitaria Félix Varela. La Habana.

Soloway, Jeff (Editor) (2001). *Grammar Smart. A Guide to Perfect Usage*. Princeton Review Publishing. LLC. New York.

Tangkakarn, Boonyarit. *CEFR and new National. English Language Teaching Syllabus*.

Venolia, Jan. (1979). *Write Right!* Ten Speed Press.

VOA radio program *Everyday Grammar*. Hosted by Adam Brock as writer and producer for VOA Learning English, and Ashley Thompson as editor.

Ward Gilman, E. (Editor) (1989). Webster's Dictionary of English Usage. Merriam-Webster Inc., Publishers. Springfield, Massachusetts.

Webster´s Dictionary. (1992). U.S.A.

Education, Values
and Patrimony

Moral Education and the Meaning of Life

PhD Manuel de Jesús Velázquez León. Full Professor
PhD Adonay Bárbara Pérez Luengo. Full Professor

The Human Quest

In Edgar Lee Masters' *Spoon River Anthology*, George Gray warns from the grave that:

> To put meaning in one's life may end in madness,
> But life without meaning is the torture
> Of restlessness and vague desire—
> It is a boat longing for the sea and yet afraid.

According to Camus' well-known quotation, "Human beings are not absurd, and the world is not absurd, but for humans to be in the world is absurd." In his view,

Humans cannot feel at home in the world because they yearn for order, clarity, meaning, and eternal life, while the world is chaotic, obscure, and indifferent and offers only suffering and death. Thus, human beings are estranged or alienated from the world. Integrity and dignity require them to face and accept the human condition as it is and to find purely human solutions to their plight. (Microsoft Encarta, 2004)

Perhaps unknowingly aligning with Camus' conceptions, Bárcena wrote that humans have the necessity of integrating their lives with the transcendent. "Man always keeps the more or less conscious will to save himself from (life's) relativities"; salvation is in the absolute. "This is the ultimate end of human life". According to this author, human need for the absolute is the foundation of the "necessity for Good, Beauty and Truth, qualities of the absolute" (Bárcena, 1956).

For Carpentier, in humans, there is a yearning for perfectibility and new life that pushes them beyond what is given them. That is, precisely, human greatness: the wish to improve what is not in the realm of heavens. "In the Realm of Heavens there is no greatness to conquer […] man can only find his greatness in the Realm of this World." (Carpentier, 1964)

The biological mission of life is to reproduce the species. Once that is attained, the human body begins to prepare for death by means of a somewhat lengthy and rather painful and humiliating process called aging. That is the biological, natural meaning of life, as ruled by nature. Human beings cannot possibly reconcile with the biological mission of reproduction as the only purpose of their lives.

The alienating condition of the world demands humans to have the courage and the moral resources necessary to take on the world as it is, and make their lives meaningful. It is essentially human to make sense of life in this world, however hostile it might be. Making sense of life is then a fundamental task, a task demanded by dignity and dignifying at the same time, a task that pays tribute to the human condition and that is inherent in that very condition.   .

Only life with meaning is worth living, the search for meaning being the most human spiritual endeavor. Many people found that wealth, fame and even artistic realization were not enough to give meaning to their lives[13]. Lucinda Matlock, in a poem that naturally accompanies "George Gray", feels deeply gratified by a life she lived intensely, however ordinary it could have been—by George Gray's standards. For this woman, living the simple joys and pains of everyday life is meaningful by itself and makes life worthy and full of sense; such living capitalizes life: "It takes life to love Life," she warns the living.[14]

"Making life meaningful is a task demanded by dignity and dignifying at the same time, a task that pays tribute to the human condition and that is inherent in that very condition"

Frankl highlights that the striving to find a meaning in life is the primary motivational force in human beings—not the striving for pleasure or power—, that what he calls the *will to meaning* is a fundamental component of the human condition.

Man's search for meaning is the primary motivation in his life and not a "secondary rationalization" of instinctual drives. This meaning is unique and specific in that it must and can be fulfilled by him alone [...]. There are some authors who contend that meanings and values are "nothing but defense mechanisms, reaction formations and sublimations." But as for myself, I would not be willing to live merely for the sake of my "defense mechanisms." Nor would I be ready to die merely for the sake of "my reaction formations." Man, however, is able to live and even die for the sake of his ideals and values! (Frankl, 1984)

In the field of values education, a preliminary idea would be that whatever is significant for the students in that, the most spiritual human quest—the search

---

[13] Elvis Presley's life could be an example.
[14] See "Lucinda Matlock" in the second section of the book.

for meaning in life—would be relevant and meaningful to them and could contribute to their values formation.

Cultural creation has been considered fundamental for providing meaning to life. For Dimitri Uznadze, the distinguished Georgian teacher, the search for happiness and individual prosperity cannot bestow the authentic meaning of life. He places such meaning at a higher level, that of culture. Only cultural creation—id est, the creation of cultural values—can give meaning to our existence, he states. The life of an individual, Uznadze writes, makes sense according to her contribution to the transformation, to the humanization of nature, and to the creation of the artificial world of culture. In his opinion, creative activity is man's predestination, the meaning of his life. (Kechwachvili, 1994)

Yurén Camarena considers that possibilities for cultural creation are essential for the realization of human dignity (Yurén Camarena, 1995). Vygotsky also regarded creative activity as crucial. In his opinion, the ultimate phase of education is to be concerned with creative activity. He described it as a human realization ingrained in imagination that creates something new on the bases of known elements. So important is creative activity, in his opinion, that all the world of culture, different from the natural world, is a product of human imagination and creation. (Vygotsky, 1973)

Cultural creation is an important source for the actualization of creative values; nevertheless, this is not the only possibility for giving meaning to life. Creativity is a randomly dispensed human faculty. Life's opportunities are broader, and they are certainly more liberally distributed. Frankl (1989) considers that besides creative values—that is, those attained by achieving tasks, such as Uznadze's cultural values—there are also those that he calls experiential values—those attained by knowing the good, the true and the beautiful or by knowing one single human being in all his/her uniqueness, id est, by loving him/her. For Frankl, even the attitude assumed by someone who faces some form of unchangeable suffering may be a form of actualizing what he calls attitudinal values, because such an attitude is a source of meaning for the life of the sufferer.[15]

What is the meaning of life?
Life is an individual endeavor, a unique experience that happens once to each human being. Obviously, there is not only one answer that satisfies everybody's spiritual needs; rather, every one faces peculiar challenges during life, tasks that

---

[15] "The way in which a man accepts his fate and all the suffering it entails, the way in which he takes up his cross, gives him ample opportunity—even under the most difficult circumstances—to add a deeper meaning to his life." (Frankl, 1984)

life demands from each of us, particular missions that are usually different and always unrepeatable. The tasks raised by life may be simply the need to strive for an education, to build a family, to raise children, or to help the family out of poverty. Many people devote long years of their lives to taking care of some sick relative that requires special dedication, and that silent daily endeavor, usually private and unnoticed, provides content and sense to their existence. In some cases, the tasks posed by life can be exceptional, as happens to people who are compelled to advance some lofty ideals. Facing those particular tasks— whichever they might be—with responsibility implies the actualization of values that satisfy radical needs, and that is what fills life with meaning.

"(...) everyone's task is as unique as is his specific opportunity to implement it...each man is questioned by life; and he can only answer to life by *answering for* his own life; to life he can only respond by being responsible." (Frankl, 1984)

Later, in a more accurate approach, this author states that beyond people's somatic and mental dimensions there is a spiritual dimension marked by the most human of all needs: that of *giving meaning to life by actualizing as many values as possible* (Frankl, 1989).

As stated above, life constantly poses challenging tasks to people. Reacting to those tasks with responsibility by *actualizing values* gives meaning to life. In other words, facing life's tasks with responsibility requires the actualization of values. Human spiritual dimension compels people to make life meaningful. To do so, they have to face the demands of life itself with responsibility *by actualizing values* since *consciousness of life's tasks constitutes the meaning of life*.

"Facing the tasks that life poses with responsibility implies the actualization of values that satisfy radical needs: that is what fills life with meaning."

Experiential values may be an important source for life's sense. Take for instance love, a basic value for the satisfaction of a radical need, socialization; its essential content is purely experiential. In her poem "Variation on the Word Sleep", Margaret Atwood indirectly addresses the question whether love is to be given, shared or taken. In images of strange beauty, the poet dives into the dream of the man she loves and rescues him from his "worst fear." She gives him the protection of hope of "the silver branch,/the small white flower," and then she turns into a rescuing vessel, into the guiding beacon of "a flame/in two cupped hands" up to a smooth return to consciousness, all the way invisible, unnoticed but necessary as "the air/that inhabits you for a moment only."

Here, love offers all and asks for nothing, not even for a noticeable presence. It is conceived as a selfless experience that does not require the creation or the development of a love relationship. This love's only intent is giving, silent and unnoticed giving; and that is enough. In fact, love, that supreme value, can only be actualized if giving is enough for the lover. Its only demand can be to be essential to the loved one, to be just "the air/that inhabits you for a moment only." Sharing yields joy, but love does not require sharing—if it is true love. Otherwise, how can love be realized when the loved one is not present, when, for instance, he or she is dead? Taking and possessing do not have anything to do with actual love; the loved one cannot be a possession or a piece of property. Love is an experiential value that gives meaning to life[16].

The actualization of experiential and creative values in class may contribute to the students' formation. Enriching one's consciousness—by actualizing experiential values, for instance—is essential to being responsible. As Frankl points out, "being human means being conscious and being responsible." The foundation of human existence is constituted by *consciousness of responsibility*, he writes. A class experience that helps students know the good, the true, the beautiful, or that helps them develop feelings of love towards other human beings may imply the actualization of experiential values. In that way, it contributes to enhance individual consciousness, that is, awareness of responsibility towards the tasks that life demands.

Values that satisfy radical needs are transcendent. Search for transcendence is essential to human nature. People do not look to religions only because of fears derived from their mortal condition, but in search of actualizing transcendent values that may satisfy spiritual needs. Human religiosity is nurtured by the need for transcendence that results from consciousness of the nature of the world and that is pertinent to human spirituality. Martí refused to accept that "this" was all. Addressing his son, he writes of his *faith* in human improvement, in future life and in the usefulness of virtue. Here, Martí did not appeal to reason that results from the knowledge of the laws of the material world —a man so reasonable. He knew of the power of the moral world, the immeasurable usefulness of virtue.

"Values that pay tribute to the satisfaction of radical needs are transcendent and henceforth they give especial meaning to life."

---

[16] García Márquez's **Love in Times of Cholera** is a classical literary case of love as an experiential value that fills a man's life with meaning. Real life offers many examples.

For Heller, as noted above, although they guide people towards ideas and practices that abolish subordination and dependence, radical needs *cannot be satisfied* in a world based on subordination and dependence. In this other world—still distant—without subordination or dependence, the satisfaction of radical needs would be natural, inseparable from human life itself. Liberty would be diastole and systole, reflex action, as necessary as the air that people breathe, according to Hayden (1913-1980). Therefore, the actualization of values that satisfy radical needs inevitably has to transcend this world.

This is a world that conditions, that "bridles" human beings according to José Martí. Martí insisted in so many ways that education is the *only* way to liberty, the guide that Heller wrote about. The fact is, in education, values that satisfy radical needs may be actualized and thus transcend this world of subordination and dependence. In the microcosms of the classroom, in the "isolated" space of the class, conditions may be built that unbridle the subject and let her realize spiritually and thus improve herself in virtue.

"In class, the subject may be unbridled and actualize transcendent values that satisfy radical needs in an essentially redeeming effort."

This space, this "values education situation" must be created. First of all the teacher must understand, must even have faith, like Martí, that the subject tends to virtue, to good and beauty, to transcendence, to moral growth. Therefore, the first thing to do in class is to unbridle the subject, to remove the blindfolds fastened by philosophy, by religions, parents' passions, political systems, to return to him his spiritual freedom, to return man to himself—as Martí wrote, and he urged redemptions be effective and essential. That is precisely the opposite of inculcating values.

"A values education situation is a process in class in which the necessary conditions for the subject to give meaning to her life are built by actualizing values that pay tribute to the satisfaction of radical needs thus educating herself to prefer values responsibly."

Such is the nature of moral consciousness, that this type of knowledge and this form of learning are only possible in conditions of actual freedom of option— attainable solely in class. At the same time, the resulting consciousness of responsibility for the satisfaction of radical needs frees the subject from her bondage to the satisfaction of natural needs because it elevates her; it places her above those needs. The question is not to achieve a blind disdain for the needs of material life, but to place those needs in their just place in the individual's scale of values who may then sacrifice their satisfaction in the face of values of a higher magnitude.

"Freedom to freely choose for personal benefit at the expense of the others' rights and justice is only the expression of submissive compliance to the conditions of dependence and subordination imposed by the world. Freedom that makes it possible to understand the usefulness of personal sacrifice in the service of the others is dignifying and liberating."

Martí's life and work were of love. For him, to give himself, to serve, were expressions of vital human growth, unavoidable forms of realization towards transcendence and liberation. Death is not certain if life's work is well done, he thought. In his unfinished letter, written the day before his death in combat, he reasserts his trust in the transcendence of his ideas after life ends, "But my thought would not disappear, nor would my darkness embitter me," he writes to his soul friend.

Therefore, if the satisfaction of natural needs makes biological life possible in a world alien and indifferent to human survival, the satisfaction of radical needs— liberty, consciousness, sociability, objectification, and universalization—pays tribute to the human spiritual quest for meaning. *A class experience in which the students actualize values that satisfy radical needs may help them grow conscious and responsible, may give meaning to their lives, and may foster their values education.*

"A class experience in which the students actualize values that satisfy radical needs may help them grow conscious and responsible, may give meaning to their lives, and may foster their values education."

Learning about issues referring to the satisfaction of radical needs may not be enough. If they are related to the intimate class experiences will develop better into values education situations that contribute to the students' values education.

(This article was taken from the book Beyond Poetry: Experiences in Values Education, written by Manuel de Jesús Velázquez León, Órgano Editor Educación Cubana. Dirección de Ciencia y Técnica – MINED. ISBN: 978-959-18-0353-5)

Bibliography
Aptheker, H. *The American Revolution*. New York: International Publishers, 1954.
Arés Muzio, P. "Familia, ética y valores en la realidad cubana actual". *Temas*. No. 15, julio-septiembre de 1998. Nueva Época. Ciudad de la Habana, 1998.
Autores varios. *Educar en valores: diez tesis en forma de dudas*. Seminari Permanent d'Educació per a la Pau de Badalona CD-ROM "25 años contigo." Ihardun Multimedia. Barcelona, 1999.

Batista Rodríguez, A. *Propuesta Pedagógicas para el trabajo con los valores dignidad nacional e identidad nacional en el Instituto Superior Pedagógico*. Tesis de Master en Ciencias Pedagógicas. Holguín, 2001.

Baxter Pérez, E. "Un estudio exploratorio acerca de la formación de valores. Instituto Central de Ciencias Pedagógicas." Ponencia presentada al simposio internacional Pedagogía 1999. Ciudad de la Habana, 1999.

Berkowitz, M. W. Ph.D. *The education of the complete moral person* www.http:tigger.uic.edu.elnucci.MoralEd.practices.findex.html, 1998.

Blanco, J. A. "Ética y civilización: apuntes para el tercer milenio". *Temas*. No. 15, julio-septiembre de 1998. Nueva Época. Ciudad de la Habana, 1998.

Cortina, A. "La educación del hombre y del ciudadano." en *Educación, valores y Democracia*, Organización de Estados Iberoamericanos para la Educación, la Ciencia y la Cultura: OEI, pp. 49-74. Madrid, 1998.

Cruz, M. *El hombre Martí*. Centro de Estudios Martianos. La Habana, 2007.

Daudinot Betancourt, I. M. *Perspectivas psicopedagógicas acerca de la inteligencia: la creatividad y los valores*. Editorial Chong, Lima, Perú, 2003.

Domènechi Francesch, J. *Educación en valores*. Federación de MRPs de Catalunya. CD-ROM "25 años contigo." Ihardun Multimedia. Barcelona, 1999.

Domínguez Rodríguez, W. L. *Actividades pedagógicas para la escuela primaria mediante las potencialidades axiológicas de la obra martiana*. Ponencia presentada al simposio Pedagogía 2007. Ciudad de la Habana, 2007.

Domínguez, M. I. "La formación de valores en la Cuba de los años 90: un enfoque social" *La formación de valores en las nuevas generaciones: una campaña de espiritualidad y conciencia*. Editorial de Ciencias sociales. Ciudad de la Habana, 1996.

Donoghue, D. *Connosseurs of Chaos. Ideas of Order in Modern American Poetry*. Columbian University Press. New York, 1986.

Fabelo Corzo, J. R. "Mercado y valores humanos". *Temas.* No. 15, julio-septiembre de 1998. Nueva Época. Ciudad de la Habana, 1998.

Fabelo Corzo, J. R. La "Crisis de valores: conocimiento, causas y estrategias de superación." *La formación de valores en las nuevas generaciones: una campaña de espiritualidad y conciencia*. Editorial de Ciencias Sociales. Ciudad de la Habana, 1996.

Fabelo Corzo, J. R. *Los valores y sus desafíos actuales*. Editorial José Martí. Ciudad de la Habana, 2003.

Fabelo Corzo, J. R. *Práctica, conocimiento y valoración*. Ciudad de la Habana. Editorial de Ciencias Sociales, 1989.

García Batista, G (Ed.) *Compendio de Pedagogía*. Editorial Pueblo y Educación. Ciudad de la Habana, 2002.

Geddes G. and P. Bruce (eds.) *15 Canadian Poets plus 5*. Oxford University Press. Toronto, 1978.

González Rey, F. "Los valores y su significación en el desarrollo de la persona". *Temas*. No. 15, julio-septiembre de 1998. Nueva Época. Ciudad de la Habana, 1998.

González Rey, F. "Un análisis psicológico de los valores: su lugar e importancia en el mundo subjetivo. *La formación de valores en las nuevas generaciones: una campaña de espiritualidad y conciencia*. Editorial de Ciencias Sociales. Ciudad de la Habana, 1989.

González Rey, F. and A. Mitjáns Martínez. *La personalidad su educación y desarrollo*. Editorial Pueblo y Educación. Ciudad de la Habana, 1996.

González Rey, F. *Comunicación Personalidad y Desarrollo*. Editorial Pueblo y Educación, Ciudad de la Habana, 1995.

González Rey, F. y H. Valdés Casal. *Psicología Humanista: Actualidad y desarrollo*. Editorial Ciencias Sociales. La Habana, 1994.

González Rodríguez, Y. *Una vía no convencional para potenciar los valores en los estudiantes de las carreras pedagógicas*. Tesis presentada en opción al grado científico de Doctor en Ciencias Pedagógicas. Instituto Superior Pedagógico José de la Luz y Caballero. Facultad de Ciencias Técnicas. Holguín, 2005.

Gutiérrez, C. "Etica y moral: teorías y principios". *Revista Parlamentaria*. Vol. 5. No. 2. Agosto, 1997. pp 49-63.

Kohlberg, L., & Turiel, E. "Moral development and moral education." En G. Lesser (Ed.), *Psychology and educational practice*. Chicago, 1971. (Citado por Nucci, 2000).

Kohlberg, L., and D. Candec "The Relationship of Moral Judgement to Moral Action," en Rurtines W. L. y J. L. Gewirtz (Eds.). *Morality, Moral Behavior and Moral Development*. New Jersey, Wiley, 1984. (Quoted by Berkowitz, 1998)

Kohn, A. "How Not to Teach Values: A Critical Look at Character Education". *Phi Delta Kappan*, Feburay 1997. p 429-439.

López Bombino, L. et al. *Ética marxista-leninista (t. I y II)* Departamento de Textos y Materiales Didácticos-Ministerio de Educación Superior. La Habana, 1985.

López Bombino, L. R. "El diálogo y la cultura del error en la formación de valores". *Temas*. No. 15, julio-septiembre de 1998. Nueva Época. Ciudad de la Habana, 1998.

Luria, A. R. "La Actividad consciente del hombre y sus raíces históricas". *Psicología General* (Dávila, Z. B. and J. C. C. Fernández, eds.) Editorial Félix Varela. La Habana, 2005.

Martí Pérez, J. *Obras Completas*. Ed: Ciencias Sociales, La Habana, 1975.

Mayo Parra, I. *La relación personalidad - sujeto: Una perspectiva psicológica de la problemática de la formación de valores*. Holguín: Ponencia para el simposio internacional Pedagogía 2001.

Nucci L. *Moral Development and Moral Education: An Overview* http://www.uic.edu/~lnucci/MoralEd/copyright.html, 2005.

Nucci, L. "The Personal Domain". (Excerpt from: Reed, Turiel, & Brown (Eds.). *Values and knowledge*. http://wwwuic.edu.~lnnuci/MoralEd/copyright.html,1997

Nucci, L. *The Promise and Limitations of the Moral Self Construct*. Ponencia de aperture al encuentro 30 de la Jean Piaget Society: Society for the Study of Knowledge and Development, Montreal, Canada, June 3, 2000.

Nussbaum, M. "Great philosophers: Martha Nussbaum on Aristotle." *BBC Education and Training*, Jill Dawson (producer). Princeton, N.J: Films for Humanities & Sciences, 1997. (Citado por Turiel, 2007)

Pérez Sarduy, Y. y M. Velázquez León. (2001) *Programa de la Disciplina Historia de la Cultura de los Pueblos de Habla Inglesa*. MINED.

Permanent d'Educació per a la Pau de Badalona *CD-ROM "25 años contigo."* Ihardun Multimedia. Barcelona, 1999.

Rodríguez Ugidos, Z. *Filosofía, ciencia y valor*. Editorial Ciencias Sociales, Ciudad de la Habana, 1985.

Rodríguez Ugidos, Z. *Obras Tomo II*. Editorial Ciencias Sociales, Ciudad de la Habana, 1989.

Velázquez León, M. A *Sheaf of Poetry: for the Students*. Biblioteca CD-ROM de los estudiantes. Ciudad de la Habana, 2003.

Velázquez León, M. *A Sheaf of Poetry: for the Teachers*. Biblioteca CD-ROM de los estudiantes. Ciudad de la Habana, 2003.

Velázquez León, M. *Beyond Poetry: Experiences in Values Education.* Editorial Educación Cubana. Ciudad de la Habana, 2008)

Velázquez León, M. *Chosen Short Stories*. Biblioteca CD-ROM de los estudiantes. Ciudad de la Habana, 2003.

Velázquez León, M., et al. *A Textbook on the History of the United States up to World War I.* Editorial Pueblo y Educación. Ciudad de la Habana, 1989.

VIII Seminario nacional para educadores. Curso escolar 2007-2008. Editorial Pueblo y Educación. Ciudad de la Habana, 2007.

Vitier, C. *Ese sol del mundo moral*. Ediciones Unión. Ciudad de la Habana, 2002.

Vygotsky L. S. http://www.orientared.com/articulos/vygotsky.php

Yurén Camarena, M. T. (2005) *Sujeto de la Eticidad y Formación Valoral*. http://educacion.jalisco.gob.mx/consulta/educar/dirrseed.html

Yurén Camarena, M. T. *Eticidad, valores sociales y educación*, Universidad Pedagógica Nacional, México, 1995.

Zinn, H. *A People's History of the United States 1492- Present*. Harper Perennial. New York, 1995.

Moral Judgment and Decision.
Construction, Choice and Intent

PhD Manuel de Jesús Velázquez León. Full Professor
PhD Adonay Bárbara Pérez Luengo. Full Professor

Learning implies developing through sequential stages. In each stage, the individuals are limited in their capacity to understand the world—their competence to make a moral judgment of the world, in this case—by the reasoning possibilities that they have developed up to then. When they find information that contradicts their current knowledge, such equilibrium is broken. They then have to change their points of view vis-à-vis the contradictions found and look for a new equilibrium with the environment by restructuring their mental constructions.

In the case of values, building knowledge about them is not enough. As mentioned above, the assimilation of texts about values does not contribute much to values formation (Gonzalez Rey, 1998). Yurén Camarena considers that actualizing values implies choosing them and doing something to make them real, for which students should be formed as "radical choosers". Radical, because their preferences must satisfy radical needs. For instance, preference for a democratic institution is radical because such institution favors the realization of liberty, a radical human need. Such "choosing" demands abilities and competences to find the necessary information, to make social judgments and to communicate ideas. Because of the level of independence and creativity required, indoctrination and inculcation are not recommended. (Yurén Camarena, 2005)

Lev Vygotsky (1926) decidedly stood against sermonizing. He considered that teaching morality is pointless. Moral precepts, in and of themselves, will, in the student's mind, seem like a collection of purely verbal responses that have absolutely nothing to do with behavior. At its best, such a system is like a motor that has not started up some device and which is doomed to remain idle [...] Moral behavior will always be that which is associated with the free choice of social forms of behavior.

Therefore, *the question is not to feed the subject with knowledge about moral norms and values*. The students must be helped to reflect on the contradictions that they find between what they know to be right and the new information obtained—an internal conflict of consciousness—and so help them rise to a higher level of moral reasoning, of moral judgment. Consequently, students should *learn to learn and to think*, they should develop abilities as processors of knowledge. Education should promote meaningful learning through reflection and discovery and encourage the development of cognitive abilities, for which the teacher has to organize activities that foster the protagonist role of the students. It is essential for the teacher to encourage the cognitive self-construction of the student by stimulating doubt, interrogation, rather than by offering finished answers to life's situations.

"Feeding the subject with knowledge about moral norms and values—teaching values—is pointless."

Consequently, moral development is a complex process in which people, because of their interaction with their surroundings, *construct and reconstruct their morality*. Piaget described that development as the transition from a heteronomous to an autonomous morality. According to his studies, children start at a level of moral reasoning in which they obey rules, comply with duties and do not consciously question the adults' authority. Young children—6 to 8/9 years olds—can do very little to oppose the will of adults. Besides, because of their cognitive structure, they are egocentric[17]; they cannot assume the others' perspectives besides their own. They also believe that misconduct is automatically followed by punishment.

As the child interacts with her peers, especially in games, this begins to change. Vygotsky (1926) considered games "the natural seedlings of future moral behavior". Children playing in a group, Piaget observed, try to do it fairly, which sometimes contradicts the rules handed down from the adults. Those interpersonal interactions by means of which children try to figure out rulings that would be fair to all, construct and reconstruct their conceptions about what is right and wrong, and result in their moral development. Gradually, children develop towards autonomy in moral reasoning—10 to 12 years olds. Autonomous moral thinking implies that the individual is able to consider rules critically, to apply them on the bases of reciprocity and mutual respect, and to coordinate her perspectives with those of the others. Piaget also believed that moral norms result from socialization in *groups of peers*—in the case of children, he observed that adults played no significant role as socializing agents. These observations confirm Vygotsky's thesis that moral education should develop in conditions of actual freedom of option, just as children do when they make decisions on the regulations that will make their dealings in games just and fair[18].

---

[17] Literally: limited in concern to one's own activities or needs.

[18] In the real world, such liberty is practically impossible. In the classroom, the conditions that allow for moral growth may be built—or restricted. This crucial issue will be further developed elsewhere in this text.

"Moral education must develop in conditions of actual freedom of option."

At variance with Durkheim, Piaget held that children do not merely internalize the norms from their interactions with the group; they define morality *individually* through their efforts to find fair solutions to their conflicts of interest in a process of construction and reconstruction of their moral concepts[19]. Consequently, Piaget pointed out, the task of the teacher is extremely complicated since, rather than indoctrinating them with moral norms, students have to be offered opportunities to make personal discoveries through problem solving. Thus, the subjects' moral norms and principles result from their moral maturation—of which they are the protagonists—, *moral norms and principles that are the fruit of experiences of their efforts to adapt to conflicting social interactions, and not external structures that they internalize.*

"Moral norms and principles are the fruit of experiences of the subjects' efforts to adapt to conflicting social interactions and not external structures that they internalize."

Kohlberg further elaborated the work of Piaget. He went beyond the idea of internalization of values by emphasizing on the human essence of morality and the protagonist role of the individual in her growth towards a full moral age. Kohlberg notes that morality is the natural product of a universal human tendency towards empathy[20], towards an intimate relation with the others, a universal human concern for justice, for reciprocity or equality in human interrelations[21]. He also found that the process of achieving moral maturation is more gradual and takes more time than what Piaget had thought.

---

[19] "Paradoxically, this autonomous view of morality as fairness is more compelling and leads to more consistent behavior than the heteronymous orientation held by younger children" (Nucci, 2002).

[20] Here understood as the capacity for understanding, being aware of, being sensitive to, and experiencing the feelings, thoughts, and experiences of another.

[21] Vygotsky (1926) considered that "man is naturally drawn to the good and the beautiful". Noam Chomsky wrote about a human predisposition towards developing complex mental systems such as language. Steven Pinker (1994) has developed a whole theory according to which language is fundamentally human instinct. For this neuroscientist, people have innate basic modules that allow them to understand the behavior of physical objects, mental maps of territories, a sense of fear that includes phobias for some animals, language, etc. Thus, the complex things that people are capable to do result from the interaction of a number of those modules. What is interesting here is that Pinker includes among these innate systems *a sense of justice, rights and duties*. However debatable Pinker's ideas could be, his proposition that there is a natural predisposition for the development of moral attributes is of interest. If that is so, human beings, by nature, tend towards empathy, cooperation and justice, whether that tendency is favored by innate modules or by very early social interactions of the subject, as other authors write.

Kohlberg also pointed out the lack of a consensus on what values to teach. He rejected the relativist position of moral clarification since he realized that moral maturity was signaled by an understanding of the importance of justice and fairness. On the other hand, in his studies of different cultures, he found that these principles were regarded everywhere as basic, as the highest expression of moral maturity. He also noted that individuals who hold more or less the same moral values sometimes take different positions regarding a moral dilemma. For those reasons, he believed that rather than concentrating on teaching given values, the role of teachers should be to give attention to moral development itself, to help the individual to develop to the next stage of moral thought.

Kohlberg described six stages of moral reasoning grouped into three major levels of moral development—preconventional, conventional and post conventional—, which he termed universal after thorough studies in different cultures. The level of moral development is determined by the arguments used by the subject when facing a moral dilemma, arguments that—in Kohlberg's opinion—are more important for determining the level of moral development than the decision itself. Though the idea of helping the individual rise to the next level has been subject of criticism by subsequent research, a summary of the levels of moral development may help the teacher understand with more precision the general trends followed by the subject in her growth towards moral maturity.[22]

Kohlberg's proposal did not rely on moral dilemma discussion only. He also considered that the subjects needed a proper context in which they could operate as moral agents. He worked with his colleagues to establish "just communities" —usually schools within a school—where students could not only discuss openly the moral dilemmas faced by the group but could also make decisions on the bases of consensus and assume the responsibility of devising and imposing rules.

"A values education situation is a class process in which necessary conditions are built for the subject to give sense to her life by actualizing values that contribute to the satisfaction of radical needs, thus educating herself to responsibly prefer values."

The effort highlights the importance of free debate in class and of students' participation in decision-making, whenever possible. Conditions of free expression will help the students realize their limitations and transcend those constraints into broader moral views. It also points to the possibilities opened

---

[22] Only with that purpose, Kohlberg's levels are summarized in an appendix, at the end of this book.

for moral formation if debate is not limited to a given situation in class but develops into a values education situation by expanding its space into the students' personal and social—global, generic—responsibilities.[23]

According to Kohlberg, moral growth occurs when cognitive imbalances take place, that is, when the cognitive perspectives of the person are not appropriate for facing a given moral dilemma. Moral dilemmas will demand individuals to look for solutions and to grow morally. When the subject faces a moral dilemma and the solution is unsatisfactory at her stage of moral reasoning an imbalance is created. Since reasoning at the following, higher level is intelligible to her; it becomes attractive and compels her to grow towards that higher level.[24]

Following Kohlberg's perspectives, the task in a university class would be to help the students consolidate a conventional level of moral reasoning and assist them in their growth towards a post conventional level. Such development, according to Kohlberg, is progressive, without skipping phases since the subjects cannot understand moral reasoning beyond the stage following their stage.

The idea of unintelligibility of further stages of moral reasoning has been challenged. It has been found that *individuals at different stages of moral reasoning can prioritize a moral perspective to analyze a situation*. Nucci and Turiel point out that, according to thorough research, the subjects—wherever they were in Kohlberg's levels—are able to judge moral dilemmas from the perspective of justice and human welfare, that is, from a moral standpoint. Turiel's researches have documented that seeming inconsistencies in the application of moral judgments may be greater in adults than in children[25]. Moral decisions, thus, will always be based on the context in which they are made; people *"do not judge or act habitually"*—emphasis by the author— (Turiel, E. and S. A. Perkins, 2004).

---

[23] According to Berkowitz (1983), discussion of moral dilemmas as an educational method has been overestimated, in particular the notion that statements by the teacher at one stage above the students' current stage of moral reasoning will help them "rise" to that stage. It has been found that the criteria of their peers have more impact in the student's moral formation than interventions by the teacher.

[24] This approach has several contemporary developments. Among relevant efforts in this field there are the works of Georg Lind at the University of Konstanz, Germany, and Jamie Phillips at the Clarion University of Pennsylvania, United States.

[25] Obviously, adults are more capable of feigning a moral stance.

If so, little is left of the hope that advancing students to higher levels of moral judgment will *guarantee* "correct" decision-making, not to talk of traditional attempts at instilling, inculcating, or fostering values—or virtues, or personality qualities, or whatever denomination might be used. If the subject will make her decision through her reason and on the bases of particular circumstances, what is important is to work with the students so that they are competent to *understand the moral elements in a given social context as well as their personal implication and responsibility for the moral issues at stake*.[26]

The teacher may help and encourage students to make moral-based choices rather than try to move them towards a higher level of moral understanding. In the end, a higher level of moral understanding will never guarantee a correspondingly high behavior, since other factors influence in decision-making. Class experience in this discipline has shown that if life is brought into class debate, if the students' complex and contradictory reality is not ignored, if they are placed vis-à-vis society's actual moral dilemmas, learning may become morally meaningful, and students may address issues from a moral stance, with considerable maturity in their reflections, whatever their level of moral reasoning.

"The subject must be helped to understand the moral elements in a given social context as well as her personal implication and responsibility for the moral issues at stake."

Ethically meaningful knowledge built by the students may broaden their potential for values reasoning and for moral decision-making. Whether the subject prioritizes elements of the moral domain or not in judging a given values dilemma, such decision largely depends on her knowledge of the context in which the dilemma takes place. Final moral decisions in favor of just causes and the well-being of others, even at the risk of personal suffering are also grounded in the subject's understanding of the situation and of her role in it. Beyond the possible—so far unproven—existence of some "character trait or virtue" forcing the subject to act morally, her behavior is organized according to *her comprehension of a given social situation and her understanding of the responsibility that she has within it as a conscious moral being*.

---

[26] Anyhow, the subject's capacity of judgment on moral issues is very important. According to Berkowitz, "there is a very substantial body of literature demonstrating a significant relation between one's capacity for moral reason and one's moral behaviour", and he quotes Blasi, 1980; Kohlberg & Candee, 1984; and Rest, 1979 (Berkowitz, 1998).

A Contextualized View

Anomalies revealed by research on Kohlberg's stage sequence led to fresh understandings in the field of moral formation, in particular the domain theory, advanced by Turiel, Nucci and Helwig. Evident inconsistencies between the level of moral reasoning and moral-oriented behavior suggested that other factors, besides moral judgment, influenced decision-making. It seemed necessary to move towards a more contextualized vision of morality.

What Kohlberg considered a single structural system is in fact composed of several systems or domains of social judgment, one of which is morality. Conceptualized moral judgments may be regulated by moral considerations or by other sorts of considerations, such as social conventions or elements pertaining to the personal domain. In some cases, the subject may give priority to the moral domain when taking a decision. In different circumstances, considerations grounded on other domains may be decisive in making a values choice. Therefore, to understand moral decisions the analysis should take into consideration moral and non-moral elements in a context in which morality is only one of the factors, however important it may be.

The domain theory distinguishes, in particular, morality from social conventions and from elements of the personal domain. Conceptions about morality and the other domains arise early in life and develop with age into distinct, separate conceptual frameworks. As noted above, morality has to do with concepts of reasoning and actions that pertain to the *welfare, rights and fair treatment of persons*. Specific moral concepts are structured around conceptions of justice, rights and human well-being that have a pretension of generic universality transcending cultures and time boundaries. Violations of moral codes result in impairment of people's rights, dignity and/or well-being.

"Morality has to do with concepts of reasoning and actions that pertain to the welfare, rights and fair treatment of persons."

On the other hand, social conventions are formations shaped by the social system that serve to organize, regulate and sustain social interactions by establishing ways of behavior agreed upon by large groups of people in a given society. They include canons regulating how people dress, forms of address among people of different status in the social order, the vast range of social standards called formal education, social norms dealing with sexuality, etc.

Conventions are rather arbitrary—in Western cultures, skirts are for women and pants are for men, for instance—and are largely dependent on particular social contexts. They are usually dissimilar in different societies and are reshaped in time without much pain or trouble by succeeding generations. Though social conventions play an important role in maintaining social order, their violation does not necessarily imply harm to people's rights, dignity or well-being. Unlike issues concerning morality, transgressions of conventions "are considered wrong not because of their intrinsic nature, but rather because of social agreement that they are wrong." (Berkowitz, 1998)

The personal domain refers to activities that the subject regards as within her area of decision, actions that define the limits of her authority over her locus of privacy and personal discretion. Such activities—hairstyles, clothing fashion, the right to choose friends, confidentiality of correspondence, tastes, etc.—that cannot be justifiably regulated by society since they are objects of personal preference and cannot be judged as right or wrong by others. The existence of that personal domain establishes the boundary between the self and society and allows the construction of what is socially individual and unique in the person. "(...) the personal represents the set of social actions that permit the person to construct [...] a sense of the self as a unique social object..." (Nucci, 1997)

Moral norms, social conventions and elements of the personal domain overlap. Sometimes, social conventions help sustain unfair social orders, such as the many conventional archetypes that support discriminatory practices towards women. Very often, moral norms and social conventions are not clearly distinguished and the latter are conferred pretensions of universality, which leads to infringements into people's privacy and violations of their rights. Sometimes long-established social prejudices, shaped as conventions, provide justification and support of discriminatory practices, such as those addressed against homosexuals on the ground that a different sexual preference is immoral. Common is the case of school regulations that sanction students—and teachers—because of violations that have to do with the length of man's hair or the length of a woman's skirt, as if fashion styles—obviously non moral issues but social conventions and elements pertaining to the personal domain—were serious breaches of public morality. Values education should help students clarify between *what is not recommendable but acceptable, in terms of social conventions, and what is unacceptable in terms of morality*.

Now, for most individuals, morality is not just another domain of social judgment; it is a central component of their personalities. For José Martí morality was an essential element in his preaching and in his praxis. "Decorum"—in his precise definition—it included internal honor, purity and honesty, the way in which those qualities were revealed encouraging the others' respect, and how those internal and external orders corresponded (Vitier, 2002). Like for Martí, moral values constitute the core of spiritual existence to many people: many live and/or die in defense of moral principles that sustain their dignity and give sense to their entire lives. Morally meaningful learning, if its intent is to influence people's moral awareness and decision-making, will have to consider this fact.

(This article was taken from the book Beyond Poetry: Experiences in Values Education, written by Manuel de Jesús Velázquez León, Órgano Editor Educación Cubana. Dirección de Ciencia y Técnica – MINED. ISBN: 978-959-18-0353-5)

Bibliography

Aptheker, H. *The American Revolution*. New York: International Publishers, 1954.

Arés Muzio, P. "Familia, ética y valores en la realidad cubana actual". *Temas*. No. 15, julio-septiembre de 1998. Nueva Época. Ciudad de la Habana, 1998.

Autores varios. *Educar en valores: diez tesis en forma de dudas*. Seminari Permanent d'Educació per a la Pau de Badalona CD-ROM "25 años contigo." Ihardun Multimedia. Barcelona, 1999.

Batista Rodríguez, A. *Propuesta Pedagógicas para el trabajo con los valores dignidad nacional e identidad nacional en el Instituto Superior Pedagógico*. Tesis de Master en Ciencias Pedagógicas. Holguín, 2001.

Baxter Pérez, E. "Un estudio exploratorio acerca de la formación de valores. Instituto Central de Ciencias Pedagógicas." Ponencia presentada al simposio internacional Pedagogía 1999. Ciudad de la Habana, 1999.

Berkowitz, M. W. Ph.D. *The education of the complete moral person* www.http:tigger.uic.edu.elnucci.MoralEd.practices.findex.html, 1998.

Blanco, J. A. "Ética y civilización: apuntes para el tercer milenio". *Temas*. No. 15, julio-septiembre de 1998. Nueva Época. Ciudad de la Habana, 1998.

Cortina, A. "La educación del hombre y del ciudadano." en *Educación, valores y Democracia*, Organización de Estados Iberoamericanos para la Educación, la Ciencia y la Cultura: OEI, pp. 49-74. Madrid, 1998.

Cruz, M. *El hombre Martí*. Centro de Estudios Martianos. La Habana, 2007.

Daudinot Betancourt, I. M. *Perspectivas psicopedagógicas acerca de la inteligencia: la creatividad y los valores*. Editorial Chong, Lima, Perú, 2003.

Domènechi Francesch, J. *Educación en valores*. Federación de MRPs de Catalunya. CD-ROM "25 años contigo." Ihardun Multimedia. Barcelona, 1999.

Domínguez Rodríguez, W. L. *Actividades pedagógicas para la escuela primaria mediante las potencialidades axiológicas de la obra martiana*. Ponencia presentada al simposio Pedagogía 2007. Ciudad de la Habana, 2007.

Domínguez, M. I. "La formación de valores en la Cuba de los años 90: un enfoque social" *La formación de valores en las nuevas generaciones: una campaña de espiritualidad y conciencia*. Editorial de Ciencias sociales. Ciudad de la Habana, 1996.

Donoghue, D. *Connosseurs of Chaos. Ideas of Order in Modern American Poetry*. Columbian University Press. New York, 1986.

Fabelo Corzo, J. R. "Mercado y valores humanos". *Temas*. No. 15, julio-septiembre de 1998. Nueva Época. Ciudad de la Habana, 1998.

Fabelo Corzo, J. R. La "Crisis de valores: conocimiento, causas y estrategias de superación." *La formación de valores en las nuevas generaciones: una campaña de espiritualidad y conciencia*. Editorial de Ciencias Sociales. Ciudad de la Habana, 1996.

Fabelo Corzo, J. R. *Los valores y sus desafíos actuales*. Editorial José Martí. Ciudad de la Habana, 2003.

Fabelo Corzo, J. R. *Práctica, conocimiento y valoración*. Ciudad de la Habana. Editorial de Ciencias Sociales, 1989.

García Batista, G (Ed.) *Compendio de Pedagogía*. Editorial Pueblo y Educación. Ciudad de la Habana, 2002.

Geddes G. and P. Bruce (eds.) *15 Canadian Poets plus 5*. Oxford University Press. Toronto, 1978.

González Rey, F. "Los valores y su significación en el desarrollo de la persona". *Temas*. No. 15, julio-septiembre de 1998. Nueva Época. Ciudad de la Habana, 1998.

González Rey, F. "Un análisis psicológico de los valores: su lugar e importancia en el mundo subjetivo. *La formación de valores en las nuevas generaciones: una campaña de espiritualidad y conciencia*. Editorial de Ciencias Sociales. Ciudad de la Habana, 1989.

González Rey, F. and A. Mitjáns Martínez. *La personalidad su educación y desarrollo*. Editorial Pueblo y Educación. Ciudad de la Habana, 1996.

González Rey, F. *Comunicación Personalidad y Desarrollo*. Editorial Pueblo y Educación, Ciudad de la Habana, 1995.

González Rey, F. y H. Valdés Casal. *Psicología Humanista: Actualidad y desarrollo*. Editorial Ciencias Sociales. La Habana, 1994.

González Rodríguez, Y. *Una vía no convencional para potenciar los valores en los estudiantes de las carreras pedagógicas*. Tesis presentada en opción al grado científico de Doctor en Ciencias Pedagógicas. Instituto Superior Pedagógico José de la Luz y Caballero. Facultad de Ciencias Técnicas. Holguín, 2005.

Gutiérrez, C. "Etica y moral: teorías y principios". *Revista Parlamentaria*. Vol. 5. No. 2. Agosto, 1997. pp 49-63.

Kohlberg, L., & Turiel, E. "Moral development and moral education." En G. Lesser (Ed.), *Psychology and educational practice*. Chicago, 1971. (Citado por Nucci, 2000).

Kohlberg, L., and D. Candec "The Relationship of Moral Judgement to Moral Action," en Rurtines W. L. y J. L. Gewirtz (Eds.). *Morality, Moral Behavior and Moral Development*. New Jersey, Wiley, 1984. (Quoted by Berkowitz, 1998)

Kohn, A. "How Not to Teach Values: A Critical Look at Character Education". *Phi Delta Kappan*, Feburay 1997. p 429-439.

López Bombino, L. et al. *Ética marxista-leninista (t. I y II)* Departamento de Textos y Materiales Didácticos-Ministerio de Educación Superior. La Habana, 1985.

López Bombino, L. R. "El diálogo y la cultura del error en la formación de valores". *Temas*. No. 15, julio-septiembre de 1998. Nueva Época. Ciudad de la Habana, 1998.

Luria, A. R. "La Actividad consciente del hombre y sus raíces históricas". *Psicología General* (Dávila, Z. B. and J. C. C. Fernández, eds.) Editorial Félix Varela. La Habana, 2005.

Martí Pérez, J. *Obras Completas*. Ed: Ciencias Sociales, La Habana, 1975.

Mayo Parra, I. *La relación personalidad - sujeto: Una perspectiva psicológica de la problemática de la formación de valores*. Holguín: Ponencia para el simposio internacional Pedagogía 2001.

Nucci L. *Moral Development and Moral Education: An Overview* http://www.uic.edu/~lnucci/MoralEd/copyright.html, 2005.

Nucci, L. "The Personal Domain". (Excerpt from: Reed, Turiel, & Brown (Eds.). *Values and knowledge*. http://wwwuic.edu.~lnnuci/MoralEd/copyright.html,1997

Nucci, L. *The Promise and Limitations of the Moral Self Construct*. Ponencia de aperture al encuentro 30 de la Jean Piaget Society: Society for the Study of Knowledge and Development, Montreal, Canada, June 3, 2000.

Nussbaum, M. "Great philosophers: Martha Nussbaum on Aristotle." *BBC Education and Training*, Jill Dawson (producer). Princeton, N.J: Films for Humanities & Sciences, 1997. (Citado por Turiel, 2007)

Pérez Sarduy, Y. y M. Velázquez León. (2001) *Programa de la Disciplina Historia de la Cultura de los Pueblos de Habla Inglesa*. MINED.

Permanent d'Educació per a la Pau de Badalona *CD-ROM "25 años contigo."* Ihardun Multimedia. Barcelona, 1999.

Rodríguez Ugidos, Z. *Filosofía, ciencia y valor*. Editorial Ciencias Sociales, Ciudad de la Habana, 1985.

Rodríguez Ugidos, Z. *Obras Tomo II*. Editorial Ciencias Sociales, Ciudad de la Habana, 1989.

Velázquez León, M. A *Sheaf of Poetry: for the Students*. Biblioteca CD-ROM de los estudiantes. Ciudad de la Habana, 2003.

Velázquez León, M. *Beyond Poetry: Experiences in Values Education.* Editorial Educación Cubana. Ciudad de la Habana, 2008)

Velázquez León, M. *Chosen Short Stories*. Biblioteca CD-ROM de los estudiantes. Ciudad de la Habana, 2003.

Velázquez León, M., et al. *A Textbook on the History of the United States up to World War I*. Editorial Pueblo y Educación. Ciudad de la Habana, 1989.

VIII Seminario nacional para educadores. Curso escolar 2007-2008. Editorial Pueblo y Educación. Ciudad de la Habana, 2007.

Vitier, C. *Ese sol del mundo moral*. Ediciones Unión. Ciudad de la Habana, 2002.

Vygotsky L. S. http://www.orientared.com/articulos/vygotsky.php

Yurén Camarena, M. T. (2005) *Sujeto de la Eticidad y Formación Valoral*. http://educacion.jalisco.gob.mx/consulta/educar/dirrseed.html

Yurén Camarena, M. T. *Eticidad, valores sociales y educación*, Universidad Pedagógica Nacional, México, 1995.

On Values Education
PhD Manuel de Jesús Velázquez León. Full Professor
PhD Adonay Bárbara Pérez Luengo. Full Professor

Values Education or Education in Values?
Different terms are used to refer to educational approaches that privilege values formation: education in values, moral education, character education, spiritual education, civic education, values education, and others, terms that do not cover the same areas of meaning and that are sometimes conflicting. In Cuba, there are no specific disciplines devoted to that field of education.[27]

Here, attention is rendered to education in values and to values education. Debate on these two particular definitions is not merely an etymological issue but is relevant to the concepts upon which this book sustains its proposals.

Nationally, values oriented education is generally called *education in values*[28]. This is also the term found in programs and methodological guidelines of the discipline History of the English Speaking Cultures. The concept of education in values refers to the incorporation of values patterns within the self as conscious or unconscious guiding principles through socialization. Normative orders that exist in the fabric of social relations are to be internalized by the individual due to her interaction with the group who exhorts, rewards, and/or punishes her to do so.

This project advocates *values education*, a term referred to the actualization of values in class, in line with Frankl's notion that values can be actualized by creating culture, by experiencing events—good, beauty, love—and by assuming an attitude towards a given situation. The actualization of values can help the student develop intellectually and morally to prefer and actualize values.

---

[27] Nevertheless, every syllabus, program and discipline contains objectives that refer to the education in values of the students, especially to the fields of ideological and political formation, implying that a formative process that takes into account values is not only possible but also desirable. Such educational effort occupies a hidden or transversal curriculum that goes through disciplines and subjects.
[28] The term "education of values" is sometimes used alternatively.

"The term values education refers to the actualization of values in class, in line with the notion that values can be actualized by creating culture, by experiencing events—good, beauty, love—and by assuming an attitude towards a given situation. The actualization of values can help the student develop intellectually and morally to prefer and actualize values."

As it is intended here, values education deals, in the main, with moral education, with the moral or character formation of the subject,[29] with moral judgment and decision-making. People in different cultures regard some forms of social behavior as moral universals, considered right or wrong independently of existing social rules. Concepts of morality are structured by underlying conceptions of justice and welfare. Thus, morality refers to the subject's concepts, reasoning, and actions that pertain to the welfare, rights and fair treatment of persons (Helwig, Turiel, & Nucci, 1997). A personality[30] is a self-regulated organism and morality is central to such regulation by providing crucial referential points for the control of behavior. Education also deals with the conventional domain of social judgment, which should be differentiated from moral issues, a definition that is expanded and fleshed out elsewhere in this book. The elements pertaining to the personal domain (choices concerning tastes, the selection of friends, etc.) should not be considered targets for education.

Neutrality or Intervention?
Before discussing methodological approaches on values education, the ethical and practical validity of such a formative effort should be briefly addressed. In particular, the controversy between neutrality and intervention, that is, between the defenders of clarification as opposed to those who believe that the teacher should take a stance.

---

[29] As stated elsewhere here, all values that contribute to give meaning to life may be relevant to the moral education of the subject, not only those that could be termed "moral values". Learning about morality implies dealing with a vast array of meanings significant to society—hence the broader term values education—but not all morally meaningful. Learning to distinguish and prioritize moral values is, nevertheless, central to moral formation.
[30] Fernández Rius (2005) defines personality as "the most complex and stable organization, integration of psychological contents and functions that deals with the regulation and self-regulation of behavior in the most relevant domains of the subject."

Those in favor of neutrality defend the idea that the formative process should take place with minimum orientation and control by the teacher, whose role should be limited to the establishment of conditions that would help the students themselves clarify their evaluative tendencies. This approach has received much criticism. A radical non-interventionist stance seems to rest on the consideration that values are neither absolute nor objective, neither correct nor incorrect, that they depend on each person's experience. If so, the actual content of the values preferred by the students is not relevant. Such neutrality would presuppose that the students, spontaneously, and under the cultural influence of their milieu, would be able to make the best decisions for themselves and for others. According to this perception, the educational system should help the students become familiar with moral reasoning, with the clarification of values, but it should not *teach* moral precepts, which would be indoctrination (Simon, et al. 1972).

Critics maintain that clarification advocates assume the relativity and subjectivity of all values and ignore the important distinction between moral values and social conventions, which would place moral values and conventional preferences at the same level. From this perspective, the teacher should not interfere in the individual's stance towards the right to display particular manners at the table, nor should the teacher interfere in the students' stance regarding rape, torture or murder.

From the perspective of values education, assuming absolute neutrality is questionable. Nevertheless, building in class proper conditions for the clarification of the student's stance towards particular values, *by the student*, may be an important step towards a conscious morality. Besides, if the construction and reconstruction of morality can only be the work of the subject herself, minimum intervention by the teacher is a necessary requirement.

For those who advocate intervention, neutrality is neither acceptable nor possible. For them, teaching about moral issues is legitimate. People's values choices are many times not only a private concern. It is considered that since people's position towards values is significant for human development, it deserves the attention of the school, and the teacher should not only take a stance but also work to help the students orient themselves in the world of values[31]. It is generally assumed that such intervention is only possible if the teacher is a paradigm of the values that she defends. There is a consensus

---

[31] Bombino (1998) writes that education must help students learn to orient themselves freely and knowledgeably by a scale of values with the mediation of their consciousness as the highest norm of behavior.

among Cuban teachers and researchers that moral judgment regarding personal dignity and human progress is necessary, and that it is possible to educate people in that judgment.

A radical stance towards intervention may lead to inculcation, indoctrination and the imposition of dogmas[32]. Considered acceptable by many[33], inculcation implies that self-evaluation is a process in which the student *has to* identify with and accept a set of moral norms that must be incorporated into her values system. This concept has received much criticism.

"When education is construed as the process of inculcating habits—which is to say, unreflective actions—then it scarcely deserves to be called education at all. It is really, as Alan Lockwood says, an attempt to get "mindless conformity to externally imposed standards of conduct." (Kohn, 1997)

In the belief that the teacher will always preach for moral good and that she is always better informed as to what is correct it is not exceptional that the formative effort trespasses into the land of dogmatism.

(This article was taken from the book Beyond Poetry: Experiences in Values Education, written by Manuel de Jesús Velázquez León, Órgano Editor Educación Cubana. Dirección de Ciencia y Técnica – MINED. ISBN: 978-959-18-0353-5)

Bibliography

Aptheker, H. *The American Revolution*. New York: International Publishers, 1954.

Arés Muzio, P. "Familia, ética y valores en la realidad cubana actual". *Temas*. No. 15, julio-septiembre de 1998. Nueva Época. Ciudad de la Habana, 1998.

Autores varios. *Educar en valores: diez tesis en forma de dudas*. Seminari Permanent d'Educació per a la Pau de Badalona CD-ROM "25 años contigo." Ihardun Multimedia. Barcelona, 1999.

Batista Rodríguez, A. *Propuesta Pedagógicas para el trabajo con los valores dignidad nacional e identidad nacional en el Instituto Superior Pedagógico*. Tesis de Master en Ciencias Pedagógicas. Holguín, 2001.

---

[32] Cortina defines "dogma" as an assertion or prescription that insulates itself from rational criticism, and whose veracity or validity rests upon authority, evidence, the immediate connection to feelings and traditions, or upon its metaphorical character (Cortina, 1990)

[33] In school practice, terms like "to inculcate values", "to plant values" and the like are common. They can also be frequently heard in symposia devoted to education in values. In these spaces, those terms are not metaphors; they are used with their literal meaning.

Baxter Pérez, E. "Un estudio exploratorio acerca de la formación de valores. Instituto Central de Ciencias Pedagógicas." Ponencia presentada al simposio internacional Pedagogía 1999. Ciudad de la Habana, 1999.

Berkowitz, M. W. Ph.D. *The education of the complete moral person* www.http:tigger.uic.edu.elnucci.MoralEd.practices.findex.html, 1998.

Blanco, J. A. "Ética y civilización: apuntes para el tercer milenio". *Temas*. No. 15, julio-septiembre de 1998. Nueva Época. Ciudad de la Habana, 1998.

Cortina, A. "La educación del hombre y del ciudadano." en *Educación, valores y Democracia*, Organización de Estados Iberoamericanos para la Educación, la Ciencia y la Cultura: OEI, pp. 49-74. Madrid, 1998.

Cruz, M. *El hombre Martí*. Centro de Estudios Martianos. La Habana, 2007.

Daudinot Betancourt, I. M. *Perspectivas psicopedagógicas acerca de la inteligencia: la creatividad y los valores*. Editorial Chong, Lima, Perú, 2003.

Domènechi Francesch, J. *Educación en valores*. Federación de MRPs de Catalunya. CD-ROM "25 años contigo." Ihardun Multimedia. Barcelona, 1999.

Domínguez Rodríguez, W. L. *Actividades pedagógicas para la escuela primaria mediante las potencialidades axiológicas de la obra martiana*. Ponencia presentada al simposio Pedagogía 2007. Ciudad de la Habana, 2007.

Domínguez, M. I. "La formación de valores en la Cuba de los años 90: un enfoque social" *La formación de valores en las nuevas generaciones: una campaña de espiritualidad y conciencia*. Editorial de Ciencias sociales. Ciudad de la Habana, 1996.

Donoghue, D. *Connosseurs of Chaos. Ideas of Order in Modern American Poetry*. Columbian University Press. New York, 1986.

Fabelo Corzo, J. R. "Mercado y valores humanos". *Temas*. No. 15, julio-septiembre de 1998. Nueva Época. Ciudad de la Habana, 1998.

Fabelo Corzo, J. R. La "Crisis de valores: conocimiento, causas y estrategias de superación." *La formación de valores en las nuevas generaciones: una campaña de espiritualidad y conciencia*. Editorial de Ciencias Sociales. Ciudad de la Habana, 1996.

Fabelo Corzo, J. R. *Los valores y sus desafíos actuales*. Editorial José Martí. Ciudad de la Habana, 2003.

Fabelo Corzo, J. R. *Práctica, conocimiento y valoración*. Ciudad de la Habana. Editorial de Ciencias Sociales, 1989.

García Batista, G (Ed.) *Compendio de Pedagogía*. Editorial Pueblo y Educación. Ciudad de la Habana, 2002.

Geddes G. and P. Bruce (eds.) *15 Canadian Poets plus 5*. Oxford University Press. Toronto, 1978.

González Rey, F. "Los valores y su significación en el desarrollo de la persona". *Temas*. No. 15, julio-septiembre de 1998. Nueva Época. Ciudad de la Habana, 1998.

González Rey, F. "Un análisis psicológico de los valores: su lugar e importancia en el mundo subjetivo. *La formación de valores en las nuevas generaciones: una campaña de espiritualidad y conciencia*. Editorial de Ciencias Sociales. Ciudad de la Habana, 1989.

González Rey, F. and A. Mitjáns Martínez. *La personalidad su educación y desarrollo*. Editorial Pueblo y Educación. Ciudad de la Habana, 1996.

González Rey, F. *Comunicación Personalidad y Desarrollo*. Editorial Pueblo y Educación, Ciudad de la Habana, 1995.

González Rey, F. y H. Valdés Casal. *Psicología Humanista: Actualidad y desarrollo*. Editorial Ciencias Sociales. La Habana, 1994.

González Rodríguez, Y. *Una vía no convencional para potenciar los valores en los estudiantes de las carreras pedagógicas*. Tesis presentada en opción al grado científico de Doctor en Ciencias Pedagógicas. Instituto Superior Pedagógico José de la Luz y Caballero. Facultad de Ciencias Técnicas. Holguín, 2005.

Gutiérrez, C. "Etica y moral: teorías y principios". *Revista Parlamentaria*. Vol. 5. No. 2. Agosto, 1997. pp 49-63.

Kohlberg, L., & Turiel, E. "Moral development and moral education." En G. Lesser (Ed.), *Psychology and educational practice*. Chicago, 1971. (Citado por Nucci, 2000).

Kohlberg, L., and D. Candec "The Relationship of Moral Judgement to Moral Action," en Rurtines W. L. y J. L. Gewirtz (Eds.). *Morality, Moral Behavior and Moral Development*. New Jersey, Wiley, 1984. (Quoted by Berkowitz, 1998)

Kohn, A. "How Not to Teach Values: A Critical Look at Character Education". *Phi Delta Kappan*, Feburay 1997. p 429-439.

López Bombino, L. et al. *Ética marxista-leninista (t. I y II)* Departamento de Textos y Materiales Didácticos-Ministerio de Educación Superior. La Habana, 1985.

López Bombino, L. R. "El diálogo y la cultura del error en la formación de valores". *Temas*. No. 15, julio-septiembre de 1998. Nueva Época. Ciudad de la Habana, 1998.

Luria, A. R. "La Actividad consciente del hombre y sus raíces históricas". *Psicología General* (Dávila, Z. B. and J. C. C. Fernández, eds.) Editorial Félix Varela. La Habana, 2005.

Martí Pérez, J. *Obras Completas*. Ed: Ciencias Sociales, La Habana, 1975.

Mayo Parra, I. *La relación personalidad - sujeto: Una perspectiva psicológica de la problemática de la formación de valores*. Holguín: Ponencia para el simposio internacional Pedagogía 2001.

Nucci L. *Moral Development and Moral Education: An Overview* http://www.uic.edu/~lnucci/MoralEd/copyright.html, 2005.

Nucci, L. "The Personal Domain". (Excerpt from: Reed, Turiel, & Brown (Eds.). *Values and knowledge*. http://wwwuic.edu.~lnnuci/MoralEd/copyright.html,1997

Nucci, L. *The Promise and Limitations of the Moral Self Construct*. Ponencia de aperture al encuentro 30 de la Jean Piaget Society: Society for the Study of Knowledge and Development, Montreal, Canada, June 3, 2000.

Nussbaum, M. "Great philosophers: Martha Nussbaum on Aristotle." *BBC Education and Training*, Jill Dawson (producer). Princeton, N.J: Films for Humanities & Sciences, 1997. (Citado por Turiel, 2007)

Pérez Sarduy, Y. y M. Velázquez León. (2001) *Programa de la Disciplina Historia de la Cultura de los Pueblos de Habla Inglesa*. MINED.

Permanent d'Educació per a la Pau de Badalona *CD-ROM "25 años contigo."* Ihardun Multimedia. Barcelona, 1999.

Rodríguez Ugidos, Z. *Filosofía, ciencia y valor*. Editorial Ciencias Sociales, Ciudad de la Habana, 1985.

Rodríguez Ugidos, Z. *Obras Tomo II*. Editorial Ciencias Sociales, Ciudad de la Habana, 1989.

Velázquez León, M. A *Sheaf of Poetry: for the Students*. Biblioteca CD-ROM de los estudiantes. Ciudad de la Habana, 2003.

Velázquez León, M. *A Sheaf of Poetry: for the Teachers*. Biblioteca CD-ROM de los estudiantes. Ciudad de la Habana, 2003.

Velázquez León, M. *Beyond Poetry: Experiences in Values Education*. Editorial Educación Cubana. Ciudad de la Habana, 2008)

Velázquez León, M. *Chosen Short Stories*. Biblioteca CD-ROM de los estudiantes. Ciudad de la Habana, 2003.

Velázquez León, M., et al. *A Textbook on the History of the United States up to World War I*. Editorial Pueblo y Educación. Ciudad de la Habana, 1989.

VIII Seminario nacional para educadores. Curso escolar 2007-2008. Editorial Pueblo y Educación. Ciudad de la Habana, 2007.

Vitier, C. *Ese sol del mundo moral*. Ediciones Unión. Ciudad de la Habana, 2002.

Vygotsky L. S. http://www.orientared.com/articulos/vygotsky.php

Yurén Camarena, M. T. (2005) *Sujeto de la Eticidad y Formación Valoral*. http://educacion.jalisco.gob.mx/consulta/educar/dirrseed.html

Yurén Camarena, M. T. *Eticidad, valores sociales y educación*, Universidad Pedagógica Nacional, México, 1995.

Zinn, H. *A People's History of the United States 1492- Present*. Harper Perennial. New York, 1995.

Promoting Reading:
The Formative Role of University Libraries

MSc Marianela Juana Rabell López. Assistant Professor
MSc Ernesto Galbán Peramo. Associate Professor
MSc Anabel La O Bacallao. Assistant Professor

The Ministry of Higher Education (MES) in Cuba has conceived a kind of university characterized by the formation of values and quality processes in order to graduate skilled professionals.

One of libraries´ milestones today is their innovative character, wide participation in scientific-technical improvement of tasks, human development, social culture, as well as their role in contributing to quality teaching, research and extra-curricular activities. Taking into account that there are still mistaken notions about university libraries being just entities in charge of providing information and bibliographical support to the teaching process, compiling researchers´ scientific production, among other functions, the present paper aims at presenting experiences that Holguin University Library "Miguel de Cervantes Saavedra" has gathered and applied since it opened its doors to the public.

A library is by definition a vital space in the promotion of reading. This practice is supported by solid work conceived, organized and implemented through a group of reading-promotion activities, alongside cultural and scientific formation offered to attain higher goals set by society in the formative map of our professionals. The systematization of these experiences resulted in their application in other university libraries, which quantitatively and qualitatively improved their management and sociocultural promotion.

This era we are living in is full of challenges, information and knowledge which are important resources for development in any field. Universities are strategic institutions for society. The university library, an essential element as an information-leading-and-managing center has to redesign both its functions and improve its management processes, particularly those promoting its activities, products and services.

The Cuban university librarian, one of the most important supporting agents of the teaching-learning process, is aware of these challenges which make him/her perform their functions more efficiently. The library is conceived as a learning-resource center at the service of students, teachers and researchers, closely related to the university syllabi. On the one hand, the library is intended, as a cultural university center, to be the core source for professional training, research and extra-curricular on-campus and community activities. On other hand, the university library has been defined as:

Center for learning, teaching, research and activities related to the running and management of the universities. It treasures bibliographical, documentary, audiovisual and digital collections gathered by the different departments, centers and services, through varied acquisition channels, including endowments and donations from other institutions. That is why the library must be in line with the current transformations within the university and society, and at the same time integrate them into its development, management and services. However, even when new concepts are added, its main objective must not be forgotten, the one accompanying libraries since they opened for community service: the promotion of reading.

The University of Holguin has stated within its strategies, key-result areas and objectives the training of a competent professional. Similarly, it aims at positively impacting integrated-university processes related to local economy and social development. Therefore, students must read more, no matter the format they access or the type of literature, as long as they learn, are informed, educated and grow as individuals with a social role.

In order to contribute this this purpose the University library revisits its working objectives and searches for new and more efficient initiatives in relation to cultural and scientific formation of the academic community, in a world where the young depend on technology more every day. Magán (2002) stated in his *Temas de biblioteconomía universitaria y general*:
"Rethinking the library not only means rethinking its service, model and management methods: it means rethinking the ethics commitment which is sustaining and leading it... Humanizing the library is a task that we must prioritize, since technological advances are of no use if they have no counterpart in the human being´s improvement... Not forgetting our mission is the only way to achieve our objectives."

Libraries are irreplaceable social spaces for reading, recreation, constant learning, research and open access to information that supports comprehensive human being formation. They are also a space for integration within the university. It offers cultural and scientific options for both students and teachers. At the same time it promotes scientific results and technology innovation, preserves heritage collections, widens the interaction spaces and cultural expansion, stimulates and promotes reading. It is so because the university library, besides developing institutional repositories, develops information products, manages knowledge production and it is a resource center for teaching and research; it also fosters activities aimed at supporting reading by the students in order to graduate a well-prepared professional able to transform his/her context. The library helps creating cultural assets, meets society´s demands and satisfies spiritual needs focused on social responsibility.

An educated lifestyle is needed, hence the necessity of activating a comprehensive orientation that prepares the human being to value his/her environment. Therefore, the librarian is one of the main changing agents when promoting reading habits in the university.

Promotion is usually understood as the resulting action of promoting, in other words, spreading. It helps people know. Every extra-curricular activity can also be identified as promotion, translated into the promotion of new products, values, and knowledge for a public that may have had no or little access to them. The main objective of promotion is spreading activities whose purpose is that people learn, enjoy, but mainly that they identify with topic and artistic expression in a participatory involvement.

Starting from the point that promotion is every promoting joint action, of giving a new motivation to an idea, product, company; it can be simultaneously understood as the purpose of spreading different activities in an specific area; then promotion complies with a number of actions spread through the media: written, visual, oral or artistic in its broadest sense.

Reading promotion is the set of actions (administrative, academic, financial, policy, social and cultural) that person, community, institution or nation develops in favor of reader formation and of the democratic access to reading. This is understood as a system of adequately planned activities in which librarian-reader-book are integrated. Every reading promotion action has to motivate reading, text interaction and critical reading.

As the promotion of reading must be an on-going process, the library staff plan and carry out activities every month taking into account literary, historical and scientific anniversaries; events held within the university; Honorary and Specialized speeches; books published by the university teachers; awards for professional achievement; cultural and scientific events (the International Book Fair, Iberian-American Culture Festival; The University Book and Reading Festival; Culture Week, among others, led the different University Faculties. Among these activities the following can be mentioned:
- Poetry reading
- Books and movies discussions
- Books and plastic art exhibitions
- Book presentations
- Conferences
- Readers and writers meetings
- Dramatizations
- Talks
- Commented readings

- Guided reading
- Literary clubs: *Escuela de la Décima Holguinera* and *Peña MotivArte* (here Cuba-Canada-Literary-Alliance writers have been promoted)
- *Ediciones Holguín en la Universidad* (*Exchange space for local authors and texts*)
- Reader clubs: here teachers, students, and workers in general are invited, as well as readers from the community
- Presentation of digital products: *Boletín de Nuevas Adquisiciones* and *Boletín Científico*

These activities of reading promotion are developed in different places at the university; however, most of them are held at the library entrance. It has a vantage position as students, professors and workers frequently meet there. This place facilitates spontaneous participation of persons passing by. Besides, it is the first user contact with the library. Such activities are aimed at all groups within the university.

Every single one activity is organized to stimulate reading in different formats, and at the same time to contribute to spiritual growth and professional improvement of students, teachers, and workers in general. This has turned the library into a referential, documentary and information center supporting teaching, research and extra-curricular pursuits, mainly the promotion of reading.

Its principal contribution lies in sharing reading habits, guiding students about what texts to read, favoring their aesthetic education, encouraging scientific research through the consultation of diverse information sources, motivating readers towards a constant, reflexive and critical approach to reading.

Conclusions
Libraries are highly contributive to reading, not only within the university, but also beyond campus. Ideas are presented on the role played by these entities regarding reading promotion. This experience has been applied in other university libraries with positive quality results in not only the teaching process, but also in research and extra-curricular ones. If the results presented here are generalized to other information centers, highers goals can be achieved within new research and teaching projects.

References
Decreto-Ley No. 271. (2010). De las bibliotecas de la República de Cuba. En *Gaceta Oficial No. 030* Ordinaria de 10 de agosto de 2010.

González, T., Alfonso, M., Castellanos, L., Ferrer, M. A., Rabell, M. J., Macías, N. P. González, K. (2013). *Proposiciones para la lectura desde la biblioteca escolar*. La Habana: Pueblo y Educación. ISBN: 978-959-13-2662-1

Magán Walls, J. A. (2002). *Temas de biblioteconomía universitaria y general*. Madrid: Editorial Complutense.

Rodríguez, A. O. (1999). *Por una escuela que lea y escriba. Taller de talleres*. Colombia.

Fostering Teacher Educational Guidance through Reading

PhD María Elena Ayala Ruiz. Full Professor
MSc Katiuska Ceballos Bauta. Associate Professor
MSc Miguel Ángel Olivé Iglesias. Associate Professor

In Cuba, efforts are aimed at increasing the quality of education towards the integral formation of current and new generations. In this context, Cuban higher education goes through deep transformations. These imply substantial changes defining the management of the teaching-learning process. It is necessary to provide good academic, professional and scientific education for college professionals.

Consequently, today's University fosters an alternative, active, developmental education supported by a pedagogical conception of diversity and equity. It presupposes educative, systemic, continuous and permanent processes where the lesson is the main organizational form, as it is considered the pedagogical stage with greater possibilities for organizing and systematizing teaching objectives. It is in the lesson where the appropriation of contents and skills takes place, together with values formation and students' cognitive and professional interests.

From this perspective, professionals in the educational area are responsible for joining efforts and facilitating the participation of all social agents to successfully accomplish the corresponding educative task. In it, which actions are to be channeled towards collective use of all educative influences. This will guarantee integration in cooperative and collaborative relations in the pedagogical process, accompanied by interaction with family and community.

Within the previous frame of reference, the primacy of educational guidance in school should be highlighted, due to its essential role in professional formation. Such guidance acquires a higher significance in a holistic approach to the teaching-learning process. Here, an overall analysis of learning is possible: new levels of relations among its components emerge, as elements of a system that allows a holistic understanding of the process, educationally and instructionally. Studies about educational guidance are diverse. This indicates its pertinence in the educational context: Puentes (1992); Calviño (1996); Collazo y Suárez (1999); Recarey (2000); Díaz (2001); Bisquerra (2001 - 2005); Repetto (2001 - 2006); González (2005 – 2006 - 2007); Molina (2005); Cubela (2005); C J. L. del Pino (2006); Pérez, R (2012), García, M. I. (2013), among others. They, from the orientation practice, point out theoretical aspects, which can be considered the foundation of the Cuban educational community.

They all structure the teacher educational guidance as a way of relating instruction and education, channeled into prevention through the integration of different performance contexts. Besides, they conceive this guidance as a scientific activity that defines and implements how to help someone in a given space and in a specific moment. Such notion will provide further personal growth, according to the level of development, within a specific social and personal situation.

The authors assume the role of the teacher educational guidance based on the *integrative trend*. It plays a role within the teaching-learning process: a dynamic element that revitalizes instruction and education, and potentiates the students' personality resources for a communicative and developmental learning.

The Teacher Education English Major at the University of Holguin assumes the requirements listed by the Professional Profile for the Pedagogical Sciences Area. It focuses on the development of communicative competence in all its dimensions. These include habit formation, the development of critical and reflexive thought, and other resources that permit the configuration of competent and independent professionals who love what they do and develop values and creative qualities, according to social demands. The concern about this objective demands analysis on a methodological conception of the lesson that goes beyond the cognitive aspect of teaching.

In this sense, a revision of the types of lessons in the teaching-learning process of English as a foreign language, rendered that the reading lesson is given priority, for its role in integrating the other language skills as indispensable tools for the students' profession. Likewise, reading is considered for its great formative potentialities and its possibilities for favoring cognitive-affective processes that facilitate the development of thought, memory, emotions, feelings, imagination and universal values.

Contemporary studies have given great importance to reading: Goodman, K. (1982); Carbonell, M. (1989); Dubois, M. E. (1986); Parra, M. (1999); Mañalich R. (1999); Ayala Ruiz, M. E. (2000-2008-2016); Romeu, A. (2002); Montano, J. R y Arias G. (2002); Sales, L M., (2004); Rodríguez, L. (2004); Brere, M. (2006); Martínez, M. (2007); Lobaina, N. (2008), Barrera, AD. (2009); Cansigno, Y. (2010); Estévez, I. R. (2011); Muñoz, E. M. et.al 2013; Forman, R. (2014).

They have approached the theme from different perspectives that expose new ways for teaching to read since the early years in curricular study map. They also reveal a new idea about the reading process. It has profound implications for a didactic approach that should deal with active and complex processes in which the final goal is to form an active and independent reader

Huge efforts are made to improve the reading teaching-learning process and take advantage of the potentialities of this type of lesson for a systemic and systematic teacher educational guidance. However, there are still limitations in the methodological and theoretical conceptions assumed by the teaching staff. These affect the outlining of actions and techniques that promote educational guidance through reading, in its own teaching-learning process.

The authors' experience, their participation in class observations and methodological sessions, as well as the application of scientific methods and techniques allow them to reveal the following:
  ✓ Lack of a set of actions in the planning of reading lessons to foster educational guidance.
  ✓ Students' poor participation in text selection that affects their motivation for reading with a purpose and the use of its potentialities to favor educational guidance.
  ✓ Poor variety of reading exercises and tasks, which promotes students' leading role in their assumptions before problem-solving situations close to their personal experiences.
  ✓ Predominance of activities going only as far as the critical level of text comprehension.
  ✓ Insufficient use of reading exercises and tasks for skill integration.

These limitations allowed the identification of a scientific problem: How to favor educational guidance in the reading teaching-learning process in the Integrated English Practice discipline; and the objective has been declared as the elaboration of an educational orientation strategy to be implemented when teaching reading in the Teacher Education English Major at the University of Holguin.

Educational guidance should be a guided process along the students' academic life, not only restricted to specific situations at the end of a stage. This will allow the students' decision-making process to come from their real needs and not from a personal wish in a given moment. It is a process of assisting the individual student to reach optimum educational development. It helps students to make right choices, as well as to make adjustments in relation to schools, curriculum, courses and school life.

Guidance aims at educating individuals to understand themselves, unfolding potentialities to their maximum expression, so that they may eventually prove themselves adjusted and practical members of a community. Guidance, therefore, is a significant educational procedure. Well-planned educational guidance helps and prepares students in making appropriate decisions. This requires a well-organized and accessible syllabus at each level of education.[34]

When dealing with educational guidance, there are conceptions to be taken into account:

- *Guidance is education in itself.* It aims at educating individuals to understand themselves, unfolding potentialities to their maximum expression, so that they may eventually prove themselves adjusted and practical members of a community.
- *Guidance is a process.* It enables individuals to discover themselves in the most satisfying and positive manner. It provides direction to enable them to exploit potentialities, abilities, interests and aptitudes.
- *Guidance is a continuous and dynamic process* in which an individual understands him/herself, learns to use his/her own capacities, interests and other abilities.
- *Guidance is life-related.* The process of guidance is related to life, its problems and challenges and how to face them. Problems and challenges are the building blocks of our personality.
- *Guidance is individual-centered.* The focus of all guidance is the individual who needs to manage him/herself by a healthy alignment of individual desires and aspirations with socially desirable aims.
- *Preparation for the future.* The guidance process is helpful in preparing a person for his future. *Guidance is based on individual differences.* Individual differences or, the fact that individuals differ significantly, forms the basis of guidance.

The strategy proposed is characterized by being:

- *Systemic:* the actions cover different stages, integrating forms and levels, which are interrelated.
- *Systematic:* centered on the different methodological levels: discipline, subject, teaching staff.
- *Interactive:* the relations established between professors and students and among them in the design and implementation of the methodological work to favor educational guidance.
- *Flexible:* it moves from an exploration phase that determines the actions to promote educational guidance according to the potentialities and necessities of the context where the strategy is implemented, so they can be regulated and improved.

---

[34] Ashish K. 2012. *Role of Guidance and Counseling at University Level*. ISSN (Print): 2249-7374.
Website: http://www.tspmt.com

Contextualized: because it is devised taking into account the historical context, where the reading teaching-learning process takes place.

Communicative and developmental: the Communicative and the Developmental Approaches are assumed as generators of the actions for guiding the Reading teaching-learning process.

Professionally approached: the conception and determination of the actions for educational guidance should favor the students' performance, in accordance with their future profession, as teachers of English.

The strategy takes into account distinctive procedures and techniques for educational guidance:[35]

Group reflection: through discussion of the selected content, departing from the students' diagnosis. The application of these techniques should be previously designed to enhance the students' participation and motivation.

Reinforcement: to make the students conscious about their potentialities and possibilities for solving problems, self-evaluating them and increasing their self- esteem.

Dialogue: for socializing experiences, knowledge, emotions, values and problem-solving solutions.

Support: it means to use the word that transmits emotions, trust, and confidence, sympathies for guiding the students to a higher level of development.

Persuasion: centered on the students' reflexive system and their reasonableness that may propitiate controversy, line of argument and meditation.

Other relevant references to model the strategy were taken into account:[36]

Knowledge and personality stimulation

Educational guidance should foster the students' personalities in their own contexts.

Guidance integrity

Its coherence and objectivity are basic conditions for this process. It refers to its integration, systematization, its systemic and holistic character.

---

[35]Ortiz, O.L. (2013). La orientación educativa para la formación de habilidades sociales en adolescentes de Secundaria Básica. UhO. Holguín.

[36]García, Aurora. (2001). Programa de orientación familiar para la educación de la sexualidad de adolescentes. ISPH José de la Luz y Caballero, Holguín.

Participation

The student is the center of the guidance process, since it departs from his/her necessities, knowledge and potentialities.

Participation has to be seen in all its dimensions, assuming how diverse is the group of teachers and students in the classroom and beyond the classroom.

Communication enrichment

Orientation should facilitate meeting people so they can interchange, identify and overcome barriers, in such a way that they can develop feelings of acceptance for living together, as well as satisfaction and interpersonal relations in and out of the group.

The strategy is aimed at getting the necessary changes to guarantee the teacher's training for developing educational guidance at the service of a competent reader's formation as a result of his/her methodological actions.

The objective of the proposal is the implementation of educational orientation actions, which are conceived for the reading process. These will potentiate the students' integral formation. It includes three phases:

PHASE I. EXPLORATION AND IDENTIFICATION

This stage is assumed as a process to search for basic information for preparing teachers to introduce educational guidance in the reading lesson. The objective is to know, analyze and value the educational guidance state and the students' reading level of development. It is also necessary to identify strengths and weaknesses to implement the proposal.

The diagnosis should be developed taking into account all the dimensions of the reading process: linguistic, discursive, strategic, sociocultural, cognitive and affective. Its point of departure lies in the characteristics of the context where the teaching-leaning process occurs.

The phase also expects to sensitize teachers on the need to implement educational guidance to foster reading. It creates the necessary conditions for preparing the teaching staff to assume the teacher educational guidance in the reading comprehension lesson.

PHASE II. PRECISION AND INTERVENTION

In this phase all the conditions for implementing the proposal are ensured. The methodology is carried out through workshops, demonstration lessons (teaching a regular lesson, with a specific didactic-cognitive aim, for students and guest teachers. After the lesson, guest teachers and the teacher meet for discussion of what was done in class) and open lessons (teaching a regular lesson for students and guest teachers where the teacher in charge presents a didactic-cognitive aims and develops it. After the lesson, they meet without the students for discussion. The difference is that guest teachers are less experienced ones, who will be receiving a special training).

For guiding the reading teaching-learning process, it is necessary to conceive different forms that benefit integrated and developmental reading tasks to favor educational guidance. They should be devised according to a systemic organization and integration. Besides, they ought to be varied and sufficient, contextualized and flexible, according to the students' individual needs. In this sense, it is recommendable:

To foster group work.

To explore additional sources.

To generate different opinions about the text.

To assume reflexive and critical attitudes.

To analyze, judge and value the information.

To transfer the information into the students' context.

To debate the text content.

To generate questions about the text.

To strengthen self-esteem, and reading problem activities.

To apply group strategies and techniques such as:

MORAL DILEMMAS: it is a moral education technique, consisting in brief narrations about conflict situations in which the students have to select from different solutions.

UNFINISHED PHRASES: it is a technique that permits students to become aware of values and options each person has for guiding his/her life, using the theme presented in the text.

COOPERATIVE GAMES: it is a useful technique for solving reading tasks. Games promote group cooperation and collaboration, in which success and failure are always collective.

CONFLICT SOLUTIONS: it is a technique that takes advantage of daily controversial situations faced by the students while working with the text.

PHASE III: ASSESSMENT

This phase determines the accomplishment of the objectives. It allows systematic evaluation on educational guidance contents, and proves the effectiveness of the methods applied. At the same time, it permits to reorient the guidance processes in the teaching-learning process of reading.

The flexible character of the strategy allows its contextualization and regulation based on the participants' own realities. Its application consists of different moments which coincide with the different levels of the methodologies followed.

Different workshops are implemented with the following conceptions:

Workshops for exchanging results in the different organizational levels of the methodologies used.

Workshops for defining and redefining methodological actions for implementing educational guidance in the reading comprehension lesson.

Workshops for socializing and making methodological decisions about agreements and precisions.

Workshops for presenting the subject´s strategy to insert educational guidance in the teaching-learning process of reading in the foreign language.

Methodological and theoretical conceptions on educational guidance and its implementation within the English lesson are not sufficiently considered in the foreign language area when teaching reading. It affects motivation towards reading and consequently the students' integral education.

Studies reveal that the texts selected by the teacher do not always offer the necessary potentialities to foster educational guidance in the reading lesson. It influences the students' interests and the development of strategies that promote contextualized meanings, which may activate different points of view about daily problems and their solution.

Educational guidance, viewed as a teacher's role in the reading comprehension lesson, is an essential element to optimize the future professionals´ formative potentialities, together with their communicative and methodological competence for the management of the teaching-learning process. Within it, reading occupies a relevant position.

Bibliographic analysis allowed the authors to assume that reading is an indispensable resource for learning in all content areas. It reinforces values formation, attitudes, aspirations, as well as other skills that activate thinking skills.

Bibliography
Ashish K. & Ranjana, G. (2012). *Role of Guidance and Counseling at University Level*. ISSN (Print): 2249-7374. Website: http://www.tspmt.com.
Cohen, M. (2007) *Guidance and Counseling Education Tool.* London, Mc Raw Hill
Cordard (1998) *Life of Guidance and Counseling in a Society*, New York, USA.
Cuenca, Y. (2010). *Orientación Educativa a estudiantes de carreras pedagógicas para el desarrollo de proyectos de vida*. Tesis presentada en opción al grado académico de Doctor en Ciencias Pedagógica. UCP. ¨José de la Luz y Caballero¨, Holguín.
Del Pino, J, & Recarey, S. (2011). *La orientación educacional y la facilitación del desarrollo desde el rol profesional del maestro*. En *Orientación educativa*. La Habana: Pueblo y Educación.
Estévez, I. R. (2011). *Estrategias de aprendizaje para la comprensión lectora en inglés para estudiantes de primer año de medicina*. Gaceta Médica Espirituana.
Gainza, M. (2016). *La orientación educativa como recurso de asistencia para el perfeccionamiento del aprendizaje en la educación preuniversitaria*. In Revista Opuntia Brava: Didáctica y Educación, I Vol. 15, No. 2, de 2016 con ISSN: 2222-081X. RNPS: 2074.
García Gutiérrez, Aurora. (2001). Programa de orientación familiar para la educación de

la sexualidad de adolescentes. Tesis presentada en opción al grado de doctor en Ciencias Pedagógicas. ISPH "José de la Luz y Caballero", Holguín.

Hooley T. (2015). *What Role Should Teachers Play in Career Guidance*. University of Derby.

Leyva, E. (2012). *Concepción de orientación familiar para contribuir a la motivación hacia la lectura, en adolescentes de Secundaria Básica*. Tesis presentada en opción al grado científico de Doctor en Ciencias Pedagógicas.

Morón et al. (2016). *The Importance of Educational Guidance at Every Stage of the Education System*. C. Universidad Politécnica de Madrid. Spain. ISBN: 978-84-608-5617-7 ISSN: 2340-1079 doi: 10.21125/inted.2016.1154.

Opfer, V. D. et al. (2010). *The Role of Teachers' Orientation to Learning in Professional Development and Teacher Education* doi: 10.1016/j.tate.2010.09.014

Ortiz, O.L. (2013). *La orientación educativa para la formación de habilidades sociales en adolescentes de Secundaria Básica*. UhO. Holguín.

Gallicisms in English: Establishing a Link to Teach Comprehensive Culture and Richer Vocabulary

PhD Pedro Antonio Machín Armas. Full Professor
BEd Yennier Greenhauff Desdín
PhD María Elena Ayala Ruiz. Full Professor

Students who graduate from the English Language Teacher Education Major at the University of Holguin are employed by different educational institutions. Among them, technical-professional schools where students are trained for occupational services such as the gastronomical services, and national and international cuisine for the Tourist Sector. In these specialties, English is taught for specific occupational purposes (EOP).

Through the consideration of the lacks and needs of English language teachers in service, it was determined that their lexical competence to teach EOP in certain semantic areas is limited, so they have difficulty in meeting the demands of the syllabuses they teach. Further empirical study with the use of observation, interview and tests applied to pre-service students in the major, revealed more difficulties: not only had they limitations in the lexical choice of specialized terminology, but they lacked a comprehensive culture in relation to areas such as food and beverages service, international cuisine, literature and arts (ballet and decorative arts).

It was also noticed that teachers in preparation had very little knowledge about linguistic phenomena related to Gallicisms in English, their meanings, spelling and pronunciation; and the links with universal culture. When interviewing teacher educators on these issues, they recognized that usually, little attention is paid to the teaching of these complex lexical items and specialized vocabulary. The complexities involve distinctive linguistic features giving an alien appearance to the lexical units because of their French origin. Therefore, there is an avoidance tendency by teachers and learners.

The research work is intended to prepare pre-service teachers for their future jobs, favoring the learning of the previously mentioned complex lexical units, as well as the adaptation and creation of linguistic materials to contextualize them. As a tangible result, a booklet containing attractive and useful texts for listening and reading with their corresponding activities was created. It has been used as an important tool to achieve the desired goal. The solution of the problem in this research work contributes to the linguistic, communicative, cultural and intercultural preparation of students who are trained to be English language teachers.

The authors reviewed the theory on barbarisms, foreignisms and particularly on Gallicisms in order to reveal a distinction among these classifications of lexical items in English and establish basic concepts to teach. Obviously, Gallicisms are words that come from French, some of which have been accepted and are part and parcel of the English lexicon and appear in dictionaries (barbarisms), Galperin, I. R. (1981); and others which have been imported and are used for stylistic and literary purposes in many important literary works (foreignisms).

The study of the bibliography allowed the systematization of essential theoretical elements related to the teaching and learning of lexical items. Among the authors who have done research in this area, one can mention: Corder, S. P. (1981, 1983); Galperin, I. R. (1981); Antich, R. (1987); Terroux, G. (1994); Ur, P. (2000); Acosta, R. (2009); Gass, S. y Selinker, L. (2008); Richards, J. (2010); Mijares, L. (2013); Medina, A. (2013); Machín, P. (2014, 2017); and Rizo, F. (2018). They have referred to methodological aspects that contribute to the processing of vocabulary (comprehension and production).

To support the solution of the problem from the pedagogical point of view, the authors carried out a systematization of the methodological procedures, enriched by developmental learning. The researchers particularly emphasized the socialization of learning strategies through the systematic use of reflection sessions in which the students exchange experiences, attitudes and procedures to retain the complex lexical units.

According to psycholinguistic studies, acquiring a vocabulary item for automaticity includes learning several aspects: meaning, phonological features, graphic and morphological characteristics, as well as collocation. The complex nature of Gallicisms underlies in their phonic and graphic nature which gives them an alien appearance that becomes a source of interference. The features they keep of the language from which they have been imported make them different from the regularities of English lexicon, thus their complexity.

In English, the number of lexical units which have French origin is high; this is estimated as a 28.3 % of the English lexicon. Therefore, it is a relevant issue in order to acquire the desired level of communicative competence for intercultural communication. The following examples illustrate how frequent English speakers and language users meet Gallicisms in their communication. In literature, if they read Dan Brown´ s *The Da Vinci Code*, they will find many the author purposefully use to achieve local color, create a particular effect or serve a special semantic function, for example: *déjà vu, monsieur, Musée du Louvre, façade, premiere, sangfroid, rendezvous, and parisienne*, among others.

In reading about ballet, language users may commonly find: *pas de deux (a dance performed by two dancers), la Fille mal garde, and Giselle (ballet masterworks), Ballet du Théâtre de l'Académie Royale de Musique, Grand Théâtre de Bordeaux (Famous institutions)*. In decorative arts*, Art Deco, facade* (from French *façade), Art Nouveau* and *Art Moderne (for New Art* and *Modern Art);* and international expositions such as *Exposition internationale des arts décoratifs et industriels modernes.*

In texts about universal history, one can find *bourgeois, memoir, regime, coup d'état, coup de grâce, aristocracy.* Some of these terms have been completely or partially naturalized while others keep their original characteristics, as it can be observed in the previous examples; i.e. the degree of assimilation may vary. Other frequent terms used in literary works involve: *repertoire, déjà vu, en passant, au revoir, laissez-faire, laissez-passer, and many others.* Gallicisms are barbarisms and foreignisms from French.

In the culinary arts, when eating at international food restaurants or specialized restaurants, costumers may usually find: *á la carte, cuisine, hors d'oeuvre, foie gras, croissant, crepes, ragout, omelette, vinaigrette, crème brûlée, mousse, among others;* and drinks *such as frappe, and crème de menthe.* Many French words have entered the English language throughout the years, since the Norman Conquest in 1066. Foreignisms, though used for certain stylistic purposes, do not belong to the English vocabulary. They are not registered by English dictionaries.

As an alternative for intervention and solution of the problem, the authors adapted and created materials supported by the principles of communicative language teaching. For devising them, the authors took into account the activation of cognitive processes and thinking through inductive-deductive procedures for discovery learning. The materials promote a contextualized and meaningful language practice of the complex lexical units through a variety of cultural topics of social significance, such as: arts (ballet, architecture, culinary recipes, and gastronomical services).

Methodology
The research was carried out with third-year students of the English Teacher Education Major. An initial diagnosis to determine their lacks and needs included the following instruments to collect information: observation, revision of lesson plans, interview of teacher educators and students, and vocabulary tests. Insufficiencies were found in relation to the poor treatment given by teachers (linguistic analysis, feedback and correction of the complex lexical units).

Teacher educators recognize the difficulties the students face to comprehend and produce Gallicisms and specialized lexicon, thus the need for teaching and making the learners practice them. The first action was to make teachers and students understand the importance of these lexical units for intercultural communication and the link with universal culture.

The researchers proceeded to select and adapt language materials that included the focused linguistic units in a range of cultural topics related to the arts and culinary services. The materials were carefully selected so that they were attractive and useful to learners. Different texts were adapted (audio-texts and reading texts) and systems of exercises created to focus the complexities. Though some of the activities centered on individual linguistic phenomena, general comprehension and oral and written processing of the information in the texts was also treated. This was done to ensure that the learning process had a transition to the development of habits and skills and favored lexical competence.

Out of the elaborated materials and exercises, a booklet to teach specialized lexicon was created. These activities were implemented to assess and validate their applicability and effectiveness. The suggested materials were submitted to assessment by experienced foreign language teachers in order to gather their opinions which were useful to improve the proposal. The authors applied the materials and exercises in the major's third-year group, and collected necessary evidence to assess the qualitative results. This also contributed to the improvement of the material.

For data collection, the authors used observation and checked the students' reaction. Also, group interview and reflection sessions were carried out based on pre-established indicators: students' acceptance of the material, motivation and interest, relevance of linguistic material, accessibility of materials, necessity of these contents for their future jobs and for their all-around culture, and contribution to their general cultural background.

In the chart below, a sample representation of material adapted and created is shown. It includes the titles of audio-texts, and a sample group of complex lexical units because of their semantic, morphological, and syntactic characteristics. Also, a set of procedures for the processing of lexical items is shown. They determine the corresponding exercises to be used.

The types of exercises comprise the following: 1) Analysis of the context in order to determine the meaning of lexical units 2) Identification of words in the text 3) Analysis of the morphological structure of the words to infer their meanings 4) Analysis of the syntactic structure of lexical phrases 5) Responding to questions formulated by the teacher educator 6) Looking up words in the dictionary 7) Reflecting about phonic, graphic and morphological features 8) Practicing the lexical items in context 9) Using the lexical items in communicative tasks 10) Reflection about their achievements and limitations.

Results

The implementation in practice of the materials and exercises allowed their validation through the transformations undergone by the third-year students. The application of empirical instruments (observation, interview, testing) favored the collection of data and the processing of information. The students:
1) Recognized their lacks in the initial state and the importance and need of the specialized and complex lexical units for their comprehensive culture and future job, 2) Manifested acceptance of the materials, exercises and implemented procedures, 3) Showed motivation and enthusiasm for learning the specialized vocabulary, and particularly the Gallicisms, 4) Were involved and interested in the implementation process, they asked questions and requested help when required, 5) Interacted actively in the solution of the exercises which moved through different levels of complexity, 6) Socialized experiences and learning strategies during the reflection sessions about their attitudes, procedures they used to retain the characteristic features of pronunciation and spelling in the complex lexical units, 7) Evidenced an enhancement in the development of their comprehensive culture as they were ready to talk about the treated topics with their future students, 8) Expressed that they would like to teach ESP courses in Technical and Professional Schools where the Culinary and Food Service Specialties are taught, and 9) Requested the inclusion of the materials and exercises in an Elective course or in any of the language practice subjects they have in the curriculum.

The application and triangulation of the results of the different empirical methods helped determine the lacks and limitations in the comprehension, pronunciation, spelling and use of specialized lexicon and specifically Gallicisms because of their learning complexities.

The use of theoretical research methods contributed to systematize the methodological aspects about the teaching and learning of lexical items in a foreign language, and essential pedagogical implications were synthesized for the linguistic treatment and practice of complex lexical units. This foundation helped in the adaptation of materials to achieve the intended purpose.

The implementation of the materials with third year students of the Major evinced their effectiveness and stimulated the motivation, interests and comprehensive culture of the students. Besides, the students´ linguistic awareness of these phenomena was developed, and the relevance for teaching English for specific occupational purposes in practice was estimated as valuable.

Bibliography

Corder, S. P. (1981). *Error Analysis and interlanguage*. London, UK: Oxford University Press.

Corder, S. P. (1983). *A role for the mother tongue in language learning.*

Galperin, I. R. (1981). *Stylistics.* Moscow, USSR: Vyssaja Skola.

Gass, S. and Selinker, L. (2008). *Second Language Acquisition. Theory and Practice.* Language Learning. S. Gass and L. Selinker (Eds.)

Machín, P. and Medina, A. (2014). *Desarrollo interlingüístico en la formación del profesional de la carrera pedagógica Lengua Extranjera Inglés.* Revista Luz. Edición 57. Año XIII. No. 3. Julio- Septiembre 2014. II Época. (Disponible en http://www.revistaluz.rimed.cu).

Medina, A. (2013). *Glossary: Improve your methodological technical register with more than 600 terms.* UCP "José de la Luz y Caballero", Holguín

Mijares N. y col. (2013*). Manual de Estrategias de Aprendizaje de Lenguas Extranjeras.* La Habana, Cuba: Editorial Pueblo y Educación.

Richards, J. y Schmidt, R. (2010). Longman Dictionary of Language Teaching and Applied Linguistics: Pearson Education Limited.

Richards, J. (1990). *Interchange I y II Workbook. English for International Communication.* London, UK: Cambridge University Press.

Rizo, F. (2018). *What Gallicisms are and why we use them.* https://www.noslangues-ourlanguages.gc.ca/en/blogue

Moral Education: The Vertex of Axiological Formation

MSc Miguel Ángel Olivé Iglesias. Associate Professor
BEd Jorge Alberto Pérez Hernández. Instructor
BA Alexei Rojas Riverón. Assistant Professor

The issue of values and values education is a number one prerogative in the agenda of social, academic and pedagogical thought within and beyond Cuban frontiers. Research has attempted to reveal the varied implications inherent in such categories, as they are part of a central component of humanity's existence and an unquestionable factor affecting human behavior.

Binaburo (1998:35) alerts us that: "Questa crisi, questo cambio di valori, si unisce alla crisi della post-modernitá: dell'economia, dell'ecologia, della politica, delle relazioni sociali e delle ideologie" ("This crisis, this values change, are part of the crisis of postmodern times: economic, ecological, political, social relations and ideology"). *(Translated by the editor)* Values have been deeply undermined in all spheres of life, therefore, their formation and safeguarding has turned into a priority issue in everty field.

International publications talk about their high concern for the problem of values education today: "La preocupación por los valores es algo latente en todos los sistemas educativos internacionales" ("A concern for values is felt in every international educational system"), and "Se advierte una preocupación generalizada por fomentar una postura ética de actuación" ("There is a noticeable general concern to encourage an ethical stance in behaving") (González, 1995:76). *(Both quotes translated by the editor)*. People´s moral and ethical position before crises sweeping across the world must ensure a return to mindfulness and respect for the survival of the human race.

An approach to the problem of values education is clear in Rojas *et al* (2002:54): "It is within the humanistic side of education where the axiological approach is promoted or integrated, which has been globally identified as education in values." *(Translated by the editor)*.The connection of these categories to many branches of science has made their understanding somehow tortuous to the layman. Obviously, a detailed itemization is necessary, setting up nexuses and systemic sinews in analytical and historic analyses that would provide the general reader with an explanation.

It jumps to the eye that education then has a role to play in the formation of the new generations. That is to say: «Éduquer c'est aussi apprendre à juger par soi-même, à rechercher la vérité, à critiquer, à faire évoluer et changer les règles, à modifier les traditions... L'éducation s'inscrit alors dans cette "brèche ouverte entre le passé et l'avenir", où se transmet la tradition et où en même temps se prépare l'exercice de la liberté» (Obin:?:9) ("To educate is also learning to judge by ourselves, to find the truth, to criticize, to make rules evolve and change, to modify traditions... Education is, therefore, that ´opening between the past and the future´ where tradition is passed on and where at the same time we prepare for the exercise of our liberties"). *(Translated by the editor)*

This paper addresses these matters and opinions by placing the problem of values education on the very vortex of a moral education that must accompany a righteous axiological formation.

Moral education encompasses two fundamental goals to be attained in the individual who receives it and the one who has the task of passing it on to other generations. An insightful knowledge of the elements of morality other more than the mere awareness of what is good and what is bad, what should be done and what should not, is implied in these two branches of the approximation to a moral education.

It is a need to *know* what moral education is, to be aware of the content of the moral values that are to be achieved. This is content formed in the individual´s experiential world: values are seen as the result of individual experience learned in situations and contradictions that the person undergoes in the process of socialization. (González Rey, 1998) But knowing is not enough to guarantee a proper education that is reflected in proper behavior. It is vital to favor ways of acting, of behaving, that stem from the adequate assimilation of moral standards not just because these have to be obeyed, but because such rules of moral and social character are part of the individual's system of convictions, he is aware of them, he knows their what and why and assumes the social regulations as his own.

This ideal is primordial in the fulfillment of any society. González Rey (1998) states that the logic of the development of social values is inseparable from the logic of the individual values, as all declared social values which are not part of the individual's system of values are cut off from practice, and become formal and empty with no sense for human behavior.

The concern for a proper activation and implementation of values education has been advocated in a variety of approaches through time, all embarked on the need of sensitizing the students towards the problem and leading them to develop a system of values that enables them to value, judge and act in life at a personal and social level:

Instilment. It is seen as the internalization of a standard or pre-established system of values through the notion that they are the ones the student must acquire. This process of internalization means that such standard values are to be taken in, not connoted according to each personality.

On this point, Camino Trapero (1993) says that values should not be instilled simply, but *formed* in the students' evaluative processes so that they create their own values hierarchies. She states that it is not enough to just *inculcate* something saying it must be done because it is good.

Moral Development. This approach exploits models of thought, stimulates debate among the students about the assumption of values and externalization of attitudes, so that such exchange leads to a transformation and progress of the system of values.

Some techniques employed here are the so-called moral dilemmas (hypothetical or real situations), and the externalization and defense of postures (the students assume certain attitudes that they must correlate with their verbalizations and deportment).

Analysis. Logical thinking is fostered here. The students approach problems of social significance at individual and group level and carry out discussions in class.

Clarification of Values. It encourages the identification of values and the awareness of one's and other people's values. Also, it favors the sharing of one's values with others and acting after one's own choices. Ways to achieve this are group discussions, dilemmas, interviews, simulations, and the steps to be followed can be choosing alternatives, electing freely and correctly, valuing the choices made, expressing the choice publicly, acting accordingly.

Learning by Acting. It encourages performing personally and socially according to one's values; shifting from thought and feeling to action. Values are fostered in the person-society interaction: interpersonal relations, action projects. The steps proposed here are: becoming aware of the problem, comprehending a problem and taking a stand, deciding on a course of action, planning strategies and stages for the action, reflecting on the actions, and considering consequences.

An analysis of this approach renders:

➢ Becoming aware of the problem: This is the first step towards the resolution of a problem, knowing what is wrong, what has to be changed.

➢ Comprehending a problem and taking a stand in respect to it: The understanding of a problem allows facing it with a more positive outlook, when a phenomenon is understood, an entirely different position towards it is adopted, and its different angles are considered.

➤ Deciding on a course of action: Such course of action implies a process resolution of a problem, what will bring about a change of perspective towards the object under analysis.

➤ Planning strategies and stages for the action: This part is a result of the previous one. The tasks proposed allow the organization of the work towards their fulfillment and the solution of the problem. This planning becomes steps that gradually lead to such solution.

➤ Reflecting on the actions and considering consequences: This moment is crucial for the affective commitment of the students as they are asked to reflect on what they have done, that is, a course of action has been charted, carried out and implemented. Now is the time for reflection and considerations, effected at group dimension. Values are formed in the process of socialization of the human being.

Thus, an axiological view of education opens a window overlooking the moral aspects that shape it. Moral education encompasses two fundamental goals to be attained in the individual who receives (student) it and the one who has the task of passing it on to other generations (teacher).

Knowing is not enough to guarantee a proper education that is reflected in proper behaviour. It is vital to favour ways of acting, of behaving, that stem from the adequate assimilation of moral standards not just because these have to be obeyed, but because such rules of moral and social character are part of the individual's platform of convictions. He or she is aware of them; they know what and why and assume social regulations as their own.

A discussion of values and values education cannot escape today's priorities at a historical, philosophical, social, psychological, or educational level. Such is the imperativeness of the issue that it becomes necessary to approach it and present it so that its essences are discernible and comprehensible to those in charge of implementing and materializing values, paving the way for a more conscious and coherent effort towards this goal.

The social role and responsibility of education in the matter – a task of society as a whole – must start with an adequate understanding of the categories from a theoretical point of view. On this ground, education must focus on the particular contexts in which professionals operate.

Bibliography
Baxter Pérez, Esther (1989) *La Formación de valores: una tarea pedagógica*. La Habana, Editorial Pueblo y Educación.

Camino Trapero, María (1993) *Valores que priorizan los docentes en su acción pedagógica y cómo son percibidos por sus alumnos: una experiencia investigación-acción*. Uruguay, Universidad Católica, Departamento de Educación e Investigación Educativa.

Colectivo de autores MINED (2000) *Aprendizaje y la formación de valores*. In Seminario Nacional para el Personal Docente. La Habana, Ministerio de Educación. (Tabloide).

Domínguez, María Isabel (1996) *La Formación de valores en la Cuba de los años 90: un enfoque social*. Ciudad de la Habana, Editorial de Ciencias Sociales.

Fabelo Corzo, José Ramón (1989) *Práctica, conocimiento y valoración*. La Habana, Editorial de Ciencias Sociales.

González Maura, Viviana (1995) *Psicología para educadores*. La Habana, Editorial Pueblo y Educación.

González Rey, Fernando (1985) *La Personalidad: su educación y desarrollo*. La Habana, Editorial Pueblo y Educación.

López Bombino, Luis R. *et al* (1985) *Ética marxista-leninista* (two volumes). MINED. La Habana.

MINED (1989) *Programa director de ética pedagógica para los Institutos Superiores Pedagógicos*. La Habana, Ministerio de Educación.

MINED (1998) *Orientaciones metodológicas para el desarrollo del programa dirigido a la formación de valores, la disciplina y la responsabilidad ciudadana, desde la escuela*. La Habana, Ministerio de Educación.

Olivé Iglesias, Miguel Ángel (2000) *Simulated Situations and Methodological Suggestions to Implement them in the Speaking Lesson of the Subject Integrated English Practice to Foster Values in the 4th-Year Students of the Major at the Teacher Training College of Holguín*. Tesis en opción el título académico de Máster en Ciencias pedagógicas. ISP Holguín.

Olivé Iglesias, Miguel Ángel (2014) *An X-ray Journey into Values Education Across the Subjects Integrated English Practice 7 and 8 of the Specialty at the University of Pedagogical Sciences of Holguin*. Article. UPS Holguin.

Olivé Iglesias, Miguel Ángel (2014) *Tipología de tareas para un enfoque axiológico de la clase de Práctica Integral del Inglés en la especialidad en la UCP Holguín*. Artículo. UCP Holguín.

Velázquez León, Manuel (2000) *Reflexiones sobre la disciplina Historia de la cultura de los países de habla inglesa desde la perspectiva de la educación valoral. Texto Didáctico*. Holguín, I.S.P. Holguín.

Velázquez León, Manuel (2010) *La educación valoral en la disciplina Historia de la cultura de los pueblos de habla inglesa*. Tesis en opción al título científico de Doctor en Ciencias Pedagógicas. Universidad de Ciencias Pedagógicas de Holguín.

Teaching English through Profession-Related Axiological Simulations for Students of the Teacher Education English Major of Holguin University

MSc Miguel Ángel Olivé Iglesias. Associate Professor
MSc Guillermo Ronda Velázquez. Associate Professor
PhD Jorge Ronda Pupo. Full Professor

A foreign language lesson focuses on the formation and development of skills that will guarantee the appropriate use of the language. But authors on the topic, and teachers, have always defended that notion that such lesson is also a context to pass on culture and educate the students. The topics proposed to them in class for speaking, reading, listening to or writing are in line with the idea that for the exchange of opinion, moral and ethical issues are usually hot items for classroom debates (Brown, 1994). Brown also provides a list of topics:

1. Women's Rights.
2. Choosing a Marriage Partner.
3. Cultural Taboos.
4. Economic Theories.
5. Political Candidates.
6. Abortion.
7. Crises.
8. War and Peace.

These topics nurture the awareness of the need to foster values in the lesson, which is in agreement with the contentions proposed by researcher and teachers. It has been stated that the classroom is the ideal setting to set the bases for the education of ethical attitudes and behavior. The classroom therefore turns into a place where students from a teacher education major discuss profession-related matters. The proposal made in this article exposes theoretical and practical ideas on this.

Why the profession-related axiological simulations (PRASS)

The elaboration and implementation of profession-related axiological simulations (PRASS) in the lessons to help foster values in the students is an alternative that will be discussed in this article. They were conceived to help foster values in teachers-to-be, exploiting the professional side of their lives and taking experiences from the real contexts where they carry out their practicum as part of their pre-service formation in a teacher-training major.

The simulations are called PRASS and modeled PRASS. A distinctive element is that the PRASS are directly taken from – even sometimes proposed by – the students´ actual contexts; while the modeled PRASS are simplified variants designed by the professor, who knows the characteristics of his/her students.

It has been contended elsewhere that a foreign language lesson is viable for values education. With the boost of communicative concepts in the teaching of foreign languages and the updated methodological conceptions on the matter, it has potential to carry out this type of education. An analysis of the principles of communication renders that the contextualization of the situations is a favoring factor: the tasks proposed respond to a thematic unity which allows focusing on their resolution.

Another aspect of communicative teaching is that the topics should be appealing, meaningful, that is, relating the students, to their own lives, to situations taken from emotionally close events that purport some relevant meaning according to their needs and hopes. Their experiences should be exploited for debate, reflection and a conscious assimilation of the contents. Simulation activities with situations taken from reality should be proposed.

The PRASS are mostly elaborated based on the realities faced by the students in their practice teaching, and on modeled situations prepared by the professor (modeled PRASS). However, this distribution is not a straightjacket. An axiological view of education opens a window overlooking the moral aspects that shape it. Moral education encompasses two fundamental goals to be attained in the individual (student) who receives it and the one who has the task of passing it on to other generations (teacher). Taking this standpoint into consideration, this item is devoted to the presentation of the PRASS to foster values in the students in class.

They are the result of years of endeavor taking as sources in the first place a study made of situations that are brought to the students in the so-called "meetings of reflection and debate". Secondly, the thirty-year experience of the author of this paper in practice teaching visits. This allowed gathering a wide variety of incidents, anecdotes, problems faced by the students in the schools. In the third place, the registering of the students' own experiences in their schools, told by themselves. This variety was then studied, decanted and organized to create thematic units that contain different yet related situations to be brought up in class.

Defining modeled PRASS and PRASS

A definition at this point seems necessary. The repertoire of situations obtained has been termed **modeled PRASS and PRASS.** A simulation in the teaching-learning process of English is seen as an activity where the learners discuss a problem or perhaps a series of related problems within a defined setting (Byrne, 1989). Simulations can be expanded to what is discussed and to why_it is discussed, giving more precision and contextualization to it. These situations can be enriched as an activity where the students discuss a series of related or critical problems within a defined setting.

The PRASS given to the students so that they solve a problem are realistic as the learners are likely to find themselves in them. In the case of the modeled PRASS, they are not real in the sense that the students have to work in perspective with incidents that may happen to them in their future professional life, and for which they will have to be ready before hand. Therefore, given the specific context and the purpose of the situations, the terms are defined as: *Profession-related situations, either modeled or more realistic, posed to the students for their assessment and resolution in class (or outside it, in a later follow-up), with a values-oriented connotation that prepares them for their future roles.*

Criteria for the elaboration of the modeled PRASS and PRASS
They were elaborated keeping in mind some basic rules established to give them a more solid ground to stand on. Together with the source component introduced before, special criteria were respected and are explained here.

> What to teach through the situations. Assuming that values can be known, felt and acted accordingly, it is possible to have the students learn from these situations and be open to the educative influence underlying the situations. The students have to cope with values and anti-values depicted, judge attitudes, get personally involved, help others, etc. This will have an impact on their ways of thinking and behaving. The author stands by the notion that more general educational benefits can be found and exploited in language learning, such as social learning. This social learning is referred to as the tool for acting in life socially, that is, in the context under analysis; it is the preparation to act in the social role assigned.

> Correlation between what the students face in the PRASS and their own capacities and experiences to solve the problems. It has already been explained that the realities recreated precisely describe problems to come up in the future, or surrounding the students at present. There is a valuable background to start with in both cases. Based on the students' level, the teacher will use the PRASS to prepare them to "act" in such situations. It must be added that solving a problem facilitates a personal connection with the object of the problem and paves the way for demands of higher outcome: the establishment of patterns of conduct to resolve the situations. The relation established by the subject with this object should bring about changes in the individual.

> Language at disposal. The students use the language progressively with an acceptable degree of accuracy and are led to develop activities to attain more fluency. Here the language command the student has should be exploited and used purposefully. Solving problems presupposes that

the students assimilate little by little the system of the language and have an acceptable accuracy and fluency. The language that is used and how it is used will have an incidence on the way the activity develops and the outcome of the interactional analyses made. Brumfit (1985:54) specifies that "The conversion of the tokens of the language learnt into value-laden systems with genuine communicative potential requires fluency activity."

As a partial conclusion, a few elements must be an integral part in the elaboration of the PRASS: a communicative perspective where the students can exchange ideas and contribute solutions. The functions of communication cannot be ignored in the realization of the task (communication must be put at play for participation, interaction, debate). There must be a contribution to develop critical thinking in the students as they value phenomena, people and events. Substantial criticism, meaningful learning, constructive confrontation of points of view must be a constant in the process.

Motivation is a must in the presentation of PRASS which are meaningful, life-related and touch the personal experiences and the emotions of the students: the process has an emotional character leading and motivating the student to know more and learn what he/she does not know.

This process builds a foundation for the preparation of the student for his/her future role. In this sense, problem solving involves not only cognitive but also emotional factors. A concrete educative connotation aimed at influencing the students' behavior must be present: setting modes of professional action and developing conscience and conduct are fundamental in the conceptions sought after. The PRASS should present the undergraduate with a gamut of happenings which encompass many of the social, human, psychological, pedagogical and ideological issues his/her future students undergo in real life.

Relating to these problems from the position of a teacher who strives to solve or at least palliate them in the real/imaginary pupils he/she has or will have, creates a rapport with them and the profession and a conscience of behavior towards the resolution of such problems. It eventually leads to the modification and improvement of the students´ values system and consequently their behavior. This rapport towards the profession enhances their willingness to learn more, act better, as their relation with their own students improves too.

The values to be fostered should cover the same spectrum as the aim of the PRASS. They are a system that cannot be severed. Thus, if a situation emphasizes the need for solidarity, then humanism, friendship, love and team work are also fostered. In addition, if the professional value *being communicative* is activated, then it carries along other professional virtues such as *being emotionally attached to the person you are trying to help in the resolution of his/her problem.* Such moments develop a connection at the affective domain.

The PRASS are to be centered on a problem, authenticity-oriented and applicable. Out of this situation is activated the repertoire of the student aimed at solving the problem. The PRASS recreated should allow, in fact they do, a cross-disciplinary approach. This characteristic is in line with the new conceptions of an integrated work from all disciplines and subjects in the schools, leading to a balanced educational influence.

The work with the PRASS must be a reference mosaic for the undergraduates once they go to their practice. The answers provided (the solution given to the problem) ought to permit them to carry out a more efficient work and save time when confronting problems. They will only have to adapt them to the new situations which logically will be richer and far more complex than the ones used in class, but will also be a valuable reference for what is done in the classroom. This approximation to what will happen in real life, the fact that the student must act to solve the problems before him/her, brings gradual changes, what qualifies to purport a system of moral and professional values inherent in the type of graduate any society is intent on forming today.

The conception of the personal involvement of the student in what will be his /her professional life is an important part and is connected to the moral connotation that emerges from the problem being dealt with. The student discovers and develops a moral angle in what he/she has to do, what also af-fects personality and behavior.

Examples of modeled PRASS and PRASS

A. Modeled PRASS
You have senior high students with many different opinions about having sexual relations. One boy says that to have sex with many girls is good because he learns more. A girl says to use condoms will hurt her and she won't feel the same.
    I.   What can you do to help them and the group in general?
    II. Prepare a list of solid reasons to prove the boy he is wrong and show him the dangers he exposes himself to, and to show the girl the advantages of the condom.
    III. Would you discuss your students' doubts with their families? When? Explain; remember you are a teacher and an educator. Use scientific information.

IV. Write a letter to prospective students you will have next year, who you know are beginning to have sexual relations, recommending them to be sure of the important step they are taking, and to use condoms and IUDs. Explain to them in detail why it must be so reading materials about using contraceptive devices and the condom.

B. PRASS
VARIANT ONE

* The group of students you teach in your school has one member whose reputation is not very clear. He is allegedly a pilferer, even though there is no concrete evidence. The boy is a quiet and isolated one, and stays alone most of the time. The group is despising him already. He is not a bad student.
* A debate opens in your lesson as to the role of women in society. Some male students claim that women cannot perform certain jobs (builder, bus driver, sports narrator, high-ranking military official), and the girls respond by mentioning woman-dominated jobs (nurse, telephone operator, typist, secretary).
* A boy in your class despises a girl who is known to have had many boyfriends. He tries to publicly label her as a "promiscuous one" alleging her instability. The girl, an excellent student, defends herself saying that the boys who have many girlfriends are considered heroes, not promiscuous.

Activities to be developed based on the situations

1. Read the situations analytically and detect all the conflicts, dilemmas and problems encountered by the characters. List them.
2. Explain what values are missing/present in the attitudes and behaviors of all the characters mentioned and referred to, according to their view.
3. Substantiate what they understand by these values and why they believe them to be absent/present.
4. Prepare a five-item strategy that leads to the accomplishment of the following actions: Showing a degree of solidarity and support with the affected character, Approaching critically the behavior of all the characters, Proposing concrete ways (steps) to influence on the characters' verbalizations, attitudes and behaviors, Finding possible solutions to all the problems posed in each situation, Elaborating a plan to help and guide the affected students and support the families.
5. Write out a report on the work done to be presented orally in plenary session, before a critical audience (the other small groups which will also present theirs in turns).

6. Write notes, letters or customized points to be told to the families that include: How he or she feels about the problem as a teacher, member of an educational institution, and as a human being; How the family should face the problem and help the young boys and girls; An outline of the difficulties ahead and how they can be overcome; An offering of unconditional counseling and help.
7. Prepare expositions that comprise the elements: Contrasting the bad models given in the situations with good ones, bringing the latter ones to the foreground, taking them from personal experiences, anecdotes, emphasizing the good points of the characters and how these can be channeled positively for common welfare, presenting other situations that escape the contents of the ones they have faced in the simulations, which become new points of departure for analyzing and resolving.

VARIANT TWO

- You have a student who is always telling the others she will be a doctor in the future. A boy tells her he would rather be a teacher. She laughs at him arguing doctors enjoy wider social respect than teachers. The class splits in two sides: those for and those against her position. What would you do as a teacher in the midst of this situation? Offer arguments to the whole class that place both (and any) profession in their right standing. Ask your students to "interview" their elders and how "maestros" were viewed back in their time. Ask them to interview then young people on the street and find out what they think of teachers today. Prepare a report.
- You are a teacher. A student of yours gets angry and highly offended in class at Darwin's theory because he claims he is a devoted Christian. How do you approach a situation like this in class and out of class? Explain. Prepare a conversation with the student from a respectful but educational standpoint. Write a note to the student's parents to talk about the situation and discuss solutions. They are devoted Christians too.
- A pupil of yours is having trouble to concentrate and is getting C's in exams. You try to contact her parents, but they never come to school. It seems there is neglect on their part. What do you do as a teacher in a case of parental neglect? What consequences may this bring to this girl? Make a list of ways to help the girl. Write a careful letter to the parents describing the situation and asking for support. Prepare to meet with the girl. Introduce worries and suggestions to help her out.
- You have two students who had a disagreement about a topic they were discussing. They no longer talk to each other because of that. It is even affecting their performances in class. As a teacher, how would you react to such problem? Think of, and list, procedures you would follow to bring the two together again. Elaborate arguments to convince the students those issues are solved with maturity and communication.

The prerogative character of finding ways in class and in society to form values makes it necessary to approach the issue and present it so that its essences are discernible and comprehensible to those in charge of implementing and materializing values, paving the way for a more conscious and coherent effort towards this goal.

The present paper aimed at presenting arguments on the need to foster values education in class, and demonstrating how it should be done. First, theoretical and notional foundations of the proposal were laid out; second arguments and examples were provided for a complementation and support of the PRASS, as a tool to form values in students of the Teacher Education English Major of Holguin University. The proposal may be useful in other majors and fields of education and beyond, with modification and contextualization.

Bibliography

Baxter Pérez, Esther (1989) *La Formación de valores: una tarea pedagógica*. La Habana, Editorial Pueblo y Educación.
Brown, H. Douglas (2001) *Teaching by Principles*. University of San Francisco. U.S.A.
Colectivo de autores MINED (2000) *Aprendizaje y la formación de valores*. In Seminario Nacional para el Personal Docente. La Habana, Ministerio de Educación. (Tabloide).
Domínguez, María Isabel (1996) *La Formación de valores en la Cuba de los años 90: un enfoque social*. Ciudad de la Habana, Editorial de Ciencias Sociales.
Byrne, Donn (1989) *Teaching Oral English*. La Habana, Edición Revolucionaria. Cuba.
Fabelo Corzo, José Ramón (1989) *Práctica, conocimiento y valoración*. La Habana, Editorial de Ciencias Sociales.
Finocchiaro, Mary and Christopher Brumfit (1989) *The Functional-Notional Approach. From Theory to Practice*. Edición Revolucionaria.
González Maura, Viviana (1995) *Psicología para educadores*. La Habana, Editorial Pueblo y Educación.
Medrano Samaniego, Concepción (1994) *Cuándo y cómo se trabajan los valores morales en la transversalidad*. In Aula de Innovación Educativa. Año II No. 32, noviembre. España: Imprimeix S.C.C.L, Barcelona.
MINED (1989) *Programa director de orientación profesional pedagógica para los Institutos Superiores Pedagógicos*. La Habana, Ministerio de Educación.
MINED (1989) *Programa director de ética pedagógica para los Institutos Superiores Pedagógicos*. La Habana, Ministerio de Educación.
MINED (1998) *Orientaciones metodológicas para el desarrollo del programa dirigido a la formación de valores, la disciplina y la responsabilidad ciudadana, desde la escuela*. La Habana, Ministerio de Educación.
Olivé Iglesias, Miguel Ángel (2000) *Tesis en opción al grado académico de Máster en Ciencias Pedagógicas. Situaciones Simuladas para formar valores*. University of Pedagogical Sciences. Holguin, Cuba.
Olivé Iglesias, Miguel Ángel (2006) *Valores: ¿Formación, Aprendizaje, Educación?* Artículo. *atlante.eumed.net/formacion-aprendizaje-educacion*
Velázquez León, Manuel (2000) *Reflexiones sobre la disciplina Historia de la cultura de los países de habla inglesa desde la perspectiva de la educación valoral*. Texto Didáctico. Holguín, I.S.P. Holguín.

Heritage of Values: A Comprehensive Approach in Cuban Education

MSc Miguel Ángel Olivé Iglesias. Associate Professor
PhD Libys Martha Zúñiga Igarza. Full Professor
MSc Marisela Rodríguez Calzadilla. Associate Professor

Cultural legacy is constantly created and recreated through a complex and encompassing process that leads to the making of a cultural mosaic. We call it heritage of values, or values patrimony, and define it preliminarily as a systemic whole, enriching previous views on patrimonial analyses and opening a fresh alternative to the conception. Deeper scrutiny on these aspects reveals an interdisciplinary angle, seen from education as a need and a right vital for human development.

Therefore, the study made discloses the nexuses discussed theoretically, aided by research methods such as analysis-synthesis, induction-deduction, abstract-concrete. The paper attempts, firstly, at unveiling the new links between values, patrimony, interdisciplinarity and education. Secondly, in achieving the first purpose, it wishes to contribute to an awakening of the awareness for the preservation of culture as a key pillar of human existence.

An accepted notion of an integral culture believes in preparing young people to be useful in social terms, consequently to act adequately in their contexts: There is much to be done to have an integral culture and to channel the formation of values in youngsters, so they respond to the realities where they live and work. Nelson Mandela said, "Without education, your children can never really meet the challenges they will face…"

Humans, society and the environment – both natural and nurtured – are closely connected. It is humankind's duty to safeguard such patrimony so they bequeath it to their offspring in a historic line of legacy.

Interdisciplinarity

The term *interdisciplinarity* comes to light for the first time in 1937, in the works by Louis Wirtz. The word *discipline* comes from Greek and Latin "to learn." Interdisciplinarity refers to the notion of "inter"-learning of these aspects. *Inter* implies that interdisciplinary approaches contain learning from various sources that complement each other, exchange directed not just to learning alone but also to an interdisciplinary search, to solving problems taken from real life.

Interdisciplinarity borders along the act of mutual sharing among disciplines or among the contents within those disciplines. Research on the concept presents it as an interactive cross-disciplinary strategy, as a collaboration towards a new echelon of knowledge. It is frequently deemed as complicated but must become an object of interest and common study.

Departing from the previous analyses, we propose a definition of the term: "Epistemological re-organization of knowledge, method, subjects, from a systemic and systematic perspective – global and complex – given in an integration of educational thought and praxis, in an interweaving of behavior, qualities, values and opinions derived from different sciences, towards an insight of and a solution to concrete social problems". This definition is in line with the objectives of the paper, further concretized in the analyses below.

Values and Patrimony

The problem of values is an opening point in the agenda of intellectual and educational thought in and outside Cuba. Most research has attempted to disclose the manifold implications inherent in the category, as it deals with a vital component of humankind's existence and is an unquestionable social factor pertinent to human beings and their behavior.

Values, as a part of the patrimony of culture and educational institutions, belong with the knowledge people learn. To Fabelo (1996:73) values are: "The socially positive significance of objects and phenomena of social praxis" *(Translated by the editor)*. Fabelo sees values as that which favors social progress, health and social life.

Fabelo (1996) mentions three fundamental values of the Cuban Revolution: justice, solidarity and independence. Upon these values, the principles of Cuban social development rest. Justice presupposes equity of distribution and opportunity for education and spiritual growth. Solidarity implies mutual help and caring for others not only at family or national levels, but also at an international level, building bonds of cooperation and support for those in need. Independence is the basis to develop and exist as a nation free from foreign restraints and rules. It is a key value to foster other values.

Ortiz and Mariño (1995) propose a set of values to be formed and fostered in the individuals: General Human Values: collectivism, perseverance, honesty, uprightness, dignity, austerity, solidarity, discipline, industriousness, patriotism, modesty, independence, self-control, delicacy, enthusiasm. Professional Values: *being* communicative, creative, loving towards the profession, observant, sagacious, studious, motivated towards researching, optimistic, tender, active, organized.

Values cover areas as varied as economy, politics, ethics, aesthetics, law, religion, environment, patrimony (*tangible*, the material one; *intangible*, the nonmaterial one).

A discussion of values and values education cannot leave out today's priorities at historical, philosophical, social, psychological, anthropological, patrimonial and educational levels. Such is the imperativeness of the issue that it becomes necessary to approach it and present it so that its essences are discernible and comprehensible for the safeguarding of values, paving the way for a more conscious and coherent effort towards this goal.

The social role and responsibility of education in the matter, a task of society as a whole, must start with an adequate understanding of the categories from a theoretical point of view. On this ground, a clarification of the terms values, patrimony, interdisciplinarity and education in their general and particular senses can help pave the way to becoming aware and growing actively involved in the preservation of our heritage.

Briefly, we assume that all cultural heritage passed on to humanity in each historic moment acquires value inasmuch as it is socially accepted and carries significance in human activity. We refer to both the physical and the spiritual heritage. De la Torre & Mason (2002:3) explain that: "Value has always been the reason underlying heritage conservation. It is self-evident that no society makes an effort to conserve what it does not value."

Moreover, this heritage stands as a patrimony. The word is Latin *patrimonium*, that is, *what comes from the parents*. In broader language, social and individual patrimony are traces and values – either material or not. They comprise cultural and natural landscapes and seascapes, cultural traditions, languages, religious beliefs and manifestations, archaeological sites, museums, folklore, celebrations, social mores, agricultural patterns, even local populations, traits of flora, fauna, geological formations, etc. These components are patrimonial values, which according to De la Torre & Mason (2002) stem from the usefulness and ends of patrimonial wealth that makes up an all-around culture.

These values, resulting from human activity, include material and immaterial products, and qualify as the objective legacy of a society within a socio-historic moment. They are both a physically and spiritually created inheritance.

Nevertheless, there is a higher level of analysis in reference to the elements discussed about values and patrimony. It moves logically from the tangibility to the intangibility designs. At the same time, these involve human beings, places and society. The tangible-intangible relations, focused from the view of complexity, emerge into a degree of wholeness. Wholeness is the capability of humanity to discern their identity, their culture. Once these premises are clarified, humanity will see itself as a whole, from identity and cultural approaches that unfold from individuality to family to environment to nation. Educational and systemic perspectives on these ideas open a door to the understanding of a values patrimony of both people and nation.

The authors of this paper propose the term, *values patrimony,* as "A human attribute of possession and preservation to safeguard through a "socially-built" process. It has an educational, complex, multifarious, objective, subjective and institutional character, concretized in its tangible and intangible components – marked individually and socially – central to human existence and growth, and with potential to transcend and become universal."

There is evident social recognition to a values patrimony of the material type. Since the mid-20th century, sites and edifices have been labeled as tangible patrimony and inducted to the rank of National Monuments in Cuba: Havana Cathedral in 1934; Mantua, 1935); St. Ifigenia Cemetery,1937 and Bayamo City in 1939. These referred to *areas* – not physical patrimony (erected or built) – due to past historic events that took place there. In the category of natural values was included the Sierra Cristal National Park in Holguin, in 1930, because of its forests and the worth of the pinewoods.

Since the 1959 revolutionary triumph, a serious policy was set afoot in Cuba for the promotion and conservation of the national patrimony. On the material side, special mention goes to declaring as National Monuments the first seven villages founded in Cuba: Baracoa, Bayamo, Puerto Príncipe, Trinidad, Havana, Santiago de Cuba. This well thought-out policy led four Cuban cities to be in the UNESCO list of Humanity´s Cultural Patrimony: the Old City of Havana along with its fortresses, in 1982; Trinidad and the *Valle de los Ingenios*, in 1988; Santiago de Cuba´s San Pedro de la Roca Castle, 1997; Cienfuegos Urban Historic Downtown, 2005 and Camagüey Historic Downtown, 2008. Natural resources also cited are: *Desembarco del Granma* Park in Bayamo; Mankind´s Cultural Landscape in Pinar del Rio, *Valle de Viñales* in 1999 and the archaeological landscape of the first coffee plantations in southern Cuba, in 2000 and 2001.

On the nonmaterial side, UNESCO recognized *La Tumba Francesa,* a folkloric dance, in 2008; *La Rumba Cubana,* a festive mixture of dance and music, in 2016 and the Cuban *punto* (farmers´ form of poetry and music), in 2017.The latter side expands into other spiritual manifestations. These values were formed through the influence of the revolutionary and educational processes undergone by Cuban society.

Education towards the Preservation of a Values Patrimony

The materials consulted make constant reference to the general concern for the loss, deterioration and vulnerability (manifold causes) of values. As well, there is a sustained allusion to the need of preserving a country's values patrimony, which treasures the cultural vessel inclusive of the natural and the built resources of a spiritual and physical denomination. The alarm sets off in every context:

Binaburo (1995), cited by Olivé (2012:2) warns that: "Questa crisi, questo cambio di valori, si unisce alla crisi della post-modernitá: dell'economia, dell'ecologia, della politica, delle relazioni sociali e delle ideologie." *(See page 232 for translation)*. González (1995) also cited by Olivé (2012:3) states that: "The concern about values is present today in every international educational system... there is a general urge for fostering ethical attitudes and behavior." "A values-based approach is the current most preferred approach to heritage conservation, adopted, and advocated by major conservation authorities, both at national level (e.g., USA, Canada, Australia, and UK) and at international level (e.g., UNESCO World Heritage Centre), and by major research and educational institutions (e.g., Getty Conservation Institute)" (Poulios, 2010:1). "... demands of the region to keep the historic foundation of a city via an urban organization that respects the inherited values. These values are resources..." (Zúñiga & Pérez, 2013: 69).

Education is primordial to protect our values patrimony. Nelson Mandela stated that it is "The most powerful weapon which you can use to change the world." Olivé (2012) refers to the role of education to prepare people so they face the challenges of life, co-existence, conservation of resources and post-modernity issues. Education is a conception, by extension a produce of human activity. Its role aims at forming men and women so that society can operate and progress.

The premises to reach that goal base on respect to otherness and biodiversity, on a sense of commitment to nature and to historic development, on an awareness of the continuity of culture and national identity. Values and patrimony are linked to Cuban educational roots and intellectual thought: José de la Luz y Caballero, Enrique José Varona, Féliz Varela and José Martí, among many others. These "maestros" were advocates of human values in harmony with nature and national identity, unity and modesty.

Environment-related values have also been connected to interactive, dynamic and developmental processes of nature, human and inter-cultural relations. Key categories are meaning, representativeness, singularity and authenticity, viewed from the aspects of form, function, space and time, plus their economic and social worth, integrity of form and environment.

An interdisciplinary approach today is vital to meet the call of realities like technology and communication, new trends of teaching in primary, secondary and tertiary levels, to which are added special and adult teaching. An educational look at the way a nation´s – and the world´s – values patrimony is preserved would be contributive to identity, national culture and the very transcendence of humankind.

Summarizing, interdisciplinarity is an appropriate tool to gain an insight into real problems that emerge from the values-patrimony formula, and into solving them from an educational perspective. Values patrimony must be approached as attribute and possession developed by humans in a temporal framework, complex and educational in character, multifarious, objective-subjective and set in a system of tangible and intangible values to be fostered. It will contribute to formative practices both individually and nationally.

Education is a changing phenomenon, historically and culturally established. It has a mission in helping develop and salvage a values patrimony and general human values – personal, professional, environment-friendly – so that we preserve our resources and are ready to face the challenges Mandela warned us about.

Bibliography
Binaburo Iturbide, J.A. (1998) *La Dimenzione Morale Dell'educazione*. Http://Lgxserver.Uniba.It/Lei/Sfi/Convegni/Reggioemilia/Iturbide.Htm.
De la Torre, Martha & Randall Mason (2002). *Assessing the Values of Cultural Heritage*. The Getty Conservation Institute. Research Report. Los Ángeles, EEUU. https://www.getty.edu/conservation/publications_resources/pdf.../pdf/assessing.pdf
Fabelo Corzo, José Ramón (1989). *Práctica, conocimiento y valoración*. Editorial de Ciencias Sociales. La Habana. Cuba.
Fabelo Corzo, José Ramón (1996). *La Crisis de valores: conocimiento, causas y estrategias de superación*. La Formación de valores en las nuevas generaciones. Una campaña de espiritualidad y de conciencia. Editorial Ciencias Sociales. La Habana.
González Alfayete, Manuel (1995). *Hacia un sistema de valores básico compartidos en el PEC*. Aula de Innovación Educativa, Año IV No. 38, mayo. España, Imprimeix SCCL, Barcelona.
Lacerda, Norma (2005). *Los valores de las estructuras ambientales urbanas: Consideraciones teóricas.* En CECI (2005). Gestión de la conservación integrada urbana y territorial. Programa Integrated Territorial and Urban Conservation (ITUC), Rio de Janeiro, Brazil.
Olivé Iglesias, Miguel Ángel (2012). *Experience-Based Tips for Planning and Teaching an Integrated English Practice Lesson in the Specialty at Holguin University of Pedagogical Sciences.* Holguin UPS, Cuba. (Article)
Ortiz, Emilio & María Mariño (1995). *¿Cómo educar la personalidad?* Holguin Teacher Training College (manuscript). Holguin, Cuba.
Mandela, Nelson. https://www.forbes.com/.../20-inspirational-quotes-from-nelson-mandela

Mandela, Nelson. https://www.brainyquote.com/quotes/nelson_mandela_621327

Mason, Randall (2002). *Assessing values in conservation planning: Methodological issues and choices.* En Research Report. The Getty Conservation Institute, Los Angeles, California, EE.UU.

Poulios, Ioannis (2010). *Moving Beyond a Values-Based Approach to Heritage Conservation.* Hellenic Open University. https://www.researchgate.net/.../233621722_Moving_Beyond

Zúñiga Igarza, Libys Martha y Pérez, (2013). *Los recursos construidos de valor patrimonial en un modelo de gestión ambiental urbana.* Disponible en www.eure.cl. Edición Nº117, mayo de 2013. (p. 69-90).

Zúñiga Igarza, Libys Martha y Pérez, (2013). *Los recursos construidos de valor patrimonial en un modelo de gestión ambiental urbana.* Disponible en www.eure.cl. Edición Nº117, mayo de 2013.

Zúñiga Igarza, Libys Martha (2013). *Gestión ambiental urbana de recursos construidos de valor patrimonial.* Editorial Académica Española; Bonn, Alemania. ISBN 978-659-06440-1.

Professional Skills in the Teaching-Learning of English as a Teacher Education Major at Holguin University

MSc Miguel Ángel Olivé Iglesias. Associate Professor
MSc Guillermo Ronda Velázquez. Associate Professor
PhD Julio César Rodríguez Peña. Associate Professor

This paper aims at exposing that skill formation and development in FLT, the theory underlying both processes and their didactic crystallization, has been a must on the map of foreign language teaching. Central to a discussion on the matter is the notion that skills are defined as the *know-how*, or are called the learn-to-do according to UNESCO standards. This is translated as putting to use the knowledge acquired.

In an educational context, skill development means that the student acquires knowledge and applies it in a specific field. Cuban researcher Álvarez de Zayas (1996) states that skills, as a part of the contents, allow to characterize, didactically speaking, the operations performed by the students, as they interact with their object of study, transforming it, passing on to it their human influence.

The mastering of a foreign language involves, for example, knowing the rules for verb conjugation. The learner must also practice it to internalize habit and skill so that language command reaches expected levels. Therefore, foreign language teaching gives special prominence to skill development through the integrated practice of the language in communicative situations. The previous statement is fundamental for an understanding on how the process operates. As a constituent of contents, skills are the individual's practical performance within a specific field of knowledge amassed in the vast cultural mosaic of humankind. A preliminary approach from a psychological standpoint reveals that skills are the actions and operations mastered by that individual – the learner – with a definite objective in mind.

It must be pointed out that skill formation and development are by no means the exclusive possession or prerogative of foreign language teaching. Any learning activity presupposes the acquisition of knowledge and the development of general and particular skills, depending on the reality and perspective of the process.

Recent studies on skill formation and development carried out in the field by researchers from the Teacher Education English Major, rendered elements that explain why this work came to life. While it is a fact that official documents analyzed show clearly the multifarious aspects related to teaching and learning, and the teaching staff is one of seniority and dedication, there is still much to be explored in the areas of theory and contextualized practice to improve the process. This paper is an endeavor towards that end. The major aspires to develop general communicative skills inherent in learning a foreign language. However, the goal goes beyond that: developing a set of profession-related skills, the so-called *professional skills*.

This article explores skill theory in general and delves into the specific term *professional skills*, contextualized in the teaching and learning of English as a teacher education major in Holguin.

Material and Methods
The theoretical methods used were historic-logical, analytic-synthetic, inductive-deductive, and documentary study. The work done allowed the authors to reveal essential aspects on the category and their theoretical, methodological and professional implications. Skill development means that the student acquires knowledge and applies it in a specific field. English as a teacher education major gives special prominence to skill development through the integrated practice of the language, and aims at the development of skills that are part of the specific field of study, the so-called professional skills

Results and Discussion
Stepping into the concept of skill implies, primarily, an analysis based on a compilation of definitions. Obviously, this paper cannot list all of them. It will propose a selection and disclose coincidental points.

Petrovsky (1978) states that skills are the mastery of a system of psychical and practical activities, which are necessary for the conscious regulation of activity, knowledge and habits. Danilov & Skatkin (1978) clarify that skills are an extremely encompassing and complex pedagogical concept, and view them as the capacity acquired to use creatively knowledge and habits in theoretical and practical activity. They were able to summarize the definition in saying that skills are knowledge in action.

González (1995) defines these as the mastery of psychical and practical operations that allow rational control of activity. She adds that they are the result of systematization of actions under such conditions that their constant development is guaranteed. They are actions, which are embedded in learning and assure efficient human performance.

Álvarez de Zayas (1996) says that skills are the mastery of the content that reveals human behavior in a specific context. For him, they are actions and operations mastered by the individual, with a goal in sight. Oramas (?) posits that skills are developed within the activity, therein are included cognitive activity, practical activity and valuation activity. Ortiz & Mariño (2009) present them as a dimension of contents showing human behavior in a specific field of knowledge.

A critical reading of these definitions leads to mark words that are essential to the analysis: action, practice, activity, use of knowledge and habits, behavior, acquired capacity. In other words, the study of the very concept brings to light that the process occurs as follows: from practice to the psychical plane and back again. Furthermore, skill development is a full combinatory exchange between the outside and the inside, a dialectical harmony between psyche and reality. It should be noted that Danilov and Skatkin refer to "capacity."

A constant in the definitions is the fact that many authors include skills within the contents, discerning what is to be taught and what is to be learned. For González, Recarey & Addine (2004) contents are the product of humanity's contribution during its historic development. They include:
- ✓ Systems of knowledge.
- ✓ Systems of skills and habits.
- ✓ Systems of relations with the world (values, feelings, attitudes).
- ✓ Systems of experiences (affective and motivational) in activity.

There are no skills and no habits without previous knowledge: the latter is the foundation upon which the former form and develop. Knowledge comes first then you teach how to operate with it in a given reality and a given practice context. Knowledge and skills are coherently connected. These are modeled and developed. Rephrasing it, knowledge is a key premise for the development of the skills.

Skills are a form of assimilation of activity. Alongside with habits, they enable individuals to carry out a task. So when they apply to an activity they acquire a system of procedures and methods that are useful for the performance of a variety of tasks. They also begin to master actions piecemeal, as they exact their performance. Only with a feedback on what they have already learned – knowledge and habits – will they be able to perform better.

Skill manifests itself in the most perfect and elemental way of acting. At a higher level, it is considered as the mastering of the whole process, and presupposes the acquisition of knowledge and the formation of habits as essential components. An effective skill formation includes systematization through repetition of actions and steady reinforcement, together with continual improvement.

Skills are therefore a systematization of actions and these are subordinate processes of a conscious objective, as was previously stated. It can be said that in the case of the skills, automatization is not reached: this is a characteristic of habits. The fulfillment of skill-related actions demands conscious regulation by the individual. Skill development implies the possibility to choose and put in practice different methods and knowledge acquired in correspondence to the final goal and the conditions of the task.

Further analyses of skills in the teaching and learning of a foreign language should refer to Leontiev *(Taken from Antich et al)*. He states that the learning process is a complex activity with two aspects, a methodological and a theoretical one:

1. The acquisition of knowledge (the premise of the existence of previous knowledge to move to the next level).
2. The formation of habits and skills (formed and developed based on previous knowledge).

To understand how teaching and learning work and which their cycles are for presentation and exploitation in a lesson, we must depart from the theory of verbal activity. It is founded on the general theory of activity defined by Vygotsky and his followers (Leontiev, Luria, Galperin). Verbal activity has four aspects: listening, speaking, reading and writing. From these elements, the system of teaching is organized, that is, we speak about a reading comprehension, a speaking, a writing and a listening comprehension lesson, depending on the leading skill involved.

It should be pointed out that even when there is a leading skill in a lesson, they all act in combination through the process: it is impossible to develop a pure skill when in real life they overlap in communication. It is clear that there is no such thing as a pure one-skill lesson. Students will do tasks of all types and will navigate back and forth the skills of the language during the hours allotted. However, there is a predominant skill, because that is what you seek as a teacher and that is what the syllabus suggests as contents to be taught. That skill is the header in each lesson.

Now, skill development in the teaching and learning of English as a teacher education major in the university implies an inherent pedagogical-professional, interdisciplinary and formative premise. Skills are not developed *per se* but as means to upgrade communicative competence, which in turn will enable teachers-to-be to use indispensable "tools" to lead the teaching-learning process of English once they graduate: the necessary development of professional skills.

These tools are referred to in the directive documents the major responds to. They state the teachers-to-be must have reached upon graduation an ethical and professional formation that will allow them to lead the pedagogical process from an analytical perspective of their professional contexts towards the solution of problems, debate and research. Students will solve pedagogical, social, scientific problems, as they must have formed and developed technical skills to apply them creatively in their professional scenarios.

It should be noted that the documents emphasize the students´ development of communicative skills to enter a further skill dimension, that of professional skills.

Llanes (?) offers definitions of *professional skills*:

> "Skills that guarantee success in an activity and the solution of multifarious problems in the major."

> "Skills included in the syllabus contents related to role models to be developed during the teaching-learning process. They require a degree of systematization, which, once acquired, will allow the student to face and solve all sorts of professional problems."

> "Logical content of actions done by the professionals in interacting with the objects of their profession."[37]

Llanes states that in approaching each definition, it can be noticed authors coincide this type of activity is in line with the role models of a profesional. This guarantees the solution of problems in each specific field.

The definitions reveal the intentional character of this type of skill development. Two aspects are essential: direct connection with the profession and it modelling to solve problems. At this point in the analysis, the authors consider it pertinent to present a distinguishing working definition of *professional skills*. Thus, *professional skills in the teaching and learning of English as a teacher education major* are:

"Skills formed and developed during the teaching and learning of English as a teacher education major, which will allow future teachers to learn and teach English and solve academic, contextual, social, pedagogical issues related to their profession." (Olivé, 2021)

---

[37] *Taken from Llanes Montes, Aleida. Estrategia educativa para el desarrollo de las habilidades profesionales desde las prácticas pre-profesionales en la especialidad contabilidad. Page 1 (Definitions given by Márquez, page 18; Mestre, page 21; Fuentes, page 48, respectively).*

Activities to develop professional skills
The following activities are examples to show how the pedagogical-professional aspect is channeled in class.

Simulated Situations: Women in Society Today[38]
I. One of your students has verbally attacked his former girlfriend. She is shocked. He claims that she offended him and deserves "even a spanking." She defends herself explaining he tried to force her to come back to him and regarded her as a person with no rights.

II. A debate opens in your lesson as to the role of women in society. Some male students claim that women cannot perform certain jobs (builder, bus driver, sports narrator, high-ranking military official), and the girls, respond mentioning female-dominated jobs (nurse, telephone operator, typist).

III. A boy in your class despises a girl who has had "many boyfriends." He tries to label her publicly as a "promiscuous one" saying she is "too unstable". The girl, an excellent student, says boys who have many girlfriends are considered heroes, not promiscuous.

Profession-related activities derived from the situations above:
1- Read the situations analytically and detect the conflicts and problems seen through the characters. List them.
2- Prepare a five-item strategy that leads to achieving:
   - A degree of solidarity and support in favor of the affected characters.
   - A critical approach to the characters' behavior.
   - A concrete proposal (steps) to influence on the characters' verbalizations, attitudes and behaviors.
   - Possible solutions to the problems posed in each situation.
   - A plan to help and guide the affected students and to support their families.
3- Write out a report on the work done to be presented orally in plenary session.
4- Write notes to be told to the families that include:
   - ✓ How you feel about the problem as a teacher, a member of an educational institution, and as a human being.
   - ✓ How the families should face the problem and help the boys and girls.
   - ✓ An outline of the difficulties ahead and how they can be overcome.
   - ✓ An offering of unconditional counseling and help.

---

[38] Taken from Miguel Ángel Olivé Iglesias. Simulated Situations in the English Lesson for Advanced Students at the Teachers' College of Holguín. Page 7.

5- Prepare expositions with the elements below:

❖ A contrast between the bad models given in the situations and good ones, bringing the latter ones to the foreground, taking them from personal experiences, anecdotes.

❖ An emphasis on the good points of the characters and how these can be channeled positively for the students´ personal growth.

❖ A presentation of other situations that escape the contents of the ones they read and analyzed, which become new points of departure for solving.

Research done on the matter of skill formation and development rendered the need to go further in the fulfillment of specific professional objectives in the Teacher Education English Major of Holguin University, within the Discipline *Integrated English Practice*. The present paper aimed at contributing a properly contextualized proposal.

An approximation to the problem started with the contextualization of the analyses made. Empirical and epistemic inquiry into the category led to systematization, assumption and modeling of a theoretical corpus where skills are viewed beyond the initial communicative element into the professional component. As well, practical activities to channel the results didactically were offered according to the professional needs and realities of the Teacher Education English Major of Holguin University.

Bibliography

Addine Fernández, Fátima; Ana María González Soca; Silvia C. Recarey Fernández (2202) *Principios para la dirección del proceso pedagógico. In Compendio de Pedagogía*. Editorial Pueblo y Educación.

Álvarez De Zayas, Carlos (1996) *La escuela en la vida*. Editorial Pueblo y Educación.

Antich De León, Rosa; Dariela Gandarias Cruz; Emma López Segrera (1986) *Metodología de la enseñanza de lenguas extranjeras*. Editorial Pueblo y Educación.

González Soca, Ana María; Silvia Recarey Fernández; Fátima Addine Fernández (2004) *La dinámica del proceso de enseñanza aprendizaje mediante sus componentes*. In *Didáctica. Teoría y práctica*. Editorial Pueblo y Educación.

Ceballos Bauta, Katiusca; Miguel Ángel Olivé Iglesias (2013) *Aproximación al desarrollo de las habilidades comunicativas en inglés en los estudiantes de la carrera de lenguas extranjeras inglés*. Monografía. Research Project. University of Holguin, Cuba.

Medina Betancourt, Alberto (2004) *Modelo de competencia metodológica del profesor de inglés para el perfeccionamiento de la dirección del proceso de enseñanza-aprendizaje del nivel medio*. Doctoral Thesis. University of Holguin.

Olivé Iglesias, Miguel Ángel (2011) *Writing: The Cinderella? Experiences with Fourth-year Students of the Teacher Education English Major of Holguin University*. Paper presented in WEFLA-SECAN, International Event. Holguin, Cuba.

Olivé Iglesias, Miguel Ángel (2013) *Programa Analítico de la Asignatura Práctica Integral de la Lengua Inglesa para 4to año, CRD*. Syllabus. Teacher Education English Major of Holguin University. Holguin, Cuba.

Reading for Values: From Conceptual Analyses to Concrete Illustration

MSc Miguel Ángel Olivé Iglesias. Associate Professor
BA Yudisleidys Sánchez Roque
BEd Madelín Feria Torres. Instructor

Impacted by international events echoing across our national frontiers, and the socio-economic framework into which Cuba has been thrust, the 'cordon sanitaire' that protected the ideals and values of the nation has been threatened to such an extent that a massive campaign is afoot today aimed at preserving and developing values inherent in the Cuban society for years. The issue emerges on the evidence that, due to the twists of economy, individuals tend to dissociate from high-standing values of a spiritual and social order, shifting towards the immediate satisfaction of more "down-to-earth" matters. This evidence is essential to understand the effects of a so-called *values crisis* on the ethical attitude of individuals and on how their values scales are affected, what reflects in their behavior.

Thus personalities from all provinces of knowledge discuss the values problem that has been outlined. Considering that the road to travel is hard before the Cuban economy reaches a steady increase, it is a must that all entities, organizations and institutions embark on an educational "battle" for the salvation and enrichment of the values of the Cuban society, especially of children and youngsters.

This work attempts to disclose the author's views on some theoretical and practical elements. The main objective is to offer the reader an overview about *values* as a category, how the process of values education operates, where to direct our endeavour within a foreign language lesson to form values, as well as examples for the reading comprehension lesson – where the author has focused most of his research in the past years. Given the relevance of the topic and the importance of reading as a formative tool, the paper offers reference material in English, theoretical and practical, to prove the viability of forming values through reading, a priority for all times, places and people.

An overview on values and values education

Webster's Dictionary, 1992 edition, registers the word <u>value</u> with ten different entries. The second one reads: *"(often plural) something regarded as desirable, worthy, or right, as a belief, a standard, a precept: the values of a democratic society"*. The word derives from Latin **valere** (to be of worth). This concept is of assistance in a first approach to the topic as it clarifies a value is originally the position/attitude of an individual in respect to something.

This notion is approached by García (1996): *"to have values is to appreciate an object, a principle. It is to place things hierarchically in order of importance. It is to decide what is more relevant in a certain moment. It is to place spiritual and material riches in their rightful order..."* (Translated by the editor)

The definition stresses the hierarchical character of the scale of values for the human being, i.e. individuals look at the world around them with prerogatives not only from a material stance but also from a spiritual one, prioritizing those values which come first for them conditioned by reality and their subjective apprehension of that reality.

A Spanish researcher, Concepción Medrano, provides a definition of values as: *"meaningful priorities reflecting the inner world of the individuals, and manifested in our behaviour."* (Translated by the editor) This concept may be dissected in three basic components:

Meaningful priorities: priorities that have an emotionally strong impact on people, because they are part and parcel of their lives. They are essential to them and move them in a special way.

Reflection of the inner world: the expression of the construal of a world which, on a subjective level, individuals assimilate in their interaction with peers and objective reality.

Behavioral manifestation: outward manifestation of an established subjective notion in the form of attitudes, actions, conducts.

It can be stated that the conception of values is centered on the contention that they are attitudes, behaviors conditioned by the personal interpretation in an individual's conscience of relations, events and phenomena of the surrounding world.

Many have been the ways used by international and national specialists to refer to education in values. Some are: values education, education in values, construction of values, formation of values (most frequent term in Cuba), education for values, education in respect to values, axiological education, etc. Related terminology employed by a variety of authors is: axiological situation, axiological campaign, axiological scales, axiological models and values scales.

An approach to values education as a term is that by Rojas Arce et al (2002), who state: *"In this humanistic tendency of education (...) is where the integration or promotion of the axiological approach is proposed through what is known worldwide as values education..."* (Translated by the editor)

Yurén (1995) explores the problem and proposes the following: values education includes education in values (socialization), education on values (transmission of information about values, education for values (intellectual and moral development to be informed, prefer and choose values), education through values (formation of values through the materialization of values). This author accepts the different terms when she says: "... *education according to values, also called values education (...) the education according to values is above all a formative process...*" (Yurén, 1995) *(Translated by the editor)*.

Forming values at school, particularly during a lesson, presupposes the integration of a series of principles and requirements which go beyond the borders of a specific subject and its contents, and move within the realm of a pedagogical conception of a lesson and the system of influences and fundamentals that have an incidence on the personality of each individual.

A lesson aims at exploring and activating values within a communicative atmosphere through not only exchanging opinions, points of view, judgements, but also doing independent work, assuming an attitude, solving hypothetical situations in simulation activities taken from life and presented in the classroom, offering practical suggestions and solutions and getting ready to "act" in real-life contexts.

The lesson of English, as any other, is viable for values education. With the boost of communicative concepts in the teaching of foreign languages and the updated methodological conceptions on the matter, it enjoys favorable conditions to carry out this type of education.

The principles of communication are not obviated: contextualization of the situations; students should interact with one another; topics should be appealing, meaningful (that is, relating the students to their own lives, to situations taken from emotionally close events that purport some relevant meaning), according to the students' needs, hopes; their experiences should be exploited for debate and reflection and a conscious and volitive assimilation of the contents to be received; simulation activities with situations taken from reality may be proposed.

As our main objective is the formation of values in the classroom, through the lesson, it is important to consider that the lesson is a process of communication with three fundamental functions: informational, regulatory and affective. In fact, to form values, attitudes inside a classroom, it must become a scenario of communication and dialogue, debate and problem-solving activities, where students interchange among themselves and with the teacher, moulding their own systems of values, adopting a position and helping to solve a social predicament they will be eventually confronted with in their practice teaching.

Potentiating a lesson towards values education is possible as has been proven even in a variety of subjects, which seem circuitous for the task (Mathematics and Chemistry). What remains a truth is that the so-called social disciplines do lend themselves more feasibly, given their characteristics. A History lesson is excellent for all kinds of educational efforts to channel the contents of the subject on a values-oriented path. This has been demonstrated by research on the matter (Velázquez, 2000).

The principles of communication cannot be obviated:
  ➢ Contextualization of the situations. Activities proposed are to spin about a thematic unity, which allows focusing on their resolution.
  ➢ Students should interact with one another. Interaction is understood as *"collaborative exchange of thought, feelings or ideas between two or more people, resulting in a reciprocal effect on each other."* (Douglas, 1994)
  ➢ Topics should be appealing, **meaningful**, as was explained before. *"We understand as meaningful what activates the students' interest, what relates to their lives and by extension to their experiences. For values education (...) the experiential element, what is connoted and significant, becomes primordial, because values are assimilated by individuals who gradate in ranks that object which is, precisely, meaningful to them."* (Olivé, 1998)

Camino Trapero (1993) cites Touriñán in saying that the pedagogical consideration of values is in "beholding man as 'perfectionable'" (Touriñán, 1977), a definition that enters the area of pedagogy. She states that the objective character of values allows:
  ➢ Knowing these values, that is, values are an object of appreciation, they can be known.
  ➢ Teaching these values, that is, the experiential relationship with other people, the subject-subject nexus that allows the shaping of an object-subject connection inherent in the formation of a system of values.
  ➢ Materializing these values, that is, values can become rules (not forced but followed by conviction) to be observed by people.

García (1996) analyzes the pedagogical angle of values formation involving students, parents, family and representatives of all social organizations in:
  ➢ A "process of clarification" about which are the values to be assumed.
  ➢ The responsibility acquired out of patterns of conduct (that is, accounting for one's assumed conduct).
  ➢ The verbal expression of the values already defined.
  ➢ Acting according to these values.
  ➢ Finding their meaning and hierarchical order.

Specialists' views on values education in the pedagogical process
Many are the authors who study and publish on the matter. A brief selection is given below as a representation of what has been said on values education.

González Maura (?) states that it is necessary to:
- Make room for reflection, so that the student learns to value, substantiate viewpoints and defend them.
- Find a space of freedom of speech, adequate debate and initiatives.
- Listen to and understand others.
- Face problems with self-assurance and independence to achieve goals.

Chacón (2002) advocates for the need for a cross-disciplinary approach to the lesson, while Castellanos (2003) posits the need for: *"An activation and control of learning, meaningfulness of the students' own learning, motivation and diversity in class."* (Translated by the editor)
Silvestre (?) reflects on the issue stating that it is necessary to:
- Diagnose.
- Activate knowledge search.
- Devise activities that lead to reflective standpoints.
- Motivate.
- Stimulate logical thinking and problem-solving skills.
- Consider individual differences.
- Relate contents with social praxis.
- Stimulate valuations from an educative perspective.

The previous author and Zilberstein (2002) emphasize that the tasks assigned to the student must be centered on key elements, provoke reflective analyses, lead to growing demands of the students' intellect, and favor self-control and valuation of reality.

Arias and Dominguez (2004) see the formation of values in school with:
- Teaching as part of life and human activity.
- The students at the center of the process.
- The axiological universe and cultural heritage at their disposal.
- The psychological organization of the process.
- Individual and personalized activities.
- Integration of education and life, school and society.

All the authors coincide on the need to stress values education and see the lesson as a crucial moment, where they must:
- Interact among them.
- Respect others' opinions and views.
- Reflect on life and problems from a social stance.

> ➤ Activate their mental processes.
> ➤ Be considered as individuals with common but also different traits.
> ➤ Relate their learning with life and social issues.
> ➤ Solve problems.

Reading as a tool for values education in the lesson of English

General considerations on reading

Understanding a written text means extracting required information from it as efficiently as possible. For example, we apply different reading strategies when looking at a notice board to see if there is an advertisement for a particular type of flat and when carefully reading an article of special interest in a scientific journal. Yet locating the relevant advertisement on the board and understanding the new information contained in article demonstrates that the reading purpose in each case has been successfully fulfilled. In the first case, competent readers will quickly reject the irrelevant information and find what he is looking for. In the second case, it is not enough to understand the gist of the text, more detailed comprehension is necessary.

Reading is a constant process of guessing, and what one brings to the text is often more important than what one finds in it. This is why, from the very beginning, students should be taught to use what they know to understand unknown elements. There are two main reasons for reading:
  - Reading for pleasure.
  - Reading for information (in order to find out something or in order to do something with the information you get).

The process of reading comprehension is a phenomenon in which the student-reader interacts with the written material to extract information and get to the point of evolving information. This process moves from decoding up to critical assessment, which is part of the comprehension process.

Phases for the didactic treatment of this ability:
  1 - Students prepare to interact with the text.
  2 - Student interaction with the text to process information for comprehension.
  3 - Critical assessment of the text.

Phases to be followed to achieve a good reading-comprehension (Medina, 1999):
"1. Sensitiveness phase: A first approach to the text with the aim of preparing students for reading. The following procedures must be taken into account:
  > ➤ To select topics and texts appropriate for their needs.

➢ To determine elements which may hinder comprehension of the essential ideas in the material.
➢ To have a purpose for reading.
➢ To formulate possible hypotheses for the process.

2. Processing phase: Where students interact with the text on bases created during the previous phase:
➢ Distinguishing central ideas.
➢ Prioritizing ideas.
➢ Searching for meaning in the dictionary.
➢ Answering questions from the teacher or classmates.
➢ Comparing ideas.
➢ Relating the text content to their backgrounds.

3. Redefinition phase: Students go beyond comprehending the elements from the text, and are able to express viewpoints about the author with critical assessment:
➢ Summarizing.
➢ Carrying out inferences from the subject.
➢ Assessing the content of the text.
➢ Speculating about the content." *(Translated by the editor)*

Antich *et al* (1986) talk about activities to work with the "subtext," and offer these suggestions:
"- To link facts and doers.
- To draw conclusions about facts.
- To value attitudes
- To link what was read to personal experiences.
- To interpret facts, attitudes or feeling or criticize them.
- To discover and express the author´s intention." (Translated by the editor)

For the post-reading phase, Ayala (2000) proposes to call it:
*"**Integration and transference stage:***
It is the critical-reading phase where the most important aspect is assessing what was read based on background experience and reading competence. It involves all actions prior to full comprehension of the text. Through these, reading is integrated with the rest of the language skills and the information acquired is transferred to new situations.

Reading skills:
Assessing text content.
Summarizing and recalling what was read.
Drawing logical conclusions.

Cross-referencing information with other texts.
Expressing orally what was read expanding the information.
Expressing in writing what was understood.
Transferring reading strategies to other texts." (Translated by the editor)

This author presents valuable ideas when approaching reading comprehension in this final phase. Assessing contents and drawing logical conclusions pave the way to develop logical and critical thinking, reflection and then working on creative activities where students "transform" that reality and help people around them. Valuative thinking may also be activated as a way to form adequate values in the students.

Potential of reading comprehension to foster values education

Reading for comprehension as a communicative skill is vital for fostering values (read an article in this section of the book about the formative character of reading) since readers assume the written text in their inner world according to their interests and motives. Reading also helps form life-long abilities and habits.

Through reading for comprehension, readers are capable of understanding many facts that sometimes seem unworthy in the objective world. Readers can also modify their views of the objective world as well as all the things they thinks may be useful in life. Ayala Ruiz (2000) summarizes this idea as follows: *"Through reading, people become cultivated, they become good readers who notice and appreciate the wealth and effect of what they read and channel it in attitudes and behaviour... it is unquestionable that reading influences the shaping of feelings as well as moral and political ideas; it moulds aesthetic development in young people and the formation of convictions that will bring harmonic growth to human beings." (Translated by the editor)*

Post-reading as a values-forming stage

Post reading, or redefinition phase, is a key phase for developing values education through reading comprehension. Students have the opportunity to critically express their viewpoints on the authors' message. They also summarize, infer from the subject, assess the content of the text, and the teacher can ask them to transpose situations in which they voice their opinions or use the language in a more productive form.

All phases may be oriented towards this kind of education but there is no doubt that once students have fully understood text and message, they are in a favorable position to assess it and embark on deeper reflections on matters recreated in the text. This possibility opens the way to debates and exchanges that are auspicious for values education.

What reading activities best favor the formation of values?
The analyses made so far show that the activities devised to achieve an adequate values education must:
- Consider and spur the student's own experiences in life.
- Promote a reflection on the issues dealt with in the texts presented.
- Provoke an interactive exchange among students and teacher.
- Bring up debate and clarification of ideas that are necessary for the understanding of the situations depicted in the texts.
- Make room for respect among speakers, individual contribution and consideration of the subjective and personal character of values, which are finally "accepted" on an individual level, even when social influence is the foundation for the growth of the personality of each student. It is not only what the group can do for the individual, it is a two-way path where one must know that he/she can offer something in return to the class, and they will feedback and assist in building his/her system of values.
- Facilitate communication, cooperation, support, comprehension.
- Develop critical and assessing thinking and a scientific world-view.
- Exploit when necessary the student's mother tongue and cultural background to clarify ideas and tick emotional aspects, reinforcing the affective domain.
- Avoid one-side answers and imposition of ideas.
- Cultivate listening and attentive behavior.
- Explore and kindle the students´ emotions, their innate ones, and the ones underlying the texts at hand.
- Cover different skills.
- Concentrate on the inference and the applicative stages of reading to elicit values-centered viewpoints.

Possible types of reading comprehension activities to form values
Based on what was disclosed above, the author considers the following can be of help in elaborating values-forming activities:
- Dramatization of text-related "axiological situations" (where aspects about values and antivalues are presented).
- Dramatization of situations to describe emotional aspects related to the text.
- Inference questions (reading between the lines) and above all application questions where students have to exploit their personal experiences in life, reflect on facts and events related to the text, interchange, criticize on a constructive basis, respect others' criteria considering the theme of the text.
- Presentation of anecdotes of an emotional character related to the text.

Writing out of notes or letters:
- ✓ Praising people or events in the text for their values.
- ✓ Criticizing and giving advice to people or events for their misbehavior or explicit mistakes.
- ✓ Contrasting with examples of great human values.

Also, the lesson can offer the following possibilities:
- ♦ Finding and getting ready to tell poems related to the text.
- ♦ Offering alternatives of solutions to possible problems (positive or negative connotation) derived from the themes of the text.
- ♦ Presenting books, poems, articles, art in general, which describe exemplary events or virtuous persons, related to the text.
- ♦ Developing workshops and/or round tables to debate and discuss themes related to the text.
- ♦ Analyzing situations to help form a world-view about historic events and phenomena related to the text.
- ♦ Narrating facts that show evident identification with family, school, neighborhood, local and territorial values, related to the text.

Examples of reading and post-reading activities to form values
The activities presented below can be modified depending on the needs of each student group, objectives and the teacher. All of them have been implemented in class (only one text is included as a concrete example, which is presented in its original Spanish version t the students yet debates are in English):

(Text about time travel)
1. Find out information about who made possible the construction of the Egyptian pyramids. Summarize the information you found based mainly on: living conditions, working conditions, the origin of the workers.
2. Do you think the conditions were the best for developing that kind of work? Support your answer.
3. Which are the conditions of the workers in Cuba? Find out and report to the class.
4. Although the Egyptian pyramids are considered one of the Seven Wonders of the ancient world, their construction brought about the suffering of many people. Do you agree with that? Prove your answer. Consult your History teacher.
5. Write a letter to a friend telling him/her what you have learned about the construction of the pyramids, based on the information you have already found. Invite your friend to cultivate him/herself. Give reasons for doing so.
6. Find out about historic constructions in Cuba that have special significance for us. Present your findings in class.

(Text about the environment)
1. Think of other possible titles for the text. Why these?
2. Answer:
   Do you consider it important to protect the environment? Why? Give five reasons.
   What advice would you give the people of Thailand to continue their fight?
3. Work in groups and list six things you can do in your community to protect the environment. Say why you selected them.
4. Write a list of bad things people do in your neighborhood against the environment.
5. Write:
   A) A note of congratulation to the people of Thailand for their efforts to save the land.
   B) A critical note to those who are destroying the forest.
   C) A note of congratulation to eco-friendly people.

(Text about a Cuban historic figure. Example text)
"Terminada la cena, Marcos entrega al capitán los mejores caballos de que dispone, todo el dinero que había en la finca...
- Y de los muchachos ¿cuál me da?
No hay respuesta sino un paso al frente de Antonio, José y Justo...
Cuando parten los muchachos, Mariana le dice al marido: - Y tú Marcos, ocúpate de "acotejar" las cosas, que aquí todos estamos en guerra... Mariana entra en la sala con un crucifijo en la mano, habla con seguridad emocionada:
- De rodillas todos, padres e hijos, delante de Cristo, que fue el primer hombre liberal que vino al mundo, juremos libertar la patria o morir por ella.
María Cabrales hinca la rodilla junto a Mariana. Todos juran. Todos cumplirán el juramento..." *(See Appendix for translation)*
(Taken from Hombradía de Antonio Maceo, by Raúl Aparicio, 1974, pp. 47-48)

1. Putting the text in context (exchange with the students about the historic setting of the events and family context)
2. Answer:
   a) What do you think of giving all you have for a cause, for other people? Is it worthwhile? Explain.
   b) Prepare with your partner an assessment of the courage shown by Maceo and his family.
   c) Give your opinion on Mariana's position and her sacrifice.
3. Comment on the phrase: "... Here we are all at war." What is its significance historically speaking?
4. Find out with your History professors if the statement "Todos cumplirán el juramento" ("Everyone will keep their pledge") was finally true.

5. During the preparations for the Moncada Garrison attack, other young people sacrificed many things. Do research on this respect. Find help from your professors.
6. What did you feel when reading this text? Explain in writing then share your emotions with the group.
7. How would you present and work with this text so the emotions stirred through it are activated in your students too? Demonstrate.

A discussion of values and values education cannot ignore today's priorities on a historical, philosophical, social, psychological or educational level. Such is the imperativeness of the issue that it becomes necessary to approach it and present it so that its essences are discernible and comprehensible to those in charge of implementing and "materializing" values, paving the way for a more conscious and coherent effort towards this goal.

The social role and responsibility of education in the matter – an undergoing of society as a whole – must start with an adequate understanding of values-related categories from a theoretical point of view. On this ground, education in its general and particular senses can embark on a values "crusade" where scientific support and research facilitate work.

Values education is possible in social and educational contexts. This paper has aimed at proving this assertion. Reading is a basic skill. Its objectives may be focused on forming a personality that meets the needs and aspirations of society. Therefore, both the theoretical and practical goals set forth with this article have been brought off. The task ahead is now in the hands of those for whom the work was conceived, those concerned with and about the education of the new generations.

Bibliography
1. Ayala Ruiz, María Elena (2000) La enseñanza-aprendizaje de la comprensión lectora en el Departamento de Humanidades de los institutos preuniversitarios. Master´s degree Thesis. Holguin Pedagogical University.
2. Camino Trapero, María (1993) Valores que priorizan los docentes en su acción pedagógica y cómo son percibidos por sus alumnos: una experiencia investigación-acción. Universidad Católica, Departamento de Educación e Investigación Educativa. Uruguay.
3. Addine Fernández, Fátima; Ana Ma. González Soca; Silvia Recarey Fernández (2002) Principios para la dirección del proceso pedagógico. In Compendio de Pedagogía. Editorial Pueblo y Educación.
4. Antich De León, Rosa; Dariela Gandarias Cruz; Emma López Segrera (1986) Metodología de la enseñanza de lenguas extranjeras. Editorial Pueblo y Educación. La Habana.

5. Arias Guevara, Ma. de los Ángeles; Wanda L. Domínguez Rodríguez (2004) ¿Cómo favorecer la formación de valores en los escolares? Fondo Editorial del Pedagógico San Marcos. Perú.
6. Chacón Arteaga, Nancy (?) La formación de valores morales. Retos y perspectivas. ISPEJV. Electronic support.
7. Chacón Arteaga, Nancy (2002) Dimensión Ética de la Educación Cubana. Editorial Pueblo y Educación. Ciudad de la Habana.
8. Douglas Brown, H. (1987) Principles of Language Learning and Teaching. U.S.A, Prentice-Hall Inc.
9. Douglas Brown, H. (1994) Teaching by Principles. An Interactive Approach to Language Pedagogy. U.S.A, Prentice Hall Regents.
10. García Batista, Gilberto (1996) ¿Porqué la formación de valores es un problema pedagógico? In La formación de valores en las nuevas generaciones. Una campaña de espiritualidad y de conciencia. Editorial Ciencias Sociales. La Habana.
11. González Maura, Viviana *et al* (1995) Psicología para educadores. La Habana, Editorial Pueblo y Educación.
12. González Maura, Viviana (1999) La Educación en valores en el currículo universitario. Un enfoque psicopedagógico para su estudio. In Revista Cubana de Educación Superior. No. 2, 1999. CEPES. Universidad de la Habana. http://www.campus-oei.org/valores/maura.htm.
13. González Maura, Viviana (1999) El Profesor universitario: ¿un facilitador o un orientador en la educación de valores? In Revista Cubana de Educación Superior. Vol. XIX. No. 3, 1999. Universidad de la Habana. http://www.campus-oei.org/valores/viviana.htm.
14. González Rey, Fernando (1996) Un análisis psicológico de los valores: su lugar e importancia en el mundo subjetivo. In La formación de valores en las nuevas generaciones. Una campaña de espiritualidad y de conciencia. Editorial Ciencias Sociales. La Habana.
15. González Soca, Ana María (2002) El Proceso de enseñanza-aprendizaje ¿Agente del cambio educativo? In Nociones de Sociología, Psicología y Pedagogía. Editorial Pueblo y Educación.
16. Medina Betancourt, Alberto (1999) La competencia metodológica del profesor de inglés para dirigir el proceso de enseñanza-aprendizaje del Inglés en el Nivel Medio. Master´s degree Thesis.
17. Medrano Samaniego, Concepción (2003) ¿Es posible enseñar y aprender los valores en la escuela? Universidad del país Vasco. E.H.U. España. www.yahoo.es.
18. Olivé Iglesias, Miguel A. (1998) La comunicación y el desarrollo de la personalidad de los sujetos. Paper.
19. Olivé Iglesias, Miguel A. (1998) Values Education. An Approach to Theory and Practice in the Lesson of English. Paper.
20. Olivé Iglesias, Miguel A. (1999) Favoring values Education in the Spectrum Series. Pedagogical Foundation and Methodology through Teaching Tasks. Paper.
21. Olivé Iglesias, Miguel A. (2000) El Trabajo político-ideológico en el mundo y la Cuba de hoy. Su implementación en el plano pedagógico. ISP Holguín. Artículo.
22. Olivé Iglesias, Miguel A. (2000) Simulated Situations and Methodological Suggestions to Implement them in the Speaking Lesson of the subject Integrated English Practice IV to Foster Values in the 4th-year Students of the Specialty at the Teacher Training College of Holguin. Master´s degree Thesis.

23. Olivé Iglesias, Miguel A. (2001) La expresión oral como habilidad comunicativa en función de la formación de valores en la clase de inglés. Master´s degree Thesis. Olivé Iglesias, Miguel A. (2002) Values-forming Teaching Tasks. An Analysis and Exemplification. Paper.

24. Olivé Iglesias, Miguel A. (2003) Situaciones simuladas para formar valores en las clases de expresión oral del inglés para nivel avanzado en los estudiantes de la especialidad del ISPH. Paper.

25. Olivé Iglesias, Miguel A. (2003) A Monograph on Values and Values Education. ISP Holguín. Treatise.

26. Olivé Iglesias, Miguel A. (2004) Crisis de valores. Aprender los valores. Una reflexión al respecto. Paper.

27. Olivé Iglesias, Miguel A. (2004) Lo Axiológico en la Pedagogía cubana. La educación como macrovalor. Paper.

28. Olivé Iglesias, Miguel A. (2004) Tareas y textos emotivos sobre Antonio Maceo para el fortalecimiento de valores en estudiantes de primer año. Paper.

29. Olivé Iglesias, Miguel A. (2005) La Psicología como fundamento y la Historia como núcleo de una aproximación interdisciplinaria a la investigación sobre la identidad como valor. Paper.

30. Olivé Iglesias, Miguel A. (2006) Valores: ¿Formación, Aprendizaje, Educación? Paper.

31. Olivé Iglesias, Miguel A. (2006) Tareas docentes interdisciplinarias para la práctica integral de la especialidad de inglés. Breve esbozo teórico y ejemplificación. Paper.

32. Olivé Iglesias, Miguel A. (2006) La formación ideopolítica en el trabajo científico-metodológico y su concreción en la clase desde la disciplina Práctica Integral del Inglés para la especialidad en el ISPH. Paper.

33. Sigarreta Almira, José (2001) Incidencia del tratamiento de los problemas matemáticos en la formación de valores. Holguín. Cuba. PhD Thesis. Holguín Pedagogical University.

34. Silvestre Oramas, Margarita (1999) Aprendizaje, Educación y Desarrollo. Editorial Pueblo y Educación. Ciudad de la Habana.

35. Silvestre Oramas, Margarita (2002) El proceso de enseñanza-aprendizaje y la formación de valores. In Compendio de Pedagogía. Editorial Pueblo y Educación. Ciudad de la Habana.

36. Silvestre Oramas, Margarita; Pilar Rico Montero (2002) Proceso de enseñanza-aprendizaje. In Compendio de Pedagogía. Editorial Pueblo y Educación. Ciudad de la Habana.

37. Silvestre Oramas, Margarita y José Zilberstein Toruncha (2002) Hacia una didáctica desarrolladora. Editorial Pueblo y Educación. Ciudad de La Habana.

38. Silvestre Oramas, Margarita (?) Exigencias didácticas para dirigir un proceso de enseñanza-aprendizaje desarrollador y educativo. Monografías.com.htm.

39. Terroux, Georges; Howard Woods (1991) Teaching English in a World at Peace. Professional Handbook. Mc Gill University. Faculty of Education. Canada.

40. Velázquez León, Manuel (2000) Reflexiones sobre la disciplina Historia de la cultura de los países de habla inglesa desde la perspectiva de la educación valoral. Texto Didáctico. Holguín, I.S.P. Holguín.

41. Velázquez León, Manuel (?) Educación valoral. Pretensiones y posibilidades. Artículo. ISP. Holguín.

42. Yurén Camarena, Ma. Teresa (1995) Eticidad, valores sociales y educación. Universidad Nacional. Distrito Federal. Ciudad de México.

Appendix

Translation of the text in Spanish (Translated by the editor)

Setting: The outset of the Cuban 19th-Century Independence War in 1868. The *mambises* (Cuban fighters) visit Antonio Maceo´s home looking for supplies and recruits for the war.

(Mariana is Antonio Maceo´s mother. Marcos is her husband. Antonio, José and Justo their sons. María Cabrales is Antonio Maceo´s wife)

After dinner, Marcos gives the captain the best horses he has, all the money in the farmhouse...

"And the boys, which one will you give me?"

There is no reply but a step forward by Antonio, José and Justo...

When the boys leave, Mariana tells her husband: "Marcos, you prepare everything, we are all at war here..." Mariana comes to the living room with a cross in her hands, she speaks with emotion and certainty:

"On our knees all of us, parents and kids, before Christ, who was the first progressive man on earth, let´s pledge to free our homeland or die for it."

María Cabrales kneels beside Mariana. They all take the vow. All of them will honor it...

Teaching English as a Foreign Language in Cuban Local Communities

PhD María Elena Ayala Ruiz. Full Professor
MSc Miguel Ángel Olivé Iglesias. Associate Professor
MSc Katiuska Ceballos Bauta. Associate Professor

With the acceleration of globalization, learning foreign languages is becoming progressively important. Nowadays, it is just a condition to be a good professional in any field. This rank is probable due to the continuing expansion of English, which has influenced language teaching and learning. As it is considered a powerful tool for communication and contact with people from different cultural and linguistic backgrounds, it is assumed as the international language or lingua franca, and the language of science, economy, politics, commerce and financial affairs.

Consequently, Cuban schools have declared the study of English as a priority from very early childhood. It has promoted huge changes to improve the development of the students´ communicative competence, and this has generated continuous improvement processes aimed at a better effectiveness of the scientific management of the teaching-learning process, with positive outcomes cognitively, socially, affectively, as well as in knowledge, skills, attitudes and values.

The study of English as a foreign language has been given special significance in the Cuban National System of Education. That is why many efforts are made to improve teaching methods, so students reach adequate levels of language proficiency according to a set of defined points of reference provided by Common European Framework of Reference Framework, along with the a cultural formation and the fostering of human values that the Cuban project requires. In this way, the teaching of English as a foreign language has become one of the strategic directions for the enhancement of higher education processes to favor the training of professionals-to-be.

English is so significant that strategies have been conceived by the university to assure the formative aspect of highly qualified professionals in the foreign language area, for training teachers-to be to create innovative methodologies to teach the language effectively according to the students´ reality. This challenge puts in the agenda profound didactic reflections on updated conceptions for teaching and learning the language from a social standpoint, which takes into consideration the community the students belong to (families, peer groups, schools, neighborhoods) and its culture, for its influence on learning.

The aforementioned ideas guide the purpose of this paper and provide this work with social significance and pertinence. It is oriented towards the design of language courses just in the context where the teaching-learning process occurs, in response to the country´s policy of expanding the possibilities that new spaces have to involve children in the study of the foreign language. It aims at increasing their motivation and guiding them to become autonomous learners with implications in their future academic, personal and professional life.

In the history of the Cuban educational system, the improvement of English learning syllabuses has been a constant preoccupation, bringing about plans to open out the range of this language throughout the country. However, students reveal many communicative limitations, which are generally the result of their lack of motivation. The belief that the school is the only responsible institution for these limitations in language learning can be considered a debatable criterion, since homes and communities must also be involved.

Many studies reveal a number of innovations intended for more efficient and comprehensive learning contextualized programs. Intentionally, the syllabus and guidelines proposed in this work have been designed taking into account current conceptions for the implementation of community courses specifically aimed at children. Their singularity lies in their being conceived in the community where they live. The proposal is directed at presenting motivational activities to activate the participants' interest for language studies as they accomplish the first level of language proficiency. It intends to change structural teaching styles into communicative and creative designs from a new angle for the accomplishment of more fruitful language teaching and learning.

In this type of course, a number of influences contribute to the differences of learner performance such as age, gender, attitudes, motivation and learning style, among others. Therefore, it is crucial for teachers to revise their teaching strategies when planning and selecting the materials to be used in class to avoid passivity and demotivation and guarantee the student´s enjoyment of the way English is taught. This is only possible if flexibility is taken as a principle for creating a credible atmosphere of collaboration and trust and all necessary conditions for authentic teaching, centered on learners' daily experience, personal values and attitudes, in their own community.

Teaching heterogeneous groups is a challenge for teachers. They must think about adapting and grading contents according to learners´ levels of development, devising activities for keeping them interested, and providing individual attention in the classroom to talented, overachieving, average and slow learners. Also, it can be achieved by adapting books, materials and activities, and deciding strategies for assessing the students' integral development.

The syllabus and guidelines have been created according to the notional and functional categories of language. They concentrate on interactions for using the language to perform holistic communicative tasks and for placing the learner's interests and needs at the foreground. They focus on all the dimensions of language (Brown, 1987).

From a psychological point of view, the support is found in Vygotsky´s historical-cultural approach. It is based on the dialectical-materialistic theory, focused on its main contributions, the law of double formation, the development of the human psyche; the zone of proximal development, and its meaning in the learning process of a foreign language, as well as the relationship between cognitive and affective-motivational aspects (Vygotsky, 1982).

The Common European Framework of Reference for Languages, created by the British Council of Europe (CEFR, 2011), offers a common basis for the elaboration of language syllabuses considered a powerful tool to assist in the planning of community courses. The CEFR is a guide for determining what learners need to be able to do in the foreign language. It describes in an integrative way what language learners need to learn to do in order to use a language for communication and what knowledge and skills they have to develop so as to act effectively. This approach also takes into account the cognitive, emotional and volitional resources and full range of specific abilities to be applied by the individual as a social agent.

The proposal also bases on the CEFR since it is a syllabus to be implemented in a community. It considers forms of relationships with overlapping social groups, which as a whole define identity features. It responds to the objective of promoting satisfactory development of the learner's whole personality and sense of identity in response to the enriching experience that inter-subjective relationships facilitate in the community. Its conception is eminently communicative, so attention is directed to the development of communicative competence in its four dimensions, and the development of thinking processes. It enlarges the participants´ general formation as they comprehend the culture and ideology of the community and promote relations among its members, feelings and attitudes.

CEFRL principles of good practice are also valued. They emerge from the Communicative Action-Oriented Approach, which is comprehensive and coherent with the aims of most school language learning referring to cognitive, emotional and volitional resources and the full range of abilities specific to and

---

applied by the individual. They also serve in guiding the syllabus to consider participants' needs and motivations, focused on real-life tasks and constructed around selected functions, viewing learners primarily as members of society who have tasks (not exclusively language-related) to accomplish in a given set of circumstances, in a specific environment and within a particular field of action.

The proposal goes as far as getting learners to do activities with language for carrying out communicative acts of various kinds. These activities demand learners to participate dynamically through cooperative and collaborative relations in which the students engage in meaningful interaction, negotiate meaning, use communication strategies, and try to overcome limitations while working in pairs or small groups. Tasks are appreciated as the actions performed by one or more individuals strategically, using their own specific resources to achieve a given result (CEFR, 2011).

In this paper both approaches are assumed from a holistic perspective that includes a diverse set of principles reflecting a communicative view of language and language learning, which can be used to implement a diversity of classroom procedures (Richards & Rodgers, 2001). These precepts are accompanied by a methodological conception that encourages creative, unpredictable and purposeful use of language as communication outside the classroom (Kumaravadivelu, 2006).

The approaches mentioned above are combined with the Developmental Approach. They facilitate a process that promotes creativity and learner´s development, through the appropriation of linguistic-communicative and sociocultural knowledge, the development of basic habits and skills enabling students to comprehend and produce coherent and simple texts that contribute to their comprehensive formation. These assumptions help teachers conceive developmental teaching and learning as the systemic process of culture transmission, which is organized taking into consideration the students' real and potential levels of development that lead to the learner´s continuous growth in order to form an integral and self-determined personality in a historical, concrete context (Castellanos, 2001).

This theoretical framework orients teachers to use innovative classroom activities (games, role-plays and scenarios) designed for creating and sustaining learner motivation from more context-situated and teacher-developed methodologies. Teachers have autonomy and responsibility for guiding the teaching-learning process by means of classroom procedures and principles they construct based on the approaches for foreign language teaching and their own teaching experience, instead of following prescribed methods.

A communicative, developmental and action-oriented didactics for teaching English in a local community, takes into account the nexuses between teaching and learning, instruction and education, development and formation. Besides, it capitalizes on the importance of an integral diagnosis, the role of communication, the sort of activity and the establishment of interactions and interrelations in which cognitive, affective and volitional aspects are implied. It follows a theoretical support for planning correct communicative tasks, which should be planned in accordance with the students' level and peculiarities, and the sociocultural environment where the teaching-learning process takes place.

The syllabus design includes all the didactic components of the foreign language teaching-learning process, as follows: *objective, content, method, teaching media* and *assessment*. It also includes *guidelines:*

Objective. This is the ruling category that determines contents and methods together with the rest of the components of the teaching-learning process. It defines communicative functions, knowledge, skills and values to attain; the interrelationship between language forms, meaning and use. Three main general objectives have been determined:

- o Get familiar with the foreign language and its culture, fostering love and motivation for studying English.
- o Understand simple oral and written texts about realistic themes.
- o Express themselves orally and in writing about the communicative functions studied at an applicative-creative level. (taken from the CEFRL precepts)
- o Foster friendship, solidarity and love for their relatives, their neighbors and their community.

Content. The content is structured to form in the learners communicative competence in English. It is a combination of knowledge, skills, attitudes, feelings and values to carry out communicative acts. The content of the syllabus responds to **Level A1,** which is described in the CEFR as the lowest level of generative language use, the point at which the learner can interact in a simple way, ask and answer simple questions about themselves, where they live, people they know, and things they have, initiate and respond to simple statements in areas of immediate need or on very familiar topics, rather than relying purely on a very finite rehearsed and lexically organized repertoire of phrases for specific situations.

- ▪ *Listening*: Recognizing familiar words and very basic phrases concerning themselves, their family and immediate concrete surroundings when people speak slowly and clearly.

- *Reading*: Understanding familiar names, words and very simple sentences for example in notices, posters and catalogues.
- *Spoken interaction*: Interacting in a simple way provided the other person is prepared to repeat or rephrase things at a lower rate of speech and help him/her what is being tried to say; asking and answering simple questions in areas of immediate need or on very familiar topics.
- *Writing:* Writing a short, simple postcard for example sending holidays greetings; filling in forms for personal details, for example entering their names, nationality and address on a hotel registration form.

Method. Communicative, developmental and action-oriented procedures and techniques in their most effective combination in accordance with the students´ necessities and potentialities in their own community. It conceives communication as its main goal, keeping in mind methodologies centered on skill integration and the accomplishment of meaningful and authentic communicative tasks related to the community.

Teaching media. Some of them are selected while others are elaborated for supporting teaching methods and techniques to improve learning effectiveness and motivation by the combination of different sensory analyzers: auditory and visual analyzers. They include authentic materials, such as movies and songs, television programs and recordings and a wide range of visual aids that might help, pictures, drawings, photos from magazines, flash cards, picture cards, models, pocket charts, flannel boards, realia, worksheets. The students can participate in their creation.

Evaluation. Oral evaluation is to be prioritized although holistic assessment is effective to value the accomplishment of objectives. It highlights good results and involves children in a nice improving atmosphere. The amount of unpleasant stress associated with a test is avoided. It highlights how well the learners are prepared and how confident they feel of success, instead of focusing on giving marks.

Quizzes can be administered during a unit and at the end of a unit. During-a-unit quizzes are integrated into the activities included in the learning process. End-of-a-unit quizzes sum up the objectives of the unit. The project work is assumed as an end-of-a-unit evaluation. Both types of evaluation can be used for diagnostic, pedagogical, formative, developmental and motivational purposes.

Guidelines:

Create an enjoyable and flexible atmosphere. Try to get the students out of their classrooms, whenever possible, in open areas that most communities have. Use games and songs whenever reasonable to favor interaction, cooperation and collaboration through pair and group work.

Engage students, relatives and neighbors in pleasant activities in the community, fostering group acceptance, together with a harmonious coexistence that enhances the students' emotional development.

Relate the contents to learners' real communicative situations in their community.

Aim activities at values education according to the characteristics of the community.

Provide students with enough declarative input. Introduce meaningful, contextualized language communicative functions through simple techniques: short monologues and brief dialogues, real conversations between the teacher and the students, simple micro-situations, etc.

During the controlled practice stage, *include* graded exercises to provide learners with the opportunity to practice and fix the language. As a pre-communicative stage, the teacher may insist on phonological and grammatical accuracy. Pre-communicative and communicative activities should be developed in a holistic way; in almost every lesson (except for the first lesson of the study unit), the student listens, understands, talks, reads and writes. They should be graded according to their level of assimilation and their position within the system of rehearsing lessons: recognition, reproduction, partial production. They prepare the students for the creative practice where authentic communicative tasks at a production level are implemented, the stag

Give the students plenty of opportunities for working in groups or pairs to transfer meaning in real life-like situations to foster interaction in the classroom and outside it.

Judiciously *select* which mistakes to treat and the correction techniques to be used, to avoid demotivation.

Include activities or materials that illustrate the connection between language and culture.

Introduce everyday communication expressions: simple words such as **please** and **thank you**, **sorry**, **pardon** etc.

Do not use abstract terminologies or explain grammar using terms, as children do not know how to use them while communicating. E.g., verbs, adjectives, singular, plural... present progressive or future tense...

Assign a project work at the end of each study unit and invite parents and neighbors to the discussions thereafter.

Include the Portfolio as a powerful essential metacognitive tool.

Community courses can be implemented as an alternative for putting English at the service of the community with the sense of bringing sound activities to people in their spare time, as they increase their motivation for learning this foreign language. It responds to the policy of expanding the learning of English throughout the country to improve the comprehensive cultural formation of the Cuban people. They may be considered effective means for teaching English as a foreign language with instructive and educative intentions to favor children's motivation for the study of this language with positive impact in all elementary schools in the community. It is important for the university to improve teachers-to be training for their future responsibility in making didactic choices for combining methods and procedures according to the community where the syllabus is implemented.

The basis of the Common European Framework is vital for devising community courses, since it describes what language learners need to learn to do in order to use language for communication, and what knowledge and skills they have to develop so as to act effectively. Students' needs, motivations, characteristics and resources are considered.

The principles of a communicative, developmental and action-oriented didactics allow teachers to be effective for designing and introducing community syllabuses to practice, because they reveal a view of language and language teaching-learning that supports authentic classroom procedures, techniques and methodologies oriented towards skill integration and authentic meaningful communicative tasks according to general and specific objectives.

The syllabus and guidelines are recommended to teachers-to-be and professionals from the English foreign language area. Its introduction into practice and the use of different methods such as observation, interviews, surveys and focal groups reveal its pertinence, feasibility and applicability.

Bibliography
Acosta. R (2005) Didáctica desarrolladora para lenguas extranjeras. IPLAC. La Habana.
Ayala, M.E. (2017). Enfoques contemporáneos para la enseñanza-aprendizaje del inglés como lengua extranjera. En Convención Científica Internacional y Expoferia Las Tunas.
Instituto Cervantes. (2017). Acerca del Marco Común Europeo de Referencia para las lenguas (MCER). Cambridge English. Cambridge English Language Assessment.
Aldridge, J. & Goldman, R. (2007). Current issues and trends in education (2nd Ed.). Boston.
Bishop M. (2013). It's all relative. 10 ways to teach about family. Jet program. English in elementary school. Teaching materials collection. www.Genki English.com.
Brown D. (1987). Principles of language learning and teaching. Englewood Cliffs, New Jersey, H. Douglas Prentice Hall

Brown, D. (2002). English language teaching in the post-method era: toward better diagnosis, treatment, and assessment. Methodology in Language. Teaching: An Anthology of Current Practice. Cambridge: Cambridge University Press.

Castellanos D. (2001).Hacia una concepción del aprendizaje desarrollador. La Habana, Cuba.

University of Cambridge. (2011) ESOL Examinations. Using the CEFR: Principles of Good Practice. Green in press.

Council of Europe. (2017). Common European Framework of reference for languages: Learning, teaching and assessment. Cambridge University Press.

Kumaravadivelu, B. (2006). A Post-Method Perspective on English Language Teaching. In: Forum Language Pedagogy. World English.

Kumaravadivelu, B. (2006). TESOL methods: Changing tracks, challenging trends. TESOL Quarterly, 40 (1), 59-81.

Larsen-Freeman, Diane. 2000. Techniques and principles in language teaching. 2nd edition. Oxford: Oxford University Press.

Nunan, D. (2002). El diseño de tareas para la clase comunicativa. Madrid. Cambridge University Press.

Penny Ur & Haim O. (2019). Teaching English in Mixed-ability Classes - a booklet of Practical Suggestions. State of Israel. Ministry of Education. Language Department. English Language Education.

Py-Ching Chen. (2019). The Effect of English Popular Songs on Learning Motivation and Learning Performance. Department of Foreign Languages and Literature National Cheng Kung. En WHAMPOA - An Interdisciplinary Journal 56.

Richards, J. C. & Rodgers S. T. (2006). Approaches and Methods in Language Teaching, Second Edition. USA. Cambridge University Press.

Urdanigo, E. D. (2016). Hacia un nuevo enfoque en la metodología para la enseñanza-aprendizaje del inglés ISSN 2528-7842, Revista Mikarimin. Publicación cuatrimestral. Vol. 2, Año 2016, No. 3 (septiembre-diciembre).

Vázquez, F. (2010): Enseñanza de las Lenguas. Un enfoque orientado a la acción. CPR Huelva-Isla C. Descargado de: http://www.slideshare.net/franvazquez/enseanza-de-las-lenguas-un-nfoque-centrado-en-la-accion.

Vygotsky, S. (1982). Pensamiento y lenguaje. Ciudad de La Habana: Editorial Pueblo y Educación, 1982.

Warrington, S. D., & Jeffrey, D. M. (2005). A rationale for passivity and de-motivation revealed: An interpretation of inventory results among freshman English students. Journal of Language and Learning.

Yen-Hui, W. (2010). Using Communicative Language Games in Teaching and Learning English in Taiwanese Primary Schools. Kainan University. Journal of Engineering Technology and Education, Vol. 7, No.1 March.

Applied
Information and Communication
Technologies (IT)

Learning Objects to Foster the English Teaching-Learning Process in the University

MSc Anabel La O Bacallao, Associate Professor
PhD Julio César Rodríguez Peña, Associate Professor
MSc Marianela Juana Rabell López, Associate Professor

Along with the introduction of Information Technologies (IT), many have been the changes carried out in the teaching-learning process to improve the students' learning. In this sense, the virtual era reaches every aspect of life, with a significant role in learning. On the other hand, when training professionals society requires, particularly so when learning foreign languages, the use of IT is a feasible solution: practical and interactive resources are generated, motivating IT users.

Nowadays, schools are more likely to use IT in the teaching-learning process than decades ago. However, this technology alone has no meaning, and it does bring actual benefits to the educational context. It is a must for both teachers and students to contextualize IT use in teaching and managing educational pursuits in order to improve them. Despite what has been achieved, there are still things left to do.

The University of Holguin, Campus José de la Luz y Caballero, started a research on the use of IT. Learning resources was increasing based on the application of generalized experiences by the Cuban Ministry of Education (MINED) oriented towards the initial training of professionals, and the introduction of IT strategies. All these elements corroborate the fact that both professional updating and efficient performance increase as they efficiently implement technology, especially so in mastering English as a foreign language. In Cuba, just like the rest of the world, mastering a foreign language is a priority within globalization and breakthrough discoveries in IT. Hence, the Cuban Educational System gives importance to English language learning as new challenges arise in professional training performance-enhancement.

The application of empirical methods and studies, the analysis of regulation and specialized material on the topic worldwide (Willey (2000); IEEE (Institute of Electrical and Electronics Engineers) (2002); Polsani (2003); García (2005); APROA, (2005); Callejas, Hernández & Pinzón (2011); Portilla (2015); La O (2017), as well as interviews to teachers and other education-related personnel, allowed researchers to detect that IT resources through learning objects (LO) at the university were not exploited. In addition, the existing resources were barely put to use.

The above reasons brought to the surface the need to develop an experience with LO to foster the English teaching-learning process in times when learning through IT has a significant role to play in higher education in the country.

As part of the research project "Development of educational applications," in its second research line "Development of learning resources in the virtualization context in the University of Holguin," the following objectives were stated:

1. Creating and designing LO, through the author tool OPALE (Open Academic Learning)
2. Branching out to further researching fields leading to the granting of a Master´s degree.

Taking as a point of departure the results derived from the project, it was decided to start research on modelling new LO for the learning process of grammatical aspects taught to English teachers-to-be in pre-service students from the English major. Therefore, this paper aims at presenting the experience related to the elaboration of LO to support the English learning process, specifically, grammatical aspects throughout the author tool OPALE, in times when learning English is central in teacher training.

Using IT in education and elementary forms of usage
Using IT within education has been defined by different starting points. Many have designed profiting from use and potential. In this sense it must be clear that most of the students know or have access to some kind of technology, an issue that makes technology very popular among them. To develop the required elementary skills when using technology it is necessary to consider:

- Productivity: to take advantage of what these resources offer when: taking down notes and solving exercises, searching information, communicating (e-mail, chat, etc.), spreading information, studying, among others.
- Innovation in teaching practices: to take advantage of the teaching possibilities these resources offer for the students to reach a higher learning status.

In this regard, it is necessary to LEARN ABOUT *IT*, LEARN *IT* and WITH *IT*. In the first case, according to Coloma, 2012, it is related to IT literacy and its use as a productivity instrument, which assumes the use of computers and general programs and the acquisition of good work habits. The second one includes IT within the framework of each subject, to inform, transmit content interactively through the resources created for each subject and the use of didactic materials. The third one would use IT as a cognitive instrument and for group interaction and collaboration.

It is about using IT to motivate learners towards responsible and creative learning. Universities currently face the challenge of expanding the range of responses in correspondence to social demands, as well as the increasing requirements presented by students in training, who must be able to fully engage in social, productive and scientific processes, in a noticeably diverse society of technological changes. As part of all this discussion to improve learning, specifically the learning of English grammar, a command of grammatical aspects is essential for understanding the foreign language. Grammar gives the necessary elements to proficiently act in their future performance as teachers with a high communicative competence.

Many factors define teaching English to non-native speakers: effort, proficiency in the foreign grammar, lexicology, didactics, etc. All of them offer the possibility of teaching; however, this does not guarantee success. It all depends on the teacher's expertise, his/her competencies, performance, teaching media he/she brings to class, etc. The teacher must be a teaching-learning process leader and stimulate the students' active participation in class. Another positive aspect is that teachers can devise the teaching units and media to use in the English class, taking into account the characteristics and demands of the syllabus. Likewise, they develop skills when creating learning resources, flexible and open to the real students' conditions.

In that sense, authors like Lowther *et al* (2008), Further, Serhan (2009), Gee (2007, 2011) have dealt with topics related to including learning resources when learning foreign languages and their role in learner development. They have highlighted the development of high quality teaching and learning through IT. Lowther *et al* (2008) have stated that there are three main characteristics to develop such teaching and learning: autonomy, capability, and creativity.

Autonomy means that students take control of their learning through IT so they become more capable of working on their own and cooperatively. Thus, LO focus the students on the aforementioned process, making them the center and holding them responsible agents in their learning process. One of the objectives of creating this kind of resource is not only that teachers can use them in class, but also that students can access them without the teachers' help. In other words, this is student based learning (Castro Sánchez & Alemán 2011). Further, Serhan (2009) concluded that IT fosters autonomy by allowing educators to create their own material. This helps language teachers design and create their own LO and channels the created resources in giving teachers a better control over contents and students' real needs.

According to Further, Serhan (2009), "with regard to capability, once students are more confident in learning processes, they can develop the capability to apply and transfer knowledge while using new technology with efficiency and effectiveness" (*Apud*. Shan Fu (2013), pp. 114). As a result, the teaching learning process enriches the student's learning skills and widens their knowledge beyond what they already know. Through IT, student creativity is promoted. Along the process they can also find other resources and materials, even create others from available styles for them such as, games (Gee 2007, 2011), CD and television. Combining student autonomy, capability and creativity using IT, upgrades and improves not only the teaching quality, but also learning.

It is important to remember that when designing the LO one fact stands out: IT have full meaning combined with other resources and materials, along with the teacher's help, and they represent a powerful tool in the learners' hands to foster independent study and learning the foreign language.

Deficiencies were identified regarding the low number of learning resources to foster the English teaching-learning process. There is a significant amount of digital materials for the students to use them: books, dictionaries, etc. Yet there are no palpable resources to interact and appropriate themselves of the contents or via the teachers' help. Furthermore, there is little knowledge on LO to support the English learning process, specifically treating grammatical aspects. Consequently, developing this kind of resource will allow planning and organizing the learning process with an interdisciplinary and human approach, and will also foster the use of IT in such process with productive methods.

Presenting Learning Objects
Taking as a starting point the documents analyzed, it was stated that several authors have studied this topic. Following, the main characteristics LO have are listed below, stated by García (2005) and quoted by Portilla (2015) in the article "OPALE an Alternative to Develop Learning Objects": assumptions adopted in this research as they respond to the Cuban conditions of education, and the teaching-learning process. Reuse, educative purpose, accessibility, duration, independence, autonomy, generativity, flexibility, versatility and functionality.

Proposal of LO for introducing basic elements of English Grammar I
When designing the LO proposed it was taken into consideration the ones resulting from the project "Development ..." and a Master Thesis by La O, 2017. Parts of speech was one of the topics included in the LO created. When learning grammar, this is one of the first things taught. It includes: the noun (See Image 1), adjective, the verb. During the creation process were considered and included links enriching the aspects presented in the LO; which are also related to contents studied in the subject Integrated English Practice, so a relation is evidenced between grammar and communication when learning this specific language.

Image 1. LO The Noun

Within the LO above, students can find vocabulary which helps them enrich communication, as cognate words, among others, which in some cases they can easily relate in order to use them, as well further vocabulary in their English dialogues. Furthermore, the semantic quality of the content guarantees the acquisition and attention to contents through the tags OPALE facilitates: Definition, information, example, etc. (See Images 2 and 3).

Image 2. Examples of tags in OPALE

Image 3. Examples of Tags in OPALE

Here learners will find general structures of different grammatical tenses, affirmative and negative sentences, conjugation of verbs, regular and irregular verbs, among other aspects of interest presented in a simple way that will allow them to know and review the contents taught in class. They include audio and images, enhancing the information presented; all of which is possible because OPALE permits the inclusion of different resources.

The learner will interact with the tool and surf through the menu, where the referred information will be found. This LO contains objectives orienting what students must achieve once they finish consulting it. Also an introduction motivating them to use the LO and learning specific contents. Within this resource, the student will find a learning activity with the content element, which is the LO part with the content as such, also presented in a simple way students can understand with or without the teachers' help. Finally, there is a conclusion summarizing the content in the LO. There are also included other cross-tools fostering the information within. Out of two known versions of OPALE: 3.3.0.07 and 3.6.100, the second one was chosen as it is in English and since the proposals were designed and created for English Major Students

Professional training is one of the priorities in Cuban higher education institutions along with the use of IT in the English teaching-learning process. In this direction, designing and creating a tool which can help students with or without the teachers' help to develop their skills and enhance their professional performance through LO, is a strong point. At the same time, it will reinforce learning the English language and adequate levels of communication to face their professional and social life successfully.

The proposal presented here improves the students' English learning process, with or without the teacher's assistance. Thus, the importance of the elaboration of LO would contribute to the learners' preparation in their appropriation of basic elements of English grammar. Considering the potential this kind of resource offers and the results derived from this research and previous ones, it can be posited that LO through the author tool OPALE constitute a feasible solution to use IT within the English teaching-learning process in the virtual era.

Bibliography
APROA. (2005). *Aprendiendo con objetos de aprendizaje.* Proyecto chileno. Recuperado de http://www.aproa.cl/1116/channel.html
Callejas, M., Hernández, E. J. & Pinzón, J. N. (Enero – Junio, 2011).Learning objects: a state of the art. *Entramado 7(1), 176-189.*
Coloma, O. M. (2012). *La Transversalidad de las Tecnologías de la Información y las Comunicaciones en la formación del docente vs acreditación de carreras e instituciones. Experiencias, UCP "José de la Luz y Caballero".* Holguín.
García, L. (2005). *Objetos de aprendizaje: características y repositorios.* [España]: BENED, 2005. Recuperado de
http://www.tecnoeducativos.com/descargas/objetos_virtuales_deparedizaje.pdf
IEEE (2002). *Estándar para Metadatos de Objetos Educativos.* Recuperado de http://www.gist.uvigo.es/~lanido/LOMes/LOMv1_0_Spanish.pdf
La O, A. (2017). *Propuesta de Objetos de aprendizaje para el desarrollo del proceso pedagógico-profesional del idioma inglés en la carrera de Licenciatura en Educación Laboral e Informática.* Tesis en opción al título académico de Máster en Pedagogía Profesional. Universidad de Holguín.
La O, A., Granado, M. & Portilla, Y. (2017). *OPALE User's Handbook. Steps to follow to create learning objects with the OPALE tool.* Unpublished material.
Polsani, P. R. (2003). Use and Abuse of Reusable Learning Objects. *Journal of Digital Information, 3(4).* Retrieved fromhttp://www.info2.uqam.ca/~nkambou_r/DIC9340/seances/seance10et12/Standards%20et%20LO/http___jodi.ecs.soton.ac.pdf
Portilla, Y., Labañino, C. & Granado, M. (2015). *OPALE una alternativa para el desarrollo de objetos de aprendizajes.* Manuscrito no publicado, UCP José de la Luz y Caballero, Holguín, Cuba.
Shan, J. (2013). ICT in Education: A Critical Literature Review and Its Implications. *International Journal of Education and Development using Information and Communication Technology (IJEDICT), Vol. 9, Issue 1, pp. 112-125.*
Wiley, D. A. (2000). *Learning object design and sequencing theory.* (Doctoral dissertation). Department of Instructional Psychology and Technology Brigham Young University.

Multimedia to Improve Oral Expression in English

PhD Julio César Rodríguez Peña. Associate Professor
BEd Kenia Páez Tamanes
MSc Miguel Ángel Olivé Iglesias. Associate Professor

The nature of oral communication is a two-way process between speaker and listener. It involves the productive skill of speaking and the receptive skill of understanding (or listening with understanding). The main goal in teaching speaking is oral fluency. This can be defined as the ability to express oneself intelligibly, reasonably, accurately and without too much hesitation. Oral expression is considered the most important skill in teaching foreign languages. In order to develop the skill, we have to cope with a number of obstacles such as:

- Class size (often thirty or more learners).
- Classroom arrangement.
- The number of hours allotted for teaching the language.
- Limitations in the syllabus.
- Testing formats.

This topic has been approached by linguists, professors and researchers internationally, nationally and locally: Widdowson, 1978; Littlewood, 1981; Harmer, 1983; Byrne, 1983; and Finocchiaro, 1983; Antich 1975 and 1986 Acosta, 1996; Faedo (1988, 1994, 1997 and 2003); Santiesteban, 2004; Medina, 2004; and Pérez, 2008; Teruel et al 2006; Torres, et al 2007; and Rodríguez, 2008.

Communicate comes from the Latin verb *communicare* meaning to make common to many, share, impart, divide. This concept is central in understanding communication. When persons communicate, they share or make common their knowledge and ideas with someone else. According to Vygotsky and Rubinstein, 1982, "(...) communication is an exchange of thoughts, feelings and emotions." These authors reveal three functions of communication: informational, emotional and regulatory.

Communication is also defined as "(...) the sharing of ideas, information and feelings. It is a two way process that involves a sender, a receiver, and a message. Communication also involves feedback - the response that tells if the receiver got the message". (Emma Plattor et al, 1989) González Castro, 1989, defines it as "(...) an interchange; an interrelation; a dialogue; life in society; a process associated to men's needs that cannot exist without language."

Communication, according to Wilkins, 1953, includes knowledge of grammar and the ability to be grammatical but as a highly complex skill, it involves more than the sub-skills of being grammatical. (It is worth saying here that the term grammatical involves the levels phonology, grammar and lexicology." Byrne,

1989, defines communication "as a process of two ways between a sender and a receptor or receptors and it requires the productive ability of comprehension or listening ability with comprehension." Gordon, 1995, defines communication as "the processes of codification and decodification of signals; all the verbal messages are codes of the language and they are equivalent to feelings and not the feelings themselves."

McCain, 1998, states "communication is not just about more bulletin-board announcements and reports from management. It is about sharing information (….) communication is also about obtaining points of view from others and not only listening, but hearing what others say." McShane, 1998, communication is the process by which information is transmitted and understood between two or more people. González, 1998, states that communication represents a way of human interrelation. It expresses interaction among human beings and it is a way of interaction itself, which is closely related to the men's activities. It has an active character for both the sender and the receiver, it is for that reason that it can be said that it is a dynamic process.

Beebe et al, 2000, say "communication is the process of acting upon information. It is the process of interacting simultaneously and sharing mutual influence with other persons." Borges, 2004, quoted by Emma Plattor, considers that communication "is to share ideas, information and feelings." Medina, 2004, considers oral communication as the main skill in the teaching of foreign languages and its development depends on the verbal skill-integration between cognitive and affective-motivational elements.

Communication is a necessary and indispensable condition for man's existence. It is one of the most important factors for personal development. Communication is a key process for any human activity, it reflects the objective necessity of human beings to associate, cooperate and interact among themselves. Since the very beginning of humankind, the human-nature link has been marked by the relationships among humans.

According to Acosta, 1996, the communicative approach of language teaching takes as its starting point the use of communicative purposes of the language. This approach, therefore, strongly advocates use rather than form/meaning. It is an approach to foreign or second language teaching, which emphasizes that the goal of language learners is communicative competence.

The intuitive mastery that the native speaker possesses to use and interpret language appropriately in the process of interaction and relation to social context has been called by Hymes, 1972, communicative competence. In his words, it is a competence that tells "when to speak, when not, and as to what to talk about with whom, when where, in what manner." "Communicative competence involves grammatical (or linguistic) competence, sociolinguistic competence strategic competence, discourse competence and socio-cultural competence."

The conception about communicative competence given by Rodolfo Acosta, 1996, states: competence in any circumstances. It must include not only the linguistic forms of a language but also knowledge of when, how and where it is appropriate to use these forms. Oral expression is the key to communication. By considering what oral expression tasks can be used in class, and what specific needs learners report, teachers can help learners improve their oral expression and overall oral competence.

Littlewood, 1981, presents four broad domains that make up a speaker's communicative ability and calls for their consideration in foreign language teaching. They are presented here synthetically:

- o Learners must develop the skill of manipulating the language system to the point where they can use it spontaneously and flexibly in order to express their intended message.

- o Learners must distinguish between the forms mastered as part of their linguistic competence and the communicative functions to be performed.

- o Learners must develop skills and strategies for using language, to communicate meanings as effectively as possible in concrete situations. They must learn to use feedback to assess levels of success, and if necessary remedy failure by using different language forms.

- o Learners must be aware of the social meanings of language forms. This entails the skill to use their own speech to suit different social circumstances and avoid offensive ones.

To be effective when teaching oral expression, some methodological aspects should be kept in mind:
(Byrne, 1989):
1. Demonstrate the learners that they are making progress in the language all the time.
2. Correction should not discourage the learners.

3. Encourage the learners about how to complement the knowledge they have got in the English language.

4. Teach patterns of real interaction.

5. Give guided preparation.

6. Teach interactional language.

(Baobing Zhao, 1998):

1. Environment is essential: It is essential to build an atmosphere where students no longer feel shy, where they will voluntarily raise their hands to ask a question and where they will freely voice their own opinions. Teachers can do the following:

   a) Try to arrange seats in a circle or in groups with the students facing each other not in rows and lines.

   b) Let the students speak English sitting in their seats not standing. They will feel more comfortable this way.

   c) Try to divide the students into pairs and groups according to the different topics if you can, and also you can let them prepare their "opinion," and then have a group spokesman deliver the opinion.

   d) Set a day for no native language spoken. Students prepare a certain number of cards and they can write down those words or expressions, which they cannot convey in English if they have. Later on, the teacher and students discuss those words and expressions in class.

   e) Let students have 5-10 minutes of free talking at the beginning of every class. Students can talk about any interesting events, news or stories they have read, listened and watched recently.

   f) Let students have an English lesson out of the classroom with such activities as a class barbecue, picnic and a party.

   g) Build an English corner at the school and let students talk freely with those who are interested in learning English.

2. Encouragement is necessary: After students finish their oral expression in class, teachers should encourage them and let the students feel they have made some progress with a sense of their fulfillment. Teachers should point out some apparent mistakes in their oral expression after they finish their speech. Try to do these:

   • Be firm in a gentle way and give students praise whenever they are doing anything close to a good job.

   • Be sincere and look for opportunities to find something right in the answers of your students. Never get frustrated, angry or impatient.

   • Be a nice, sensitive and approachable person at all times. Never single students out or put them on spot.

   • Treat students with kindness and respect. Smile a lot and value their opinions.

- Allow the students to be themselves rather than expecting them to comfort to your preconceived ideas about how they should behave. Build their trust, take your time, and let students come to you.

3. Many tasks can be used while teaching English to your students in a better way. Some of them can be the following ones: Free talk, Retelling, Role-playing, Story telling, Talking according to the picture, Description, Games, Problem-solving.

4. Guidance is helpful: the guidance of the teacher can help learners get more motivated and interested making the teacher's job inevitable in the classroom:

   a. Try to use many gestures, vivid language and clear expressions in class.
   b. Act as an actor as well as a conductor giving demonstrations.
   c. Give students enough time to prepare what they want to speak about. Provide students with a conversation planning worksheet for this purpose. The conversations can vary in length depending on the level of the class. Give students time to plan what they want to say.
   d. Let students know the day they will be expected to participate in the next day.
      Sometimes give a handout that asks for opinions and tell the class that the teacher expects each student to have at least one with a very low level or particularly shy students.
   e. Ask students to try to memorize the whole thing, but if it smells rote, teachers can break it up by asking questions and try to let them think and say in their own words.
   f. It is not uncommon for learners to feign understanding when they are having conversations with one another. Also, believe that when learners feign understanding, they have lost important opportunities to practice conversation strategies. Encourage students to say "I beg your pardon" if they fail to understand their partner.
   g. Try to teach students to concentrate their attention on the important information of the speech rather than every word that your partner says.
   h. Try to explain some cultural background before students talk about a certain subject. Let them know differences between the two cultures.
   i. In oral expression, ask the students to focus their attention on fluency over accuracy and not to think too much of grammar.
   j. Try to call those students who express and act better to serve as examples. Then, call the ones who are poorer in English expressing and acting.

If the teacher encourages the students to speak by using as many ways as possible and creating a good language – oral expression environment, students will speak actively, willingly and naturally. Oral expression can only be mastered through practice.

The use of the Multimedia in the teaching-learning process of oral expression in English

In 1980, UNESCO defined the term educational technology as a systematic application of the resources of scientific knowledge to the process that each person needs to acquire and use knowledge. The term information comes from Latin *informatio-onis*, and it means action and effect of informing communication and acquisition of knowledge that are possessed about a determined subject; communicated or acquired knowledge. Technology does not guarantee with its own presence the pedagogical success, it is necessary to design carefully the educational program where it will be used. Teachers have the unavoidable duty to define and contextualize technologies of information and Communication (IT) in the educational sector.

Teaching media are all natural and artificial elements that contribute to objectify the interrelation between teachers and students in the process of transmission, acquisition, formation and development of knowledge, habits, skills, and capacities. They are the basis for making more effective the methods and procedures used in lessons. Teaching media transmit information combining eyesight and ear: the amount of information that students can get through movies, videos, TV and computers increases

Computers favor the teaching-learning process. They are used as didactic resources for teachers and aids for students´ learning. They provide teachers with the necessary tools to teach. Students can use them to know, analyze and assess reality.

Browsing the Web *(http://searchsoa.techtarget.com/definition/software)* the authors found useful information on software:
Software is a general term for the various kinds of programs used to operate computers and related devices. (The term hardware describes the physical aspects of computers and related devices).

Software can be thought of as the variable part of a computer and hardware the invariable part. Software is often divided into application software (programs that do work users are directly interested in) and system software (which includes operating systems and any program that supports application software). The term middleware is sometimes used to describe programming that mediates between application and system software or between two different kinds of application software (for example, sending a remote work request from an application in a computer that has one kind of operating system to an application in a computer with a different operating system).

An additional and difficult-to-classify category of software is the utility, which is a small useful program with limited capability. Some utilities come with operating systems. Like applications, utilities tend to be separately installable and capable of being used independently from the rest of the operating system. Labañino and M. Rodríguez, 2001, in their book "Multimedia para la educación", define educational software as: "(...) computer application that is supported in a well-defined pedagogical strategy. It supports directly the teaching-learning process; it constitutes an effective tool for educational development (...)"

It is necessary to highlight the effect that the use of a software (or multimedia) produces in the motivation towards learning, because of the review of contents that these media offer (activities, videos, music, games, images, etc.).

In Junior and Senior High Schools in Cuba are used Rainbow and Sunrise, two software programs designed to support the lesson taught in English. Computers and educational software, as teaching media, are efficient media for teachers in the preparation and teaching of lessons.

Multimedia is a set of several elements that facilitate communication (texts, images, video, audio, etc.) to transmit a good idea to achieve its objective, that is, to make people learn (Castro, 1997). Ganity and Sipior, 1992 said "Multimedia is the set of technologies of sensorial stimuli. It includes visual elements, audio and other capacities based on the senses, and they can increase knowledge and the user's comprehension." These authors said that in multimedia, several kinds of communication media are involved as well as several formats like texts, graphic data, images, video and audio. Multimedia help to find information in different ways (Electronic Computer Glossary).

For the elaboration of the multimedia that is described in this paper, Mediator was used, which is software used for the creation of applications as multimedia. It is able to combine graphics, sounds, animations, texts and video. The visual environment that it has is intuitive, that is why creation, importation, animation and media control can be easily and quickly fulfilled. For the work with multimedia presentations, Mediator is a powerful tool, which gives a professional tonality to them. It provides the user with the necessary tools for the creation of presentations with special effects and also to begin working with variables and the use of scripts. In addition, it allows programming, writing codes and achieving presentations with a refined aspect.

The Author System used is based on the construction of media resources, created with other applications for different purposes. All these resources have to be put effectively together to present the final application.

To design and work with images in general, Adobe Photoshop CS is used because of its advantages over other known applications for graphic design. Adobe Image Style 1.0 is used for higher speed in response and also Microsoft Word for text edition.

With the creation of IT, educational software (or multimedia), is introduced in the teaching-learning process of English. It constitutes an essential element for improving the teaching of English. They are a support that stimulates the students' motivation.

Description of the multimedia to improve oral expression in English
The name of the Multimedia is "Let´s Talk."
Analysis of the elements shown in the image:
- **Gallery:** It has images to help teachers to present new content and vocabulary.
- **Activities:** It allows accessing the activities designed related to contents included in the English books for the level.
- **Music:** Songs to help the teacher to carry out activities related to different topics. (To make pupils center their attention on and motivate them towards the lesson, and to sensitize them.
- **Help:** To help the teacher with doubts on how to use different elements included in the multimedia.
- **Exit:** It allows exiting the multimedia.

Then is presented the logical sequence that the user follows to use the multimedia:
How does the multimedia work?
1. To execute the application the principal screen appears.
2. The buttons with the different options are shown. When the user moves the mouse pointer in the different elements, a comment with information appears about the content of the option and different options are unfolded.
3. The user selects an option.
4. The corresponding screen with the selected option appears.
5. The user interacts with the application and gives answers according to the option selected.
6. If the user needs to continue interacting with the system, she/he must go back to the principal screen and select the desired option, the one who is going to guide the user to new screens. It gives the possibility to repeat

the selection process until the user decides to leave the system, so the user closes the application.

Minimum requirements for the running of the software:
- Microprocessor: Intel Pentium, AMD o Celeron a 133 + Megahertz
- Depth of color: 16 or 24 bits
- A mouse
- A sound card or device
- A CD-ROM reader
- Operative System: Windows 98, Windows NT, or Windows XP
- Minimum RAM: 64 Megabytes, but its behavior is excellent in 128 or 256 Megabytes.

How to use the multimedia
The multimedia can be opened in any Windows platform in normal conditions and it does not show messages of error. It determines if the conditions of the computer are good for its correct function. Its setup prepares the computer with the necessary resources for efficient running without affecting the parameters of the operative system. It works well in the lab configurations in the Cuban primary schools. It can be installed in the hard disk and run from the CD-ROM independently. The interface of the Software is easy-use, the code system used is clear, without interferences, the structure of the program allows to enter without any difficulty to its components, the media used are harmonically distributed. This product also has an interface with attractive images and it offers levels of help.

Methodological guidelines for the use of the Multimedia
Teachers are aware of the necessity to stimulate and develop in their pupils the necessary skills to express themselves orally that is why, the multimedia was conceived to develop oral expression. It is recommended to use the activities as reviews, images for teaching new vocabulary and music (songs), for stimulating and creating in them good feelings towards nature (animals, persons, etc.) Also, the activities proposed can be used as homework. Teachers must check the activities through their execution, to define the way to control the activities.

For the use of the multimedia is recommended to pay attention to:
1. The level of assimilation, the physiological and psychological maturity of the students, as indispensable conditions for the acquisition of oral expression skills.
2. The use of computers, in the teaching-learning process, helps to improve the assimilation of contents and the development of skills in the pupils.
3. The activities can be adapted or modified taking into account the teachers and pupils' necessities.

4. The implementation of activities in a practical way permits to use the computer as a teaching media so pupils give their best for finding solutions.
5. Pay attention to pupils individually; also make them reflect about the answers given.
6. Evaluate the activities included orally and in a written form, giving more stress to oral evaluation.
7. Evaluate the activities included individually or in pairs.

Multimedia to improve the development of oral expression. Activities included in the Multimedia

Activity # 1
Title: Be creative and dramatize.
Objective: Pupils should be able to create mini-dialogues to dramatize them, focusing the attention on speaking.
Heading: Select one of the cards and be ready to carry out the instructions.
Examples of situations:
Card 1
Dramatize the following situation:
Pupil A: You see your friend, greet him/her, ask how he/she is, say good bye.
Pupil B: A friend greets you, greet your friend back, answer how you are and ask the same to him or her, say good bye.
Card 2
Pupil C: You are a teacher, ask one pupil his/her name, and ask him/her how she/he spells it.
Pupil D: You are a pupil, your teacher talks to you, say your name, and spell your
name.
Card 3
Pupil E: You and a friend of yours are at the theater and you meet an ex-classmate, greet him/her, ask how he/she is, ask what he/she is doing, introduce your friend, say good bye.
Pupil F: You are at the theater and you meet an ex-classmate who is accompanied by a friend, greet him/her, ask how he/she is, ask what he/she is doing, meet your friend's friend, say goodbye.
Card 4
Pupil A: You arrive to a classmate´s house, you greet him/her and you ask him/her how he/she is. Your classmate introduces you a friend, tell him/her that it is a pleasure for you to meet him/her. The new classmate tells you about a party, ask him/her where and when it is.
Pupil B: A classmate arrives at your house, greet him/her. You have a friend who is visiting you and you introduce your friend to him/her.

Pupil C: You are visiting a friend. He introduces you a classmate who arrived to greet him/her, tell him/her that it is a pleasure for you to meet him/her, tell him/her about your party, and tell him/her where and when it is.

Activity # 2

Title: Let's select.

Objective: Pupils must select a card from the multimedia and talk according to the instructions given.

Heading: Select a card, answer the questions, and be ready to dramatize the situations with a partner.

Card 1

It is nine O'clock. You meet one of your friends on the street. How do you greet him/her? Make a mini-dialogue using this information and dramatize it with a partner.

Card 2

You met a person a few minutes ago. How would you ask him/her name in English? Make a mini-dialogue using this information and dramatize it with a partner.

Card 3

You meet one of your friends walking on the street with his/her mother. How would you ask your friend the name of his/her mother? Make a mini-dialogue using this information and dramatize it with a partner.

Card 4

You arrive at the school and you meet the head of the department. How would you greet her/him? Make a mini-dialogue using this information and dramatize it with a partner.

Card 5

Edward and Angel want to play baseball and they ask Kevin to play with them. What would they say to him? Make a mini-dialogue using this information and dramatize it with a partner.

Activity # 3

Title: Think about...

Objective: Pupils have to complete with the correct form of greetings already studied.

Heading: Complete the following conversation according to the forms of greetings you know. Be ready to practice it with your partner.

Two friends meet at school.

Axel: _____, Amy.

Amy: Hi, Axel.

Axel: Are you prepared for the Spanish test?

Amy: Yes, I am.

Variant:
A pupil greets the Principal at school.

      Pupil: _____!
      Principal: Good morning! How are you today?
      Pupil: Fine, thank you, how are you?
      Principal: Very well, thank you.

Theoretical and methodological considerations about oral expression in English reveal that these should be taken into account for elaborating activities that improve the development of this skill. Multimedia helps to increase pupils' motivation and plays a significant role in the improvement of speaking.

Bibliography
ABBOTT G. et al. 1989. The Teaching of English as an International Language. A Practical Guide. Edición Revolucionaria. La Habana.
AKAHORI, KENJI. 1985. Evaluation of educational Computers software in Japan (I y II): Methods and results.
BAUMGARTNER AND PAYR. 1996. Educational multimedia, Association for the Advancement of Computing Education, Charlottesville, V.A.
BEEBE, S. A., BEEBE, S. J., & REDMOND, M. V. 2002. Interpersonal Communication: Relating to Others. Boston: Allyn & Bacon.
BOEHM, 1978. Characteristics of Software Quality. Nueva York. North Holland.
BROWN G, 1 989. Teaching the Spoken Language. Edición Revolucionaria. La Habana.
BROWN, D.H. 1994. Guided cooperative language learning and individual language acquisition, Hillisdale, EE.UU.
BYRNE D, 1989. Teaching Oral English. Edición Revolucionaria. La Habana.
COLECTIVO DE AUTORES. 2000. Introducción a la Informática Educativa.
ELECRONIC COMPUTER GLOSSARY.
FAEDO, A. febrero del 2001. Comunicación Oral en Lenguas Añadidas: Un reto pedagógico actual. Curso 36, Evento Internacional "Pedagogía 2001". La Habana.
GARRIDO M. 1991. Diseño y creación de software educativo.
GANITY, E AND SIPIOR, J.1992. Multimedia II: Conceptos básicos de Multimedia.
GONZALEZ CASTRO VICENTE, 1980. Medios de enseñanza. La Habana: Ed: Pueblo y Edición.
GONZALEZ, J.; MARTINEZ, F.; BRADSHAW, R.; GOMEZ, A. y TORO, M.1994. Tecnología interactiva. Desarrollo y consecuencias para la escuela. Centro de Estudios de Software para la Enseñanza (CESoftE), ISPEJV, La Habana.
LANDROVE, GONZÁLEZ, JORGE L. 2012. Tesis en opción al título de Máster en Nuevas Tecnologías para la Educación, Geomap, Multimedia para favorecer el aprendizaje de la geografía de la localidad.
LABAÑINO RIZZO, CESAR A. y DEL TORO RODRIGUEZ MARIO. 2001. Multimedia para la Educación. Editorial Pueblo y Educación. Ciudad de La Habana, Cuba.
LABAÑINO, C. 2006. El Software Educativo. Disponible en CD Maestría Ciencias de la Educación. Módulo I.
LABAÑINO RIZZO, CESAR A.2002. Multimedia para la Educación. La Habana. Editorial Pueblo y Educación.

MARQUÉS, P. 1995. Software educativo. Guía de uso y metodología de diseño. Barcelona: Estel.

MEDINA BETANCOURT, ALBERTO. 2004. Modelo de Competencia Metodológica del Profesor de Inglés para la dirección del proceso de enseñanza-aprendizaje en el nivel medio. Tesis Doctoral en opción al grado científico de Doctor en Ciencias Pedagógicas. UCP Holguín.

MEDINA BETANCOURT, OLDY. 2008. Metodología para el uso del software educativo Sunrise por los estudiantes de 10mo grado del municipio Mayarí. Tesis en opción a título académico de Máster en Ciencias de la Educación. UCP Holguín.

PONS, J. 2004. La Formación Superior y el Reto de las Nuevas Tecnologías de la Información. Nuevas Tecnologías y Educación.

Revista Electrónica de Tecnología Educativa (EDUTEC). 1997. Nuevas competencias para la formación inicial y permanente del profesorado.

RODRÍGUEZ PEÑA, JULIO CÉSAR. 2008. Sistema de tareas de aprendizaje para posibilitar la formación y desarrollo de la habilidad de expresión oral en Inglés en los estudiantes de décimo grado en el IPVCP "Lucía Iñiguez Landín". Tesis en opción a título académico de Máster en Ciencias de la Educación. UCP Holguín.

SIPIOR, J.C. AND E.J. GANITY. 1992. Merging Expert Systems with Multimedia Technology, Database, Winter.

SQUIRES, D. Y MCDOUGALL, A. 1997. Como elegir y utilizar el software educativo. Madrid, Morata.

TORRES, GUERRERO, OSMANI. 2012. Tesis en opción al título de Master en Nuevas Tecnologías para la Educación, El software educativo como alternativa en la adquisición de la lectura en los escolares de primer grado de la Educación Primaria.

VISUAL BASIC PARA WINDOWS. 1994. Ediciones Anaya Multimedia S.A.

ZHAO, BAOBIN.1998. How to motivate students to speak English.

Learning Tasks as Learning Objects to Effect Interdisciplinarity in Holguin University Teacher Education English Major

BEd Yanelis María Fonseca Ayala

PhD Julio César Rodríguez Peña. Associate Professor

MSc Yannia Torres Pérez. Associate Professor

General elements concerning interdisciplinarity

Interdisciplinarity has been at the center of research for decades now. It defines much of the work done in many fields, including education. Different authors study interdisciplinarity as d'Hainaut L. (1986), Klein and Newell (1997), Boix Mansilla and Dawes Duraisingh (2007), Diana Rhoten (2008), Erin O `Connor, and Edward J .Hackett (2009), Vess (2009), Repko (2009) and Ayala M. (2018). They analyze interdisciplinarity as the capacity to integrate knowledge and modes of thinking in two or more disciplines or established areas of expertise to produce cognitive advance.

Psychology is a subject of the curriculum of study in first-year students of the Teacher Education English Major at Holguin University. Psychology is key for teachers-to-be because a teacher must play different roles in school, not only in the implementation of learning, but also as mentors for students. Guidance is the kind of assistance for students to solve problems they confront. Knowledge of educational psychology allows teachers to provide educational and vocational guidance necessary for students at different ages.

The term *interdisciplinary* arose for the first time in 1937 and attributed its invention to the sociologist Luis Wirt. Interdisciplinary can be broken into its parts: inter-, which means "between" in Latin, and disciplinary, which is from Latin "disciplina" and means teaching or knowledge. Klein and Newell´s (1997) definition describes what students and scholars do when they deal with interdisciplinary studies. It is noticed that this definition refers to an educational practice that is process oriented, emphasizing integration and problem solving.

Rhoten, O'Conner & Hackett (2009) offer a definition emphasizing that interdisciplinarity is a communal activity, both purposeful and result driven: "We understand interdisciplinarity as both a process and a practice by which a set of purposive arrangements and a sense of community are established and ultimately integrates ideas with others to form an end product" (Rhoten, O'Conner and Hackett, 2009, p. 87).

The foregoing definitions are related to the actual nature of interdisciplinarity. They have different aspects of interdisciplinarity to adopt as a criterion. Boix Mansilla and Dawers Duraising (2007) define interdisciplinarity as the capacity to integrate knowledge and modes of thinking in two or more disciplines or established areas of expertise to produce a cognitive advancement–such as explaining a phenomenon, solving a problem, or creating a product–in ways that would have been impossible or unlikely through a single disciplinary means. In their definition, they include five characteristics of interdisciplinary studies:

1. Involves a process for addressing questions or solving complex problems.
2. Draws on multiple disciplinary perspectives.
3. Works toward the integration of multiple disciplinary insights through the construction of a more comprehensive perspective.
4. Goal is to construct a more comprehensive perspective in answering questions or addressing complex problems by producing a greater understanding, advancing existing knowledge, or creating a new product that could not have been created by drawing from a single discipline.
5. Results in correcting, complementing, and supplementing the limits of disciplinary approaches.

Interdisciplinary learning should create knowledge that is more holistic than knowledge built in discipline-specific studies. Interdisciplinary approaches, while arguably less effective than traditional approaches for building the depth of single-subject knowledge, emphasize higher-order thinking (e.g., analyzing, applying, generalizing) and seek meaningful connections between and among disciplines. Lake (1994) has argued that learners in interdisciplinary programs are guided beyond simpler forms of knowledge acquisition to a deeper assimilation of cross-disciplinary concepts.

As learners attain mastery in interdisciplinary studies, they use interpretive tools to combine and integrate information into a complex interdisciplinary knowledge structure focused on the program's theme. This knowledge structure reflects many central facets of the program: its integrated theories, essential concepts, effective modes of inquiry, and primary paradigms. The interdisciplinary knowledge structure is honed through a gradual advancement in higher-order cognition—specifically, metacognitive skills, critical thinking, and personal epistemology.

Interdisciplinary studies facilitate higher-order cognitive processing by motivating students to engage in deep learning. When students take a deep approach to learning, they seek meaning, reflect on what has been learned, and internalize knowledge by creating personal understanding (Entwistle & Ramsden, 1983). Deep learning is often contrasted with surface learning (e.g., memorization of facts) and characterized by important and long-standing changes in intellectual development.

Critical thinking is another outcome of interdisciplinary programs Researchers have demonstrated a relationship between college attendance and critical thinking, particularly concerning weighing evidence, determining the validity of databased generalizations or conclusions, and distinguishing between weak and strong arguments (e.g. Pascarella & Terezini, 1991). These findings extend to both traditional college students and adult learners (Klassen, 1983–1984).

If students have developed critical thinking, they are good at "gathering, analyzing, synthesizing, and assessing information, as well as identifying misinformation, disinformation, prejudice, and one-sided 'monological' argumentation" (De Costa, 1986, p. 2). In integrated programs, students are challenged to determine the basis of arguments and analyze truth claims across disciplines (Kelder, 1992).

In Cuba, different researchers have studied the interdisciplinary approach. For example, Garcia Bertha (2000), Caballero Cayetano (2001), Fiallo Jorge (2001), Diaz Tereza (2003) and Lombana Raúl (2005), Briñas Yulieth (2007), Cruzata Nancy (2010) and Zaldívar Nadia (2017), Pérez Yunier (2005) and Ayala Maria (2018).

Learning objects and learning tasks
A learning object is a modular resource, usually digital and web-based, that can be used and reused to support learning activities. (Marco Spienelli, 2019).

The learning object was designed in Opale (Open Academic Learning). Opale is used for the production of educational digital contents. The author's first step was to characterize the age of his students. Taking into account the characteristics of this stages for the preparation of the learning object.

The following graphic illustrates how the researcher´s notion is implemented in the Web page she created:

The author recommends the elaboration of a glossary with Psychology terms. It should be oriented by the Psychology and the Integrated English Practice professors with the objective of developing the students' vocabulary and research skills. The work with the glossary should be systematic and those terms should be practiced in the Integrated English Practice lessons. The importance of the elaboration of the Psychology glossary is that it allows students to transfer what they have learned to different situations.

Traditionally, the terms used to designate the means of interaction between learners and the foreign language content are exercises and activities. The term learning tasks has also been present. In general, learning tasks are the means of interaction subject-object, that is, between the learners and the language content, under the guidance of the teacher.

Learning tasks to be used as learning objects
Structure of the learning tasks:
> Title
> Objective
> Description of the learning task
> Heading of the learning task
> Evaluation

Learning Task 1 the students are going to watch a video three times. The first time they will identify the general elements of the video, the second time, the students will take notes for answering questions and the third time, they will organize the information.

Topic: What is personality?

Objective: To characterize the personality category at a critical level of comprehension.

1- Watch the video and answer the following questions.
> A- What is personality?
> B- Where did personality come from?
> C- Is it important for your future profession to know that all of us are unique?

2- Write a paragraph about the importance of knowing the personality category for your future work as teachers.

Learning Task 2 is developed in the subject Integrated English Practice. The students are going to watch a video three times. The first time has they will identify the general elements of the video; the second time, the students will take notes for answering questions and the third time, they will organize the information.

Objective: To characterize the communication category at critical level of comprehension fostering solidarity.

Learning Task 3 the students are going to work in groups. They will select a learning theory and do research about it.

Objective: to develop research skills through learning theories at a critical comprehension level.

In the next learning task (number 4), the students are going to read a story as starting point. The objective for reading this story is to make the students reflect about disability. Firstly, they are going to read then they are going to answer questions.

Objective: To develop reflection about differences between people at a critical level of comprehension fostering equality.

Learning Task 5 the students are going to watch a video as starting point. The objective for watching this video is to make the students reflect about the importance of responsible sex. Firstly, they are going to watch then they are going to answer questions.

Objective: To develop reflection about responsible sex at a critical level of comprehension fostering responsibility.

The current state of the interdisciplinary relations between English and Psychology in the teaching-learning process of English permitted to precise that there are only a few interdisciplinary activities developed between these subjects in the teaching-learning process.

To elaborate and implement learning objects (tasks) to contribute to the interdisciplinary relations between English and Psychology is an imperative aspect today in first-year in-service students of Teacher Education English Major, so it is crucial for teachers to assume the interdisciplinary approach as the basis to guide actions and conceive activities on this respect.

Bibliography
Álvarez Pérez, Martha. (2004). Interdisciplinariedad. Una aproximación desde la enseñanza-aprendizaje de las ciencias. Editorial. Pueblo y Educación.
Ariel, S. (1987). An information processing theory of family dysfunction. *Psychotherapy, 24,* 477-495.
Ayala Ruiz, María Elena. (2007). El trabajo metodológico interdisciplinario en función de la competencia humanística del profesional en formación. En Evento Universidad 2008. Universidad de Holguín.

Barangan, C. (2008). Adolescent Psychological Development. Consulted in May, 2019, in: http://pedsinreview.aappublications.org/cgi/content/full/29/5/161

Betancourt, Alberto R. (2004) Modelo de competencia metodológica del profesor de inglés para el perfeccionamiento de la dirección del proceso de enseñanza-aprendizaje del nivel medio. Doctoral Tesis at UPS Holguín.

Briñas Y (2007) Tesis en opción al grado científico de Doctor en Ciencias Modelo pedagógico para la prevención de alteraciones de la conducta del escolar. Universidad de Holguín.

Bruns, D and and Disorbio, Mark J.(2003)Glossary Of Terms Related To The Psychological Evaluation Pain.by Pearson Assessments. All rights reserved.

Caballero Camejo (2001). La interdisciplinaridad de la Biología y la Geografía con Química : una estructura didáctica .Universidad Enrique José Varona , Facultad de Ciencias Naturales .Ciudad de La Habana.

Corbacho, Ana M. (2017). El aprendizaje interdisciplinario, intensivo e integrado como herramienta para el desarrollo de conocimientos, habilidades y actitudes en estudiantes de grado. Interdisciplina 5, n° 13 (septiembre–diciembre 2017): 63-85.

Colectivo de autores (2019). Estrategia Educativa para el primer año: Licenciatura en Educación Lenguas Extranjeras Inglés 2018-2019.

Collective of authors (2014). The Teaching of Psychology through learning activities from a multidisciplinary approach: Increasing motivation and performance. University of Jaén Spain. In http://pedsinreview.aappublications.org

Cruzata N. (2010). Interdisicplinariedad en la escuela cubana. Universidad de Oriente.

D'Hainaut L. (1986) Interdisciplinarity In General Education. Division of Educational Sciences Contents and Methods of Education.

García B. (2000). *La interdisciplinariedad como base de una estrategia para el perfeccionamiento del diseño curricular de una carrera de ciencias técnicas y su aplicación a la Ingeniería en Automática en la República de Cuba.Instituto Superior Politécnico "José Antonio Echeverría"*

Humphreys, A. H., Post, T. R., & Ellis, A. K. (1981). *Interdisciplinary methods: A thematic approach*. Santa Monica, CA: Goodyear.

Ivanitskaya L, Clark D, G Montgomery and Primeau, R.(2002). Interdisciplinary Learning: Process and Outcomes. Innovative Higher Education, Vol. 27, No. 2.

Klein and Newell. (1997). Advancing Interdisciplinarity Studies.

Medina Betancourt, Alberto R. (2006). Didáctica de la lengua extranjera con enfoque de competencia. UCP Holguín.

Lake, K. (1994). Integrated curriculum. In *School Improvement Research Series*, (CloseUp #16). Retrieved from *http://www.nwrel.org/scpd/sirs/8/c016.html*

Pascarella, E. T., & Terenzini, P. T. (1991). *How college affects students: Findings and insights from twenty years of research.* San Francisco, CA: Jossey-Bass.

Pérez Sarduy, Y. (2005).El desarrollo del modo de actuación interdisciplinario en la formación inicial de profesores de lenguas extranjeras. Holguín.

Rickett, B and Woolhouse,M. (2015). Psychology, Gender, Sexuality, Class. In: https://www.researchgate.net/publication/49

Sally W. Aboelela, Elaine L arson, Suzanne Bakken, Olveen Carrasquillo, Allan Formicola, Sherry A. Glied, Janet Haas,and Kristine M. Gebbie. (2007) Defining Interdisciplinary Research:Conclusions from a Critical Review of the Literature. Health Research and Educational Trust.

Speinelli Marcos (2019).What is Learning Managment System ?

Van den Besselaar, P. and Heimeriks, G. (2001). Disciplinary, Multidisciplinary, Interdisciplinary Concepts and Indicator. Social Science Informatics Program, University of Amsterdam Roetersstraat 15, NL- 1018 WB Amsterdam, The Netherlands.

Vess and Repko (2009). Why teach with an interdisciplinarity Approach?

Zaldívar, Nadia (2017). La formación inicial del licenciado en Educación Primaria para la atención educativa integral a los escolares con retardo en el desarrollo Psíquico. Facultad de Educación Infantil, Psicopedagogía y Arte departamento de Educación Especial / Logopedia. Universidad de Holguín.

Zhou, M., & Brown, D. (Eds.). (2017). Educational Learning Theories. affrdablelearninggeorgia@usg.edu.htts://oer.galileo.usg.edu/education-textbooks/1

A Learning Hyper-Environment to Improve the Teaching of English Grammar in Senior Students of the Teacher Education English Major of Holguin University

BEd Katherine Mora Chacón. Instructor
PhD Julio César Rodríguez Peña. Associate Professor

General Remarks

Medina (2013) defines teaching media in foreign language learning as images or representations of objects and phenomena specially elaborated for teaching. They are auxiliary or instrumental devices that teachers use for the particular purpose of presenting, illustrating, or reinforcing perception and observation of a given knowledge. They can be natural or industrial objects. They support teaching methods and improve the effectiveness and attractiveness of the language content and the process itself. They facilitate a direct contact between the objective reality and its reproduction, so they help to achieve authentic communication.

Wikipedia (2016) when referring to audiovisual media defines them as a valuable resource for teaching, whichever level of education they are used. They are about a collection of visual and auditory techniques that support educational processes, facilitating a better comprehension and interpretation of the ideas presented by the teacher. The efficiency of the audiovisual media in education lies in the perception of contents through the senses.

Media reduce time and effort in the teaching-learning process, since students get motivated. They simplify the process of acquisition and comprehension of message and allows the students to build their knowledge. Likewise, media make it possible to have feedback within the group, and increase the volume of information retained in the brain from a short to medium term. Media develop the critical sense in the students and their imagination is stimulated and encouraged. Another benefit they supply is the fact that students´ attention is kept for longer periods, improving interaction among the students during the practice sessions in the classroom.

Dirk (2016) states that "Media can be a component of active learning strategies such as group discussions or case studies. Media could be a film clip, a song you hear on the radio, podcast of a lecture or newspaper article. Students can also elaborate their own media. For example, student video projects can be a powerful learning experience. The use of media to enhance teaching and learning complements traditional approaches to learning. Effective instruction builds bridges between students' knowledge and the learning objectives of the course. Using media engages students, aids student´s retention of knowledge, motivates interest in the subject matter, and illustrates the relevance of many concepts."

In this context computers play a prominent role in the teaching-learning process, as media function as material supports of methods (instructive-educative) with the aim of reaching certain goals. Computers demand a constant renovation of the current concepts of teaching and its traditional definitions. Moreover, they include the discovering of organizational ways for the teaching-learning process, the appropriate time for using them and the technical training of teachers and students for their use.

Personal computers are key in the teaching-learning process in the Cuban institutions. Their use as didactic resources for teachers and aids for pupils´ learning is fundamental in improving language learning. They have supplied teachers with the precise tools for teaching effectively and transforming the teaching-learning process into an easier and more complete one.

The teacher´s educational effort cannot be dismissed in favor of computers, since computers do not replace them. They are tools in their hands to achieve a goal. Further into what has been exposed, it is necessary to define software. It refers to the logical equipment or logical medium of a digital computer. It comprises the necessary logical components to make possible the realization of specific tasks, in comparison with the physical components of the system, called hardware. So, it is the computer programs, procedures, rules, documentation and associated data that integrate the operations of a computing system (Ecured, 2015).

EduTech Wiki (2009) considers the term Educational Software can refer to most educational technologies, i.e. all software designed or used to facilitate teaching and learning. Likewise, the definition provided by Ecured (2015) educational software are programs destined to support the teaching-learning process. They contribute to increase its quality and are aimed at providing attention to the specific characteristics of every student, based on an accurate projection of pedagogical strategies to follow in the process of implementation as in its exploitation. They are an effective instrument for the educational development of the individual.

The quality of the software it is expressed by its suitability or usefulness and by the level of satisfaction of the demands of its users: the quality of the process is reached when student, teacher and family expectations are satisfied as a major achievement in social expectations.

It is necessary to remark the benefits obtained with the use of educational software (or Learning Hyper-Environments) in which can be mentioned the increase of the motivation towards learning, because of the spectrum of contents these media offer (activities, videos, music, games, images, etc.). Computers and educational software, as teaching media, are excellent tools for the teachers in the preparation and teaching of their lessons. They are sources of methodological advantages and represent a major realization of teacher and student activities.

The integration of informatics into the Cuban National System of Education has been done in three main branches: as a research object, as a tool for working and as a teaching media. The latter is linked to the elaboration of educational software for teaching and learning in the different levels. Nowadays, it is valued as an alternative in the reinforcement of knowledge in the students and has become an alternative to foster abilities and values.

Learning Hyper-Environments

As mentioned before, since the appearance of the first computers, several computer applications started to be developed for the educational field. That was the beginning of what is commonly known today as Educational Software, widely spread with the arrival of multimedia technology. Authors have provided diverse classifications of Educational Software and these resources are grouped as tutorials, simulator trainers, games and evaluators, or as tutorials, intelligent tutorials, hypermedia systems, simulations and micro worlds, just to mention some examples.

From the need generated by the development of the teaching-learning process – which demands ways, methods and strategies in agreement with the unique typical characteristics of each student, the type of content to be taught, motivation and interests, the moment and scenario of every educational activity, the learning styles, the levels in which the activities were performed and the levels of assimilation, among other factors – the development of these kinds of educational materials demanded that they reveal potentialities to adequate each one to the characteristics described above.

When in 2001 the Cuban Ministry of Education decided to develop a collection of educational software for Primary School, the concept of Learning Hyper-Environment assumed was that defined in 2001 by Labañino: "Harmonious combination of different Educational Software typologies supported on Hypermedia technology, conceived for granting a computing basis to different functions of the teaching-learning process, mainly characterized by constituting a full support to the school curriculum of a certain educational system." *(Translated by the authors)*

Communicative tasks were included in the learning hyper-environment elaborated by the researchers, for the students to practice their knowledge of grammar. These appear below the content developed in the pages of the learning hyper-environment.

Description of the structure of the Learning Hyper-Environment
The Learning Hyper-Environment presented was elaborated with SAdHEA-Web. This is a Web-Authoring System for the development of Learning Hyper Environments. It was developed by the Center for Studies of Software and their Educational Applications (CESOFTAD) from Holguin University (Campus José de la Luz y Caballero). It drew primarily from a collaboration with the Center for Studies of Educational Software Pepito Tey in Las Tunas, Cuba. The name of the Learning Hyper-Environment (LHE) is Grammore (a neologism meaning "more grammar") (see Appendix).

Analysis of the elements in Grammore:
Different modules, services and facilities proper of these systems constitute the LHE and the user can access them from the home page.

Module Contents: The Module contents constitutes a hypermedia book, the equivalent to a textbook, by means of which the author has access to all the information related to the contents of the subject to which the LHE was destined to. It can be found in different formats such as texts, static or moving pictures, sound and videos.

From this module, the user can access the part corresponding to the Module library, to deepen on the information related to the selected media, which can be pictures, animations, sounds, videos, etc. The way of surfing is structured in a simple way to facilitate navigation, with a hierarchical level of content.

For example: Firstly, the user finds the general topics, then the breakdown by epigraphs and finally the contents of the epigraphs.
This module can be accessed either through the menu Contents that is on the upper part of the application or through the access button that is placed on the left side of the application.

Module Exercises: these make possible the development of skills in the students by means of rehearsing the contents studied in class, the evaluation of their knowledge through a proposal of exercises in form of questionnaires (interactive exercises) or training exercises (through the presentation of exercises, cognitive aids for their solution and the answer itself).

It must be highlighted that for the treatment to the responses given by the students to the interactive exercises or questionnaires in this LHE, a Pedagogical conception has been used. By means of this, attention to individual needs has been possible, according to the mistakes made and the characteristics of the questions. This is carried out thanks to reflexive feedback or levels of help, as well as by deepening on the content through the access to information related to a specific content in the question.

For the case of the questionnaires or interactive exercises, several typologies of exercises are implemented, such as simple choice, multiple choice, true or false, fill in the blanks, to arrange, to match and draw, among others.

The summary of the user´s performance has three stages. First, a summary of the contents faced by him, providing him the number of exercises answered with evaluation of good, regular and bad. Second, the exercises with their grades are shown to the user with the chance of going to watch them with the user´s answer and interchange with the right one, and third, the graphic representation of the amount of exercises performed correctly, those performed with some irregularities and those failed.

Module Virtual library: It grants access to all the multimedia information contained in the Educational Software, through galleries (of pictures, sounds, animations, videos, diaporamas and electronic presentations), glossaries (of terms, definitions, biographies, etc.). Other elements are available, such as documents of interest for the users, access to important dates in history and access to websites of educational interest, etc. Moreover, from the module the student can surf to the corresponding section of the Module Contents, where a reference to that specific subject is made, thus becoming a new way of surfing on the contents comprised in the Educational Software.

This Module has been called sometimes Virtual Library and this responds to the diversity of criteria offered by different authors versed in the field, but its essence does not change in any of the cases since there is information in it that enriches the topics dealt with in the LHE. This is one of the advantages of this media in respect to the traditional textbook.

Module Games: they allow the use of the ludic element in the process of acquisition of knowledge or development of skills in specific contents, bearing in mind the particular interests of the users of each LHE. The games incorporated are of the following types: Hidden text, discovering the character, crossword puzzle and word search games, among others.

These games, in general, have the particularity of interacting with the user through a configuration screen, facilitating, the topics, the number of matches or the level of complexity, the user desires, such as checking or knowing the right answer. The results achieved are stored in a database for the professor to know students' difficulties. The best results are shown on a board that is published in every match, in order to encourage the player to become a part of it.

SAdHEA-Web web-authoring tool enables the assembly of these games through two ways: in lots or one after another, supported on an assistant depending on the method chosen. Opting for the way of lots, the user has the opportunity of assembling amounts of matches of the game selected, automatically and rapidly, just creating the game sources with the structure required. These choices demand the study of the structure for the source the game needs. At the same time, when assembling the matches one by one, the pattern orients exactly what to do and elaborates one by one each match. This way it is possible to elaborate, edit and eliminate specific matches.

Module Results: It provides the user with a powerful tool that allows to evaluate performance with the Educational software, including mistakes made in the answers provided for the exercises, and allowing progressive analysis of interaction with the material. Likewise, this information is available for teachers and family. Possibilities of stratification of the trace, reconstruction of the answers given by the students to each of the exercises faced, statistical analysis of the results of the training sessions, etc. are also included.

The products elaborated with this web-authoring tool, which have this module activated, have the opportunity that all users, students and professors that check the product, automatically obtain at the end a summary containing the main elements of their work section with the LHE, in which the following information is provided:

    1 - Section Information: Name, date and hour of checking.

    Schedule: where a sequence of the modules visited by the user with dates and hours of the visit is presented.

    2 - Visited links: the name and the time a user was in each one of the information nodes accessed (pictures, sounds, videos, animations, diaporamas and glossary terms or hot words from the Module Themes, among others) are stored.

    3 - Exercises: in this section the general results of the training are shown. It offers the number of exercises the user answered as right, fair, wrong, and those that have no evaluation, such as the possibility of consulting the exercise, the same way it was answered by the user, and in the cases the answer was not correct, it is possible to visualize the correct one.

4 - Games: The games in which every user has participated and the results obtained in them are stored by the system.

For the registered users all the information of every section in which they used the educational software will be stored and later they will have the chance of consulting the information of any section and comparing the results obtained. Besides, teachers will also have access to the users´ sections for analyzing the results obtained by them, as well as the use given to the educational software.

Module Professor: It equips the teacher, apart from the administration facilities proper of systems of this nature, with other services such as the subjects´ syllabus, methodological orientations, articles of interest and additional information.

The subjects´ syllabus: it includes the contents to be developed in the curriculum of the year or years for which the learning-hyper environment is being elaborated.

Additional information: it provides access to topics related to the use of the Technologies of Information and Communication (IT) in the teaching-learning process in general and particularly about their use in the specific subject the LHE is to be applied.

Methodological orientations: apart from providing the guidance of how to apply and deal with the contents of the subject, they suggest ways for the treatment of the content by means of the use of the learning hyper-environment as a means to facilitate the learning process.

Articles of interest: didactic, scientific and methodological materials and some other materials, which, according to the author, provide a better use of the potentialities of this web-tool by the users.

Developing tools and technical requirements for the running of the LHE
SAdHEA-Web (Web-Authoring for the Development of Learning Hyper Environments) is an open source multiplatform elaborated with free web-tools like:
PHP (PHP Hypertext Pre-processor) launched under the license PHP License considered free software by The Free Software Foundation.
Java Script, included in the modern web browsers.
MySQL released under the licenses GNU GPL and a commercial one.
AJAX (Asynchronous JavaScript and XML), which is a technique for the web´s development for the elaboration of interactive applications.
For the correct functioning of SAdHEA-Web it is necessary to have access to the following technical requirements:

Data base web server (MySQL version 5 or superior)
http://www.mysql.com
PHP (version 5.0.0 or superior)
http://www.php.net
Web server (Apache)
http://www.apache.org
Web browser (Firefox)
http://www.mozilla.com

Methodological guidelines for the use of the Learning Hyper Environment "Grammore"

Since teachers are aware of the grammatical problems students face due the lack of bibliography for the subject Linguistic Studies III (English Grammar), they have been working to find a solution, and thus meet this need. The learning-hyper environment has been elaborated: to improve the teaching-learning process of this subject in senior students of the Teacher Education English major at Holguin University.

The tasks were elaborated to motivate and help students improve their knowledge on this subject. They can be used as a rehearsing section, the articles of interest contain bibliography that expands on the contents received in class and the songs presented intend to immerse students in a reflexive and meaningful learning context while enjoying singing.

The tasks proposed can be assigned as homework or as part of the workshops corresponding to each of the lectures of the subject. Besides, students will have other spaces fro recreation and learning, such as games and exercises pertaining to the web-authoring tool. The author suggests using the learning hyper-environment as a teaching media and support for the subject aforementioned.

For the use of the learning hyper-environment it is advisable to pay attention to:
1 - The use of computers in the teaching-learning process, which noticeably increases its quality (since it helps to improve the assimilation of the contents already learned in class).
2 - Tasks can be adapted or modified taking into consideration the needs of students and teachers.
3 - The practical use of the tasks proposed allows using the learning hyper environment as teaching media.
5 - Evaluate the tasks assigned orally and in the written form.
6 - Evaluate the tasks individually, in pairs or small groups.

Examples of tasks implemented in the hyper-environment

Task # 1

Title: Rehear-Sing section

Objective: Students should be able to classify the nouns contained in the song ´Hit the lights´ while they are encouraged to accomplish their life goals without fear.

Heading: Watch the following music video entitled ´Hit the lights´ by American Singer Selena Gómez:

1- Read the lyrics of the song and say if the ideas below are included (I) or Not Included (NI) in the song. Support your answers.

____ Life is about having fun without thinking about anything else.

____ Life is too short and it is necessary to live it to the max.

____ Trips, money and youth are essential to be happy in life.

____ It is never too late to reach your dreams.

____ It is necessary to be bold and fight for what we want.

    a) Have you ever lost something important to you because of fear? Do you regret it?

    b) What do you think the singer means by "Hit the lights"?

    c) What pieces of advice would you give to those who have lost important opportunities in life because of fear? Write down at least three.

2- Read the lyrics of the song again and pick out at least eight nouns.

    a) Classify them according to the type of nomination they express.

    b) Explain the role each one of them plays in the song.

3- Prepare a brief rap that contains the nouns you chose in the previous exercise. Get ready to read it in front of your class. (Work in pairs)

Task # 2

Title: All I Remember

Objective: The students should be able to explain how gender, number and case are expressed through nouns for the comprehension of the fragment of the text "All I remember" fostering love for family and friends.

Heading: Read the following text taken from the book "Chicken soup for the soul."

All I Remember

Suddenly my mother's face appeared—my mother, as she had been before Alzheimer's disease had stripped her of her mind, her humanity and 50 pounds. Her magnificent silver hair crowned her sweet face. She was so real and so close I felt I could reach out and touch her. She looked as she had a dozen years ago, before the wasting away had begun. I even smelled the fragrance of Joy, her favorite perfume. She seemed to be waiting and did not speak. I wondered how it could happen that I was thinking of my father and my mother appeared, and I felt a little guilty that I had not asked for her as well.

I said, "Oh, Mother, I'm so sorry that you had to suffer with that horrible disease." She tipped her head slightly to one side, as though to acknowledge what I had said about her suffering. Then she smiled—a beautiful smile— and said very distinctly, "But all I remember is love." And she disappeared.

    a) What is the text about?

    b) What do you think about the author's experience with her dead mother? Would you like to see someone who passed away? What would you ask if you were given the chance to see him/her again?

    c) Pick out those nouns that are essential for expressing the main idea of the text. Support your answer.

    d) Classify them.

    e) Explain the categories of gender, number and case expressed in the text.

    f) Write an end for this story. Be ready to report it to the rest of the class.

Task # 3

Title: Rehear-Sing section

Objective: Students should be able to classify the nouns contained in the song "Thinking Out Loud" at the time they reflect on the necessity of showing love to family and friends no matter the age.

Heading: Watch the following music video entitled "Thinking Out Loud" by the British Singer and songwriter Ed Sheeran:

1 - Read the lyrics of the song and say True (T), False (F) or I Don't Know (IDK). Support the false items.

    a) The singer expresses his desire to take care of his lover until they get old.

    b) The singer dedicates the song to his mother.

    c) The singer expresses his tiredness for sharing his life with someone for so long.

    d) The singer affirms that people fall in love in ways we cannot imagine.

    e) The singer could find love far from where he is right now.

2 - Read the lyrics of the song once more and answer the following questions:

    a) Does the singer want to remain next to his loved one until they get old? Why do you think so? Give at least five reasons stated in the song that support your answer.

    b) Would you like to find someone to share your life with? Why?

    c) Is commitment important to you? State your reasons.

    d) As a teacher to be, how would you explain your junior and senior students the risks of promiscuity?

3- Read again the lyrics of the song and select from it at least five nouns:

    a) Classify them according to the reference they make in the song.

    b) Classify them according to their grammatical categories of gender and number. Say whether the other grammatical category is present or not in the song.

Task # 4

Title: The Gentlest Need

Objective: The students should be able to classify the pronouns present in the text "The Gentlest Need" emphasizing on the affection they, as teachers-in-training, must show to their students.

Heading: Read the following text taken from the book "Chicken soup for the Soul"

The Gentlest Need

At least once a day our old black cat comes to one of us in a way that we've all come to see as a special request. It does not mean he wants to be fed or to be let out or anything of that sort. His need is for something very different. If you have a lap handy, he'll jump into it; if you don't, he's likely to stand there looking wistful until you make him one. Once in it, he begins to vibrate almost before you stroke his back, scratch his chin and tell him over and over what a good kitty he is. Then his motor really revs up; he squirms to get comfortable; he "makes big hands." Every once in a while one of his purrs gets out of control and turns into a snort. He looks at you with wide open eyes of adoration, and he gives you the cat's long slow blink of ultimate trust.

After a while, little by little, he quiets down. If he senses that it's all right, he may stay in your lap for a cozy nap. But he is just as likely to hop down and stroll away about his business. Either way, he's all right. Our daughter puts it simply: "Blackie needs to be purred." In our household he isn't the only one who has that need: I share it and so does my wife. We know the need isn't exclusive to any one age group. Still, because I am a schoolman as well as a parent, I associate it especially with youngsters, with their quick, impulsive need for a hug, a warm lap, a hand held out, a coverlet tucked in, not because anything's wrong, not because anything needs doing, just because that's the way they are.

There are a lot of things I'd like to do for all children. If I could do just one, it would be this: to guarantee every child, everywhere, at least one good purring every day. Kids, like cats, need time to purr.

(Fred T. Wilhelms)

1 -After reading the text, tick which of the following ideas you consider best covers the main idea:

a) Everybody should show love to animals and people.

b) No matter age, humans and animals need to be loved.

c) Cats need to be purred by their owners.

2-Read the text one more time and answer the following questions:
   a) Do the members of the author´s family share the same need of the old black cat? Why?
   b) As a teacher-in-training you not only teach but also educate. How do you associate your educational work with the content of the story you just read?
   c) What aspects from the ones learned by you in Psychology and Pedagogy will you put into practice when dealing with teenagers who need affection?

3-Read the text to find at least eight pronouns:
   a) Classify them and say their function within the text.

Conclusions

Working with grammar acquires a special significance according to the objectives for teaching languages today and the use of new technologies of information and communication (IT) in the teaching-learning process of English. There are still limitations for devising teaching media to improve the treatment of grammatical contents in English as a foreign language in senior students of the Teacher Education English major at Holguin University. To design a learning hyper-environment to improve the teaching-learning process of the subject Linguistic Studies III (English Grammar), in the aforementioned students, is a challenge and a need in the current development of applied IT today.

Bibliography

Acosta, R. y Hernández. (2011) Didáctica interactiva de lenguas. La Habana: Editorial Pueblo y Educación.

Ayala, M.E. (2015) Reunión Metodológica interdisciplinaria: El diseño de tareas, ejercicios y actividades desde un enfoque comunicativo, desarrollador e interdisciplinario.

Canale, M. and Swain, M. (1980). The communicative competence. (Available in http://www.auburn.edu/nunnath/engl6240/dhtml)

Canfield, J. and Hansen, M. Chicken soup for the soul. (Available in http://www.chickensoup.com).

Coloma, O., Mariño, D. (et.al). (2011) El desarrollo de Software Educativo sin costo de programación. ¿Utopía o realidad? Curso 71. Sello editor Educación Cubana. Ministerio de Educación.

Dirk, G. (2016) Using Media to Enhance Teaching and Learning. (Available in http://serc.carleton.edu/econ/media/how.html)

Educational Software-EduTechWiki. (2009) (Available in: edutechwiki.unige.ch/en/Educational_software)

Ecured. (2015).Hiperentornos de Aprendizaje.

Hutchinson, T. and Waters, A. (1996). English for specific purposes: a learning-centered approach. Cambridge: Editorial Cambridge University Press.

Hymes, D. (1972). On Communicative Competence. Editorial J.B. Pride and J. Holmes (eds.) Sociolinguistics, Harmmondsworth, Penguin.

Labañino, C. (2001). Primer Seminario Nacional de Guionistas. Cojímar, Oct., 2001. La Habana.

Mariño, D. (2013). SAdHEA-Web: alternative for achieving technological independence in the development of the Cuban educational software.
Innovación tecnológica vol.19, No.4 octubre-diciembre 2013 (ISSN 1025-6504)
Mariño, D. and Coloma, O. (2013). Los Hiperentornos de Aprendizaje para la web (HEAWeb): Paradigma actual del software educativo cubano. Revista plac. No.6 noviembre-diciembre, 2013. Artículo científico. (ISSN 1993-6850)
Medina, A. (2006). Didáctica de los idiomas con enfoque de competencias, ¿Cómo enseñar el castellano y los idiomas extranjeros en cualquier nivel de educación? Ediciones CEPEDID, Barranquilla, Colombia, 2006.
Medina, A. (2013). Glossary: Improve your methodological technical register with more than 600 terms. UCP "José de la Luz y Caballero", Holguín.
Mijares N. and col. (2013). Manual de Estrategias de Aprendizaje de Lenguas Extranjeras. La Habana: Editorial Pueblo y Educación.
Paz, Y. (2016). Hiperentorno de Aprendizaje para el estudio de los medios de trabajo en la asignatura de Educación Laboral en la Secundaria Básica "Abel Santamaría Cuadrado". (Term Paper) Universidad de Holguín, Sede "José de la Luz y Caballero".
Páez, K. (2014). Multimedia to improve oral expression in English in sixth grades from Patricio Emeri Lumumba Primary school in Báguanos. (Diploma Paper). University of Pedagogical Sciences "José de la Luz y Caballero". Department of Foreign Languages, Holguin.
Pulido, A. (2005). Hacia un concepto de competencia comunicativa integral: Un novedoso acercamiento a sus dimensiones, (Available in http://apuntes.rincondelvago.com/competenciacognitiva.html), 2005.
Richards, J. and Schmidt, R. (2010). Longman Dictionary of Language Teaching and Applied Linguistics, Pearson Education Limited.
Rodríguez, J.C. (201 4). La Competencia Comunicativa Oral Profesional Pedagógica en Inglés en estudiantes de la Carrera Licenciatura en Educación Especialidad Lengua Extranjera (Inglés), (Tesis doctoral). Centro de Estudios de Educación Superior, Holguín.
▯ Rodríguez, M. (2016). Estrategia Educativa para cuarto año. Facultad de Educación Media Superior. Carrera Licenciatura en Educación Lenguas Extranjeras Inglés (Curso 2016-2017). Universidad de Holguín.
Rodríguez, R.A. (2005). Concepción Teórico-Metodológica para el Diagnóstico-Formación de las generalizaciones gramaticales en la Carrera Licenciatura en Educación, Especialidad De Lengua Inglesa. (Tesis doctoral). Instituto Superior Pedagógico "José de la Luz y Caballero". Facultad de Educación media Superior Departamento de Lengua Inglesa, Holguín.
Rodríguez, R.A. (2016). Programa de la asignatura Estudios Lingüísticos del Inglés III. Curso Diurno (201 6-201 7). Primer semestre. Carrera Licenciatura en educación, Especialidad Lenguas extranjeras Inglés. Universidad de Ciencias Pedagógicas "José de la Luz y Caballero", Holguín.
Rodríguez, R.A. (2014). Course on Linguistic Studies III (English Grammar). University of Pedagogical Sciences "José de la Luz y Caballero", Department of Foreign Languages, Holguin.
Wikipedia. (2016). Medios audiovisuales.

Pedagogical Sciences

Appendix

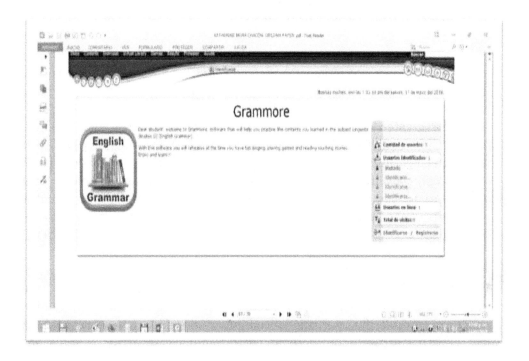

329

Exploiting Authentic Videos to Enrich Vocabulary in Students from the Teacher Education English Major of Holguin University

MSc Nuria Montero Samada. Associate Professor
Senior Student Henry García Mariño
BEd Anabel González Ricardo. Instructor

The world is an increasingly globalized place where individuals of different cultural backgrounds communicate each day. Today, an individual has access to a vast array of information from a variety of world cultures by only pressing button. For those in the English-speaking world, access to this information is taken for granted. Elsewhere, however, much of the world's information is beyond their reach, locked in English. That is one reason why learning English as a foreign language has become very popular. In fact, English is now the world's most widely spoken language, surpassing all others. As a result, there has never been a greater demand for classes to learn English as a foreign language. English is the gateway to a world of knowledge, commerce, and culture, a lingua franca that gives a student access to the world in a way that other languages do not.

Teaching English as a foreign language is an important task with a number of powerful rewards. Firstly, there is the feeling of pride that as a teacher you have made a difference in the life of a student. Secondly, there is the contribution you have made to the international community by "adding" a new speaker of the English language, one who can now communicate across cultures and worldwide in the lingua franca of the modern age.

It has been proven that our brains learn faster when we are having fun and enjoying the activity we are carrying out. As teachers, we must take this advantage into action. It is a great achievement in a language lesson if teachers are able to make their students laugh when teaching them new content. With this, teachers will easily manage to make their students feel deeply connected and interested in the lesson's topic. Furthermore, students will learn easier and the content will be remembered for a longer time. Knowing all of this, how can teachers carry out a developmental lesson in which the students truly have fun and develop their language skills and vocabulary?

Teaching vocabulary is a vital part of any English language course. Many teachers are concerned about how to teach vocabulary. New words must be introduced in such a way as to capture the students' attention and place the words in their memories. Students need to be aware of techniques for memorizing large amounts of new vocabulary in order to progress in their language learning.

English vocabulary learning can often be seen as a laborious process of memorizing lists of unrelated terms. However, there are many others much more successful and interesting ways to learn and teach vocabulary in an EFL classroom.

The benefit of using videos over other types of media is the integration of the auditory aspect as well as visuals. According to Canning-Wilson (2000), being able to see the speakers, their context and body language is a huge advantage to listeners. Videos provide not only the auditory element to be listened to but also visuals. This factor will facilitate the students' acquisition of new vocabulary by observing the speakers' body language or gestures.

Videos are considered an effective aid used by teachers in teaching vocabulary. Being a rich and valuable resource, videos have an amusement component for both students and teachers. Teachers use videos because they provide rich features such as text, pictures and sounds that can activate the learners' interests. They also help teachers in the teaching-learning activity.

Articles and general bibliography were consulted to receive input on the topic. Among them, the following can mentioned: Plavio, 1971; Wilkins, 1972; Finocchiaro, 1983; Allen, 1983; McCarthy, 1990; Brett, 1995; Egbert and Jessup, 1996; Harley, 1996; Khalid, 2001; Talaván, 2010; Medina, 2012; Figuerosa, 2017.

Using videos in the teaching-learning process of a foreign language
New advances in general technology and particularly, in multimedia, play a key role in facilitating foreign language teaching and learning. Multimedia technology (like television, computers, cellphones, tablets, the Internet, etc.) assist teachers largely by providing authentic material that, at the same time, promotes better language acquisition.

Many researchers have studied and presented proof that multimedia has useful effects on language learning due to rich, reliable and comprehensible input (Brett, 1995; Egbert and Jessup, 1996; Khalid, 2001; Talaván, 2010). Furthermore, the importance of providing learners with understandable input has been stressed in foreign language teaching-learning theories. According to Krashen (1985) input hypothesis, learners can learn a large amount of language unconsciously through abundant comprehensible input.

Videos are becoming one of the most popular multimedia tools that can be used in language classrooms because they can easily help to display the content; they facilitate a deeper comprehension and make it possible to enhance lexical and grammatical learning. Every day, more teachers are encouraged to use multimedia tools such as audios or videos in language classrooms because they are considered more convenient, entertaining, and most of the time, very handy.

From previous research, authors have made emphasis on the effectiveness of combining audio and visual aids in language classrooms. They have discussed that visual input combined with other technology tools stimulate deeper comprehension of the text and promote the interaction between the target language and the learner's mind, which, in return, allows learners to predict the target language more easily and to recall more entirely (Stevens, 1989; Underwood, 1990). In addition to its effects on increasing learner's overall language ability, the strength of using multimedia tools in enhancing vocabulary has also been studied and reported.

Subtitled videos representing words and pictures in oral and visual form more effectively activate both coding systems in the processing than words or pictures alone. As is stated in the dual coding theory proposed by Plavio (1971), when images are associated with meaning, the amount of signals linked to the message increases. The result is that viewers will more probably keep the message in mind. Therefore, the results of the previous researches seem to sustain the aspect that the use of subtitles causes multi-sensory processing, interacting with audio and video mechanisms. These information input foundations make the process of language learning enhanced, improve the comprehension of the content and increase the learner's vocabulary by looking at the subtitled words in meaningful and stimulating circumstances.

Related to this theme, Figuerosa, A. (2017) provides the following advantages of the use of videos in the English lesson:
- Videos reduce time and effort to the teacher and the students.
- Students are usually motivated by videos.
- They expand students´ knowledge.
- They allow the representation of reality by promoting and stimulating students´ imagination.
- They permit to keep the attention of the students for a long time.
- Videos can open up the classroom and bring more variety and interest into lessons.
- They stimulate students to speak the language as well as to read and write it.

Criteria for selecting video
When selecting an authentic video for use in the classroom, certain general criteria should be kept in mind:
- Watchability. Is the video interesting? Would a young native speaker want to watch this video?

- Completeness. For a video to be useful, it should tell a complete story. This idea of completeness is important for young learners whose primary motivation for watching a video is enjoyment.
- Length. The length of the clip is important. It should not be too long, perhaps between 30 seconds and 10 minutes depending on the learning objective.
- Appropriateness of content. The content should be suitable for young learners. How has the video been rated, 'Universal', 'Parental Guidance', for ages '13'or '18'? Would the video be suitable for viewing in all cultures?
- Level of maturity. Children mature very quickly so a group of 7-year-olds watching a video made for 5-year-olds would probably regard it as 'too babyish'. On the other hand, using a video intended for older children with a group of younger children might lead to children not being able to understand the concepts in the video.
- Availability of related materials. Many authentic videos now come with ready-made materials that can be used for language teaching. Other videos may have been adapted from books, which could be used in the classroom to support the video. If, however, the video is being used for presenting language or for comprehension tasks there are further factors to be considered when selecting it.
- Degree of visual support. A good idea is to choose scenes that are very visual. The more visual a video is, the easier it is to understand.
- Clarity of picture and sound. If the video has been copied from television it is important to make sure both the picture and sound are clear.
- Density of language. This refers to the amount of language spoken in a particular time. Videos where language is dense are more difficult for learners to comprehend.
- Speech delivery. Among the factors in determining how difficult a video excerpt will be for students to comprehend are clarity of speech, speech rate and accents.
- Language content. An important factor to consider in using videos to present language is the linguistic items (particular grammatical structures, language functions, or colloquial expressions) presented in the scene.
  Another important factor is the amount of repetition of language content. Authentic videos for young learners will often contain a lot of repetition. It is also useful to see if the linguistic content in the video can be linked to that of the language curriculum or the course book thus providing a way to integrate video work into the course as a whole.

- Language level. The language level of the video should be appropriate for the level of the class without the teacher having to explain too much.

Why authentic videos?

A great advantage of a video is that it provides authentic language input. Movies and TV programs are made for native speakers, so in that sense the video provides authentic language input (Katchen, 2002). Besides, the learner can concentrate on the language in detail and interpret what has been said, repeat it, predict the reply and so on. The learner can also concentrate in detail on visual clues to meaning such as facial expression, dress, gesture, posture and on details of the environment. Even without hearing the language spoken clues to meaning can be picked up from the vision alone.

The other point is that in foreign language to interpret attitude is very difficult owing to the fact that the listener concentrates himself on the verbal message, not the visual clues to meaning. Video gives the students practice in concluding attitudes. The rhythmic hand and arm movements, head nods, head gestures are related to the structure of the message. Moreover, the students have a general idea of the culture of the target language. It may be enjoyable for the learners to have something different for language learning apart from the course books and audios for listening.

Example of using videos to build vocabulary

Unit 6 Dialogue "Shopping for vegetables"
Unit 4. Dialogue. You're in great shape
Communicative Functions: Talk about weight, talk about height, talk about exercise, talk about likes and dislikes, invite someone, ask where to get something, talk about your family
Grammar Forms: infinitive vs. gerunds, possessive after *of*. The past with *used to*
Video sequence: Monica's Boot Job

Exercise 1. Read the introductory information. What do you expect the video might be about knowing how the characters of the series behave?
Exercise 2. Watch the video. Verify your expectations

Exercise 3. Watch again and say if these ideas are Right or Wrong
   a) Monica and Chandler asked Joe some money
   b) Monica want a boot job
   c) Chandler is happy with the idea of Monica having a boot job
   d) Monica and Rachel know what Chandler is talking about
   e) What is the characters´ confusion?

Exercise 4. Work with the pronunciation segment of the video

Exercise 5. Watch the video paying attention to vocabulary. Find how the characters say:
- f)   To take money with the intention of returning it later
- g)   Expression used to imply an habitual action that doesn't happen anymore
- h)   Expression meaning you are winning or getting everything right
- i)   Breast implants
- j)   Don't ask me for an answer, I don't know anything
- k)   To understand and find his jokes funny
- l)   To say nice things about someone's appearance or behaviour
- m) Expression meaning someone unexpectedly passed their limits
- n)   What caused that to happen
- o)   Get really nervous, anxious and scared
- p)   Affectionate name used by couples
- q)   This will happen independent of your opinion
- r)   To buy something at a discount price because you get the whole package
- s)   If you really want this, I will support it
- t)   If you can't support this, if you are not comfortable with this
- u)   Coming out really quickly, like a gun shouting
- v)   I have spent $ 4000

Exercise 6. Work with the vocabulary section of the video

Exercise 7. Work with the cultural references

Exercise 8. Watch the video sequence again with no subtitle

Exercise 9. Would you go through a boot job? Why or why not?

Vocabulary teaching is an important aspect of language teaching. The vocabulary acquired by students directly affects their development in listening, speaking, reading, writing and translating skills. Vocabulary mastery and application is a prerequisite for language learners to improve their English language skills. Furthermore, vocabulary learning can promote the improvement of English proficiency.

Even though students are generally accustomed to the use of audio-visual material for personal, recreational purposes, there is still a long way to make the use of this kind of material as something generalized. Therefore, it should be said that there is still more to be exploited and research yet to be done when talking about the use of audio-visual material in foreign language learning classrooms.

Bibliography

- ALLEN, VIRGINIA FRENCH. (1983). Techniques in Teaching Vocabulary. New York: Oxford University Press.
- BRETT, P. (1995). Multimedia for listening comprehension: The design of a multimedia-based resource for developing listening skills. System 23(1), 77-85.
- CANNING-WILSON, C. (2000). Current Theory on the Use of Video as an Educational Medium of Instruction. The Internet TESL Journal, Vol. VI, No. 11
- Egbert and Jessup, 1996;
- Figuerosa, 2017
- FINOCCHIARO, M. & BRUMFIT, C. (1983). The Functional-National Approach: From Theory to Practice. Oxford: Oxford University Press.
- HARLEY, B. (1996). Vocabulary learning and teaching in a second language. Canadian Modern Language Review,53, 3-12
- KATCHEN, J. E. (1996). Using authentic video in English language teaching: Tips for Taiwan's teachers. Taipei: The Crane Publishing Company, Ltd Video in ELT—Theoretical and Pedagogical Foundations. Proceedings of the 2002 KATE (The Korea Association of Teachers of English) International Conference (pp. 256-259)
- KHALID, A. (2001) The effect of multimedia annotation modes on L2 vocabulary Acquisition: A comparative study. Language Learning and Technology, 5(1), 202-232.
- KRASHEN, S. (1985), The Input hypothesis: issues and implications, New York, Longman.
- MCCARTHY, R. (1990). Language Teaching. A Scheme for Teacher's Education. Vocabulary (Language Teaching: A Scheme for Teacher Education
- MARZANO, ROBERT J. (1988). A Cluster Approach to Elementary Vocabulary Instruction. USA: International Reading Association.
- Merriam Webster´s Dictionary (2020)
- RORTY, RICHARD. (1989) Contingency, Irony, and Solidarity. Cambridge: Cambridge University Press. ISBN 0-521-36781-6
- SNOW, C. E., GRIFFIN, P., & BURNS, M. S. (Eds.). (2005). Knowledge to support the teaching of reading: Preparing teachers for a changing world. San Francisco, CA: Jossey-Bass.
- STEVENS, G.C. (1989), "Integrating the Supply Chain", International Journal of Physical Distribution & Materials Management, Vol. 19 No. 8, pp. 3-8.
- STEMPLESKI S & P ARCARIO (undated) Video in Second Language Teaching and Learning TESOL Inc
- TOMALIN B (undated) 'Teaching young children with video' in Stempleski S & Arcario P (eds)
- TALAVÁN, N. (2010), Claves para comprender la destreza de la comprensión oral en lengua extranjera, in «EPOS», XXVI, pp. 198-216.
- WILKINS, D.A. (1972) Linguistics in Language Teaching. Australia: Edward Arnold.

Exercising-type Educational Software

PhD Yunior Portilla Rodríguez. Full Professor

The first steps in the exercise of learning through computers arise with behaviorism as the psychological support of programmed teaching and teaching machines. This was developed at the beginning of the 20th century, and among its main representatives are Watson (1926), Tolman (1932), Thorndike (1935), Hull (1943, 1951, 1952) and Skinner (1938, 1953, 1954, 1960, 1961), among others. These psychological foundations were materialized in the different types of programs according to the type of response (elaboration and choice) that they demand from the students. In this regard, Fry (1971, pp. 19-20), states: *"In response elaboration programs the student must complete a sentence that has remained unfinished; in those of choice, he must select the appropriate answer from among the several that arise."* These conceptions prevailed in the ascending and accelerated development of computers, and their application in the educational field, put into practice in drills and practice.

With the introduction of computers in education in the late 1960s, a set of terms appeared, in correspondence to the various uses they were put to, specifically, Computer Assisted Instruction (CAI). This is determined by the applications directed to the instructional process that make up its basic structure and in which the learning theories of behaviorism, the concepts of programmed teaching and teaching machines were applied. In reference to this, Lipsitz (1973) states that in the CAI the material is presented to the student under the total control of the computer and through interaction with it.

The CAI applications are manifested as: tutorials, exercise and practice, dialogues, tests, games and simulations. In this sense, the **exercise and practice** mode is the type of software whose essence is exercise solution, which is approached by the United States Continental Army Command in 1969 cited by Lipsitz (1973, p. 11): *"In exercise and practice mode there are different levels based on the degrees of difficulty of the material presented. The instruction is therefore the measure of the needs and capacities of the person, based on their performance."*

Suppes (cited by Ellis, 1974, p. 44) states: *"The program was designed to exercise and examine students on the concepts previously presented in the classroom by the teacher."* Suppes confers an evaluator connotation to this type of software and recognizes the role of the teacher in driving the process. In this sense Watson, 1972, argues that the main advantages of the Stanford project are immediate feedback to students on each problem, the level of the exercise can be individualized for each student, and it can provide an immediate response to the teacher on the performance of each student in the exercises.

The importance of automating exercises is addressed by Ellis (1974), citing JCR Licklider, who raises four essential elements for consideration. In the first order, to the effort and time that educational systems dedicate to the construction and solution of exercises, secondly, to the potentialities of individualization of teaching using the exercise and practice software, thirdly, to the need to make the exercise classes more motivating and finally to the low investment cost that would have to be carried out in study programming and computer science.

The main limitation of this type of software lies in its behavioral conception of learning, based on the presentation of exercises (stimuli) and reinforcements to the responses issued by the students. In this sense Salomon, 1985, and Grabe, 1985, address the strategy of reinforcement based on the structuring of responses as one of the important aspects that differentiates exercise and practice software from the traditional solution of exercises.

These considerations of the exercise and practice software are limited to the repetition of the exercises as a formula to eliminate errors in learning, without focusing on the cognitive activity that the student has to develop to achieve learning, and the various ways to achieve it. It focuses on the solution and on obtaining correct responses, and reduces interactivity with the software through reinforcing messages as "Please try again," "OK" or "NG."

Related to this last approach, research appeared that began to delve into the role of feedback in exercise and practice software, its relationship with reinforcement, incentive and motivation. In this sense, Dempsey & Sales (1993, p. 55) carry out a systematization that addresses these elements and outlines that feedback is *"any information that follows a response and allows a student to evaluate the adequacy of the response itself."*

The results of the empirical-analytical research reflected by Dempsey & Sales allow to state the following characteristics of the feedback:
- Its use is important for the appropriation of knowledge.
- It is a unit of information.
- Its use to treat incorrect answers allows for better learning results.
- It can be used to confirm correct answers.
- It helps students correct mistakes made.
- Its use depends to a large extent on the level of knowledge that the students possess when answering.
- The ways to be used are expressed from the errors made by the students and the treatment of the content based on these, or from the confidence in the response of the students.
- Feedback can be immediate or delayed.

In correspondence to the characteristics previously expressed, Dempsey & Sales (1993, p. 25) propose that feedback can be expressed in five types:

- There is no feedback, a question is presented and an answer is required, but it does not indicate whether the student's answer is correct.
- Verification of simple comments or knowledge of the results, the student is simply informed of the correct or incorrect answer.
- Feedback correction of the answer or knowledge of the correct answer, which informs the students what the correct answer to the question should be.
- Feedback that provides an explanation of why the student's answer is correct or incorrect, or allows the student to review the material corresponding to the attributes of a correct answer.
- Feedback that informs the student when an incorrect answer has been made and allows the student to make one or more attempts to answer correctly.

This perspective of feedback in exercise and practice software reaffirms the reinforcing nature to which it was associated, or informative at best in some cases. This is due to the limitation that exists in its educational structure in memorizing correct answers. In this sense, its main detractors are the dichotomy of evaluation of the questions (correct or incorrect), and the integrative nature that its teaching strategy requires.

For Dempsey & Sales there are two types of feedback, the confirmation of the correct answer, which is very brief and has a reinforcement function such as "Well, you're right," and feedbacks that have an informative function .

In general, there is consensus that feedback in a computerized environment is a complex issue but fundamental for learning. However, its use in exercise and practice software has been limited in the vast majority to information on the accuracy of the answer. At most it provides clues of possible errors that lead to the analysis of the question again. This is part of the deficiencies in the theoretical order of conceptualizing the role of feedback in exercise and practice software based on an integrative didactic strategy for learning.

Consequently, practically speaking, computer tools as a generality have focused on the reproduction of a feedback model based on texts with a reinforcement character, which limits the interactivity of the exercise and practice software. In this sense, the multimedia potential is not exploited, the content of these and their characteristics corresponding to the objectives pursued, from the approach to learning situations that develop and give meaning to the learning of the student.

For Alessi & Trollip (1985, p. 52) the exercise and practice software *"is an exercise of a selection of questions or problems that is presented several times until the student answers or solves all of them at some predetermined level of mastery. Computer programs can greatly improve the effectiveness, efficiency and enjoyment of exercise."*

In correspondence to its definition, it proposes the structure and general procedure for an exercise (see Appendix I). The basic forms of selection of exercises can be random or without a specific order. As well, the culmination of the exercise can be done at the conclusion of a high number of exercises, after a period of time (30 minutes), or when the student´s performance reaches a certain level.

One of the main contributions of Alessi & Trollip (1985, p. 136) is found in what is considered as new pertinent factors for the exercises. These factors address: *the introduction of the exercise, the characteristics of the question, the question selection procedure, comments, grouping procedures, student motivation, and data collection.*

Another important aspect that it addresses (Alessi & Trollip) are the questions and answers, although the analysis is made from the tutorials, and recommends using these for the exercise and practice software. Questions are classified into two basic types, alternatives and construction questions: The former include true or false, matching questions, multiple multiple-choice questions, and markup questions. The construction questions are realization, short answer, and development questions. However, they are expressed through examples that have a marked evaluative character, and do not contemplate the relationship between knowledge and skills through actions with the software to answer each question.

In this sense, in Alessi & Trollip (1985) is recognized that one of the weakest factors of the exercising software is the treatment of the responses. This is due, among other aspects, to the complexity for the development of algorithms that contain the evaluation of different variants of answers in the same question and the strange variables that are present in the process of solution and introduction of the answer. For Levin & Kareev (1989), the exercise and practice software focuses on the acquisition of knowledge and its main problems are found in: the type of activity that is developed with them is sometimes boring; lack of variability and similarity with other school tasks and the control in the development of the activity in almost its entirety is the program. This author does not propose how to face these limitations, which can be analyzed from the potential of software as a teaching-learning medium.

In another work (Azarma, 1991) some of the characteristics of the exercise and practice software are listed: providing a variety of questions, various levels of difficulty, consideration of the possibility of providing the student with a general summary of performance at the end of the exercise sessions. Also, the student must have several attempts to answer and receive information about the answer issued. The limitation of his research is found in addressing mostly technical aspects that do not start from a didactic strategy that shows the relationships between the components of the teaching-learning process.

For Schwier & Misanchuck (1993) the exercise and practice software is a chain of exercises with the aim of reviewing the contents taught in an evaluation environment. Its main contribution is found when addressing the incorporation of multimedia elements, stating that these can be used to increase the types, quantities, layers of stimuli, as well as the feedback that is presented. In this regard, it is stated that *"... instead of using a map with the capitals of the cities... the student can be presented with an enlarged satellite photo with the destination city. If the student requires a clue, the country's national anthem or additional data could be presented. A correct answer could be greeted with a video or audio clip containing heartfelt congratulations for the selected state."* (Schwier & Misanchuck, 1993, p. 20)

In this sense, the use of different types of media (text, illustrations, images, videos, sounds, locutions, animations, and slides) and their didactic function within the exercise are aspects not addressed by Schwier & Misanchuck. Since when and how are not specified, it is advisable to use one or the other multimedia resource, or both. What will they do? What processes within learning will they favor? These are some of the unknowns that require scientific research for their conceptualization.

Brock, 1994, and Rajaraman & Rajaraman, 1996, refer to the facilities provided by this type of software to integrate into the study plan, based on its individualization potential, content verification, as well as the role of correct and incorrect feedbacks. The uniqueness of the research of Rajaraman & Rajaraman is found in the characterization for the use of this type of software, in three forms: learning stations, lesson activities in free time and group work. This perspective of use reduces the medium nature of the exercise and practice software and its role in the teaching-learning process.

For Galvis Panqueva (2000) the exercise and practice software must have number of exercises, variety in the formats in which they are presented and feedback that indirectly redirects the student's action. For him, the feedback should not be limited to reinforcing the answer, but rather be used as clues or criteria that allow the student to arrive at the correct answer. His work does not explain why the number of exercises, or the variety of formats of these and what function they perform in this type of software.

For Clarke (2001) the exercise software has the following characteristics: the structuring of the practice, the content and the speed. In the structuring different types of exercises are approached, such as: identification, selection of lists, ordering of sequences, filling empty spaces and coordination of eyes and hands; the content is influenced by time and degree of difficulty; speed is related to the concepts of competence and motivation within the application. The limitation of its considerations lies in the general structure of this type of software (see Appendix II), and does not show the types of relationships that occur with the tutorial as well as the reduction of the selection criteria that allow the teacher to follow up to the individualities of the students.

Exercise and practice software for Parshall, Spray, Kalohn, & Davey (2002), Colvin Clark (2008) and Jamrich Parsons & Oja (2011), has an evaluator character. The first state that this should consist of screens: instruction, practice items and help options. Their considerations limit the interaction with the software to the evaluation of the responses without clarifying the role of feedback in this process. Niegemann, Leutner, & Brünken, 2004, emphasize the solution of exercises through educational software as a learning task, which is made up of two elements: question or problem and the respective answer as a solution. Each exercise has to do with a specific part of the domain of knowledge and the cognitive operations that are required for the solution of the task. As well as, the role that interactivity plays through feedback to promote self-regulated learning.

In this sense, Niegemann, Leutner, & Brünken (2004) take up the role of feedback in exercise and practice software, and its effectiveness in learning. Their empirical research led them to conclude that informational feedback was more conducive to learning than simple feedback. The limitation of this study was to not include the quality of information, its relation to the content, s effects for motivation, stratification in correspondence with levels helped to students need. These aspects evidence the need for a coherent teaching strategy with Ciba interaction between the components of the teaching-learning process.

Fenrich (2005) and Futrell & Geisert (1984) consider that exercise and practice software is characterized by: being used after the content has been taught and not to teach new content. These assertions limit the role of this type of material in the teaching-learning process to introduce a class of new content, check the content that guarantees the starting level of the class, or in an exercise class itself.

Another theme addressed by Fenrich (2005) is the elaboration of different types of questions such as true or false, multiple choice, pairing, short answer and long answer. These are analyzed in its application in computed tests, in which the relationship between the content of the questions and the various types of action is not considered.

Fenrich addressed the implication of the different types of feedback and classifies them as verification and elaboration. In this direction, he proposed the guidelines for providing feedback, which can be correct, partially correct, incorrect, invalid or unforeseen. For Holmes & Gardner (2006) the practice exercise software has the potential to provide information, get the right answer and management to track student progress.

The analysis of these exercise systems proposed by Wiger & Dominguez (1998), Knowledge Share LLC (1995-2009), American Education Corporation (1998-2011), and Math Practice (2000-2005) are an important benchmark. The main advantages of these proposals are the large volume of information they have and the Web platform on which they are developed, which allows easy updating and access.

Although research has shown the efficacy of this type of material with respect to traditional methods, the research work carried out in the scientific literature and the accumulated experience in the development of this type of material allow to state some problems faced by this type of software:
- Its application is reduced as a generality in areas of knowledge such as spelling, translation of foreign languages and arithmetic calculations.
- The complex nature of working out the exercises.
- Feedbacks are used as a generality to inform about the result of the interaction with the software.
- Impossibility of administering the exercises by the teachers in correspondence to the individual differences of the students.
- A didactic strategy is conceived to supplant the teacher.
- Lack of methods for data collection, which being processed by the teacher will help diagnose and plan new activities based on the student's progress, of its characteristics and level of help needed.

On the other hand, an important aspect associated with exercise software has been the development of different authoring systems, frameworks, tools, and programming languages. They focus their efforts on the different types of questions. The study carried out on these shows the diversity of criteria in their structuring (content-form) and their classification based on the action to be carried out.

The work carried out by the researcher in this field has made it possible to introduce important transformations in the control algorithms and in the conception of this type of software. The achievements most importantly are the modifications made to the system author SumTotal ToolBook in the development of software collections educational "El Navegante" (Navigator) and "Futuro," (Future) aimed at education it is basic secondary and high school, respectively. Tools have also been developed for the implementation of exercise systems in Revolution and SAdHEA-Web, which is an approach to the teaching-learning process developer, as a result of the systematization that has been achieved in this field.

Bibliography

Alessi, SM, & Trollip, SR (1985). *Computer-Based Instruction. Method and Development.* Englewood Cliffs. New Jersey, Englewood Cliffs, United States: Collen Brosnan.

American Education Corporation. (May 23, 1998-2011). *AplusMath.* Retrieved July 12, 12, from AplusMath: http://www.aplusmath.com/

Azarma, R. (1991). *Educational computing: principles and applications.* New Jersey, Englewood Cliffs: Educational Technology Publications, Inc. Viewed at http://books.google.com.

Brock, PA (1994). *Educational technology in the classroom.* Englewood Cliffs, New Jersey: Educational Technology Publications, Inc. Viewed at http://books.google.com.

Clarke, A. (2001). *Designing computer-based learning materials.* USA: Gower Publishing Company. Viewed at http://books.google.com.

Colvin Clark, R. (2008). *Developing Technical Training.* California: Trainig and Consulting. Viewed at http://books.google.com.

Dempsey, JV, & Sales, GC (1993). *Interactive instruction and feedback.* Englewood Cliffs, New Jersey: Educational Technology Publications, Inc. Viewed at http://books.google.com.

Ellis, AB (1974). *The use and misuse of computers in education.* United States of America: Kingsport Press, Inc. Viewed at http://books.google.com.

Fenrich, P. (2005). *Creating Instructional Multimedia Solutions: Practical Guidelines for the Real Word.* Canada: Informing Science Press. Viewed at http://books.google.com.

Fry, EB (1971). *Teaching machines and programmed teaching.* Havana: People and Education.

Futrell, MK, & Geisert, P. (1984). *The well-trained computer. Designing systematic instructional materials for the classroom microcomputer.* Educational Technology. Viewed at http://books.google.com.

Galvis Panqueva, AH (2000). *Educational software engineering.* Santafé de Bogota, DC, Colombia: Uniandes.

Grabe, M. (1985). Evaluating the educational value of microcomputers. In H. Steven, *Humanistic perspectives on computers in the schools.* New York: The Haworth Press, Inc. Viewed at http://books.google.com.

Holmes, B., & Gardner, J. (2006). *E-learning concepts and practice.* Canada: Sage Publications Ltd. Viewed at http://books.google.com.

Jamrich Parsons, J., & Oja, D. (2011). *Computer Concepts.* United State America: Cengage Learning, Inc. Viewed at http://books.google.com.

Knowledge Share LLC. (1995-2009). *SuperKids Educational Software Review* . Retrieved on 2011 of 07 of 12, from SuperKids Educational Software Review: http://www.superkids.com/

Levin, JA, & Kareev, Y. (1989). Personal computers and education. In ZW Pylyshyn, & LJ Bannon, *Perpectives on the computer revolution* (p. 429). Norwood: Ablex Publishing Corporation. Viewed at http://books.google.com.

Lipsitz, L. (January, 1973). *The Computer in Education.* (T. Reisner, Ed.) United States of America, United States of America: Educational Technology Magazine. Viewed at http://books.google.com.

Math Practice. (2000-2005). *The World of Math of Online*. Retrieved July 12, 2011, from Math Practice: http://www.math.com/

Niegemann, HM, Leutner, D., & Brünken, R. (2004). *Instructional design for multimedia learning.* Germany: Waxmann Verlag GmbH, Münster. Viewed at http://books.google.com.

Parshall, CG, Spray, JA, Kalohn, JC, & Davey, T. (2002). *Practical considerations in computer-based testing.* New York: Sheridan Books, Inc. Viewed at http://books.google.com.

Rajaraman, D., & Rajaraman, V. (1996). *Computer primer. Second Edition.* Prentice-Hall.

Salomon, C. (1985). *Computer environments for children. A reflection on theories of learning and education.* New York, United States of America: Edwards Brothers Inc. Viewed at http://books.google.com.

Saskatoon Public Schools. (2004-2009). *Instructional Strategies Online*. Retrieved July 11, 2011, from Instructional Strategies Online: http://olc.spsd.sk.ca/DE/PD/instr/strats/drill/

Schwier, RA, & Misanchuck, ER (1993). *Interactive multimedia instruction.* Englewood, New Jersey: Educational Technology Publications, Inc. Viewed at http://books.google.com.

Watson, PG (1972). *Using the computer in education: a briefing for school decision makers.* United States of America: Educational Technology. Viewed at http://books.google.com.

Wiger, G., & Dominguez, H. (September 1, 1998). *Chemistry Drill and Practice Tutorials*. Retrieved July 12, 2011, from Chemistry Drill and Practice Tutorials: http://science.widener.edu/svb/tutorial/

APPENDIXES

APPENDIX I. General structure and flow of an exercise proposed by Alessi & Trollip (1985)

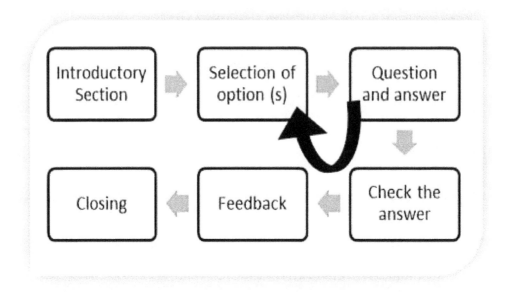

APPENDIX II. Exercise software strategy and practice proposed by Clarke (2001)

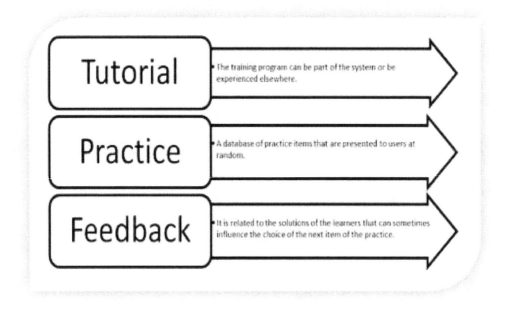

Evolution of the Exercising Software of Cuban Educational Software Collections: Case Study

PhD Yunior Portilla Rodríguez. Full Professor

In the Cuban context, the Ministry of Education (MINED) as of 2001 began to strengthen the development of Cuban educational software with the creation of the Software Studies Centers and their National Directorate. This allowed a cohesion in the elaboration of this type of didactic material based on the didactic model of learning hyper-environment specified in various collections such as "MultiSaber", "El Navegante" and "Futuro". These collections are one of the main results applied in the field of educational software in Cuba. A high number of teachers, MINED specialists, educational software developers, among others, participated in their creation. Its successive implementation in time allowed to perfect the didactic model of hyper-learning environment.

The concept of hyper-learning environment is defined by Labañino Rizzo et al (2007, p. 7) as *"a harmonious mix of different types of educational software supported by hypermedia technology, conceived to guarantee computer support for different functions of the learning process. teaching-learning, characterized fundamentally by constituting **full support to the school curriculum** of a given educational system."*

A hyper-environment can be composed of types of software such as hypermedia book, exercise and practice software, simulators, multimedia libraries (glossaries, galleries of images, videos, sounds, etc.), results and a module for the teacher with methodological recommendations. Although its conception represents a technological and pedagogical advance, it is necessary to deepen its didactic conception. This analysis must go through aspects such as the definition that focuses on technology, the nature of the hyper-environment system, the didactic functions that each of its types of software can fulfill, and the dissimilar ways for its use in the teaching-learning process, just to mention a few.

Specifically, software exercise and practice has been present in the collections of software mentioned above, with high representativeness. These have been used based on their eminently interactive character and following various didactic strategies, however, in each collection different conceptions can be appreciated.

These considerations, together with the researcher's experience in the development of educational software collections, determine the need to carry out a situational case study of the "MultiSaber", "Navegador" and "Futuro" exercising software, which aims at corroborating the main characteristics, regularities and trends of this type of software. For this, the main problems of each collection are described, in general and in particular, of the exercise software, based on the collection of quantitative and qualitative data.

To collect the data, a set of variables, dimensions and indicators was developed with the main characteristics of this type of educational software. The extraction of quantitative and qualitative data constitutes the result of an exhaustive review in two directions, first in the general conception of the exercising software, and second in the internal structure of each one of the exercises that the software possesses, aspects that are described below.

Results of the case study of the "MutiSaber" collection
With the Third Educational Revolution and the introduction of the necessary equipment in primary schools throughout the country, minimum conditions were created to use computerized teaching aids in the educational teaching process. This made possible, among other factors, the development of the "MultiSaber" collection, which, despite the great effort made, was unable to obtain a didactic model of SE, which would respond to the same guideline from the point of view of introductory design and software engineering, in such a way that the pedagogical infrastructure was the same for everyone. These aspects are reflected in the teaching educational process as follows:

- various installation paths that require multiple system resources to run the program.
- different ways of representing the educational software environments iconographically that cause the teachers and students to lose their orientation in the work.
- diverse didactic ways to implement the different types of educational software.
- various ways of authenticating in educational software by both students and teachers, which adds complexity to the modus operandi during use in the teaching process.

Multisaber collection software consists of 31 software parts. Seven are directed exclusively to the first cycle 12, to the second, and 12 can be used in both 10 subjects. Four other issues are addressed. The subjects mostly covered in the software are Spanish Language, The World Live In, History of Cuba, Artistic and Mathematical Education, as shown in graph # 1 of Appendix I.

Out of the 31 software parts of this collection, 12 do not contain exercises, representing 38.70% and the rest 92 are addressed theme-related subjects shown in Figure # 1 of Appendix II. In some software the themes were classified by levels and in others by elements of knowledge.

The analysis of the variables, dimensions and indicators in each one of the software of the "MultiSaber" collection, allows to state the following regularities:

In the *selection criteria* dimension, only one software allows the organization of sequential content, four randomly, none assigned, or predetermined configurations. The selection predominates through a number of exercises entered by the user.

In the variable *Question* in the dimension *elements of information to the user*, the mostly used indicators are those to show the name of the user and the question of the total in which they are. Only three software use time as a useful element for any software user and provides information on the amount of opportunities they have to solve the exercise.

The size *formulation of the question* is a vital link for student exercise. However, the guiding base of the action is very poor as a generality in the software, being present in only three of them, limiting the order of the question to the computer action that must be carried out to introduce the answer.

The dimension *diversity of types of questions* can be classified in terms of their use in high trend, medium trend, and low trend, as shown in graph # 2 of Appendix I. With a high tendency are the simple selection questions that respond to identification and recognition skills, and the questions to be completed by displacement that contribute to the ability to classify. With average trend are the types of multiple-choice questions, drag, selecting text and blank spaces or completion of sentences, with little tendency are questions true or false, link, order and lack of questions to put together, approach and location.

The dimension *use of multimedia resources* can be considered acceptable by the high volume of multimedia resources that are used, 19 software with exercises, 15 use. In this sense, it is not only about the existence of the resource but about its proper use in correspondence to the objective of the exercise, the learning situation and the didactic functions of the different multimedia resources.

In the dimension of *control strategy question* these are controlled through the amount of opportunities and in some software instant messages are used. Generally, control options are used for the revision of the question, with two forms of evaluation of the answer, correct or incorrect, and it is not possible to leave the exercise session to carry out external consultations.

The variable *Retroalimentación* (feeback) in the dimension *messages complementary* lacks analysis of the question, only one software enables the exchange of the answer given by the user of the system, and two software allow to access information to learn more. The dimension of *messages to the answer* is limited to the confirmation or denial of the answer as "Correct" or "Incorrect" to the question, affective messages are not perceived as generality, and once the opportunities are finished, conclusive messages are not used that help to understand the question or provide guidance on the content addressed.

In the dimension *results of the session* of exercise this resource is not used as a means to control the results, only two software allow you to access the effectiveness of the exercises carried out and these are limited to the information of the number of questions resolved, right or wrong. The dimension *tracking the results of a session* is affected by the previous dimension. The *results by contents* dimension is not in the collection, and the *Results* module only stores simple registration and permanence data in the software. This is due to the conception of the exercising software, and its strategies to enable the teacher to diagnose, plan and monitor individual ones in student learning, based on the collection and processing of data on student actions.

Results of the case study of the collection "El Navegante"
In 2003, with the imperativeness of the transformations introduced in the secondary school level, the video class and educational software were introduced as an integral part of the educational system. In this way, the "El Navegante" collection was developed, made up of 10 learning hyper-environments with an extensive curricular nature that covered all the subjects, and in which unity was achieved in various essential aspects of educational software such as:

- The same didactic design for all learning hyper-environments.
- A collection environment from installation to intrinsic levels of programming and didactic conception of the software model.
- The same global interface, only particularized in correspondence with the different disciplines.
- The same methodological conception of using the software.

In this collection, every software contains the module exercise and practice which can work 88 elements of knowledge. The study of each software reveals that there are differences in their materialization, aspects that are described below as a result of the case study.

The variable or *organization of the content* was coherently addressed by specifying the indicators of sequential, random and assigned selection and by establishing the selection of the exercises by the elements of knowledge, which facilitates the work with the exercise by objectives of the contents. The indicator default configuration is implemented only in one software, which limits teachers in addressing individual student differences.

The variable *Q registers* in the dimension *elements of information to the user* as a generality is that the name of the user is shown, the question in which he is in the total and the use of time. The number of opportunities is treated similarly for all exercises (two attempts) regardless of the difficulty level of the question, and is not offered as information.

In the *formulation* dimension *of the question,* only two software contain a well-formulated orienting base of the action, which includes the instructive and the educational. In addition, there is a predominance of the indication of the action to be carried out to introduce the answer. In the latter, incorrect indications are evidenced that do not really guide the student on the basis of the relationship between the concept of action and the executing activity.

In the dimension of *variety of question types,* the software containing more exercise are "Mathematical elements" and "The fabulous world of words" that respond to the subject of Mathematics and Spanish respectively, as shown in graph # 3 of Appendix I. Other software such as English "Rainbow" and "Learn Building" have a considerable amount of exercises.

As illustrated in graph # 4 in Appendix I, the predominant questions are *single-choice, multiple-choice, and blank*. With a medium trend are the types of drag, link and complete questions. With very little tendency there are the questions of true or false, selection of texts and ordering, and questions of assembly, approximation and location do not appear.

The dimension of *use of multimedia resources* is found at 60%. This means that more than half of the software in the collection in their exercises use multimedia resources to support the question, or as a constitutive part of the answer options. However, the exhaustive review of each exercise in the collection allows us to affirm that this is a topic of deepening in the strategy of the exercise. In this sense, the use of the multimedia resource must have a didactic and pedagogical intention, to support the learning process as a motivating or indispensable element to be able to solve the exercise, and not, as sometimes happens, the result of a process of production of a software to simply illustrate it with multimedia resources.

In *the question control strategy* dimension, four forms of implementation were used; in all, the question control was carried out by attempts. The predominant type of feedback is direct, that is, the choice of the possible response is automatically made and only one software provides feedback through the control options once it is decided. Evaluation forms are correct, incorrect and partially correct, and very few software allow the exit of the exercise session for consultations.

In the *complementary messages* dimension of the *Feedback* variable, there is no possibility of obtaining an analysis of the question. Sixty per cent of the software sporadically uses elements that expand the information about the content. On the other hand, it can be exchanged between the answer given and the one offered by the system.

The *messages to response* dimension in more than half of the software provides an affective message to it. In some of the software conclusive messages are used to guide the student towards where? and how? They can find useful information on the content of the exercise.

Eighty per cent of the software treats the *results of the session or partial* in which to obtain data can be the main difficulties by elements of knowledge, access to each exercise session with its evaluation and obtain graphical information of the overall results. The results by contents do not exist in the collection. In this sense, only very general data can be obtained from the exercise sessions such as number of exercises performed and evaluated as good, fair or bad. This limits the potentialities of the teacher in the processing of information for the diagnosis, planning, control and evaluation of student performance.

Results of the case study of the "Future" collection
In 2005, the "Futuro" collection began to be developed for High School, Professional Technical and Adult education, as a result of the experience acquired in the elaboration and conception of these resources. This collection is the fruit of years of work in introducing software in classrooms, the feedback obtained from teachers and students, and the experience acquired by the team of developers.

The results of research on the use of these software in the teaching-learning process with tools to create critical routes or directed routes, showed the following problems (Portilla, 2007):
- Software does not allow the configuration in terms of content and form to be adapted in correspondence to the contexts, needs, difficulties, motivations and interests of the major players the process, learners.
- The front organization of the class with software does not guarantee the quality of the achievement of the objectives.

- Whenever the teacher has skills to become a guide and partner in the pursuit of knowledge, so it is conditional that the student takes a more active role in their own learning role.

The collection is made up of 15 learning hyper-environments that cover all the teaching subjects to which they are directed, with an extensive curricular nature and a virtual laboratory for the teaching of Physics and Mathematics. In this, the exercising software constitutes a significant milestone, in which 13 of 15 software have interactive exercises, which represents 86.66% and 177 elements of knowledge are addressed, among all the contents of the different subjects. However, carrying out the case study allowed us to delve into the following aspects, which are described below:

Variable *ORGANIZATION content* has sequential selection indicators at random and assigned and sets the selection of exercises with elements knowledge. The selection criteria were added to the default configuration criteria, which became generalized, except for the "Substance and Field" software that was implemented with the "Director" platform.

In the dimension *elements of information to the user* as a trend, there is the use of information such as the name, the total question, the number of opportunities and the time. The latter is present in all software, except "Substance and Field."

In the dimension *formulation of the question* most software presents problems in the preparation of statements of exercises, to the not included in the formulation of the question its didactic function for understanding exercise. In this sense, the importance of the guiding base of the action is neglected and orders of exercises prevail that incite more to the executing activity than to a reflective process of the student.

The dimension *diversity of types of questions* is very well treated in software Mathematics (Eureka), English (Sunrise) and Information Technology (IT Universe) that presents the highest number of exercises and better balance work with the types of questions. With better correlation between exercise quantity and diversity of questions are software Biology (DNA), Political Culture (Convictions) and Physical (Substance and Field), aspects that are reflected in the graph # 5 of Appendix I.

In graph # 6 of Appendix I, it can be observed that the typologies that have a high prevalence are those of simple and multiple selection. With a medium trend are the typologies of complete, link and blank space. With little tendency there are the typologies of true or false, sort, drag and select text and with zero tendency are the typologies of assembly, approach and location.

On the other hand, graph # 7 of Appendix I allows to establish a comparison between the types of questions and their tendency in the collections. As a result, it can be observed that the "Future" collection is the one with the highest number of exercises in general and in particular in six types of questions. It can also be concluded that the typologies that predominate as a trend in the collections are those of simple, multiple selection, complete by displacement and blank space.

The *use of multimedia resources* dimension is present in 38.46% of the software. This reaffirms from a qualitative point of view that the didactic value of multimedia resources is not a priority in the conception of the exercises. The experience in the development of exercises for the software of these collections allows us to affirm that the use of multimedia resources is carried out from the resources used in hypermedia books or simply as a technological possibility.

In the *question control strategy* dimension, the exercises are evaluated through opportunities in correspondence with the level of difficulty of the question and the user is the one who decides through the control options when to review the answer. The messages are made according to the type of question and mostly globally to the exercise. On the other hand, the evaluation of the question may be correct, incorrect or partially correct and temporary exits from the exercise session are allowed to consult information to solve the exercise.

The *Feedback* variable in the *complementary messages* dimension lacks messages for the analysis of the response. Only seven software of 13 include messages and additional information, and these do not occur regularly in the exercise system. On the other hand, the software allow to exchange between the answer given by the user and the one that the system possesses, except the software of "Computer Universe," which represents only 7.7%.

In the *message-to-response* dimension, a mixture of affective and cognitive messages is frequently used, with a predominance of affective messages in 100% of the software. In the case of cognitive messages, they appear with a frequency of 53.84% in seven out of 13 software. In this sense, the limitation that exists in the establishment of the relationships between the elements that make up the question is evident: the objective, content, the response options, response messages, actions to be performed by the student, methods, etc.; and this in turn allows working in the zone of proximal development of the student.
In *the session results* dimension*, the* effectiveness module is incorporated, which allows, once the exercise session is over, to know quantitative and

qualitative data such as: the main elements of knowledge with difficulties and the results obtained from each exercise. In addition, you can return it to the exercises and exchange between the given and the correct response and access graphs that illustrate and I statistical analysis of the evaluation of the responses. The collection has a *Results* module for all software and is made up of tools that process the student's track record, his or her history, specific content and comprehensive analysis by subjects. Practice reveals the teacher´s recognition of its importance, although it is rarely used. A comprehensive analysis allows us to conclude that there is redundancy in the design of these tools in the collection, which can only be summarized in two: one for monitoring the session results (student trace) and another for the analysis of the results by content. The results of the case study constitute an important starting point for the search for solutions in its didactic conception.

Bibliography

Labañino Rizzo, C., Rodríguez Rodríguez, L., Coloma Rodríguez, O., Portilla Rodríguez, Y., López Perdigón, A., Ramírez Zaldivar, A., and others. (23-27 of 01 of 2007). Educational software in the context of MINED: a generalization of solutions. *Papers presented at the XV National Forum of Science and Technology.*
Portilla Rodríguez, Y. (2007). Computer mediator transforming free hyper-environments into directed ones, for its application in a teaching assisted by SofTareas. Havana, Holguin, Cuba: Cuban Education.

Appendix I

Graphic representations of the analysis from the data obtained in the case study software exercising software collections education "Multisaber", "El Navegante" and "Futuro"

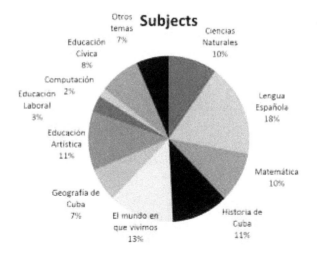

Graph # 1. Conformation of the "MultiSaber" collection by subjects.

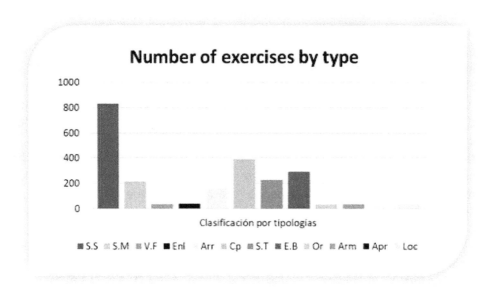

Graph # 2. Distribution of exercises by typologies of the "MultiSaber" collection.

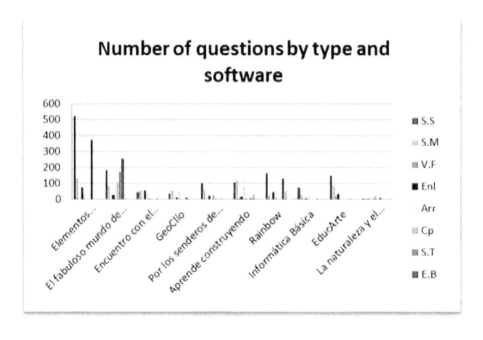

Graph # 3. Distribution of question by typologies of the software of the "El Navegante" collection.

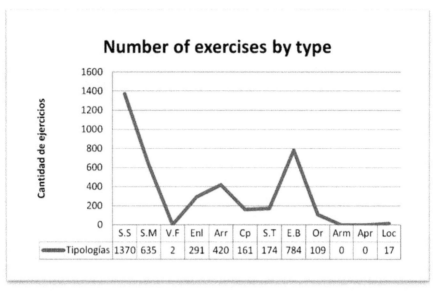

Graph # 4. Presence by question types of the collection "El Navegante".

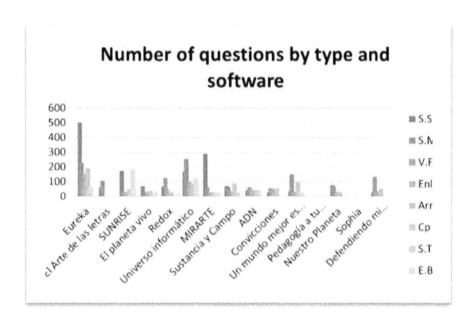

Graph # 5. Distribution of question by typologies of the softwares of the "Future" collection.

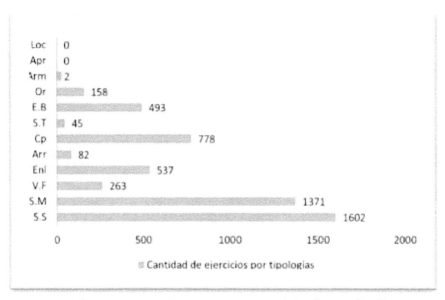

Graph # 6. Presence by question types of the "Future" collection.

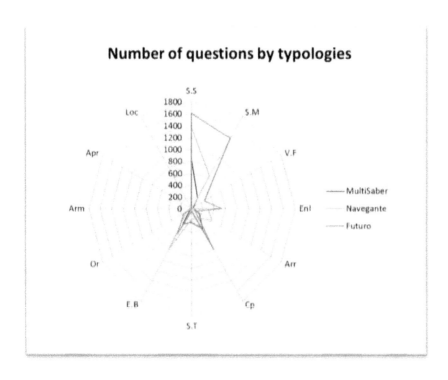

Graph # 7. Trend by question types among the "MultiSaber", "El Navegante" and "Futuro" collections.

Exercise Instructional Design of Learning through Educational Software

PhD Yunior Portilla Rodríguez. **Full** Professor
PhD Maritza Salazar Salazar. Full Professor
PhD Orestes Coloma Rodríguez. Full Professor

Exercising-type educational software has its main foundation on behaviorist theories of learning, which gave rise to teaching machines and programmed teaching. The most important investigations related to this type of software focus on its general characteristics as a methodology in which its interaction with the components of the teaching-learning process and the didactic functions that it can support are not evidenced. Although the implementation of this type of educational software can be carried out using general-purpose programming languages, in practice it is common to use computer tools, such as SumTotal ToolBook, JClic, Exe-Learning, HotPotatoes, Moodle, Question Mark, QuizFaber, ATutor, Claroline, Dokeos, OPALE, EFront, and WebQuestions. These are characterized by focusing on the various ways of presenting the exercises based on the type of computer skills that must be performed to solve the question and the structures of the evaluation algorithms for the treatment of the given answer.

The Cuban educational software collections were developed under the concept of learning hyper-environments (Labañino et al, 2007) and were structured by different typologies, among which are exercising types, which constitute a significant milestone in this line of research. However, its didactic design is the result of the practical activity of its developers, from a continuous construction that has not found solid foundations in pedagogical theory in correspondence with its evolution, as well as an insufficient integration and foundation of the results obtained in practice in its theoretical body.

On the matter, del Toro (2006) and Rodríguez (2010), refer to difficulties that this type of material presents in Cuban educational software collections, such as the graduation of the levels of difficulty of the exercises, their selection and their predominance at a reproductive level that limits attention to individual differences, the quality of help levels, distractors as response options, and learning assessment algorithms.

The investigative work of the authors for more than a decade in the conception of this type of educational software, allows to affirm that there are shortcomings in the evaluative algorithm for the control of the answers, the levels of difficulty of the questions, based on the same number of opportunities, the cognitive load of the question focuses on computer skills to answer the exercise, and the high prevalence of identification and response-elaboration exercises in contrast to the possibilities offered by technology itself, among others.

Although the educational software of the exercising type has been analyzed by different authors, there are no theoretical references that address its didactic design from the learning exercise process, in correspondence with the growing potentialities and inclusion of these media in the teaching-learning process. On the other hand, from General Didactics there is no evidence of unity of criteria in relation to the conception of the exercise, when considering it from different positions, such as educational method; procedure of the teaching-learning method, with emphasis on independent work; a special form of the fixing link of the teaching-learning process or a type of class.

The study carried out on exercise reveals that it is regularly identified from its external manifestation in the teaching-learning process, particularly in the structuring and direction of the process. It is generally associated with the continuous repetition of certain actions; it is conceived as a succession of exercises and its role in the formation of skills, habits and capacities is recognized. However, there are no theoretical references that analyze it from the conception and use in educational software in general, and of the exercising type in particular.

The theoretical and practical deepening of the subject that is addressed shows that both the exercise of learning and the educational software of the exercising type have been approached separately, without taking into account the relationships that need to be established between them, for the didactic design of the learning exercise in educational software. A reflection of this is constituted by the insufficiencies that persist in the didactic foundations for its conception, based on the use of these means in the teaching-learning process. The previous analysis allows to reveal the contradiction that exists between the need to improve the didactic design of the exercise of learning in educational software and the limitations that still exist in the theoretical and practical order for its conception.

Design of the exercise of learning in the educational software
Exercising, in general, is a process that takes place throughout the life of the human being, in the development of their own activity. When this activity is carried out in the teaching-learning process, then we speak of an intentional exercise. Its realization through educational software requires that teachers conceive a process that instructs, educates and develops, aspects that are considered current demands and needs of the school.

Based on the study carried out, exercise is defined operationally as *a procedure that can be used in reproductive and productive methods, in correspondence with the requirements of the objective and the characteristics of the content, which aims at the appropriation of knowledge and the development of habits, skills, abilities and values.*

The exercise as a procedure of reproductive methods is conceived by presenting tasks that seek to reproduce a certain knowledge with the aim of strengthening it and developing skills. In the productive methods, tasks that contemplate small challenges and the system of actions and operations to be carried out by the student are required to achieve their mobility in development, considering as important elements the different levels of aid that will be offered, the interaction with others students, group work, motivation, the search for knowledge, among others.

These considerations require that the didactic design of learning exercise in educational software is structured from tasks with an interactive nature that promote both the appropriation of knowledge as well as the formative and educational. For this, the tasks must contemplate different levels of help, reflective messages, the unity of the affective and cognitive, enable the direction of the process to the teacher for the diagnosis of the real area of development and the planning of activities in the area of potential development of the students.

Based on these ideas, it is operationally considered for this research that the educational software of the exercising type constitutes *the computer application designed to support, as a means of teaching-learning, the didactic function of fixing and improving the knowledge of the teaching-learning process, which has as a purpose the appropriation of knowledge and the development of habits, abilities, capacities and values.*

All of the above allows to define operationally the didactic conception of the design of learning exercise in educational software as *a system of ideas, concepts, demands, representations and the relationships between them, supported by the laws and categories of didactics that make design feasible, of the exercise of learning in educational software, based on the interactive nature of the teaching task and the potential of the technology used.*

Addressing the didactic design of learning exercise in educational software requires the analysis of the relationships that are established between learning exercise and educational software in the teaching-learning process, as well as its phases and functions and the main characteristics of the teaching task, which are explained below.

Relationships of learning exercise and educational software in the teaching-learning process

The exercise can be direct or indirect, it goes through the teaching-learning process, and therefore, its logic. In this way, it is identified that in the links of the teaching-learning process, **problem statement, perception of objects and phenomena, application of knowledge and analysis of achievements, evaluation and verification** is indirectly presented and expressed in the different operations to solve an exercise, observe the proof of a theorem, perform calculations, analyze solutions, establish comparisons, find the essentials of a concept, among other aspects.

In the link of **fixation and improvement of knowledge,** the exercise is direct. This constitutes the essential moment of the teaching-learning process for which teaching tasks are selected or designed, as a set of exercises, with a systemic character that can pursue various objectives, which in turn determine the type of method used. Likewise, there are two types of relationships between the types of educational software and the links in the teaching-learning process: direct and indirect. The first, from the correspondence with the main didactic function of the link and the type of activity promoted by the educational software methodology for learning. The indirect, part of the essential idea that, as in each of the links, other didactic functions are revealed to a lesser extent, these in turn can be supported by a specific educational software methodology, that is, in a class where the main didactic function is fixation, it can be introduced with a hypermedia to motivate, make clarifications or demonstrations that are considered pertinent.

Correspondingly, the direct relationship between software methodologies and the links in the teaching-learning process is manifested as follows:

- For **posing the problem,** the most recommended are hypermedia, simulation and didactic games, as they are considered to have greater potential to create a problem situation that motivates students to independently search for the cognitive task to be carried out;
- For the **perception of objects and phenomena,** the tutorial, simulation, hypermedia and didactic game can be used, due to their facilities to present, represent and analyze information with a multimedia character, since they contribute to familiarize themselves with the content and ways in which students symbolize it;
- For **the fixation and improvement of knowledge,** exercises and practice, didactic game and simulation can be used to promote the confrontation with learning situations, in correspondence with their individual differences and learning rhythms, which through exercise promote

fixation and interrelation of new links or relationships with the preceding content;

- For the **application of knowledge,** simulators, educational games and tools are very useful given their conception in which students can freely use them to carry out activities in which they have to put their knowledge and skills into practice.

- For the **analysis of achievements, evaluation and verification,** tests, simulations and tools are recommended given their intrinsic characteristics to obtain information about the student's performance during the interaction with the educational software, which properly processed allows the teacher to direct the process of teaching learning more effectively.

The relationship that exists between the exercise as a procedure of the independent work method and the educational software of the exercising type is not accidental. It is built on the systemic nature of the teaching-learning process, first in the close connection of the method with the objective and the content, which energizes them and second, in the dialectical relationship with the teaching aids. The latter constitute a support that complement the methods to achieve the objectives. Therefore, it is considered that the didactic design of the exercise of learning in educational software for a teaching-learning process that instructs, educates and develops, requires conceiving this type of didactic material as a mediating instrument of teaching and learning. This consideration requires taking into account that in educational software, due to its own characteristics, the interaction of all the components of the teaching-learning process are revealed, which are reflected in its dimensions as a teaching medium.

These ideas were addressed by Coloma (2008) who explains that educational software by its own characteristics can constitute a medium that contains and integrates all the components of the teaching-learning process. However, although the ideas raised with this author are shared, it is required to specify that:

- Educational software are designed to support one or more didactic functions, since they have specific objectives, which does not limit that due to their peculiarities they can be used to fulfill others.

- The evaluation appears in different ways, from the ways they offer to process information related to the interaction of the student in a certain content, as well as the immediate evaluation of learning situations that require their response.

- They have the character of a communicative medium, which acquires its greatest connotation through interactivity, according to the didactic strategy followed in its conception. This in turn stimulates the interaction of the components of the teaching-learning process as it allows to focus learning in a different way that contemplates the potentialities of the students, their rhythm, the mistakes they make and the help they need to eradicate them, among others.

This interaction of the components of the teaching-learning process is closely related to the dimensions of educational software as a teaching medium:

- The *semantic* dimension expresses the content from the objectives that are pursued, in which the concepts, laws and procedures are revealed.
- In the *syntactic* dimension, the didactic strategy of the software is evidenced, in correspondence with the objectives, the content structure and the didactic purpose of the multimedia resources to be used are determined, which can be presented in different ways (texts, images, videos, animations, etc.). Aspects that are specified in the type of software and are reflected in the evaluative forms that are contemplated, based on the interaction of the students with the educational software.

In the *practical* dimension, the forms of organization of the teaching-learning process are revealed, which are carried out by means of a specific method or a combination of several of them, in correspondence with the didactic strategy of the software. In addition, it expresses the interrelationships between the personal and non-personal components of the process and the relationships between teacher and students through individual, group or collective work.

Phases, functions and characteristics of the teaching task for the didactic design of the exercise of learning in educational software
The didactic design of the exercise of learning in educational software requires keeping in mind the structure that it follows in the teaching-learning process. In this regard, it starts with proposing the following phases, which will be analyzed from the demands that they impose on the didactic conception of this type of material.

In the *Diagnosis* phase, the aim is for the teacher to delve into the main achievements, difficulties and potential of the students. This constitutes the initial phase from which the exercise is structured according to the objectives to be achieved, the content in question and the forms of organization that are used. In this phase, the teacher must determine for each student what they can do on their own and with help and in this way they can select and/or design tasks aimed at achieving their development.

The *Selection and/or Design* phase begins with a process of searching and reviewing existing tasks in educational materials and software. This allows establishing an initial conceptual basis for the development of tasks. In case the search results in the existence of the exercises that are needed, then its use will simply be decided based on a certain methodology.

In this phase, it is important to take into account for the design of the tasks with an interactive nature, the following elements:

- Exercise systems are designed taking into account the diagnostic results obtained or from a general average in case of large-scale development.
- The elements of knowledge, the way in which they will be structured and the levels of difficulty that will be raised are determined.
- The general strategy to be used is determined based on the objectives to be pursued, taking into account fundamentally the following aspects: number of students who will be able to work simultaneously, minimum number of tasks for each of the elements of knowledge, the selection routes and work modalities, the type of control, the evaluative forms, the focus of the questions, the essential elements of the feedback message system, the control options, among others.
- The structure of the tools that will process the information collected in the exercise sessions for analysis is determined once these are concluded and that of those that allow the detailed study of students by content and subjects. In both cases, with the aim of determining the most significant progress made, both general and particular, and the most frequent errors, aspects that provide information for diagnosis and help decide the strategy to follow.

In the *Elaboration* phase, the tasks or systems of these are developed with an interactive nature, which will be later used in the teaching-learning process and in which attention must be paid to the following aspects:

- Avoid content errors in the formulation of the task, be written clearly and with a language according to the age group to which it is addressed, in correspondence with the objective of the task and the element of knowledge to which it responds, as well as offering the relevant guidance to provide the answer.
- Determine the use of multimedia resources based on their didactic potentialities that justify their presence in the task, either as a complementary way to clarify or support the ideas addressed by the task or as an essential element to solve it.
- Determine the type of questions based on the objective of the task, taking into account their level of cognitive complexity and the skills to be developed.
- Prepare the response options on the basis that the distractors belong to the same conceptual domain, are as plausibly correct as possible, and that the weightings are established for each of the options when

considered pertinent, in correspondence with their involvement in the task.

- Establish, based on the type of control used for the task and its level of complexity, the possibilities that will be available to solve it, whether expressed in opportunities or time.
- Elaborate the elements that are required of the feedback message strategy, taking into account, starting from the objective, the different levels of help that will be offered depending on the level of difficulty and the type of control of the task.
- Prepare tasks with a *system character,* in which the following conditions are met:
  - ✓ *System approach or part-whole relationship:* each task responds to specific objectives, leads to the performance of certain actions and operations that affect in a particular way the general objective with which the task system was conceived.
  - ✓ *Sufficient* tasks, that is, the system must have the amount of tasks necessary to achieve the objectives.
  - ✓ The tasks will be *varied,* that is, to encourage the student to make an effort in solving the tasks and stimulate their development; In this, the diversity of forms in which it is presented and its degree of difficulty is essential, where the use of different types of questions in correspondence with the skills to be developed and the actions and operations to be executed plays a determining role.
  - ✓ The tasks have to be *differentiated,* that facilitate the attention to the individual differences of the students and that promote different forms of organization of the activity, be it individual, team or collective.
  - ✓ The tasks will be carried out *systematically* to achieve the objectives gradually, on the basis of solid knowledge that lasts throughout life.
  - ✓ The task system will be *configurable* to be used for different didactic purposes such as *diagnosis, fixation and improvement, application, evaluation, training or support of playful components.*

In the *Implementation* phase, the didactic design of the learning exercise is materialized in educational software, based on interactivity as a central nucleus and revitalizer that influences the determination of the tools, systems or platforms to be used, the instructional design to follow and functional aspects. This phase requires taking into account the following elements:

- The criteria and requirements for the selection of the applications to be used based on their characteristics that allow compliance with the didactic design of the exercise of learning in educational software.
- In instructional design the coherence of the graphic interfaces (aesthetics, communication and ergonomics), navigation mechanisms, the messages it will carry, their relevance, the quality of the media and the formats to be used, the writing and spelling, among others.
- Functional elements, such as the necessary conditions for installation, execution, technical requirements for hardware and software, and maintenance during operation.

Finally, once the implementation process is concluded, it is put into practice through a methodology for its use, from which results will be obtained that will provide elements that will serve as a basis to start the process again. Related to these phases is the determination from the didactic design of the exercise of learning in educational software of the functions that it can perform in the teaching-learning process. These start from the idea of software in context and as context. In the context closely related to the links of the teaching-learning process and as a context for their independent use by students and teachers, in the latter, as a tool for subsequent work in the process.

The functions in the context refer to the *fixation and improvement, application and evaluation* of knowledge. As a context those of *diagnosis, training or support of fun components.* These in turn define the didactic strategy with which the task is designed. In the first group of functions referred to the software in the context, the exercise is carried out under the teacher's direction, in correspondence with the specific didactic function to be fulfilled, an aspect that determines the way in which the task is structured in order to fulfill the objective of the teaching-learning process:

- In *fixing and perfecting* knowledge, the task considers all its characteristics and structural elements, in order to achieve the appropriation of knowledge and the development of habits, skills, abilities and values.
- In the *application* of knowledge, the essential difference is that the tasks are designed on the basis of knowledge already formed in the students, and therefore, what is sought is that the students put into practice what they know.
- In the *evaluation,* the task is structured to control knowledge, which implies that the feedback message system is limited to the extent of the achievement of the objectives and concentrates on the results obtained in the solution of the tasks with respect to the expected.

In the case of educational software as a context, it is presented as a tool for teachers and students. The first to obtain information and support certain processes they are carrying out and the second based on their cognitive interests and self-regulation, as explained below:

- For the *diagnosis,* the teacher designs the task very similar to that of the evaluating function in the context, but can contemplate elements of the feedback message system in order to obtain criteria that allow knowing the initial state or the progress obtained.
- For *training,* the tasks can be designed with all their structural elements, but without missing those that allow flexibility for their selection, the analysis of the results, as well as the options that allow them to have control at all times, since it is the student who makes up the task system, in correspondence with their cognitive interests or according to the suggestions of their teacher.
- As a *support for fun components,* the task is structured only as a challenge that entails advances or setbacks, in correspondence with the strategy followed in the didactic game that is integrated.

Together with these criteria, it is necessary to establish the fundamental characteristics required by the teaching task for the didactic design of the exercise of learning in educational software. These constitute distinctive specifications of the task teaching in this type of material it possible to identify, explain its operation and structure and are listed as the *configurability,* the *complexity,* the *multi-focus* the *multimedia,* the *diversity of types,* the *evaluation,* the *reflective,* the *reconstruction and the interactivity.*

- *Configurability* is the quality of the task of being parameterized, allowing various routes of selection and organization of the process, which facilitates the formation of task systems, depending on support or meet certain educational functions and objectives.
- *Complexity* expresses the property of the task for its classification by the level of difficulty it has, for which various criteria can be followed, depending on the objectives pursued, based on the structuring of the task system, such as: cognitive domains, levels of assimilation of knowledge and cognitive performance, among others.
- *Multi-focus* characteristic of the task reveals the correspondence between the specific function that it will fulfill and the objective it pursues, aspects that determine the way in which it is structured and formulated, taking into account criteria such as questions of setting, of application, of evaluation, interpretation or comprehension, problematic or learning situations, among others.
- *Multimedia* refers to the different multimedia resources that can constitute a support or an essential part of the content of the task to solve it, used for a didactic purpose and in correspondence with its

potentialities, among which the following stand out: images or illustrations, phrases or sounds, videos, animations, slides, etc.

- **Diversity of typologies** requires that the design of the task be carried out on the basis of a wide variety of questions depending on its objective and closely related to the skills to be developed, in addition, they determine the operations necessary to offer the answer from the required actions. Among them we can mention *Selection of Several-One, Several-Several, Dichotomous, True or False, Relationship, Order, Classification, Completion of sentences, Selection of Texts, Location, Approach, Assemble, Identification and Open response.*

- **Evaluative** refers to the need to contemplate the activity of the students in the process of solving the task, in such a way that they take an active role in the control of the results immediately that offer the answer and can carry out analysis of this with the correct solution.

- **Reflective** refers to the need for the information system that is offered to students during the task solving process to be presented in various forms and formats, in correspondence with the didactic strategy that is used and in function of giving it a differentiated treatment of the mistakes made linking the affective and cognitive.

- **Reconstruction** is the property of the task that preserves the status of your solution at any given time, from the processing and storage of the necessary information that enables further analysis.

- **Interactivity** is the feature on which the strategy is established teaching to design the exercise of learning in educational software, based on the objectives to be met. This is shown through the communicational exchange system that the task presents and that determines the structure of the rest of the characteristics. Interactivity makes the task and has a leading role on the rest of the features that it can be considered as a regular instructional design for the exercise of learning in the educational software. This guiding condition is manifested in the degree of dependence that *configurability, complexity, multi-focus, multimedia, diversity of typologies, evaluative, reflective* and *reconstruction* of this characteristic have, from the interaction in the software educational components of the teaching-learning process.

The theoretical analysis carried out and the author's experience in the design, development and introduction of educational software in school practice, allow to affirm that the didactic design of the exercise of learning in educational software to achieve a teaching-learning process that instructs, educates and develop, requires teaching-learning tasks with an interactive nature. In this way, it is considered that a principle for this is constituted by *the interactive nature of the teaching task.*

Principle of the interactive nature of the teaching task

The didactic design of learning exercise in educational software has an educational character, based on scientific knowledge, which must be affordable and systematic, closely linked between theory and practice, which fosters a conscious and active nature of the students under the teacher's guidance, which enables the solidity of the assimilation of knowledge, skills and habits, based on attention to individual differences supported by the audiovisual nature of the process. However, these principles are not sufficient for the didactic design of the exercise of learning in educational software in a teaching-learning process that instructs, educates and develops. This is largely due to the following aspects:

1. The requirements demanded by the didactic design of the exercise of learning in educational software, specifically of the exercising type, which allow the development of tasks with an interactive character mediated by the computer.

2. The relationships on which the didactic design of the exercise of learning in educational software is based, in correspondence with its phases and functions, the characteristics of the task and the interaction of the components of the teaching-learning process in this medium, from its dimensions that have a systemic nature and are interrelated.

3. Interactivity as an essential element of the task in the educational software of the exercising type that puts dynamics into the didactic design of the learning exercise in this type of material and its interaction with the components of the teaching-learning process, which allow its structuring as an instrument learning mediator.

For the fulfillment of the proposed didactic principle, the following rules are required:

1. *Curricular consistency and integration,* that is, correspondence of the objective and content of the task with those of the curriculum.

2. *Adequate formulation of the task,* in such a way that a balance is achieved between the cognitive activity to be developed by the student and the conditions objectively necessary to solve it. In the task, both aspects must be well defined and differentiated, so that a shift towards the affective-cognitive is promoted and the students are prevented from knowing the answer, but it is very complex for them to express it.

3. *Selection of multimedia resources* (text, images, illustrations, videos, animations, slides, sounds, phrases) that justify their use in the task, in correspondence with their potentialities and the functions of orientation, help, explanatory, demonstration that they will fulfill during the solution of it.

4. *Use of the ideal type of question,* in correspondence with the objectives of the task, the cognitive activity and the skills to be developed in the

students during its execution, in such a way as to avoid an inefficient measurement of the objective and an ergonomic overload.

5. The *evaluative forms* of the task can be the following: *correct, partially correct, incorrect*, not evaluated and neutral.

6. *Strategy of the feedback message system of* the task, in correspondence with the moments in which the exercise is developed in the educational software of the exercising type, which are structured taking into account the following elements:

   - Homework can be done by opportunities or by time.
   - The message system of the task is related to the ways in which it can be evaluated (correct*, partially correct and incorrect)*.
   - Possibility of temporary exits during the exercise session in order to obtain information related to the proposed task.
   - Affective messages to raise students' self-esteem and that can be combined with cognitive ones.
   - Reflective messages to solve the task that promote the orientation of the students towards the general procedures.
   - Cognitive aid messages by levels, depending on the opportunities the task has and the mistakes made.
   - Conclusive messages regardless of the result obtained in the solution of the task, which reveal the essential elements of the task and guide how and where information about it can be found.
   - Task analysis messages, where the teacher explains the correct answers and why not of the incorrect answer options and deepens their didactic intentionality.
   - Complementary messages that make it possible to elaborate on the topic of the task, examples: curiosities, relevant historical facts, discoveries or information inquiries.

7. *The formative and educational nature* expresses that the student's transit through the task, regardless of their answers, must consequently promote changes in their knowledge system that leads to reflect, establish links and better understand social practice where they develop on solid values and feelings .

8. The *control of the task* by the student, in such a way that:

   - Choose the elements of knowledge of the tasks you want to work on, the criteria for their presentation, and the order in which you will answer them.
   - Interact with the multimedia resources proposed by the task.
   - Exchange your answer once the possibilities offered by the system have been exhausted.
   - Leave the task system at any time.
   - Analyze or not the results obtained in the exercise sessions.

The research carried out allows to conclude that:

- In the theoretical study it was found that the exercise has been the subject of research from General Didactics, in the same way there are studies of educational software, especially aimed at its use and general design. However, there is no evidence of studies that address the didactic requirements of training in educational software design, in correspondence with the potentialities of interactivity both of the teaching task and of technology.
- The relationships established between exercise and exercise-type educational software are based on the close link with the links in the teaching-learning process and the interaction of its components in educational software.
- The theoretical and practical analysis carried out and the author's experience on the subject reveal the effort that MINED and the Cuban State have made in the last 15 years to the conception and use of educational software for the development of education. Considerations that make it possible to affirm that Cuban schools are in better conditions to assimilate these results, as well as the need to continue deepening in this direction to perfect the shortcomings that persist.
- A didactic conception is proposed that sets the essential relationships for the didactic design of the exercise of learning in educational software that is based on the phases, functions and characteristics of the task in this teaching medium, learning for the exercise that facilitates the appropriation of knowledge and the development of habits, skills, abilities and values.
- Interactivity invigorates and governs the didactic design of learning exercise in educational software with a systemic character that allows considering the interactive nature of the teaching task as a principle.

Bibliography

Alessi, SM, & Trollip, SR (2001). *Multimedia for learning: Methods and Development.*

Álvarez de Zayas, CM (1999). *The school in life.* Santiago de Cuba.

Danilov, MA, Stakin, MN, Lerner, IY, Budarni, AA, Budarni, NM, Shajmaiev, NM, and others. (1980). *Teaching middle school.* City of Havana: Editorial of Books for Education.

Jensen, J. (1998). Interactivity. Tracking a new concept in media and communications studies. *Nordicom Review. Göteborg: Nordicom, Göteborg University. [Consulted March-May date at*

http://www.nordicom.qu.se/reviewcontents/ncomreview/ncomreview198/jensen.pdf] ,

Vol. 19 (No. 1), 185-204.

Marqués, P. (2003). *Design and evaluation of educational programs* . Retrieved on August 31, 2011, from Educational Software:

http://www.xtec.es/~pmarques/edusoft.htm

Portilla Rodríguez, Y., & Others. (2011). *How to elaborate Interactive Learning Questionnaires through Computers?* Holguin: Published on the CD-ROM of the International Event on the teaching of Mathematics, Physics and Computing.

Portilla Rodríguez, Y. (2013). Methodology for the didactic design of Interactive Teaching-Learning Questionnaires. Doctoral thesis as an option to the degree of Doctor of Pedagogical Sciences. Holguin.

Rodríguez Rodríguez, LA (2010). *Didactic conception of educational software as a mediating instrument for developer learning.* Santa Clara: Thesis presented as an option to the scientific degree of Doctor of Pedagogical Sciences.

Roll Hechavarría, M. (May, 2011). The interactivity. Its dynamics in the teaching-learning process with computer media. (JC Coll, Ed.) *Semester Academic Magazine Cuadernos de Educación y Desarrollo, 3* (27).

Methodology for the Didactic Design of Learning Interactive Quizzes

PhD Yunior Portilla Rodríguez. Full Professor
PhD Orestes Coloma Rodríguez. Full Professor
PhD Maritza Salazar Salazar. Full Professor

Facing the ever-increasing challenges imposed by the use of educational applications in the teaching-learning process requires a deepening of the didactics of educational software. In this direction, it is necessary to deepen on the didactic design of each of the types of educational software, in correspondence with the pedagogical foundations that sustain the educational model in which it will be used later. Educational software is classified in various ways, and the best known are those that refer to its structure. In this regard, Marqués (2003) lists them as electronic books, tutorials, exercising types, simulators, instructional games, builders and tools (Marqués, 2003).

Specifically, exercising-type educational software has its main foundations on behavioral theories of learning, which gave rise to teaching machines and programmed teaching. On this basis, Skinner raised the notion of the different types of programs that are classified in elaboration and choice of answers. These types of programs constitute the theoretical and practical base of the educational software of the exercising type based on the basic principle of E-R behaviorism, which limits their potentialities of interactivity. The most important investigations related to this type of software focus on its general characteristics as an educational software methodology in which its interaction with the components of the teaching-learning process and the didactic functions that it can support are not evidenced.

In this sense, Alessi & Trollip (1985) propose an exercise-type educational software methodology in which they propose the structure, procedure and pertinent factors of an exercise [2]. The main limitations of this work are in the use of comments only to inform about the result of the answer and the extrapolation of the question types used in the tutorials.

Although the implementation of this type of educational software can be carried out using general-purpose programming languages, in practice it is common to use computer tools, such as SumTotal ToolBook, JClic, Exe-Learning, HotPotatoes, Moodle, Question Mark, QuizFaber, ATutor, Claroline, Dokeos, EFront, WebQuestions, etc. These are characterized by various ways of presenting the exercises, in the structures of evaluation algorithms and reproduce model-based feedback text with a character reinforcement that limits the potential of interactivity in educational software.

In Cuba, del Toro (2006) and Rodríguez (2010) refer to difficulties that this type of material presents in Cuban educational software collections, among them the graduation of the levels of difficulty of the exercises, their selection and prevalence in a reproductive level that limits attention to individual differences, the quality of the levels of help, distractors as response options, and evaluation algorithms (del Toro, 2006; Rodríguez, 2010).

Together with these, there are shortcomings in the evaluative algorithm to control the responses, the difficulty levels of the questions are treated from the same number of opportunities, the cognitive load of the question focuses on computer skills to answering the exercise and in the high prevalence of exercises of the type of identification of answers and of elaboration of answers in contrast to the pos-sibilities offered by the technology itself. It is valid to point out that the exercise software of the Cuban collections "MultiSaber", "El Navegante" and "Futuro" constitutes a landmark in this line of research. However, its didactic design is the result of the practical activity of its developers, from a continuous construction that has not found solid foundations in pedagogical theory in correspondence with its progress, as well as an insufficient integration and foundation of the results obtained in practice in its theoretical body.

In addition, despite the fact that the educational software of the exercising type has been analyzed by different authors, there are no theoretical references that address its didactic design from the process of exercising learning, in correspondence with the growing potentialities and inclusion of these media in the process teaching learning. In this direction, investigative work by the author of this paper, of more than a decade in the conception of educational software, has allowed to obtain a set of scientific results to face the difficulties mentioned above. Among them, a didactic conception for the design of the exercise of learning in educational software stands out (Portilla, 2012), which constitutes the epistemic basis of the methodology for the didactic design of interactive learning questionnaires (Portilla, 2012), which is discussed below.

Materials and methods
To conduct the research, among other materials and methods were used modeling for the design and elaboration of the methodology for the didactic design of learning exercise in educational software based on interactive learning questionnaires. The analysis of documents for the description and evaluation of information regarding the didactic design of the exercise of learning in educational software that made it possible to identify the existence of inconsistencies in the conception of educational software of the exercising type from the process of exercise of learning, as well as provided information for the development of the methodology. Experimentation in the field for the

implementation of the proposal with the teachers from systematic exchanges that served to improve the methodology and obtain results about its validity.

Results and Discussion
The didactic design of learning exercise in educational software
The didactic design of the learning exercise in educational software requires the analysis of the relationships that are established between the learning exercise and the educational software in the teaching-learning process, as well as their phases and functions and the main characteristics of the task.

The exercise can be direct or indirect, it goes through the teaching-learning process and, therefore, its logic. In this way, it is identified that in the links of the teaching-learning process, *problem statement, perception of objects and phenomena, application of knowledge and analysis of achievements, evaluation and verification* is indirectly presented and expressed in the different operations to solve an exercise, observe the proof of a theorem, perform calculations, among other aspects.

In the link of *fixation and improvement of knowledge,* the exercise is direct. This constitutes the essential moment of the teaching-learning process for which teaching tasks are selected or designed, as a set of exercises, with a systemic nature that can pursue various objectives, which in turn determine the type of method used. Likewise, there are two types of relationships between the types of educational software and the links in the teaching-learning process: direct and indirect. The first, from the correspondence with the main didactic function of the link and the type of activity promoted by the educational software methodology for learning. The indirect, part of the essential idea that, as in each of the links, other didactic functions are revealed to a lesser extent, these in turn can be supported by a specific educational software methodology.

The relationship that exists between the exercise as a procedure of the independent work method and the educational software of the exercising type is not accidental. It is built on the systemic nature of the teaching-learning process, first in the close connection of the method with the objective and the content, which energizes them and second, in the dialectical relationship with the teaching aids. This requires taking into account that educational software, due to its own characteristics, reveals the interaction of all the components of the teaching-learning process, which are reflected in its dimensions (semantic, syntactic and practical) as a teaching medium.

The phases are those of *Diagnosis, Selection and/or Design, Elaboration, Implementation and Putting into Practice.* In the *Diagnosis* phase, the aim is for the teacher to delve into the main achievements, difficulties and potential of

376

the students. The *Selection and/or Design* phase begins with a process of searching and reviewing existing tasks in educational materials and software.

In the *Elaboration* phase, the tasks or systems of these are developed with an interactive nature. In the *Implementation* phase, the didactic design of the learning exercise is materialized in educational software, based on interactivity as a central and dynamic nucleus. Finally, it is put *into practice* through a methodology for its use.

The functions start from the idea of software in context and as context. In the context closely related to the links of the teaching-learning process and as a context for their independent use by students and teachers, in the latter, as a tool for further work. The functions in the context refer to the *fixation and improvement, application and evaluation* of knowledge. As a context those of *diagnosis, training or support of playful components*. These in turn delimit the didactic strategy with which the task is designed.

The fundamental characteristics of the twelve tasks constitute distinctive specifications in this type of material that allow it to be identified, its operation and structure explained:

- configurability,
- complexity,
- multi-focus,
- multimedia,
- diversity of typologies,
- evaluative character,
- reflective character,
- reconstruction and
- interactivity.

Interactivity is the feature in which the teaching strategy set out to design the exercise in educational software is based on the objectives to be met. This is shown through the communicational exchange system that the task presents and that determines the structure of the rest of the characteristics.

Interactivity defines the task and has a leading role on the rest of the features that allow to consider it as a regular instructional design for the exercise of learning in the educational software. In this way, a principle for it constitutes the interactive nature of the teaching task (Portilla, 2012), which requires compliance to the following rules:

- consistency and curriculum integration,
- adequate formulation of the task,
- selection of multimedia resources,
- use of the ideal type of question,

- evaluative forms (correct, partially correct, incorrect, not evaluated and neutral),
- strategy of the feedback message system,
- formative and educational nature and
- control of the task.

Methodology for the didactic design of learning exercise in educational software based on interactive teaching-learning questionnaires

The interactive teaching-learning questionnaire constitutes the method to structure the educational software of the exercising type that enables the objective conditions for the didactic design of the exercise of learning in educational software. This is defined as: *the system of tasks conceived with an interactive nature to be carried out through the computer, which are based on a system of communicational exchange that allows to link the affective and cognitive, in correspondence with the characteristics of the students, the curriculum and the technology to be used.*

For the educational software of the exercising type based on interactive teaching-learning questionnaires, the following procedures are determined:

- selection,
- presentation and solution,
- strategy for response analysis,
- analysis of the results of the exercise session and
- analysis of general results.

The forms of selection are *sequential, random, assigned, predetermined configuration or according to the student's performance* and can be made from the organization of work, either individually or by teams, which are described below:

- *Sequential:* allows access to the interactive tasks system based on the structuring of the content and the degree of difficulty that determines the order in which they are planned. In this case, you can select tasks that are in a range, for example, from 1 to 10, from 8 to 30, etc.
- *Chance:* enables the choice of X number of tasks from the totality for the selected topics based on the cognitive interests of the students and promotes their self-regulation, as well as their determination to check the development of their cognitive activity. In this way, the student will be able to choose, for example, 10 of 45 tasks that will be randomly generated by the elements of knowledge.
- *Assigned:* specifically designed for the teacher to designate specific tasks based on the zone of proximal development of each student to attend to their individual differences. For this, the teacher will start from diagnostic techniques that can integrate or rely on the analysis of results obtained in

other tasks with the software, as well as use the task viewer to review the new ones that will be proposed. This option makes it possible to schedule tasks from a list that do not necessarily have a consecutive order, for example: 5, 9, 18, 19, 32, 53, 55, 59, etc.

- *Default configuration:* the teacher organizes task systems based on meeting certain objectives, such as addressing the most frequent errors in the assimilation of content, specific objectives both for students who require more help and for those more advanced in order to promote their development. In this case, the student will not have the need to select which tasks to answer if it is not enough to load a file created or modified by the teacher from the task viewer.

- *According to the student's performance:* the software presents a set of tasks based on the results obtained in one or more exercise sections of a specific student. This way allows the teacher to confront the diagnosis that he has about a student with the performance in the software and thus to be able to form new systems of tasks based on their individual differences.

As explained in the last route described, the sets of tasks are formed from the results in an exercise section. However, they should not be assumed as proposed by the software, since the interaction process with it is influenced by dissimilar strange variables that are difficult to control, which generate proposals that do not adjust to the reality of the students. Hence the importance of the review by teachers of these as a way to complement the diagnosis and in order to make the pertinent corrections.

These forms of selection also include two types of work, *individual* or *team.* In the first case, more than one student may work, but each will have their assignments. In the second, the selected tasks will correspond to the work team to be solved with the collaboration and cooperation of its members. In the latter case, the results obtained in the resolution of the tasks will be registered in the name of the formed team, whose members will be known.

In the *presentation and resolution of the task* are the forms of presentation, the types of questions that determine the ways to offer the answers and the set of multimedia resources.

The objective pursued by the task system, in correspondence with the function that the exercise fulfills, influences the way in which the question is formulated, which can have a problematic approach, present a typical situation or simply a direct question. Regardless of the sense in which the task is written, it must be clear and precise, as well as include the necessary information to solve it, the actions and operations that indicate its development and how to offer the answer.

The type of questions is an important element that enables the same task to be shown in different ways depending on the objective to be achieved and the ability to develop. This presents the response options of the task that make it up, that is, the correct option (s) and the distractors. The latter must be closely related to the correct answer, that is, belong to the same conceptual or content domain and be plausibly correct. A good practice for your selection, whenever possible, are the typical mistakes that students make in situations similar to those posed by the task.

The taxonomy of questions that is proposed for the interactive teaching-learning questionnaires is based on the possible ways of structuring the task, which includes both the skills to solve it and the actions necessary to offer the answer, which are stated as follows:

- *Selection* of number-one, which can be short options, objects or long options.
- *Selection* of number-number, which can be short, long options objects or options.
- *Dichotomous,* which can be short options, objects or long options.
- *True* or *False.*
- *Relationship.*
- *Ordering,* which can be numeral, of words or phrases of sentences, steps or objects.
- *Classification,* which can be given in the following ways: One-Many or Several-One relationship.
- *Completion* of sentences, both one and several.
- *Selection* of texts, which can be words or fragments.
- *Location* of areas, which can be from Several Zones-One or from Several Zones-Several.
- *Approach.*
- *Assemble* objects.
- *Identification,* which can be one object of several, a class of objects, several classes of objects or parts of an object.
- *Open response.*

These 14 types of questions allow their presentation in up to 30 different ways, as described below:

- The *Several-One, Several-Several and Dichotomous Selection typologies* allow the realization of nine possible ways, depending on how the answer options are structured based on the objective of the exercise. In this sense, if the answer options are short then the formulation of the question must be explicit, containing the necessary elements to solve it. In the case of long answer options, these allow the use of definitions, concepts, among others, so that the students determine which one corresponds to the given conditions. In the case of answer options through objects, students generally seek recognition of three or four images that represent functions or historical events, among others, just to mention a few examples.

These *typologies* share as a common aspect the actions to be developed by the students to identify the correct answer and its operational part to emit it. The differences between them lie in the conception of the task and the objective to be pursued, as described below:

- In the *Several-One* typology: only one of the answer options is correct.

- In the *Several-Several* typologies: there is more than one correct answer option, both in this type and in the Several-One type, a third option such as "I don't know", "Maybe" or "Maybe" can be included for don't force a response.

- The *dichotomous* typology: it can be considered a specific case of the Several-One, however, it is used to put the student before a reflective situation, to determine which one meets the given conditions.

- In the *True or False* typology, the student will issue his criterion of veracity from the analysis of the set of propositions that are raised, which must be closely related to each other, which promotes the cognitive activity of students, these are presented for the student to write "V" as true and "F" as false.

- The *Relationship* typology is commonly known as the linking or matching question, in which the students are presented with two columns A and B in which there may be options, with texts or images, for the student to establish the relationships between the elements of both sets and corresponds to those of column (A) a single element of column (B). Relationships will be established through arrows imitating reality, as happens in school practice.

- The typology of *Ordering* enables the approach to two types of situations: the first from texts to order grammatically or under other conditions; the second from tasks that require an established order for a set of steps or procedures. In the first case we talk about questions of ordering words or phrases of a text, in the second it can be manifested in different ways, examples: situations in which it is required to order chronologically a set of historical events by writing the order numerically; order a set of steps to solve a quadratic equation but exchanging their position; order a set of images that represent the steps to carry out a chemical experiment, exchanging their position; among others, such as: by functions, cause-effect or stages in which an event occurs, in any subject based on the requirements of the task.

- The *Classification* typology aims for the student to solve certain situations to classify elements of the same conceptual domain or content. These are presented as a set of disordered elements in a certain area to be classified by dragging themselves towards the designed place on the screen. It is structured on the basis of two relationship criteria: one to many and many to one. In the first, each answer option to be classified may correspond to different categories, in the second it corresponds to only one of several. Also, the answer choices can be dragged a specified number of times into a ranking set, if desired.

- The *Phrase Completion* typology presents one or more blank spaces in which a word or phrase must be written directly on them. In this type of question, it is important to consider as many correct answers as possible and the typical spelling errors for each answer option. This will prevent the task from being evaluated incorrectly before a correct answer and in turn will make it possible to treat spelling errors through the feedback message system.

- The *Text Selection* typology allows the elaboration of tasks based on two types, one so that students, from a text or set of them, select certain words, and in the other, fragments. This type of question is useful to find words, determine central ideas, concepts, as well as very useful for the use of the language, in determining the lexical-syntactic classes of words.

- In the typology of *Location,* the task is structured from the use of graphics or selectable areas that require students to locate one or more areas, in correspondence with the given conditions. These questions are frequently used in the study of History and Geography.

- The *Approach* typology allows the presentation of questions in which the values of the solution are in a range established in correspondence with the demands of the task. In this type of question, a scrolling bar can be used to indicate the change of the values in the range, and sometimes, if desired, it can be accompanied by areas where the resulting value is updated.

- The *Armar* typology allows the design of tasks in which the situation requires assembling an object that is provided broken down into different parts. It is possible to determine one or several parts of the object that initially appear in their corresponding place.

- The *Identification* typology allows the presentation of different situations for the student to identify: of an object the parts that make it up or of a set of objects, the only one, the class or several classes that meet the given conditions. In the first case, for example, to identify the parts of a photographic camera, the human body or a combustion engine, in any of these cases, the image representing the object and the name of each of the parts that It is formed by those that must be correctly located on the part of the object that corresponds to it. In the second case, for example, of a set of traffic signs and under certain conditions, the correct one may be: a single (identify from the group of prohibition signs, which one does not allow parking), a class (identify a group of signs, which ones respond to danger signs) or several classes (identify from a group of signs, which ones belong to prohibition signs and which ones to danger signs).

- The type of *open-ended* questions makes it possible to design tasks that will not be immediately evaluated by the control strategy, that is, situations are presented to the student so that they can express their evaluations, positions, etc. The results of these tasks will be stored for later review by the teacher.

These question types can be used in any subject, depending on the teaching level, the objectives and the content. Some are easy to do for any content, others require greater pedagogical expertise, however, there are question types that, due to their characteristics, are more suitable for the treatment of a certain content than for another. On the other hand, multimedia resources constitute an essential element in the design of tasks with an interactive nature, depending on the objectives of the exercise and the function it performs. These can be presented in two ways based on their didactic structuring, as a constitutive part of the content as they form part of the set of information provided in the task or as support elements necessary for their solution, as described below:

- *Texts:* in the tasks you can use fragments of texts, poetry, among others.
- *Images and illustrations:* they are used both for the location in time and space and for the development of the observation; For example, in a mathematics task dealing with the content of quadratic equations, a graph of the function can be presented and equations representing it proposed as possible answer options.
- *Sounds and phrases:* songs, speeches, among others, are used that reaffirm the ideas that the student's orientation requires to solve the task; For example, in Art Education, a sound that represents a musical instrument can be presented and a set of answer options is provided for the student to identify which of them corresponds.
- *Videos:* are resources that represent the objective reality of a given moment and can be used as necessary elements in solving the task, since the analysis of their information is vital to be able to offer the answer.
- *Animations:* these are resources that reconstruct a certain process or event, from a sequence of images. These allow to describe a theorem, a law or phenomenon. For example, in a Chemistry task the reaction of several substances is proposed and the possible formulas of the resulting compounds are given as answer options, in this case, an animation can be used that shows the transformation process of the substances.
- *Slide shows:* it is the synchronization of a soundtrack with a set of illustrations, images, diagrams, concept maps, notes, among others, and that can incorporate interactive elements. This explains a process, a law, a phenomenon or the class itself and enables students to have a support resource during the task to achieve the success of the objectives set. Its

characteristics make it a valuable means to guarantee the starting level of the knowledge that is required to reach the solution of the task.

The strategy for the analysis of the response is made up of the control strategy and the feedback message system that are interrelated and that support the general didactic strategy of the task, as well as the optional control mechanisms, such as: accessing the display of the correct answer, making information inquiries if desired, among others.

The control strategy constitutes the way that allows the development of an algorithm by means of which the software will internally evaluate the answers offered by the student. This will generate feedback information, in correspondence with the feedback message system followed in the general didactic strategy of the task system. These can be evaluated in three possible ways: correct, partially correct or incorrect.

The forms of evaluation are based on the analysis that each answer option has its importance within the task. Therefore, it is key that the distractors are as plausibly correct as possible, based on their close relationship with the same conceptual domain of the task. For its elaboration, a good practice is to take into account the most frequent mistakes that students make.

For the user, each answer option is between the dichotomy of corresponding or not with the given conditions. However, for the control algorithm, the response options are considered as a whole, that is, both the number of correct options offered and the number of distractors that are not included as correct in the response are taken into account.

The total sum of both is obtained through the selection factor that is calculated from the comparison between the pattern vector V_p and the input vector (V_e) of the task to consider the answer as correct. Each of the answer options can be assigned a weight that increases or decreases its importance in the task. If not established, the most frequent is to assume the equitable distribution among them based on 100.

For example, in a Selection of Several-Several task with five answer options, two of them correct, without establishing weight and assuming that:
$V_p = (1, 0, 0, 0, 1)$ and the $V_e = (0, 1, 0, 0, 1)$, the value of 1 is for the correct options and 0 for the distractors, it would be obtained by the control algorithm: three correct options and two incorrect ones.

Finally, the selection factor (F_s), is obtained which is calculated as follows:

$$F_s = \sum_{i=1}^{n}(Pitem_i), \text{ si } V_{p(i)} = V_{e(i)} \ (1)$$

where " n " constitutes the number of response options for the task and " *Pitem* " the weighting of each response option considered correct by the control algorithm that will be traversed by " i ". Hence, the following conditions have to be met to determine the different evaluative forms:

- The answer is *correct* if $F_s = 1$.
- The answer is *partially correct* if that is true $1 - F_s \geq 0{,}6$.
- The answer is *incorrect* if $1 - F_s < 0{,}6$.

In this way, in the previous example, a selection factor (F_s) of 0.6 would be obtained, since the answer is partially correct.

These evaluative forms of work are related to the number of opportunities and system feedback messages raised in the didactic principle proposed and are associated with the teaching strategy (Figure 1) and operating interactive questionnaire of learning (Figure 2). In this sense, the number of opportunities should be determined from the level of difficulty of the task, in correspondence with the objective of the task, in such a way that different levels of help can be provided that make it possible to address the individual differences of the students.

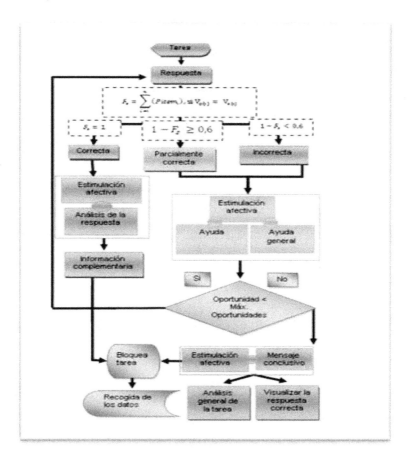

Figure 1. Flow diagram of the control strategy for the evaluation of the tasks of the interactive teaching-learning questionnaires

The *analysis of the exercise session* is made up of the main difficulties in each of the elements of knowledge that were worked on, a detailed evaluation of the exercises and the general results, aspects that are described below:

- *Main difficulties:* you must explain of each element of knowledge the amount in each one of them and how many were evaluated as Good, Fair and Bad.
- *Results by exercises:* it should make it possible to obtain the evaluation obtained from each exercise and offer information about it: the time it took the student to solve it, as well as the possibility of reconstructing the question and exchanging between the given answer and the correct one, among others.
- *General results:* it must offer a global vision of the results obtained, from the use of graphs that show the results obtained in the exercise session.

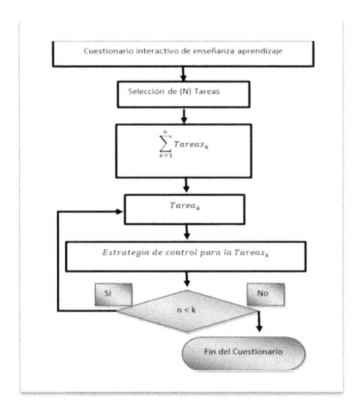

Figure 2. Flow diagram of the operation of the interactive learning questionnaires

These elements described about the results of the exercise session are structured from the idea that the student is the one who will have immediate access to them. The foregoing does not deny that they can be used under the direction of the teacher or parents to carry out a collective analysis on the conclusions of an exercise class using educational software of the exercising type.

The **analysis of the general results** allows the teacher the interpretation of all the data of the exercise sessions that are saved for each student, as well as being able to carry out analyzes of a single, a group or a sample. Then they describe which types of analysis that can be used from its structure.

The **General Analysis** can be performed from two forms that have called *Individual Analysis* and *Group.* The first allows the selection of a student to perform an analysis of the results obtained in the contents of a specific session, the history of their sessions or of various subjects. The second makes it possible to select a group, a team or a random sample of students that can pursue other research purposes, in both a study can be carried out from the results obtained in certain contents or in different subjects.

In the **Individual Analysis**, both in the specific session and in the history, the detailed results of the contents addressed in the tasks are shown, showing the number of good, average and bad answers. In the specific session, it is allowed to reconstruct each exercise, observe the answer given by the student, as well as exchange with the correct answer. In the history, the results of different sessions can be visualized and graphs are obtained that illustrate the evolution over time of the students in a certain content from the selection of one, several or all sessions.

In the case of the analysis by subjects, the *Individual Analysis* enables the study of the results of a student with different tasks of different subjects. For this, it is necessary to select the subjects of which the number of tasks in each of them will be shown and their respective evaluative results that will make it possible to establish comparisons based on the use of graphs that illustrate them.

The analysis by contents of the *Group Analysis* allows the teacher once he defines the group, team or the sample and selects the contents with which he wants to work, obtain the evaluative results by quantities in each of them, as well as access graphics that he indicate in which specific contents the students have presented the greatest difficulties, an aspect that will allow them to look for the possible causes that generate them and to draw up strategies to solve them.

The analysis by subjects of the *Group Analysis* shows the results in the same way as in the same way of the *Individual Analysis,* with the difference that these belong to the group, the team or the sample of selected students. This way facilitates the teacher the follow-up of a group of students, in correspondence with the objectives that are proposed or to obtain information that allows him to reach conclusions that will give rise to the application of new methodological strategies that include interdisciplinarity in order to achieve better learning outcomes.

In order to specify, by teachers or educational software developers, the design of tasks with an interactive nature in educational software based on interactive teaching-learning questionnaires, it was necessary to develop a computer tool called HdCuestIA (Portilla, Coloma & Mariño, 2013) that facilitates its implementation, without programming requirements, which is generalized in the Authoring System for the development of Learning Hyper-environments (Mariño, Portilla and Coloma, 2013). A set of worksheets were also prepared that specify the fundamental elements that are required for their development (Coloma, Mariño, Portilla, Rodríguez, Cuba, Torres, Lazo and Ruiz; 2011).

The methodology for the didactic design of interactive teaching-learning questionnaires constitutes a way to develop the educational software of the exercising type with the character of a learning mediator instrument, which has as an essential feature the interactivity of both the teaching task and the potentialities of this technology. The proposed methodology has been Beach Sunset to practice in various scenarios, which has been able to ascertain its feasibility for both process development and the introduction of educational software resulting therefrom.

The methodology encompasses results with high scientific and educational value, such as taxonomy of questions, conceptualization of multimedia resources and strategy for analyzing responses (control strategy and system feedback messages). In addition, the methodology is accompanied by a set of diagrams, spreadsheets and a computer tool, which enable its development and application, without programming requirements.

References

Alessi, SM, & Trollip, SR (1985) Computer-Based Instruction. Method and Development. Englewood Cliffs. New Jersey, Englewood Cliffs, United States: Collen Brosnan.

Coloma Rodríguez, O. , M ariño Blanco, D. , Portilla Rodríguez , Y., Rodríguez Verdecia, R., Cuba Ricardo, G., Torres Olvida, Y., Lazo Sánchez, Y., and Ruiz Mulet, A. (2011) The development of educational software without cost of programming utopia or reality? Course. Volume 19. Ed. Educación Cubana, City of Havana.

del Toro Rodríguez, M. (2006) Didactic design model of teaching-learning hyper-environments from a developer perspective. Havana, Havana, Cuba.

Mariño B, Portilla Y, Coloma O. (2013) SAdHEA-Web: alternative for achieving technological independence in the development of Cuban educational software. *Technological Innovation* , 19 (4), http://innovaciontec.idict.cu/innovacion .

Marqués, P. (2003) Design and evaluation of educational programs. Retrieved on August 31, 2011, from Educational Software: http://www.xtec.es/~pmarques/edusoft.htm

Portilla Rodríguez, Y (2012) The exercise of learning through educational software. Holguin . Thesis presented as an option to the scientific degree of Doctor of Pedagogical Sciences.

Portilla Rodríguez, Y., Coloma Rodríguez, O., & Mariño Blanco, D. (2013) Tool for developing interactive learning questionnaires. *Sciences Holguin* , Vol. 19, No. 3 , 136-146 .

Rodríguez Rodríguez, LA (2010) Didactic conception of educational software as a mediating instrument for developer learning. Santa Clara: Thesis presented as an option to the scientific degree of Doctor of Pedagogical Sciences.

Tool for the Development of Learning Interactive Questionnaires

PhD Yunior Portilla Rodríguez. Full Professor
PhD Orestes Coloma Rodríguez. Full Professor
PhD Dagoberto Mariño Blanco. Assistant Professor

As a significant point in the development of educational informatics, the conception of educational software called hyper-learning environment arises, which is defined as *"Hypermedia environment composed of various types of educational software, in which the student can build their knowledge through from its interaction in a modular system,"* this concept evolves, to a great extent, driven by two fundamental directions, the demand for educational software for Cuban schools and the growing need to develop educational software in accordance with the needs of the Cuban pedagogy, this is conceived in "free environments," based on an extensive, materialized curriculum, in the collections "MultiSaber", "El Navegante" and "Futuro" that are distributed respectively in all Primary, Basic Secondary and Pre university in the country.

As one of the most important characteristics of these learning hyper-environments, it can be pointed out that they are made up of several modules, among which are, in general, the following: *"Topics or Contents, Exercises, Games, Library, Results and Teacher."* Specifically, in the **Exercises** module, the sub-modules corresponding to the interactive and non-interactive **exercises** have been incorporated, depending on each product, being in the first case where systems of exercises are included which can be presented from different strategies.

On the other hand, the study carried out on the Questionnaires or Skill and Practice, demonstrated the need to analyze the relationship that is established between the computer-pedagogical components, in accordance with the advanced learning theories and the efficient use of the potentialities of the computer as a means of teaching.

The investigative process led to applied results obtained since 2001, in the different collections developed for the various teachings of the Cuban school on CD, and the on-line versions of Navegante and Futuro collections, and the collection for high schools in Venezuela. It is also in use by various institutions such as the UCI, MININT, MINFAR, the network of INSTED Software Study Centers, among others of a territorial nature, and professionals for the development of their own media.

Materials and Methods

Methods and techniques of empirical research: primarily participant observation, survey and consulting experts, who provided information processed by theoretical methods of analysis-synthesis, induction-deduction of abstract to concrete and modeling, and as statistical procedures that made it possible to obtain results, and the need to develop the tool.

Results:

Interactive Learning Questionnaires

Questionnaires are a type of high computational complexity with strong pedagogical implications. With the objective of overcoming some of the dogmas that exist when you hear about exercises through the computer and solving educational problems, was elaborated model of **Questionnaire Interactive Learning**, which has the following essential features:

a. Interactive learning questionnaires may or may not rely on hyper-learning environments.

b. Various forms of selection considering the following strategies: *sequential, random, assigned, predetermined configuration and according to student performance.*

c. *The questions that form it are of various types such as Selection of Several-One, Selection of Several-Several, Dichotomous, True or False, Relationship, Ordering, Classification, Completion of Phrases, Selection of Texts, Location, Approximation, Assembling objects, Open question.*

d. Conceive **feedback in different formats such** as *texts, voice, still images, in motion and videos.*

e. It is based on Vygotsky´s historical-cultural theory and on the postulates of teaching and learning developer of Cuban pedagogy.

f. Enhancement of cooperative and collaborative learning.

g. It enables attention to the individual differences of the students, through mediating agents or predetermined configurations elaborated by the teacher.

The above leads to express an approach to the concept of **Questionnaires Interactive Learning** as *"set of questions that allow link the cognitive and affective., During the interactive process user-computer, whose answers provide feedback."*

Tool for the development of Interactive Learning Questionnaires

In Cuba, specifically in the Study Center of Educational Software and Applications in Holguin University, was developed the authoring system for developing hyper-environments (SAdHEA-Web), where the tool is impllemented. For development, studies were conducted on platforms as Exe-Learning, hotpot, IMS Global Learning Consortium, JClic, Moodle, Question Mark, QuizFaber, Revolution and SumTotal Toolbook.

However, it led us to reach important generalizations, find points of contact, working standards of this type of software, infrastructure typified, as well as solutions implemented in general purpose languages, which made it possible to enrich and improve the tool, of which a brief description follows.

Brief description of the tool

The tool can be accessed from SAdHEA-Web when educational software is assembled online, and it has among its main characteristics the following:

1. You can create exercises classified by *topics, headings* or *other topics* defined by the developers of the educational software.
2. Each exercise is mounted through the tool may be incorporated *additional information*, which will allow the user to know more about the topic covered in the exercise.
3. Each question can be assigned as an additional element, different types of means, images, sounds, animations, slide shows and videos. In addition, when creating interactive exercises as part of a hyper-environment, media mounted in the *Theme* or *Virtual Library* module can be reused.
4. Depending on the type of question, the messages that come out in each of the incorrect attempts of the exercise can be customized, as well as the conclusive message and that of the correct answer, which allows the user who interacts with the exercise to rework their answer depending on the information given in each attempt and achieve, at the end of the question, adequate information to the answer given.
5. It makes it possible to have a visual representation of each of the elements that make up each one of the assembled questions and that is in relation to the type of exercise selected.
6. It provides, as a summary of the process of creating an interactive exercise, the main elements defined for the question and those that are mandatory to select in order to store the question.
7. It facilitates navigation and editing of all the exercises mounted in the educational software, as well as the elimination of any of them.

The previous general characteristics of the *Interactive Learning Questionnaires* tool are specified in each of the elements that are incorporated in the different *tabs* that make it up: *General Question, Immediate, Mediate, Summary* and *Configuration*:

General tab

In this tab, the following elements are defined in each exercise (see Figure 1):

• *Knowledge elements by*: In this option, the developer must select whether the interactive exercises will be grouped according to the units of the module

Topics (Content topics), the headings (Content headings) or by another classification (defined by the developer).

- *Question type*: In this option, the developer must select the type of exercise or question between Simple selection, Multiple selection (includes True or False), Link, Drag, Assemble, Sort and Select Texts.
- *Number of opportunities*: In this option, the developer must select the number of opportunities to answer the exercise.
- *Automatic point distribution*: In this option, the developer must select whether the assignment of points to each correctly answered distractor is done proportionally according to the number of distractors.
- *Total points*: In this option, the developer must set the total points assigned to the correct answer of the exercise.
- *Random presentation of elements*: In this option, the developer must select whether the distractors of each question appear in the same order each time the question is presented or are presented in a random order.
- *Additional information* (Learn more): In this option the developer must specify the additional information, in the form of *knowing more* that will be presented to the student once the exercise has been answered.
- *Response analysis*: In this option, the developer must specify the information to provide as an analysis of the response given by the student.

Fig. 1. General data of the question (*general* tab).

Question:

In this tab, the user must define the following elements for each exercise (see figure 2):

- *Statement*: In this option, the developer must write the statement of the exercise.
- *Interactive elements*: In this option, the developer must specify the interactive elements that are presented in the exercise in the form of: image, sound, video, animation, slide show. To select the type of interactive element, its location must be specified for each type of media (if it is in the *Galleries*, the *Themes* module, the *Exercises* module, or it is a new media element, that is, it is not found anywhere of the previous components). You can create as many interactive elements as you want for the question and select the correct and incorrect ones.
- *Media Type*: This section permitted selecting a medium (image, video, sound, animation or slide), as an additional element of each question. These socks can be reused from those mounted on other modules or loaded specifically for each exercise.

Fig. 2. Structuring question (tab Question).

Immediate tab:

In this tab are defined the immediate messages before the student's response, as shown in Figure 3.

Fig. 3. Feedback to support the attempt (*immediate* tab).

Mediate:

This tab defines the messages immediately before the student's response, as shown in Figure 4. These messages can be correct, incorrect, partially correct or last chance.

Fig. 4. Support feedback at the end of the question.

Summary tab

In this tab, the user receives information about each of the elements defined in the previous tabs, that is, type of question and element of knowledge, cMoUnt opportunities, total points, immediate and mediate responses, etc. In each case, the missing elements are indicated in *red* and are essential to define the correct operation of the exercise, as shown in figure 5.

Fig. 5. Summary at the conclusion of each year.

Settings tab

In this tab, the exercises are classified according to the units of the Themes module (Content Topics), the headings (Content Epigraphs) or by another classification (defined by the developer). This should be the first action to be performed before starting the installation of the *EXERCISES*.

It can be concluded that:
a. The development of a model of interactive learning questionnaire constitutes a new stage in the development of educational software.
b. The proposed tool substantially increases the level of efficiency and productivity that is required in the development of this type of educational software for Cuban schools, multiplatform and Open Source.

c. Technological independence is achieved in the development of this type of educational software.

Bibliography

Alessi, SM, & Trollip, SR *Computer-Based Instruction. Method and Development.* Englewood Cliffs. New Jersey, Englewood Cliffs, United States: Collen Brosnan. 1985. 418 p.

Coloma Rodríguez, O. Didactic conception for the use of educational software in the teaching-learning process [digital document]. Optional thesis to the scientific degree of Doctor of Pedagogical Sciences. [2008. 233 p].

Labañino Rizzo, C., Rodríguez Rodríguez, L., Coloma Rodríguez, O., Portilla Rodríguez, Y., López Perdigón, A., Ramírez Zaldivar, A. Educational software in the context of MINED: a generalization of solutions [document digital]. *Paper presented at the XV National Forum of Science and Técnic to. [23-27 01 2007].*

Ríos, P., & Ruiz, C. Development of a computerized system to study high-level cognitive processes. *Journal of the School of Psychology (Central University of Venezuela), 1* (23): 71-102. 1998.

Vygotsky, S. Interaction between teaching and development. In *Selection of child and adolescent psychology readings*. Havana: People and Education, 1995. p. 11-21.

Multimedia Presentation to Improve Teacher Education English Major Students´ English Pronunciation in Holguin University

BEd Edilberto Laudemar Chacón Estrada

MSc Miguel Ángel Olivé Iglesias. Associate Professor

PhD Sara Estrada Sifonte. Full Professor

The learning of a foreign language generally finds its starting point in speech sound reproduction by the learner to become familiar with the phonetic sound system of the target language. To fulfill this purpose, the student is devoted to constant listening and imitation practice in the classroom or laboratory following the teacher's model, or a recording that provides the closest version of the pattern given. This process develops in single words, or short utterance reproduction, and then offers larger stretches of the target language as more complex models to imitate.

Although a focus on pronunciation is part of the curriculum in many education programs, it is often not included or practiced in class: grammar and vocabulary take the advantage. In the area of pronunciation, the following authors can be mentioned: Wallace (1971), Prator (1975), Gimson-Kenneth (1980), Cook (2000), Gilbert (2005), Baker-Goldstein (2008), Mojsin (2009). There are also some Diploma and Term Papers that have dealt with the issue of pronunciation like Páez (2013), Pérez (2013), González (2015).

How does learning pronunciation work in an environment where English is learned for teaching purposes, that is, for learners who will become teachers of English? These students take two related core subjects in their junior year of the Teacher Education English Major: *Integrated English Practice* and *Linguistic Studies I*, also known as *Phonetics and Phonology* (LSI). The former subject furnishes them with the communicative competence to act in the foreign language, the latter gives them the theoretical and didactic tools to know about and apply the phonetic aspects of the language.

Researchers have investigated the impact of the use of computer technology on education in different fields. All of these researchers agree on the efficacy of the use of computers and technology in education, and how they help improve teaching methods and students' knowledge. Through using computer technology learners are not only given the opportunity to control their own learning process, but are also provided with ready access to a large amount of information given the highly attractive motivational factor embedded in the use of technologies today, especially among young people. Prensky (2001) says students are defined as natives of the digital world, while teachers are defined as immigrants of the digital world.

On pronunciation

Since language is an oral process, pronunciation involves the ability to understand what people are saying and the ability to be understood when we are speaking to others. That is to say, the ability to recognize and produce the distinctive sounds conveying different meanings, as well as stress, rhythm and intonation.

According to A. P. Gilakjani (2012), in *The Significance of Pronunciation in English Language Teaching*, the teaching of pronunciation is a noticeable factor in foreign language. Therefore, are of noticeable importance to take into account **the didactic aspects of teaching pronunciation.** In the teaching and exacting of an international intelligibly of pronunciation, it is important that teachers guide students to do the following:

- ✓ Cultivate positive attitudes toward accuracy.
- ✓ Notice the effects of pronunciation on interactions.
- ✓ Notice prosodic features of language (stress, intonation, rhythm).
- ✓ Develop communicative competence

Theoretical basis on the use of new technologies in the teaching-learning process of pronunciation

Teaching media are all the natural and artificial elements where an object is included, or its graphic representations that contribute to objectify the interrelation between teachers and students in the process of transmission, acquisition, formation and development of knowledge, habits, skills and capacities. They constitute the basis for helping to make more effective the methods and procedures used in lessons. Teaching media transmit the information combining eyesight and hearing. That is why the amount of information that students can get through movies, videos, TV and computers is increased. The objective of teaching media is to guarantee educational practice in its global scale and to better learning dynamics. (González Castro, V. 1986). The purpose of using computer technology is to enhance the learning process. There are many benefits in computer-assisted pronunciation (CAP) instruction, which cannot be found in traditional teaching approaches. Students can have access to input through using digitized pronunciation software individually and individualized feedback can be provided to them automatically.

The PowerPoint *as a tool to present multimedia for educational purposes*

PowerPoint is one of the most frequently used tools to present multimedia for educational purposes in universities. This application provides a fast way to bring a vast range of content –not only slides are presented to students but also other media such as diagrams, photographs, audio and video sequences or animations – into the classroom. In addition, multimedia presentation on PowerPoint, particularly Microsoft PowerPoint, offers the possibility of interaction of the user with the application through a user interface (UI). Thus, the multimedia presentation contains the information of the subject LSI as a way to access the material required for students and teachers during the lesson and in self-study.

Description of the structure and content of the multimedia presentation to improve English pronunciation of in-service junior students of the Teacher Education English Major in the University of Holguin

The multimedia presentation proposal is based on PowerPoint date – particularly Microsoft PowerPoint. Graphics, audio, photograph, video sequences, charts and texts from the subject LSI are included as the material that comprises the proposal.

There are arrows that lead to the content users are looking for, and they guide to the pages related to it. Users can go back and forth freely between the instances, which permits them to review the content they need. There are audio and video sequences they can be played as many times as required.

Executing the PowerPoint file starts the multimedia presentation from Main screen (fig. 2.1), where the users find hyper-links to the Help (page fig. 2.3) and to the Home page (fig. 2.2). There is no exit interface button, so users can leave the application by pressing Escape key on the keyboard.

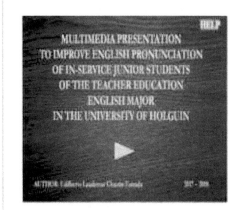

Fig. 2.1. Main screen   Fig. 2.2. Home page

The contents of the multimedia are indexed within the Home page. Users can access them by clicking on the hyper-links in the center of the instance. Each content has one or more slides and they all have hyper-links buttons that allow going back and forth between the instances of the selected content. To change the theme they are revising, users just have to go forward or backward clicking the arrows until they get to the Home page and select another topic.

The following diagram shows how users can move between the instances in the multimedia presentation (fig. 2.3):

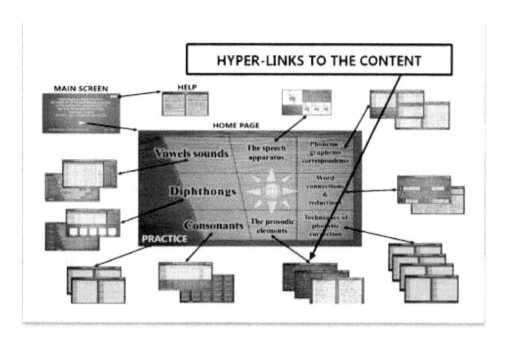

Fig. 2.3. Diagram of movement in the multimedia presentation

The audio and video sequences in the multimedia presentation are next to the buttons of a speaker for the audio reproduction, and a red bubble with a symbol of a phoneme for the video reproduction as they appear in the following picture (fig. 2.4)

Fig. 2.4. Audio and video UI

Analysis of the contents of the multimedia presentation

The speech apparatus: The content is introduced with pictures showing the speech organs as a system. The images also show the different positions of the tongue when emitting the vowel sounds. There are texts describing what vowel, diphthong, and consonant are; how and where they are produced in the mouth. *Vowel sounds*: This material consists of a vowel classification chart of the American English vowel sounds, audio sequences that reproduce the different vowel sounds in isolation and within words, the Cardinal Vowel Diagram and video sequences of the sounds as they occur in initial, medial, and final position. These videos are located in the Cardinal Vowel Diagram in the position their correspondent phonemes are produced.

Diphthongs: Its contents include a classification chart of the American English diphthongs; audio sequences that reproduce the different sounds in isolation and within words; pictures showing the movement of the glides; the Cardinal Vowel Diagram, with phonetic symbols and arrows in the direction the diphthongs move and video sequences, and demonstrations of the diphthongs when they occur in initial, medial or final position in the words.

Consonants: The contents comprise a classification chart of the American English consonants with audio sequences of the sounds in isolation. There are representations of the phonemes from the Comparison Chart of the Phonetic Alphabets of the American English. The "Bowen (1975b)" and "The International Phonetic Alphabet (Jones 1991)." There is a video section dedicated to pronunciation word examples of the consonant sounds in initial, medial, and final position.

Phoneme-grapheme correspondence: The correspondence between the American English phonemes and graphemes is presented through three charts with written words as examples of American English – vowel phoneme-graphemes correspondence, diphthong phoneme-grapheme correspondence, and consonant phoneme-grapheme correspondence.

Word connections and reductions: The topics in the section are dedicated to the connections between words and colloquial reductions – slang in American English. There are four rules for word connections accompanied by written examples of the rules and audio sequences that explain how each of the rules works. Next, users will find a whole page dedicated to the familiarization of the colloquial reductions.

Techniques of phonetic correction: The slides show charts with the different sounds in isolation for the analysis of the specific pronunciation problems for Spanish-speaker students of English. Most of the techniques offer different ways for demonstration on how a sound is produced. Furthermore, they give feasible procedures to illustrate and contrast the differences between L1 (mother tongue) and L2 (target language).

***The prosodic elements*:** To comprehend the terms and master the different techniques for teaching the prosodic features of American English, this section of the multimedia was included.

Description of the media included in the multimedia presentation

Multimedia is integration of many media into the whole. It is necessary to outline some of the especial features of the different study materials included in the multimedia presentation according to the content they comprise.

> ➢ **Symbols. The phoneme representation:** The phonemes used for the transcriptions of North American English words in this multimedia presentation are represented by the one in the "The International Phonetic Alphabet (Jones 1991)," and the "Bowen Phonetic Alphabet (1975b)."
> ➢ **Charts. The articulatory description charts:** The charts contain the articulatory classification of the vowel, diphthong, and consonant sounds in order to be helpful in the description of these sounds according to their specific criteria. (fig. 2.5, a, b, c)

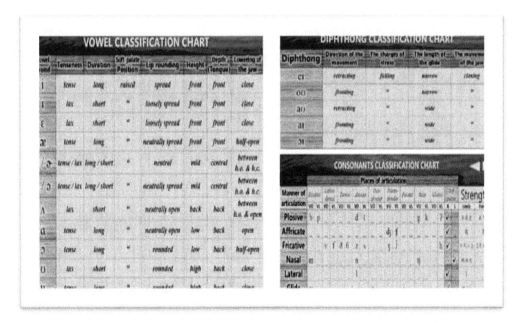

Fig. 2.5. Articulatory classification charts (a, b, c)

Charts. The phoneme-grapheme correspondence charts: These charts organize the phoneme-grapheme correspondence of the American English. There are words as examples of how a phoneme is represented by several graphemes. (fig. 2.6)

PHONEME	GRAPHEMES	EXAMPLES
i	ea ee e ey ei ie i eo	*please, tree, these, key, receive, thief, police*
I	i ie a e o u ui y	*it, cities, orange, pretty, women, busy, build, system*

Fig. 2.6. Phoneme-grapheme correspondence chart (partial)

➤ **Pictures and diagrams. The organs of speech pictures, the glides between the diphthongs pictures, and Cardinal Vowel Diagram:** The pictures and diagrams provide visual information needed. Visual learning is also faster. The multimedia illustrate information related to the organs of speech (fig. 2.7) and the vowel sound through images and diagrams (fig. 2.8):

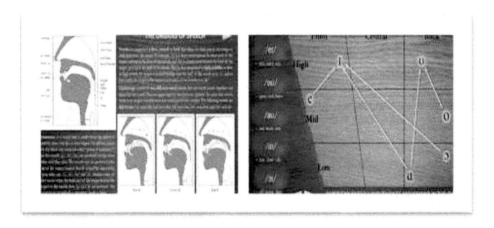

Fig. 2.7. Organs of speech   *Fig. 2.8. Diphthong movement*

The diagrams show the characteristics of the vowel sounds in the articulatory charts placed in the scale. Hence, it is possible to describe the articulatory characteristics of the sounds placed in it. Both the charts and the diagrams are related instruments for classifying the sounds according to the manner of articulation.

➤ **Sound sequences. The vowel, diphthong, consonants, word connection, and colloquial reductions:** The multimedia contain audio sequences that reproduce the sounds of the American English, offer explanations about word connections, and perform colloquial expressions in order to be recognized and practiced. Users can resort to the bookmarks within the audio sequences to practice either the sounds, words, or groups of phrases instead of having a complete reproduction of the audio.

Video sequences. Vowel, diphthong, and consonant video sequences: The video is used for clear presentation of contents or technical procedures which are reflection of real condition in technique or in everyday life. The video sequences are placed in the Cardinal Vowel Diagram to stand for the manner of articulation of the vowel sounds. They show how the sounds are produced by the organs of speech. The sequences have observable word examples that present the occurrence of phonemes in initial, medial, and final position within words. There is the possibility to carry out the analysis and observation of the mouth position playing the videos frame by frame, which is more dynamic, or using the bookmarks of the sequences. The bookmark of the videos show the mouth position as a frame (fig. 2.9).

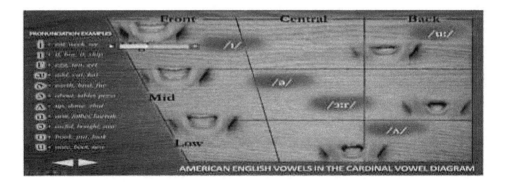

Fig. 2.9. Video sequences reproduction frame-by-frame or using bookmarks

➢ **Text. The organs of speech, Word connections and reductions, The prosodic elements, techniques of phonetic correction, notes, help, and practice section:** The texts give form to the multimedia content. The size of the text is adapted in accordance to difficulties and intention of using multimedia. Most part of the text is organized in charts in order to make it easy to understand and usage, and for delimit them from the other ones. There are notes throughout the topics adding information to clarify and extend the content revised (fig. 2.10).

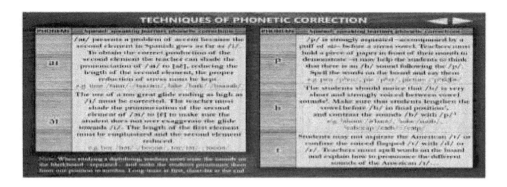

Fig. 2.10. Example of text in the multimedia presentation

Benefits of the multimedia presentation
1. The multimedia presentation gathers the information the students need to study and practice the content of the subject LSI.
2. The multimedia presentation contains authentic material in audio and video.
3. The media included in the multimedia presentation are easy to access and use.
4. The multimedia presentation offers the possibility to study either practical elements or just theory, or both.
5. Teachers can use the multimedia presentation as teaching media.
6. Learners can use the multimedia as a reference for practicing transcriptions.
7. The multimedia is easy to reproduce in the devices teachers and students have.
8. The multimedia is a digital file, so all students can copy and share.
9. The multimedia can be printed in order to work or study.

The authors have modestly tried to encompass in the proposal a multimedia to enhance the learning of pronunciation theoretically and practically. There was high concern for improving language and exploring ways to achieve that. There was minute observance of detail both in form and in the contents of the multimedia. A significant volume of hours was devoted to obtaining a useful tool for students and professors – and general learners of the language. The proposal aims at both teaching and learning. The compilation of sources for the theoretical and the input sections was also relevant. Finally, the proposal contributes to teaching phonetics, to improving linguistic competence (by extension, communicative competence), to introducing technology that is so popular these days and students favor and welcome so much, thus turning it into a powerful learning device.

Bibliography

ADAMS, C. (2006). PowerPoint, habits of mind, and classroom culture. Journal of Curriculum Studies, 38 (4), 389-411.

CELCE-MURCIA, M., BRINTON, D. & GOODWIN, J. (1 st edition: 1996, 2nd edition: 2011). Teaching pronunciation: A reference for teachers of English to speakers of other languages. New York: Cambridge University Press.

CLAYARDS, J. AND HOLMES, M. (?). A multimedia approach to learning phonetic transcription. University of Victoria, Canada.

GILAKJANI, A. P. et al (2017). English Pronunciation Instruction: Views and Recommendations. Journal of Language Teaching and Research, Vol. 8, No. 6, pp. 1249-1255, November 2017.

HILL, A., ARFORD, T., LUBITOW, A., AND SMOLLIN, L. (2012). "I'm ambivalent about it": The dilemmas of PowerPoint. Teaching Sociology, 40 (3), 242-256.

NERI, A., CUCCHIARINI, C., STRIK, H., & BOVES, L. (2002). The PedagogyTechnology interface in Computer Assisted Pronunciation Training. Computer Assisted Language Learning, 15(5), 441 -467.

PRENSKY, M. (2001). Digital Natives, Digital Immigrants. J. Horizon, 9(5).

REUSS, E. I., BEAT SIGNER, B. AND NORRIE, M. C. (?). PowerPoint Multimedia Presentations in Computer Science Education: What do users need? Institute for Information Systems, ETH Zurich, CH-8092 Zurich.

SMITH, I. (1997). Higgins: A Multimedia Program for the Instruction of the International Phonetic Alphabet. Toronto, York University.

TAMANES, K. (2013). Multimedia to improve oral expression in English in sixth graders from Patricio Lumumba primary school in Báguanos. Diploma Paper. Pedagogical Sciences University. José de la Luz y Caballero.

Web Sites

http://www.p12.nysed.gov/biling/docs/Art_as_a_Tool-for_Teachers.pdf
https://www.cal.org/caelanetwork/.../pronunciation.html
http://www.americanaccent.com
http://www.soundsofenglish.org
http://www.thesoundofenglish.org
http://learnenglishkids.britishcouncil.org/en/tongue-twisters
http://www.espressoenglish.net/silent-letters-in-english-from-a-to-z/
http://www.teachingenglish.org.uk/article/phonemic-chart
http://www.onestopenglish.com/skills/pronunciation/phonemic-chart-andapp/interactive-phonemic-chart/
http://cambridgeenglishonline.com/Phonetics_Focus/

About the Authors

María Elena Ayala Ruiz

PhD and MSc degrees in Pedagogical and Educational Sciences respectively. Full Professor of the Teacher Education English Major Department of the University of Holguin. Forty-three years of experience in the teaching of English as a foreign language. She has been in national and international events. She does research on interdisciplinary studies, the teaching and learning of English, particularly reading comprehension and humanities, with publications in Cuba and abroad. Her field of expertise is in methodology of foreign language teaching.
mariaayala@uho.edu.cu

Katiusca Ceballos Bauta

Bachelor in Education. Master´s degree in Educational Sciences. Twenty-year experience in the field of education and teaching. Currently works at Holguin University Teacher Education Department as an Associate Professor. Publishes nationally and internationally on the issues of foreign language teaching and educational topics.
katiuskacb@uho.edu.cu

Edilberto Laudemar Chacón Estrada

BEd in Education. He majored in Teacher Education, English. Has devoted his studies to the teaching and learning of English, the development of communicative skills, chiefly applied to the use of technology to improve the process. Currently leads a home-based language school and teaches English.
mastema@nauta.cu

Orestes Coloma Rodríguez

PhD in Pedagogical Sciences. Full Professor. Director of Informatics and Software for Educational Research in Holguin University. Publishes nationally and internationally on issues related to the conception, elaboration and implementation of multi-purpose software for education and broader applications.
coloma@uho.edu.cu

Daniela Aitana Domínguez Reyes

Sophomore student from the English Language major of Holguin University. She has been involved in research projects related to foreign language teaching and skill development in her specialty.
hreyesg@uho.edu.cu

Graham Ducker

Teacher, Poet, Lecturer. Retired Principal and Kindergarten teacher who published a memoir book *Don't Wake The Teacher* in 2004. He has two poetry books: *Observations of Heart and Mind*, and *Where Warm Hearts Blend*. He also published two picture books and two instructional books in 2011.
jgrahamd@rogers.com

Fara Estrada Sifonte

BEd in Education, major in Teacher Education, Chemistry-Biology. PhD in Pedagogical Sciences. Full Professor. Her research has been devoted to pedagogical themes and chemistry-related articles. Retired a few years ago and currently works as a teacher of Russian in a home-based language school.
fara@ucp.ho.rimed.cu

Madelín Feria Torres

BEd in Education, major in English. Instructor who is currently working in the Teacher Education English major Department. Her research focuses on values education, foreign language teaching and community activities to foster the teaching of English.
madelinft@uho.edu.cu

Yanelis María Fonseca Ayala

BEd in Education, major in English from Holguin University. Currently works in Senior High teaching English. Her research has been devoted to elaborating and introducing teaching tasks in the lesson of English.

Ernesto Galbán Peramo

Bachelor´s degree in the History of Arts. Holguin University Professor from the Department of Extra-curricular On-Campus and Community Activities. Associate Professor with a Master´s degree in History of Arts. Specializes in Cuban and local cultural studies. He publishes on issues regarding art and literature.
ernestogp@uho.edu.cue

Henry García Mariño

Senior student from the Teacher Education English major. The paper herein presented results from his advisor´s and his own research and findings on language teaching, and their application in the English lesson.
henrygarcia@nauta.cu

Mariluz González Borjas

Bachelor in Education. Specialist´s degree in Pedagogical Sciences. Thirty-two-year experience in the field of education and teaching. Currently works at Holguin University Teacher Education Department as an Associate Professor. Publishes nationally and internationally on the issues of foreign language teaching with systemtic presence in local, national and international events as well.
mariluzgb@uho.edu.cu

Anabel González Ricardo

BEd in Education, major in English. Instructor. She currently works in the Teacher Education English Department as a professor of English. Her research addresses issues concerning the teaching of English as a foreign language.
anabelgr@uho.edu.cu

Yennier Greenhauff Desdín

Bachelor´s degree in Education, Teacher Education English Major. He has done research on language and language teaching since he was an undergraduate and presented his findings in local events. Worked as a teacher-student for two years in the Teacher Education English Major Department. The paper included here is a result of his graduation thesis.
ygreenhoused@nauta.cu

Shireen Huq

PhD. Full Professor. Professor of English, Department of English and Modern Languages at North South University in Dhaka, Bangladesh. Senior experience in the teaching of English and foreign languages in general and author of essays on literature.
dr.shireenhuq123@gmail.com

Héctor Ernesto Jaimes Paredes

Engineering BS from the University of Mexico and MSc in Engineering in Germany. Guest lecturer on his research field. He has participated in events in Mexico, Cuba, Germany, Budapest and Moscow. He is a published author, and directs a section called "In the Language of Science" for the indexed magazine *Didáctica XXI* as a member of the Mexican Association of Language and Literature Professors.
eliaca@yahoo.com.mx

Milena Labrada Freeman

Bachelor of Arts, English major. Recently graduated, Sánchez currently works in the Teacher Education English Major Department as a professor of English and Translation. She studies and does research on language teaching and the development of communicative skills. She has participated in national events. This is her first international appearance.
milena950204@gmail.com

Anabel La O Bacallao

Bachelor in Education, English Major. Master in Professional Pedagogy. Assistant Professor. Professor from the Technical Scientific Information Department of Holguin University. She has taught, in undergraduate and graduate levels, English, grammar, reading strategies and IT, specifically the use, designing and creation of learning objects, as well as information management.
anabel.la@uho.edu.cu

Idania Leida Leyva Pérez

MSc and Associate Professor. She worked at Holguin University for 15 years in the Department of Special Education. Has participated in national and international events and published her research findings on this field.
ileyvap@nauta.cu

Pedro Antonio Machín Armas

PhD. Full Professor of the Teacher Education English Major Department at the University of Holguin. Thirty-eight years of experience in the teaching of English as a foreign language and in teacher training. He has presented different papers in national and international events. He does research on inter-language and the inter-linguistic dimension of communicative competence as well as on self-learning in foreign language teaching, particularly in English. He has publications in Cuba and on-line sites. His field of expertise is in methodology of foreign language teaching. *pedroma@uho.edu.cu*

Ronald Mackay

Master's degrees from both Aberdeen and Edinburgh Universities and a PhD from l'Université de Montréal. He has taught at the Universities of Bucharest, Newcastle upon Tyne, Toronto, and at Concordia where he was Professor of Education. Dr Mackay's research and professional work was in the interdisciplinary practice of international initiatives to promote food security and social wellbeing, especially in Latin America. He taught graduate courses in the design, management, and evaluation of development programmes. He has authored many academic and technical papers, reports, and books. Since retiring in 2002, he has published three memoirs, *Fortunate Isle, a Memoir of Tenerife*, *A Tenerife con Cariño*, and *The Kilt Behind the Curtain* as well as a score of short stories published in several anthologies. *mackay.ronald@gmail.com*

José Reinaldo Marrero Zaldívar

Professor of Research Methodology at Holguin University, Cuba. PhD degree in Pedagogical Sciences. Full Professor. He publishes and participates in national and international events on topics related to the teaching of literature and aesthetic-literary formation, comparative literary studies and the promotion of reading. *jmarreroz@uho.edu.cu*

Dagoberto Mariño Blanco

PhD in Pedagogical Sciences. Assistant Professor. Currently Works in the Software for Educational Research Department in Holguin University. Publishes nationally and internationally on issues related to the conception, elaboration and implementation of multi-purpose software for education and broader applications. *dagoberto@uho.edu.cu*

Nuria Montero Samada

Bachelor in Education. Master's degree in Pedagogical Sciences. Thirty-year experience in the field of education and teaching. Currently works at Holguin University Teacher Education Department as an Associate Professor. Publishes nationally and internationally on the issues of foreign language teaching with a steady presence in local, national and international events as well. *nuria.ms@uho.edu.cu*

Katherine Mora Chacón

BEd in Education, major in English. Instructor. She currently works in the Teacher Education English Department as a professor of *History of the English Speaking Peoples*. Her research adresses issues concerning the teaching of English from a cultural perspective.

kmorac@uho.edu.cu

Marlene Mora Delgado

Bachelor in Education. Specialist´s degree in Pedagogical Sciences. Thirty-three-year experience in the field of education and teaching. Currently works at Holguin University Teacher Education Department as an Associate Professor. Publishes nationally and internationally on the issues of foreign language teaching with a steady presence in local, national and international events as well.

mora@uho.edu.cu

Miguel Ángel Olivé Iglesias

Bachelor in Education. Master´s degree in Pedagogical Sciences related to values and values education in the English lesson. Thirty-two-year experience in the field of education and the teaching of English. Currently works at Holguin University Teacher Education Department as an Associate Professor. Publishes nationally and inter-nationally on the issues of foreign language teaching, pedagogy, interdisciplinary approaches, axiology and the preservation of humankind´s values, both material and nonmaterial, from an educational perspective.

migueloi@uho.edu.cu
cclacubanprez@gmail.com

Eladoy Oliveros Díaz

Assistant Professor currently working at Holguin University. Forty-five-year experience in the teaching of English. Spent three years in Jamaica on a mission teaching Spanish as a foreign language. Has written and published about the teaching of English and linguistic aspects.

eladoyod@uho.edu.cu

Kenia Páez Tamanes

BEd in Education, major in English. Her research has been focused on the possibilities of IT for teaching the language. Currently works in Junior High school as a teacher of English.

Elia Acacia Paredes Chavarría

Mexican researcher with a PhD in Arts from the University of Mexico and a PhD in Pedagogical Sciences from the Latin American and Caribbean Institute of the Cuban Ministry of Higher Education. Her work has focused on and published nationally and internationally about the didactics of literature and languages. She is the coordinator for the International Symposium of Teaching and Learning of Language and Literature celebrated in Mexico, and member of the Presidency of the Mexican Association of Language and Literature Professors. She is an awarded professor and author, and former Chair of the Literature Department in her school for many years.

eliaca@unam.mx

Carmina Paredes Neira

BA. Her work has been published nationally and internationally. She has participated in local and international events, such as the Symposium of Teaching and Learning of Language and Literature celebrated yearly in Mexico. She is a member of the Mexican Association of Language and Literature Professors.
eliaca@unam.mx

Adonay Bárbara Pérez Luengo

Full Professor from the University of Holguin. Master and PhD degrees in Pedagogical Sciences. Also, a poet, writer, editor, proofreader and translator. She publishes her poetry with the Canada Cuba Literary Alliance, and her academic works in numerous national and international issues and events.
adonaypl076@gmail.com

Jorge Alberto Pérez Hernández

Bachelor in Education, Major in English. Instructor. His research has been devoted to the development of skills in foreign language teaching. He worked as an Instructor for the former Pedagogical University of Holguin teaching English in the Teacher Education English Major. He has also worked at Holguin Medical School branch in Gibara teaching English for Special Purposes. Currently he publishes short stories, poetry and reviews in the Canada Cuba Literary Alliance (CCLA) formats and is Editor-in-chief of The Envoy, CCLA monthly newsletter, and Contributing Editor of The Ambassador, CCLA yearly magazine.
joyph@nauta.cu

Yunior Portilla Rodríguez

PhD in Pedagogical Sciences. Full Professor. Director of the Software for Educational Research Department in Holguin University. Publishes nationally and internationally on issues related to the conception, elaboration and implementation of multi-purpose software for education and broader applications.
portilla@uho.edu.cu

Yudisleidy Ruby Pupo Almarales

Bachelor in Education, Major in English. Her research has been devoted to the teaching of English as a foreign language. She worked at Holguin Medical School as a professor of English presenting her research results in local and international events.
yudisleidyrp@nauta.cu

Marianela Juana Rabell López

Bachelor in Education, Major in Spanish Language and Literature. Master in History and Culture of Cuba. Assistant Professor. Head of the Technical Scientific Information Department at the University of Holguin. She teaches undergraduate and postgraduate levels on topics related to Spanish language and literature, as well as information management.
mrabelll@uho.edu.cu

Hilda Reyes González

Bachelor in Education. Specialist's degree in Pedagogical Sciences. Thirty-year experience in the field of education and teaching. Currently works at Holguin University Language Center as an Associate Professor. Publishes nationally and internationally on the issues of foreign language teaching with a steady presence in local, national and international events as well.
hreyesg@uho.edu.cu

Marisela Rodríguez Calzadilla

Bachelor in Education. Master's degree in Pedagogical Sciences. Twenty-nine-year experience in the field of education and teaching. Currently works at Holguin University Teacher Education Department as an Associate Professor. Publishes nationally and internationally on the issues of foreign language teaching with a steady presence in local, national and international events as well.
mrcalzadilla@uho.edu.cu

Dalquis María Rodríguez Díaz

Professor of Language and Communication at Holguin University, Cuba. She has a Master's degree in Pedagogical Sciences and works in the Spanish Literature Department as a specialist in linguistic studies. Associate Professor. She publishes and participates in national and international events on topics related to the teaching of literature and literary analysis, especially in text construction, reading comprehension and the promotion of reading in co-curricular on-campus and community contexts.
dm.diaz@uho.edu.cu

Julio César Rodríguez Peña

Bachelor in Education. Master and PhD degrees in Pedagogical Sciences related to values and values education. Fifteen-year experience in the field of education and teaching. Currently works at Holguin University Teacher Education Department as an Associate Professor and Head of the Teacher Education English Language Department. Publishes nationally and internationally on the issues of foreign language teaching.
juliorp@uho.edu.cu

Alexei Rojas Riverón

BA, Assistant Professor currently working in the Teacher Education English Major as a professor of English and History of the English-Speaking Countries. Has cadre experience in other fields and has been translator and interpreter for years.
arojasr@uho.edu.cu

Arianna Rosa Leyva

Senior Student in Education, English major. She has done research on the teaching of English, especially related to the blind and visually limited. She has participated and published in national events on the issue.
ileyvap@nauta.cu

Jorge Ronda Pupo

PhD degree in Pedagogical Sciences, Full Professor from the University of Pedagogical Sciences in Havana and member of the National University Accreditation Committee in charge of certifying Cuban universities. He does research and publishes on issues related to education and the teaching of English as a foreign language.
rondapupo@ucpha.edu.cu

Guillermo Ronda Velázquez

MSc degree and Associate Professor from the Havana University. He has taught English as a foreign language and History and Culture of the English Speaking Peoples. He does research and publishes on language-teaching-related topics.
bill@flex.uh.cu

Maritza Salazar Salazar

Pychology degree. PhD in Pedagogical Sciences. Full Professor. Scientific and Methodological Advisor working in the Methodological Department of Holguin University. Publishes nationally and internationally on issues related to her fields of expertise.
msalazar@uho.edu.cu

Yudisleidys Sánchez Roque

Bachelor of Arts, English major. Recently graduated, Sánchez currently works in the Teacher Education English Major Department as a professor of English and French. She studies and does research on language teaching and the development of communicative skills. She has participated in national events. This is her first international appearance.
yudisr@uho.edu.cu

Yannia Torres Pérez

BA in Psychology. Associate Professor. MSc degree in Educational Sciences. Currently works with the Pedagogy-Psychology major, certified specialty, in Holguin University. Her research has been devoted to explorations on psychology and pedagogy.

Miguel Velázquez Hidalgo

Professor of Didactics of Literature at Holguin University, Cuba. Master´s degree in Planning and Supervision of Educational Systems. Associate Professor. He publishes and participates in national and international events on topics related to the teaching of literature and Spanish, especially in text construction, reading comprehension and the promotion of reading in co-curricular on-campus and community contexts.
miguelv@uho.edu.cu

Manuel de Jesús Velázquez León

PhD in Pedagogical Sciences, Full Professor who worked at the University of Holguin for more than forty years, currently working in a Chinese university teaching English and cultural studies. Professor of the History and Culture of the English Speaking Countries. Poet, writer, essay writer, translator. Has published his literary and academic works in numerous national and international issues and events.
manueld@stu.edu.cn

Sheikh Zobaer

MA (University of Surrey). Lecturer in the Department of English (DEML) at North South University (NSU). Teaches, does research and writes on issues related to language teaching. He is also a poet and writer.

Libys Martha Zúñiga Igarza

Architect. Master and PhD degrees in Technical Sciences. Thirty-three-year experience in urbanization and design leading and carrying out projects all over Cuba as well as in Europe, Africa and Latin America. Currently works at Holguin University Construction Department as a Full Professor. Publishes nationally and internationally on the issues of patrimony, urbanization, architecture and preservation of patrimonial culture, both tangible and intangible.
lmzi@uho.edu.cu

About the Editor

Miguel Ángel Olivé Iglesias is a professor, researcher and poetry, fiction and non-fiction author. He is a Canada Cuba Literary Alliance (CCLA) editor, *The Ambassador* Editor-in-chief, *The Envoy* Assistant Editor, and President in Cuba of the CCLA. He does translation, proofreading, reviewing and revision for the CCLA, along with compilation and anthologizing.

He is a member of the Mexican Association of Language and Literature Professors, of the William Shakespeare Studies Center and guest member of the Canadian Studies Department of Holguin University in Cuba.

Born in 1965 in Bayamo, Cuba, he travelled to Holguin in 1977 for his Junior, Senior High and College studies. Today he is an Associate Professor at the University of Holguin, with a Bachelor's Degree in Education, Major in English, and a Master's degree in Pedagogical Sciences. He has been teaching for thirty-three years and writing academic papers, literary reviews, poems and stories in Spanish and in English.

Miguel has written and published numerous academic papers in Cuba, Mexico, Spain and Canada. He publishes nationally and internationally on the issues of foreign language teaching, pedagogy, interdisciplinary approaches, axiology and the preservation of humankind´s values, both tangible and intangible, from an educational perspective.

He publishes his poetry, short stories and literary essays with Canadian publishing entities, like Hidden Brook Press and SandCrab Books, Canadian Stories Magazine, and Adelaide Group Lisbon-U.S.A., and translates, edits, reviews and proofreads newsletters, magazines, anthologies and books of Canadian and Cuban poetry and prose for the Canada Cuba Literary Alliance, project for which he is the President on the Cuban side. So far he has been the editor of more than five CCLA books, has published more than a hundred poems, six short stories and over forty critical reviews of poetry books and novels in different issues:

The Ambassador, official flagship of the CCLA; *The Envoy*, official newsletter of the CCLA; The Bridges Series Books, published by Hidden Brook Press and SandCrab Books; Adelaide Group in New York-Lisbon, and other anthologies by Hidden Brook Press and SandCrab Books and *Canadian Stories* magazine. He published a literary review book, *In a Fragile Moment: A Landscape of Canadian Poetry* (Hidden Brook Press, 2020) and his first full-length solo poetry book (bilingual), *Forge of Words* (Hidden Brook Press, 2020).

His poetic themes touch upon women, people, life, family, love, nature, and human second review book, *A Shower of Warm Light Upon this Land and Us*; his second solo poetry book, *This Pulse of Life, The Words I Found*; editor and translator for the Bridges Series Book V, *The Heart Upon the Sleeve*, presenting two Canadian and two Cuban poets; editor and author in *The Divinity of Blue*, an anthology of seventeen Canadian and Cuban poets; and editor and translator for *Flying in the Wings of Poetry*, a compilation of four well-known Canadian poets.

SandCrab books recently published, 2020, the e-book he edited, *These Voices Beating in our Hearts: Poems from the Valley* (English-Spanish), where his poems and haiku appear together with the poetry of other ten Holguin poets.

He works in the Teacher Education English Department as a professor of English, English Stylistics and grad courses. He is also Head of the English Language Discipline. He uses his academic papers, essays, stories and poems in class for reading, debating and practicing the language, adding a didactic and formative element to his scientific and literary production. He also does poetry reading in co-curricular on-campus and community activities.

Previous books by
Miguel Ángel Olivé Iglesias

Title – In a Fragile Moment: A Landscape of Canadian Poetry
Author – M.Sc. Miguel Ángel Olivé Iglesias
Genre – Reviews and Essays on Canadian Poetry
ISBN – 978-1-927725-92-4 = 9781927725924 – Soft cover
Publisher – Hidden Brook Press   **Phone** – 905-376-9106
Email – hiddenbrookpress@gmail.com
Publisher URL – www.hiddenbrookpress.com
Pages – 240   **Size** – 7 X 10

This book is a significant study of Canadian poetry. This scholarly perceptive book truly is a one of a kind.

Poetry in English and Spanish.

Title – Forge of Words / Fragua de palabras
Author – Miguel Ángel Olivé Iglesias
Genre – Poetry / Cuban
ISBN – 978-1-927725-71-9 = 9781927725719
Publisher – Hidden Brook Press   **Phone** – 905-376-9106
Email – hiddenbrookpress@gmail.com
Publisher URL – www.hiddenbrookpress.com
Pages – 134   **Size** – 6 X 9

CPSIA information can be obtained
at www.ICGtesting.com
Printed in the USA
BVHW011407070721
611354BV00011B/180